Prosecuting Slobodan Milošević

This book offers a comprehensive analysis of the trial of former Serbian leader Slobodan Milošević at the International Criminal Tribunal for the Former Yugoslavia (ICTY).

With the premature death of Milošević in March 2006 his trial was left unfinished. Although the traditional objectives of criminal law, such as retribution, justice for victims, and deterrence, were not achieved, the Milošević trial archive is a significant historical resource for researchers from various fields. This book extracts details from the collection of documentary and transcript evidence that makes up the trial record – sources which would be almost impossible to extricate without an insider's guiding hand – to allow readers to trace the threads of several historical narratives. The value of this methodology is particularly evident in the Milošević case as, acting as his own defence counsel, he responded to, and interacted with, almost all witnesses and evidence presented against him. By providing snapshots of the behaviour displayed by Milošević in court while conducting his defence, in combination with passages of carefully selected evidence from an immense archive familiar to few scholars, this volume reveals how these trial records, and trial records in general, are a truly invaluable historical source. The book underlines the premise that any record of a mass atrocities trial, whether finished or unfinished, establishes a record of past events, contributes to interpretations of a historical period and influences the shaping of collective memory.

This book will be of much interest to students of the Former Yugoslavia, war crimes, international law, human rights, international relations, and European politics.

Nevenka Tromp is lecturer in East European Studies at the University of Amsterdam (UvA), Netherlands, and was a member of the Leadership Research Team (LRT) at the International Criminal Tribunal for the Former Yugoslavia (ICTY); from 2000 to 2006 she was the principal researcher in the team prosecuting Slobodan Milošević.

Contemporary Security Studies

Series Editors:
James Gow and Rachel Kerr
King's College London

This series focuses on new research across the spectrum of international peace and security, in an era where each year throws up multiple examples of conflicts that present new security challenges in the world around them.

Understanding NATO in the 21st Century
Alliance strategies, security and global governance
Edited by Graeme P. Herd and John Kriendler

Ethics and the Laws of War
The moral justification of legal norms
Antony Lamb

Militancy and Violence in West Africa
Religion, politics and radicalisation
Edited by Ernst Dijxhoorn, James Gow and Funmi Olonisakin

Mechanistic Realism and US Foreign Policy
A new framework for analysis
Johannes Gullestad Rø

Prosecuting War Crimes
Lessons and legacies of the International Criminal Tribunal for the former Yugoslavia
Edited by James Gow, Rachel Kerr and Zoran Pajić

The NATO Intervention in Libya
Lessons learned from the campaign
Edited by Kjell Engelbrekt, Marcus Mohlin and Charlotte Wagnsson

Truth Recovery and Transitional Justice
Deferring human rights issues
Iosif Kovras

Reconstructing Afghanistan
Civil–military experiences in comparative perspective
Edited by William Maley and Susanne Schmeidl

Strategic Narratives, Public Opinion and War
Winning domestic support for the Afghan War
Edited by Beatrice De Graaf, George Dimitriu and Jens Ringsmose

Liberal Wars
Anglo-American strategy, ideology, and practice
Edited by Alan Cromartie

Prosecuting Slobodan Milošević
The unfinished trial
Nevenka Tromp

Prosecuting Slobodan Milošević

The unfinished trial

Nevenka Tromp

Routledge
Taylor & Francis Group
LONDON AND NEW YORK

First published 2016
by Routledge
605 Third Avenue, New York, NY 10017
4 Park Square, Milton Park, Abingdon, Oxon OX14 4RN

First issued in paperback 2017

Routledge is an imprint of the Taylor & Francis Group, an informa business

British Library Cataloguing-in-Publication Data
A catalogue record for this book is available from the British Library

Library of Congress Cataloging-in-Publication Data
Names: Tromp, Nevenka, author.
Title: Prosecuting Slobodan Milošević : the unfinished trial / Nevenka Tromp.
Description: New York, NY : Routledge, 2016. | Series: Contemporary security
studies | Includes bibliographical references and index.
Identifiers: LCCN 2015045204| ISBN 9781138961357 (hardback) | ISBN 9781315659848 (ebook)
Subjects: LCSH: Milošević, Slobodan, 1941-2006–Trials, litigation, etc. | Trials (Crimes against humanity)–Netherlands–Hague. | War crime trials–Netherlands–Hague. | Yugoslav War, 1991-1995–Atrocities. | International Tribunal for the Prosecution of Persons Responsible for Serious Violations of International Humanitarian Law Committed in the Territory of the Former Yugoslavia since 1991.
Classification: LCC KZ1203.M55 T76 2016 | DDC 341.6/90268–dc23
LC record available at http://lccn.loc.gov/2015045204

ISBN 13: 978-0-8153-4760-6 (pbk)
ISBN 13: 978-1-138-96135-7 (hbk)

Typeset in Bembo
by Wearset Ltd, Boldon, Tyne and Wear

To my tolerant and understanding children, Mara and Hylke, for their love and forbearance in my time of preoccupation.

Contents

Maps

Preface

It was early Saturday morning, 11 March 2006. I was just finishing breakfast before leaving to spend yet another weekend in the office, when the telephone rang. On the phone was Geoffrey Nice, the Principal Trial Attorney in charge of the team – of which I was a part – that was prosecuting Slobodan Milošević at the International Criminal Tribunal for the Former Yugoslavia (ICTY). Very calmly, he told me: "You won't need to go into the office today. He's dead. He died last night. There's no need to do any work today, or any other day. That's it. That's the end of the trial."

It took some time to comprehend what this meant; and before I could make any sense of it, a colleague who was already in the office, and who had just heard the news on television, called me inquiring about what we were to do. That weekend, Prosecution researchers had been set to begin preparing for the cross-examination of Momir Bulatović, who was being called by Milošević as a Defence witness.[1] In fact, preparation for a witness such as Bulatović was exactly what those of us in the Leadership Research Team (LRT) had been hired to do.[2] I became a member of the LRT in May 2000 and thereafter worked exclusively on the Milošević case, until his death. The LRT and the MAT (Military Analyst Team) were part of the ICTY's Office of the Prosecutor (OTP), consisting mostly of non-legal experts and researchers who provided information and expertise on historical, political, and military topics for Prosecution trial teams that were made up mostly of police investigators and lawyers.

Bulatović was a dream witness for the Prosecution and we could hardly believe that Milošević was being so reckless as to call him. He had knowledge of more or less everything the Prosecution needed to prove in order to establish its case, and he had been a trusted associate and protégé of Milošević since his election as the President of Montenegro in 1990 at the age of 34. Bulatović had also been present at many of the most important high-level meetings that had determined Serbia's role in the three conflicts for which Milošević was indicted and, during cross-examination, could be asked by the Prosecution to confirm the authenticity and accuracy of documentary evidence.

Milošević died in his prison cell less than two months before the trial was set to end. His death was by no means entirely unexpected; his ill health was well known and his medical condition was not helped by his choice to represent himself in court. Acting as his own advocate, he had read, watched, and listened to every piece of evidence presented against him. He had written his own opening addresses, readied cross-examinations, organised and conducted the Defence case, and prepared Defence witnesses before examining them in court himself. These would have been difficult tasks, physically and mentally, even for a healthy person in his or her prime.

But with the trial so abruptly concluded, indeed – as my colleague had asked – what were we to do? How were we to think about, and what were we to learn from, an unfinished trial? And, how might the sudden end of the trial obscure the truth? With these questions in mind, the end of the trial became the stimulus for some of us to start a new journey of discovery; this time, reviewing the frozen record of the trial outside of sealed courtrooms, where we had breathed stale but exhilarating air filled with the anticipation of what witnesses would, or would not, say. Now, we knew what had been said, and what could not be said. Yet, in hundreds of thousands of pages of our own research, and in the court record, we had the makings of history.

The death of Milošević marked more than the end of a man. It was also the end of our chance to reveal more about Milošević and his plan, and to force him to face truths he never expected to confront. In the immediate aftermath of his passing, it seemed that these truths would be hidden forever and that Milošević's death would be yet another demonstration that trials of individuals in international courts leave insignificant records of historical events. But, following his death before the end of the trial, there came an unforeseen discovery – that records of such trials may actually be invaluable points of departure to levels of historical discovery, possibly deeper than trial lawyers can ever reach. Court conclusions are limited by technical rules that require a balance to be made according to formulaic tests of proof, rules of a court and decisions of judges that all channel decision-making into narrower tracks of reasoning for determining one single and most important question – is the Defendant guilty or not. The record itself, under broader academic analysis, can permit other routes to more conclusions.

I wondered what would happen to all the research, testimony, and documentary and other evidence that had been collected. After all, I had handled material on a daily basis that uncovered the historical and political context in which mass atrocities had occurred. Might it disappear into oblivion because the trial did not come to a close? At the least, it seemed a huge amount of the material already assembled and analysed for use in court was destined to remain unexploited.

As the product of a legal proceeding dealing with individual criminal responsibility, the Milošević trial record contains a comprehensive – possibly the largest existing – collection of materials related to the political and criminal responsibility of individuals for the disintegration of Yugoslavia, and for the mass atrocities by which it was marked. Although the traditional objectives of criminal law, such as retribution, justice for victims, and deterrence, were not achieved in the Milošević case, the trial produced an extensive archive of testimonies, expert reports, hearings transcripts, and other documentary evidence. Indeed, there is no doubt that the Milošević trial record is a significant historical resource for researchers from various fields; and, any record of a mass atrocities trial – whether finished or unfinished – establishes a chronicle of past events and contributes to interpretations of a historical period and the shaping of collective memory. In this way, mass atrocities trials do not have merely a legal purpose, they also have a pedagogical function.

Examining the Milošević trial record for academic purposes, I experienced advantages and disadvantages as an 'insider' to the subject of my research. One clear advantage was my familiarity with the trial record – the principal source for this study. But, at the same time, I had to be sure to remain true to the academic requirements of objectivity, academic distance, and impartiality. This dilemma, over the appropriate measure of distance or proximity for those writing about mass atrocities, has been described occasionally by scholars like Mark Osiel, who questioned:

> How to strike an authorial posture that is scholarly, yet humane; 'disinterested,' yet not disengaged? How to represent the victims' suffering, for instance, in a way that is neither luridly salacious nor unduly solicitous and sycophantic? For the victims turn out to be perpetrators as well. How to render the perpetrators' self-understanding at once as supremely malevolent yet humanly intelligible? How to depict the zealotry of international prosecutors in both its sincere humanitarianism and its professional self-aggrandizement?[3]

From my own experience, neither an insider nor an outsider can be preferred as a matter of principle, nor can either be assumed to maintain appropriate detachment more capably. Any author and researcher must engage academic discipline, consisting of critical thought, rigorous scrutiny of sources, and a mind open to new discoveries.

My journey in trying to make sense of the trial record was a difficult one, not least because of the enormous volume of material the trial produced. The trial lasted 467 days, leaving behind 49,191 pages of transcripts, during which over 400 witnesses were called, 5,759 documentary exhibits amounting to approximately 150,000 pages were tendered by the Prosecution, and 2,107 exhibits of some 25,000 pages were tendered by the Defence. Thus, I sought guidance and insight from scholars who have studied Nazi war strategy by scrutinising the records of Nuremberg war crimes trials. The Nuremberg Tribunal produced a very specific historical interpretation of the Nazi plan, ascribing responsibility for the war chiefly to one person and the ruling elite; but, historians realised over time how the evidentiary focus of proceedings in Nuremberg had unwittingly influenced their analysis in favour of what came to be known as the 'intentionalist' interpretation of the period, which maintains that the Holocaust resulted from an explicit master plan created by Adolf

Hitler himself and implemented from the top down.[4] Only later was attention directed to the role of minor bureaucrats and functionaries at all levels of German society – an approach known as the 'functionalist' interpretation and concerned with the complicity of ordinary Germans in the Holocaust, to such an extent in the case of some scholars that they ascribe the adoption of the Final Solution primarily to social and political pressures from the bottom up.[5] Milošević's trial focused on his leadership and the trial record inevitably contains material that could point to an 'intentionalist' interpretation of Milošević's role in the disintegration of Yugoslavia in the 1990s and in the origins of mass atrocities. This book searches the trial record for traces of the existence of such an 'intentionalist' master plan where, at various stages, plans were articulated ahead of events. Evidence showing a 'functionalist' interpretation might explain how at other stages and times decision-making was a reaction to ongoing political processes that led to mass violence through interaction between the Milošević – groomed as a politician in an authoritarian system – and his followers on one hand and other parties in the conflict, Serbia's adversaries, on the other hand. Seeking the answers to some of these questions, I narrowed my examination of the trial record to the exploration of three major topics – the *leader*, the *ideology*, and the *plan*.

I also considered more generally that any criminal investigation and the trial that may follow deal with three elementary questions: *Who? What?* and *How?* These questions are revisited by judges when weighing the evidence for a judgement and are also of interest to historians researching a particular period. In this case, the question of *Who?* addresses the role of Milošević as the Accused; the question of *What?* addresses the ideology and the plan behind the leader; and the question of *How?* elicits a search for answers about what led to the violence and mass atrocities that occurred, and at what point they were sanctioned.

Notes

1 The testimony of a witness consists of three parts: testimony in chief, cross-examination, and re-examination. Testimony in chief is the term used in legal jargon for adducing evidence from a witness in court by the party – the Prosecution or Defence – that calls the witness. It is followed by a cross-examination by the opposing party. After the cross-examination of a witness, the party that originally called the witness and conducted the examination in chief has an opportunity to re-examine the witness on topics addressed by the opposing party during the cross-examination, for clarification or correction.

2 Members of the LRT came from different national and academic backgrounds, with expertise in the Balkans. The author maintained her position as a lecturer in European Studies at the University of Amsterdam throughout her employment at the UN.

3 Mark Osiel, *Making Sense of Mass Atrocities* (Cambridge: Cambridge University Press, 2008), xvii.

4 The terms 'intentionalists' and 'functionalists' were coined by Timothy Mason in his 1981 essay 'Intention and Explanation: A Current Controversy about the Interpretation of National Socialism,' in *The 'Fuehrer State': Myth and Reality – Studies on*

Structure and Politics of the Third Reich, eds G. Hirschfeld and L. Kettenacker (Stuttgart: Klett-Cotta, 1981). Mason criticised authors who focused too much on Hitler in explaining the Holocaust, calling them intentionalist. He called the opposing school functionalists because they saw the Holocaust as a consequence of the way the Nazi state functioned. Mason himself proposed, as an alternative, an investigation into a broader perspective of the period with a distinct focus on the economy.

5 See for discussion: Ruti Teitel, *Transitional Justice* (New York: Oxford University Press, 2000), 74; Mark Osiel, *Mass Atrocities, Collective Memory and the Law* (Piscataway: Transaction Publishers, 1997), 100; and Daniel Goldhagen, *Hitler's Willing Executioners: Ordinary Germans and the Holocaust* (New York: Alfred A. Knopf, 1996).

Acknowledgements

I am grateful to Professor Hylke Tromp for introducing me to the study of political violence, peace and human rights and for unselfishly sharing his knowledge and ideas over many years. I am indebted to Sir Geoffrey Nice for encouraging me to write this book; our many discussions about the law and English language inspired thoughts and shaped ideas.

The Hague, 3 November 2015

Acronyms

BiH	Bosnia and Herzegovina (*Bosna i Hercegovina*)
DB	State Security (*Državna bezbednost*)
DEPOS	Democratic Movement of Serbia (*Demokratski pokret Srbije*)
FRY	Federal Republic of Yugoslavia
HDZ	Croatian Democratic Union (*Hrvatska demokratska zajednica*)
IC	International Community
ICC	International Criminal Court
ICFY	International Conference for Former Yugoslavia
ICR	ICTY Court Record
ICTY	International Criminal Tribunal for the Former Yugoslavia
JATD	Special Anti-terrorist Unit (*Jedinice za anti-teroristička dejstva*)
JCE	Joint Criminal Enterprise
JNA	Yugoslav People's Army (*Jugoslavenska narodna armija*)
JSO	Unit for Special Operations (*Jedinica za specijalne operacije*)
JUL	Yugoslav United Left (*Jugoslavenska udružena levica*)
KLA	Kosovo Liberation Army
KOS	Military Counterintelligence Service (*Kontraobveštajna služba*)
KVM	Kosovo Verification Mission
LC	League of Communists (SK: *Savez komunista*)
LDK	Democratic League of Kosovo (*Lidhja Demokratike e Kosovës*)
LRT	Leadership Research Team
MAT	Military Analysts Team
MICT	Mechanism for International Criminal Tribunals
MUP	Ministry of Internal Affairs (*Ministarstvo Unutrašnjih Poslova*)
NATO	North-Atlantic Treaty Organisation
ND	New Democracy (*Nova demokratija*)
NDH	Independent State of Croatia (*Nezavisna država Hrvatska*)
NIOD	Netherlands Institute for War Documentation
OSCE	Organisation for Security and Cooperation in Europe
OTP	Office of Tribunal's Prosecutor
PJP	Special Police Units (*Posebne jedinica policije*)

PSFRY	Presidency of the Socialist Federal Republic of Yugoslavia
RS	Republika Srpska
RSK	Republika Srpska Krajina
SAJ	Special Anti-terrorist Units (*Specijalna anti-teroristička jedinica*)
SANU	Serbian Academy of Sciences and Arts (*Srpska akademija nauka i umetnosti*)
SAO	Serbian Autonomous Region (*Srpska autonomna oblast*)
SBSW	Slavonia, Baranja and Western Syrmia (*Slavonia, Baranja i Zapadni Srem*)
SDA	Party of Democratic Action (*Stranka demokratske akcije*)
SDC	Supreme Defence Council (*Vrhovni savet odbrane*)
SDS	Serb Democratic Party (*Srpska demokratska stranka*)
SFRY	Socialist Federal Republic of Yugoslavia (*Socijalistička federativna republika Jugoslavija*)
SIV	Federal Executive Council (*Savezno izvršno veće*)
SPOK	Serbian Resistance Movement of Kosovo (*Srpski pokret otpora Kosova*)
SPS	Socialist Party of Serbia (*Socijalistička partija Srbije*)
SRS	Serbian Radical Party (*Srpska radikalna stranka*)
SVK	Serbian Army of Krajina (*Srpska vojska Krajine*)
TO	Territorial Defence (*Teritorijalna odbrana*)
UB	Security Administration (*Uprava bezbednosti*)
UDBA	State Security Administration (*Uprava državne bezbednosti*)
UN	United Nations
UNHCR	United Nations High Commissioner for Refugees
UNPAs	United Nations Protected Areas
UNPROFOR	United Nations Protection Force
UNSC	United Nations Security Council
VJ	Army of Yugoslavia (*Vojska Jugoslavije*)
V–K–K	Virovitica–Karlovac–Karlobag
VOPP	Vance–Owen Peace Plan
VRS	Army of Republika Srpska (*Vojska Republike Srpske*)

Notes on language and translation

This text is based on and frequently includes quotations from transcripts of proceedings, evidence presented in the courtroom, and materials collected as part of the criminal investigation in the Milošević case. These materials and courtroom testimonies originated in various languages, and in variants of languages (for example, in Bosnian/Croatian/Serbian or UK/US English), and many have been translated. Non-English primary materials tendered as evidence in court were translated into English and make up the official court record. Yet, many of these first translations went through a later audit process – in which meaning was clarified and syntax corrected – that produced a second revised version. Every attempt has been made to quote these revised translations when possible.

As a researcher on the Milošević case, the author dealt with primary documents in both local languages (B/C/S) and in English, but where her original research was done with local language materials, the official English translation of those materials is presented in this text. In other words, the author did not translate those materials herself in the process of writing this text. Still, as a native B/C/S speaker fluent in English, the author had the advantage of being able to identify when official English translations were in some way inaccurate. One example of this is in the English transcript of the testimony of Stjepan Mesić. Mesić discussed Franjo Tuđman having compared the shape of Croatia to a *kifla*, the B/C/S word for a crescent-shaped roll that is traditional in Eastern Europe. In the English trial transcript, a slip-up in homophones resulted in this being translated as 'oblong role' instead of 'oblong roll' – a confusing error. In the courtroom, translations were also sometimes corrected on the spot by participants in the trial. In one such instance, an English translation of a letter written by Milošević was found online and referred to in court by the Prosecutor; it was corrected by the courtroom interpreter who explained the word 'rats' was an inaccurate translation for the B/C/S word *hulje*, which means 'scoundrel' and has a more sinister connotation. Milošević himself subsequently addressed the court to concur that 'scoundrel' was the more appropriate translation.

Translation is a challenging task because languages not only have different vocabularies, but different personalities, cultural influences, and structures.

Translating any text, but especially materials that deal with complicated political concepts and contain a number of linguistic subtleties, requires finding the balance point between what are known as 'faithful' and 'idiomatic' translations. A faithful translation is a literal rendering of a source text, without revisions that accommodate the nuances of the target language. An idiomatic translation is more focused on producing a text that conforms to the syntax and idiomatic character of the target language, so that a reader feels the text was originally written in their language. Sometimes, word-for-word translations simply do not convey meaning because idioms are a common way of communicating within languages but are not universal. Where translations are paraphrased in this text, attention has been paid to honouring the idiomatic meaning of the original.

Finally, this text is written in UK English – for example, 'Defence' instead of 'Defense' and 'analyse' instead of 'analyze' – but direct quotations of materials originally written in US English are used verbatim. This text also uses diacritical marks for words or names drawn from B/C/S, which clarifies their pronunciation (see the Pronunciation Guide for what these marks indicate). Because ICTY trial transcripts and some materials from the trial record do not include diacritics, they have been added in this text, even to quoted testimony, for consistency. Also, words that originated in B/C/S and are now widely used in their English transliteration – such as 'Chetnik' (in B/C/S, '*četnik*') – appear in their English form.

Pronunciation guide

Bosnian, Croatian, and Serbian are closely related but subtly different languages, all variants of a common pluricentric language. Though Bosnian and Croatian use the Latin alphabet, and Serbian uses the Cyrillic alphabet, the languages are sometimes referred to as one and abbreviated as B/C/S. Unlike in English, vowels in B/C/S are pronounced consistently and some consonants are marked with diacriticals to indicate their pronunciation. Diacritical marks are used in this text and so their pronunciation, as well as that of vowels, is indicated below.

a	a, as in b***a***r
c	ts, as in ca***ts***
č	ch, as in mu***ch***
ć	ch, as in ***ch***osen (this sound is softer than č)
dž	j, as in ***g***in
đ	j, as in ***j***ewelry (this sound is softer than dž)
e	e, as in p***e***n
i	ee, as in m***ee***k
j	y, as in ***y***es
o	o, as in ***o***men
r	the r is rolled
š	sh, as in pu***sh***
u	u, as in r***u***le
ž	zh, as in vi***si***on

Introduction

Why were expectations so high for the Milošević trial? Why was disappointment about its premature end so widespread? What did victims and the public hope for from the judgement or the verdict? Did they wish to see Milošević found guilty and sentenced to a long prison term? Would the text of a judgement have provided answers as to why mass atrocities had occurred, and at the instigation of whom? Is the 'right to know' as important for victims as the punishment of alleged perpetrators? And, most importantly, can the record of his unfinished trial meet any of those expectations?[1]

Answers to some of these questions can be found in literature on mass atrocities trials; trials which, *inter alia*, are meant to adjudicate individual responsibility and establish a record about controversial events from the past. The authority of these records depends to a great extent on the legitimacy of the criminal courts at which these trials are held and on the fairness of the trial. In Chapter 1, the legitimacy and the legality of the ICTY will be explored. For, the Milošević trial (as well as others at the ICTY) has been labelled by some as a 'political trial,' and this criticism deserves attention, because it reflects on the integrity of the trial record left behind.

This study relies primarily on that trial record and advances the notion that such a record, even where the trial is unfinished, can – and will – influence and shape the narrative of a conflict. And the Milošević trial record not only contains evidence of great value, but it also offers snapshots of the behaviour displayed by Milošević in court, making it a truly invaluable source of history. Still, missing source materials that were requested by legal teams but were never produced represent a gap; meaning that the trial record, while vast, is not exhaustive. The record is so large that it cannot be analysed in a single academic study, and is not examined in full here, and yet it was insufficient for the task of this research, and thus sources from outside the trial proceedings – known as extratrial material – were also analysed.

Legal approaches to the Milošević trial revolved around Milošević's leadership and whether or not he had articulated and implemented a criminal plan that led to mass atrocities. This study introduces three interconnected topics – the leader, the ideology, and the plan – that are essential to understanding the intricacies of competing courtroom narratives. In Chapter 2, the leader and the ideology are examined.

Long before his trial started in 2002, there was an ongoing debate among scholars, journalists, politicians, and diplomats about the extent of Milošević's historical and political responsibility for the violent disintegration of Yugoslavia; and there has been near consensus among these authors that Milošević personally bore the greatest share of blame for it.[2] Still, one might argue that the dominant Yugoslav political culture – which relied on strong leadership – had allowed him to develop very extensive *de jure* and de facto powers. And so, notwithstanding his personal mark on Serbia's path to war, the trial record also contains a wealth of material about the ideology to which Milošević tied his political destiny, best described for the purposes of this text as a variant of Serbian state ideology.[3]

When Milošević became the leader of Serbia on a wave of Serb nationalism, his taste for power developed rapidly and, having united Serb nationalists from other republics, he was soon accepted as the de facto leader of all Serbs. Serb nationalism had long dreamed of an enlarged Serbian state and advocates of this ideology – including Milošević – had to have known that its implementation would most likely, or even inevitably, lead to the commission of mass atrocities. The Prosecution argued that all of Milošević's political plans derived from his attempt to create a state that would incorporate all Serbs; and further, that the history of efforts to achieve this enlargement has been marked by mass violence against non-Serb populations. The Prosecution argued that Milošević had promoted Greater Serbia ideology without using the term, but that his rhetoric in the late 1980s and the platform of his party in 1990 had prioritised the protection of Serbs living outside of Serbia and had espoused the right of Serbs to self-determination – which some called the 'All Serbs in a Single State' strategy. Arguing that self-determination for Serbs would indeed expand the territory of a Serb state, the Prosecution introduced the term 'de facto Greater Serbia' to describe the ideology promoted by Milošević.

Chapters 3, 4, 5, and 6 address different stages of the plan. This was the means by which Milošević sought to create a state which would encompass all Serbs, through attempts to reach five successive goals set between 1987 and 1999, beginning with the successful centralisation of Serbia – which he achieved by revoking the autonomy of its two formerly autonomous provinces, Kosovo and Vojvodina. The Serbian Constitution of 1990 reflected those changes, and its revision launched Milošević to new political heights among Serbs. He was less successful in efforts to centralise the Yugoslav Federation and secure Serb domination, through control of the Communist Party and federal institutions of the Socialist Federal Republic of Yugoslavia (SFRY). Attempts to realise this second goal instead brought the disintegration of the SFRY, after Slovenia and Croatia declared their independence in 1991.

Milošević's third goal was set in reaction to his failure to preserve a centralised Yugoslav state. The disintegration of the Federation spurred efforts to preserve a Rump Yugoslavia that would consist of all the former SFRY republics save for Slovenia and parts of Croatia.[4] This Rump Yugoslavia was projected to include 'Serb-designated territories' in Croatia and, to that end, a bid to secure those territories by force was made as early as mid-1990, leading to an escalation of violence and a full-fledged war in Croatia in 1991.[5] In this process, Croatian Serbs proclaimed their own quasi-state entity, the Republika Srpska Krajina (RSK), which was envisaged to extend to the Virovitica–Karlovac–Karlobag (V–K–K) line – a boundary that is the very representation of Greater Serbia ideology – and the borders of the RSK were more or less achieved by December 1991.

In Bosnia and Herzegovina (BiH), a February 1992 referendum on independence had made it clear that a majority of the population there was in favour of independence. And the failure to achieve a Rump Yugoslavia that included BiH led Milošević's to his fourth goal. The republic of Serbia and Montenegro, which had not given up on Yugoslavia as the name for a common state, constituted the Federal Republic of Yugoslavia (FRY) in April 1992; but the FRY Constitution allowed for other territories to join in later, and Bosnian Serbs – following the example of Croatian Serbs – were simultaneously forming their own quasi-state in BiH, the Republika Srpska (RS). Unlike the formation of the RSK, which was achieved after several months of fighting, the formation of the RS took more than three years and led to mass atrocities against non-Serbs. Eventually, though, the peace agreement for BiH that was signed by all parties in December 1995 allowed the RS to maintain its territorial autonomy despite the fact that its borders were established by crimes that included genocide.

The fifth of Milošević's goals was control of Kosovo, but escalating conflict there in 1998 exposed his failure to rule the province from Belgrade, even after he had revoked its autonomy in the 1990 Serbian Constitution. An escalation of violence between the Kosovo Liberation Army (KLA) and Serbian forces in 1997 had been used by Serbia to justify a violent campaign against the Kosovo Albanian population. By the end of December 1998, Milošević's determination to keep Kosovo in Serbia – and on his terms – resulted in war, causing a humanitarian catastrophe that was finally brought to an end by NATO military intervention. NATO's defeat of Serbian forces led to Serbia's loss of Kosovo in June 1999 and, eventually, to the downfall of Milošević in October 2000.

In Chapter 7, this downfall is analysed. Milošević's ten-year reign had resulted in more than 100,000 dead and many more displaced; but while Bosnian Serb leaders Radovan Karadžić and Ratko Mladić were indicted by the ICTY in July 1995, Milošević was given a second chance by the international community. Indeed, some saw Dayton as marking his metamorphosis from the 'Butcher of the Balkans' into a peacemaker. Yet, the Prosecution contended that Milošević had managed to avert or end military interventions against Serb forces by supporting a policy that was *ostensibly* cooperative and focused on peace but which actually masked his criminal motivation to formalise Serb war gains. But Dayton was a victory for Milošević, and as he grew obsessively concerned with power and showed increasing intolerance towards fellow party members, he believed his newly acquired patronage by the West meant he could afford a domestic standoff.

Like many other authoritarian leaders over time, Milošević relied on an ever-shrinking circle of associates. As he became more authoritarian and exceedingly alienated from reality, he made a series of mistakes – in his dealings with the international community over Kosovo, and in his military approach to the province – that reversed any good will he had earned at Dayton. His apparent belief that he could remake the demography of Kosovo exposed the irrationality of Milošević's political strategy; and of course, Serbia lost the province.

By 2000, Milošević was isolated and out of touch. At the end of his presidency, a series of political murders against his former allies were perpetrated, reflecting his desperate efforts to retain power as his political base crumbled. Once in The Hague, Milošević refused to see the consequences of his political actions, framing himself and his family as victims of a 'savage' smear campaign. He never demonstrated that he understood the extent of suffering he had inflicted through the violence of war, but played the role of a wronged politician, enthusiastically if not always skilfully defending himself.

A decade of violence had not brought the results that Serbian state ideologues had hoped for; and by 1995, Serb territories in Croatia had been abandoned by Serb forces and a majority of Croatian Serbs had emigrated to Serbia, Kosovo, or the Republika Srpska. And in 1999, when international agreements stipulated that Serbian forces must leave Kosovo, that territory was lost to Serbia as well. The only war gain that Serb nationalists still claim is the existence of the Republika Srpska as a separate political entity in BiH.

Notes

1 Some of these questions have been dealt with in Nena Tromp, "Understanding the Milošević Case: Legacy of an Unfinished Trial," in *The Genocide Convention: The Legacy of 60 Years*, eds H.G. van der Wilt, J. Vervliet, G.K. Sluiter, and J.Th.M. Houwink ten Cate (Leiden: Martinus Nijhoff, 2012), 27–39.

2 Jasna Dragović-Soso "Why did Yugoslavia Disintegrate? An Overview of Contending Explanations," in *State Collapse in South-Eastern Europe: New Perspectives on Yugoslavia's Disintegration*, eds Lenard J. Cohen and J. Dragović-Soso (Indiana: Purdue University Press, 2008), 1–39, 14.

3 Some authors also use the term "Serbian State Project" to denote the various forms that aspirations for a Serb state have taken since the nineteenth century. For example, see: Sonja Biserko, *Yugoslavia's Implosion: The Fatal Attraction of Serb Nationalism* (Oslo: Norwegian Helsinki Committee, 2012) and James Gow, *The Serbian Project and its Adversaries: A Strategy of War Crimes* (London: Hurst, 2003). I have used the less specific *Serbian state ideology* to underline that the ideology has produced a number of different geopolitical designs.

4 The term 'rump' can be applied to describe the remainder of any state after the separation of a region or regions. In B/C/S, the term *krnja Jugoslavija* was used to refer specifically to the former Yugoslavia less Slovenia and parts of Croatia. The

word *krnja* means "truncated." Here, Rump Yugoslavia is used in English as a proper noun to reflect the particularity of how *krnja Jugoslavija* was used in the early 1990s in the former SFRY.

5 'Serb-designated territories' was the term used by the ICTY Prosecutor to denote the areas in Croatia and BiH that Serb leaders had claimed on ethnic, historical, or geostrategic bases.

1 Theoretical framework, scope of the research, and sources

There is no universal prescription for how societies should deal with legacies of mass atrocities and political violence.[1] Yet, studies in the field of transitional justice offer some guidance on the ways a state may address mass violence or human rights abuses through various mechanisms.[2] These mechanisms range from vetting or lustration processes to truth commissions and criminal trials, and are meant to "address the need for accountability."[3]

Scholars have noted that while war crimes are committed around the world every day, laws designed to punish these acts are invoked only under favourable political circumstances. Still, this has resulted in some well-known international legal initiatives aimed at addressing the individual criminal responsibility of high-level political and military officials.[4] In 1945, for example, ad hoc military tribunals in Nuremberg and Tokyo were established to try command-level German and Japanese perpetrators. But it was not until nearly 50 years later that international political circumstances again allowed for another international tribunal – to address individual criminal responsibility for crimes committed in the former Yugoslav republics.

The ICTY was founded in the spring of 1993, as the violent conflict in BiH raged. In February, parties to the conflict were presented with the Vance–Owen Peace Plan (VOPP), which would have divided an independent BiH into ten ethnically-defined cantons. But negotiations failed on 5 May when Bosnian Serb leaders definitively rejected the VOPP.[5] Less than three weeks later, the UN Security Council (UNSC) announced the establishment of the ICTY.[6]

The UNSC had laid the groundwork for creation of the ICTY in two Resolutions. In February, Resolution 808 announced the establishment of an international tribunal to prosecute those "responsible for serious violations of international humanitarian law" in the former Yugoslavia.[7] The initial mandate of the ICTY was to put an end to such crimes and take effective measures to bring the persons guilty of them to justice. Resolution 827 of May 1993 confirmed this mandate and asserted that the Tribunal would "contribute to ensuring that such violations of international humanitarian law are halted and effectively redressed," and further, that one of the objectives of the ICTY was "to contribute to the restoration and maintenance of peace."[8]

Once brought to life, the ICTY was afforded considerable power; it had been established under Chapter VII of the UN Charter, which compelled all UN states to cooperate.[9] Soon, other ad hoc tribunals – for Rwanda, Cambodia, Sierra Leone, and Lebanon – followed, and in 2002, the International Criminal Court (ICC) was finally established. It is the first permanent court with jurisdiction to address crimes committed in armed conflicts.

The legitimacy and legality of the court

The ICTY's creation was qualified by some as a fig leaf – alluding to the international community's inability, up to that point, to stop the commission of crimes in BiH through peace negotiations or military intervention.[10] And it was true that the creation of the Tribunal did not bring peace nor did it deter the warring sides from committing further crimes. In fact, the gravest crimes of the war in BiH were committed by Serb forces in the summer of 1995 in and around Srebrenica and Žepa, two years after the Tribunal was established; and the Kosovo conflict came another three years later.

The ICTY has also faced questions regarding alleged political undertones and partiality, and about its legitimacy and legality.[11] This is due in no small part to the fact that the Tribunal is run by the UN, which was involved in peacekeeping efforts during the conflicts in question and was present on the ground when some of the most severe crimes occurred; crimes that were witnessed – but not prevented – by the UN's own personnel. Some observers wondered if the UN should be in charge of an ostensibly independent court at which criminal culpability for these very crimes is determined. But scepticism about the capacity of national courts to deliver justice, and a growing sense of urgency, meant there were few alternatives.[12]

Still, the creation of the ICTY and other of ad hoc tribunals did open the door to a new field of research situated at the crossroads between law and politics.[13] In scholarly discussion about its foundation, so-called liberals, concerned with violations of human rights and the crimes committed in BiH, saw the Tribunal as a victory of liberal ideals; in this case, of what was referred to in the literature as 'liberal legalism.'[14] On the other hand, realists saw the Court's foundation through the lens of *Realpolitik* and as the result of more concrete political interests such as ensuring international stability.[15] But, what is the role of such a court? Should the ICTY – or any international criminal court for that matter – be expected to compensate for political, diplomatic, and military failures to end an ongoing military conflict, to secure a long-lasting political solution, or to contribute to reconciliation after the end of a conflict? In other words, should legal remedies be expected to resolve political and military problems?

No matter the answer, the creation of the ICTY raised high expectations, both locally and internationally, that have gone far beyond the original mandate or capacities of the Tribunal and have been difficult if not impossible to meet. This was compounded for years by a lack of appreciation among those working in the ICTY that it serves a region with a specific and unique legal culture. Indeed, several 1999 studies revealed that members of the public as well as legal professionals in the former Yugoslavia did not understand the scope of the Court's work or its processes and procedures.[16] Regional domestic legal systems are based on Continental European or Civil Law, which uses an *inquisitorial* system; and initially, the ICTY was based on Anglo-Saxon or Common Law, which uses an *adversarial* system.[17] While the adversarial system is primarily concerned with proving and ultimately winning a case, the inquisitorial system instead focuses more on determining the truth and was thus considered by some scholars and practitioners to be more suitable for mass atrocities trials. Proponents of an inquisitorial model for the Tribunal also asserted that it would allow judges to be more active in the evidentiary part of trials, which could shorten their duration, and over time this appears to have been the motivation for several rules changes that did incorporate elements of Civil Law.[18]

Support and acceptance of the Tribunal by its 'real constituency' – understood here to be people from the region where the crimes were committed – has generally been seen as an important measure of its success. The international criminal system is a normative system with a strict framework, specific legal theories, lengthy court sessions, and terminology that make many aspects of the courts inaccessible to local communities. And the fact that the proceedings are held abroad and often must be interpreted and translated is an additional barrier to constituents' comprehension of ICTY trials. As Prosecutor Geoffrey Nice asked, "Would you go in for a surgery in which you had a Brazilian doctor, a Ugandan nurse, a Canadian anaesthesiologist, and the operation took place in a Japanese hospital?"[19] Maybe not; and this is a fitting analogy for the challenging international character of the Tribunal.[20]

Responding to critical assessments of the Tribunal, Gabrielle Kirk McDonald, the ICTY President at the time, launched the Tribunal's battle for hearts and minds in 1999, establishing an Outreach Programme that aimed to encourage communication between the Court and its constituents.[21] But after a promising, if slow, start, understaffing of the Outreach Programme made its mandate impossible to fulfil. And this limited support for ICTY outreach activities reflects the UN's general, and the ICTY's particular, propensity to cautiously protect the professional and public image of the Tribunal by minimising contact between court officials and the outside world, even with – or perhaps specifically with – victim constituents.[22] Nevertheless, one of the first empirical studies assessing the impact of ICTY outreach in BiH between 2000 and 2005 concluded that the ICTY had a relatively positive impact in Bosnian society during that period. The author stressed, however, that attitudes do and will change, and that any study on the subject of public attitudes is valuable only if research continues over time.[23]

Reasonably, people of the former Yugoslavia, especially bereaved relatives of victims and surviving victims themselves, assumed that criminal accountability would be achieved at the ICTY more swiftly than it was. And efforts at the ICTY to apply an 'equivalence of guilt'[24] – by which all the warring parties were said to have committed equally grave crimes that deserved equal punishment – were criticised.[25] Indeed, disappointment among victims, who are probably the ICTY's most interested and constant observers, has often been articulated after acquittals; and predictably, reactions depend on which "side" victims see themselves.[26] In BiH, for instance, Bosnian Muslims have expressed dissatisfaction and anger over the acquittals of high-ranking Serbian indictees Momčilo Perišić, Jovica Stanišića, and Franko Simatović.[27]

The ICTY's work was never going to be easy, given the unique internal and external circumstances that framed its creation. With no institutional equivalent since Nuremberg, the ICTY pushed its way forward in what was aptly described as "learning by doing."[28] The Tribunal's indictment policy, long trials, and sometimes disappointing judgements have all led to doubts about whether the ICTY and its *retributive justice* mechanism – which concentrates on perpetrators and punishment – delivers the justice sought by victims. Now, after years of retributive justice efforts, there is growing appreciation that this form of justice may in fact be insufficient and that more weight should be given to *restorative justice* mechanisms, which address the immediate needs of victims.[29]

Among those who have voiced concern that victims need more support is Judge Patrick Robinson, who served as President of the ICTY from 2008 to 2011. He pleaded in 2010 before the UNSC for the establishment of a trust fund that would "complement the Tribunal's criminal trials by providing victims with the necessary resources to rebuild their lives."[30] Victim communities regularly stress the importance of knowing why violence against them occurred; and say they want to understand details of crimes, such as where their family members were killed and buried, but also how the crimes could have happened at all.[31] At its outset, it seemed that the Milošević trial would be a paradigm for this kind of justice, determining not only his criminal responsibility but also answering many questions about what happened and why.

Criticism of the ICTY by the Defence

When he was first indicted by the ICTY in 1999, Milošević was still a sitting head of state and few people believed he would actually be tried in The Hague. Even when he lost power in 2000, the Tribunal – which was not imbued with the law enforcement mechanisms to arrest indictees on its own – was dependent on the cooperation of the successor regime in Serbia to apprehend him. But in March 2001, Serbian authorities did arrest Milošević. They handed him over to the ICTY after detaining him for three months in a Belgrade jail, during which time they investigated him for abuse of power charges.

Milošević's 28 June 2001 transfer to The Hague was made on the authority of the Serbian (republic-level) government, but federal authorities led by

President Vojislav Koštunica declared the transfer illegal. They argued that, as a unit of the FRY, Serbia was not an international subject and could not engage in international politics, which was the exclusive domain of the federal government. But Serbian Prime Minister Zoran Đinđić took responsibility for the decision to transfer Milošević, claiming that the Republic of Serbia could legally trump the FRY's authority per Article 135 of the 1990 Serbian Constitution, which indeed stipulated that Serbia could disregard federal law in certain circumstances. The Article – originally included by Milošević's own constitutional experts – allowed Đinđić to sidestep federal authorities.[32]

Once in The Hague, Milošević raised questions about the legality of the ICTY during his initial pre-trial appearance on 3 July 2001, arguing that the Court had been illegally constituted because it was not established by the UN General Assembly.[33] Within weeks, a motion challenging the legitimacy of the Tribunal was filed on Milošević's behalf by a court-appointed *amicus curiae*, though it was dismissed by the Trial Chamber in November 2001.[34] The Chamber ruled that although the Tribunal's creation by the Security Council was without precedent, it had been founded under the Council's broad powers to act to maintain international peace and security.[35] And besides, Milošević had effectively recognised the legitimacy of the ICTY when he signed the 1995 Dayton Peace Agreement, in which all parties had agreed to cooperate fully with the Tribunal.[36]

The trial

The trial of Slobodan Milošević began on 12 February 2002, less than eight months after he was transferred to The Hague – swiftness unprecedented at the ICTY. The quick start date of the trial was cheered by some, but others questioned if there had been enough time to properly prepare the case provided the extent of the charges. Once the trial ended unfinished, more questions arose – about its length, its structure, its procedures, and the evidence – opening up a debate on how to best try political leaders for crimes alleged to have occurred over protracted periods.[37]

Milošević faced charges in three separate indictments – for crimes in Croatia, in BiH, and in Kosovo – including charges of grave breaches of the Geneva Convention, crimes against humanity, violations of laws and customs of war, and genocide. He was first indicted by then Chief Prosecutor Louise Arbour on 24 May 1999 for crimes committed in Kosovo from January of that year through the date of the indictment. Arbour's successor Carla del Ponte took up investigations into the two earlier wars, resulting in two additional and separate indictments in 2001: the Croatia indictment, filed on 1 October, and the Bosnia indictment on 22 November. As a consequence of this piecemeal approach, three separate legal teams had been created, each dealing with one of the three conflicts. This led to an unfortunate lack of harmonisation – as well as a number of discrepancies – among the indictments.

The most obvious of these discrepancies was that only the Croatia indictment referred to a Serbian policy of expansionism in terms of Greater Serbia geopolitical designs. Greater Serbia ideology could just as easily be used to explain the wars in BiH and Kosovo and was, in fact, critically significant to all three conflicts. But the three legal teams led their own investigations and, although joint meetings were held on a regular basis to discuss policy and expert witnesses, inconsistencies persisted.

In November 2001, just a few months before the opening of the trial, Geoffrey Nice, a British barrister, was named as the Principle Trial Attorney for the case. His appointment manifested a change in strategy, and steps were promptly taken to unite the three indictments in a single case. On 27 November, a request was submitted to the Trial Chamber to join the indictments. The submission argued that all three of the wars covered in the separate indictments were driven by common, premeditated Serb political strategy. The Joinder filing failed before the Trial Chamber but succeeded on appeal; and yet the Appeals Chamber ruled just over a week before the trial opened, leaving no time to restructure the substance of any of the constituent indictments. And moreover, any significant amendment to any of the indictments would have given Milošević an argument for adjournment of trial on that part of the case.

The Milošević case became the largest at the ICTY by far, with 66 counts in the indictments, allegedly committed in Croatia, BiH, and Kosovo over a period of nine years. It is useful to keep in mind the distinction between the terms 'count' and 'charge.' A charge represents a potential basis for the imposition of liability, while a count alleges the commission of a statutory offence on the basis of one or more charges, related to many different individually named victims, different geographic locations, and different forms of responsibility. A count has been described as "nothing more than a means by which the Prosecution organises the charges in an indictment." Further, an accused person "may be convicted of a count if only one of the charges under that count is established. It is each charge therefore that holds the potential of exposing the accused to individual criminal liability."[38] The 66 counts for which Milošević was indicted reflected many hundreds of charges.

Soon after Nice took over leadership of the case, a discussion about genocide charges unfolded. Milošević was charged with the crime of genocide only in the Bosnia indictment, but the Bosnian team considered dropping those charges for crimes committed in several municipalities in the north and east of BiH in 1992 and 1995. Lawyers, investigators, and analysts from all three Prosecution teams were divided on the issue. Some argued that there was no evidence to charge Milošević with genocide, proposing to strike it from the indictment and instead charge him with crimes against humanity. It would be easier, they reasoned, to demonstrate the 'widespread and systematic' element required to prove crimes against humanity than the 'intent to destroy a group in whole or in part' required for genocide.[39]

Nice, who had not been at the ICTY when the indictments were filed, tasked a lawyer to review all the evidence on genocide, then to seek out any straightforward evidence of Milošević's criminal intent as well as evidence of his awareness of unfolding events. For, if Milošević had been 'on notice' through information that came to him from governments and NGOs and yet had done nothing to change policies that resulted in mass atrocity crimes, perhaps he knew of and intended precisely those crimes. Indeed, a critical question became how long Milošević and his closest collaborators had known about critical events – for example, the Srebrenica genocide – before they took place. With this in mind, Nice initiated a 'Request for Assistance' from Serbia, asking for new evidence, such as diplomatic cables sent from embassies around the world to Milošević and other high-ranking officials between 1992 and 1996, particularly assessments of the situation before, during, and after the takeover of territories in Eastern Bosnia in the summer of 1995. Nice was concerned that if genocide charges were pressed without sufficient evidence and Milošević was acquitted of the charge, it would also have consequences on the legal and historical appraisal of the role that Serbia might have played in what had happened at Srebrenica and other places where genocide may have been committed.[40]

From the outset, the number of crime sites alone indicated that the Milošević trial would be a major test for any court, especially one as new and inexperienced as the ICTY. Once the trial ended, and without a judgement, both professionals and the public wondered how the scale of the indictments and the extent of the charges had impacted the speed and management of the trial.[41] But the extensive nature of the charges had caught the attention of the judges, too, and under instructions of the Trial Chamber, the Prosecution had amended all three indictments between November 2001 and October 2002, reducing the number of counts and crime sites.[42]

In an attempt to manage the trial, the Court also imposed a time limit on the parties in presenting their cases, resulting in a further cutback of the evidence presented, which meant that evidence for some crimes was not presented at all. At the end of the Prosecution case in February 2004, the *amici curiae* filed a Defence Motion for Judgement of Acquittal arguing that some charges should be dismissed on the basis that the Prosecution had not presented enough or any evidence to prove that they occurred.[43] In June 2004, the Trial Chamber issued its Decision on the Motion for Judgement of Acquittal (hereinafter, the Half-Time Judgement) and a number of crime site incidents, most of which related to crimes alleged in the BiH indictment, were dismissed.[44] The Prosecution had to hope that they had provided enough evidence to meet the 'widespread and systematic' test required to establish crimes against humanity and illustrate an overall plan.[45] Yet, the Prosecution was unsure of what this test was or how to guarantee that they had offered evidence for enough crime sites to prove a pattern of crimes.[46]

Arguably, the Trial Chamber's constraint on the time allotted to each party should have ensured a brisk pace. The Prosecution's part of the trial went smoothly and was within the time limit imposed by the Chamber; which, by its own calculation, determined that the Prosecution spent 360 hours proving its case, not counting hours used for cross-examination and procedural/legal arguments but including the testimonies of 296 *viva voce* witnesses.[47] Altogether, for the three indictments, if the time used for cross-examinations by Milošević and all procedural arguments was accounted for, the Prosecution case would have occupied 294 full eight-hour working days.[48]

Milošević was given the same amount of time to present his Defence case, but there was a considerable difference between the efficient way the professional Prosecution team presented evidence and Milošević's slower progress, and this was partly because he insisted on examining all his witnesses orally, often at length, and chose not to make use of written testimonies. Milošević presented the testimonies of only 42 Defence witnesses, covering mostly the Kosovo indictment, and was just starting to call witnesses for the Croatia indictment when he died. Several months beforehand, in November 2005, the Trial Chamber had calculated that Milošević had already used 75 per cent of the 360 hours allotted to him, in which he had dealt almost exclusively with the Kosovo part of the case.[49] Even if the trial had reached its conclusion, the Defence case could not have been completed by April 2006, as mandated by the Trial Chamber, because no evidence for the Bosnia indictment would have been presented by then.

Self-representation

In August 2001, the Trial Chamber granted Milošević the right to represent himself in court. This is allowed under the Statute and Rules of the ICTY; however, no mechanism, guidance, or protocol regulates the right of self-representation.[50] And in such a complex case, this would have been a challenge for the court even in the most ideal circumstances, but in combination with Milošević's deteriorating health condition, it became a major obstacle to efficiency. Delays attributed to Milošević's recurring health problems highlighted issues of fairness that exist in a trial of this kind. Is fairness delivered only if the right of the Accused to represent him/herself is preserved even if he/she is physically unfit? Is fairness delivered only when victims have the right to see justice done, even if that requires the forced imposition of defence counsel on a sick accused person and continuation of the trial proceedings in his/her absence? Can both be achieved or must one concept of fairness yield, in whole or in part, to the other? The judges tended to resolve this question by affording extensive rights to Milošević, whatever additional difficulties this caused.

Adding to confusion over Milošević's legal representation, the Trial Chamber invited the Registrar to assign three *amici curiae* to the case. The Chamber's Order explicitly stated that the *amici* did not represent the

Defendant but were there to assist the court to ensure that the case was conducted properly.[51] Yet, no concrete instructions were given as to how the *amici* should play this role and Milošević chose not to give them such instructions himself. Still, they managed to file hundreds of motions, and all three *amici* took part in cross-examining Prosecution witnesses.[52] Milošević also had a team of legal advisors of his own choosing, who met with him regularly and assisted him with preparations.[53]

Self-representation by Milošević slowed the pace of the case in part because of the time he spent questioning witnesses, often addressing issues that had no probative relevance – something for which he was cautioned by judges on a regular basis.[54] But his health was also regularly on the agenda of the court. In November 2002, nine months after the start of the trial, the parties were invited by the Trial Chamber to submit their views and proposals on how to deal with the effects of Milošević's health on trial proceedings. The possibility of appointing counsel to assist Milošević was discussed, something that would have been very different than the appointment of *amici curiae*. He resisted this proposal and defended his right to self-representation, saying that under no conditions would he abandon his fight in the courtroom. "You yourselves have provided for that possibility in your Rules and regulations," he noted, saying that "although I don't consider this Tribunal of yours to be legal … I assume you adhere to the Rules you laid down yourselves."[55]

The Trial Chamber decided against imposing Defence counsel, but Milošević's health did not improve over time and delays became more frequent as the case progressed. In September 2003, the Prosecution again pushed for counsel to be appointed to assist Milošević, at least with crime site evidence. The trial had been interrupted 13 times just during the Prosecution's part of the case and the Prosecution argued that the appointment of Defence counsel would allow proceedings to continue when Milošević was unable to attend court as a result of ill health.[56] Nonetheless, Milošević's resistance persisted and the Trial Chamber repeatedly decided against appointing counsel.

The Defence part of the case, originally scheduled to start on 8 June 2004, was postponed on five occasions.[57] It eventually began on 31 August 2004, and in September 2004, the Prosecution once again called upon the Trial Chamber to reconsider the right of the Accused to self-representation.[58] The Chamber responded with an order that adjusted the court schedule to accommodate Milošević's failing health, reducing the working week from five to three days; and it finally assigned legal counsel to assist Milošević. The ruling stated, *inter alia*, that there was a "real danger" that the trial would not conclude otherwise.[59] The decision allowed Milošević to continue to participate in the conduct of his case, "with the leave of the Trial Chamber," and to examine witnesses after the assigned counsel had done so.[60] However, this was effectively overturned by the Appeals Chamber, which agreed in principle on the necessity of assigning legal counsel but modified their responsibilities so as to minimise their impact. In reality, nothing changed.[61]

In April 2005, Milošević again fell ill, during the testimony of Defence witness Kosta Bulatović, and the Trial Chamber decided for the first time to proceed in Milošević's absence. But the attempt failed, as the witness refused to answer questions in cross-examination by the Prosecution, saying that he had come to testify at the request of Milošević, whom he still considered his President. As long as Milošević was absent from the courtroom, Bulatović refused to cooperate.[62] Contempt of court charges were levelled against Bulatović on 20 April 2005, but his four-month prison sentence was suspended for two years due to his own poor health.[63] And by the time Bulatović returned to give evidence on 25 April, Milošević had recovered sufficiently, so that Bulatović's testimony was concluded in his presence.

Temporary continuation of the trial *in absentia* would have represented a major breakthrough in resolving the problems caused by Milošević's ill health. But witnesses like Kosta Bulatović forced the court to submit to Milošević's notion of how the trial should be managed. A workable and effective solution to continue the trial with assigned counsel did not materialise; and many interruptions due to Milošević's health problems extended the duration of the trial beyond the total of its actual courtroom hours, so that it carried on for over four years. If sessions had been held five days each week, from 9:00 to 16:00, the trial could have been concluded in two to three years.

Joinder or severance?

The scope of the indictments also remained an important issue in debates about best management of the trial. The difficult question was whether all three indictments should have been tried together or in two separate trials – one for the Kosovo indictment and one for the Croatia and Bosnia indictments. The Prosecution's December 2001 motion seeking joinder had argued that all three be addressed in a single trial on the basis that they were all part of the same overarching plan, but the Appeals Chamber ruling in February 2002 had left open the possibility of severing one or more of the indictments if the trial threatened to become unmanageable at a later stage.[64] And indeed, the Trial Chamber did later raise the possibility of severing the indictments, in July 2004, when it proposed two trials.[65] The Prosecution strongly rejected severance, though, arguing that inefficiencies arose not from Milošević's ill health but from his insistence on self-representation and contending that this would be remedied by the imposition of professional legal counsel to conduct his defence.[66]

This topic was again on the Court's agenda in November 2005, as the judges grew concerned about the time the trial was taking and the prospect that it might never conclude. The Trial Chamber invited the parties to consider severance of the Kosovo part of the trial in order to secure a judgement for Kosovo, leaving the Croatia and BiH crimes to be tried later.[67] Yet, at a hearing held on 29 November 2005, both the Prosecution and Defence argued – for different reasons – that all three indictments should continue to be tried together. Milošević maintained that there had been a single war, in which Yugoslavia had been intentionally destroyed by external forces, and that his trial was a continuation of that war and the ICTY one of its weapons.[68] The Prosecution made a case for "judicial economy," noting that many high-level witnesses would need to be called twice if there were two trials; but the most persuasive argument articulated by the Prosecution was that trying events "back to front" could prejudice both parties to the case in unpredictable ways. By this reasoning, the Trial Chamber's December 2001 Decision to start the trial with the Kosovo part of the indictment had effectively made severance impossible. In any Kosovo-only trial, evidence from the Croatian or Bosnian wars that could illuminate Milošević's developing state of mind as it applied to the Kosovo conflict would have been excluded from consideration. And, if evidence was presented in the Kosovo trial that related back to events in the earlier conflicts, any associated findings might have had to be accepted without challenge in the subsequent trial covering earlier events.[69] The Prosecution's position was that the trial could have been severed only if the Croatia and Bosnia indictments were tried first, following the chronology of events from 1991 to 1999.

The indictments were not severed, and by November 2005, the time allocated for the Defence had been used in such a way that Milošević had just 25 per cent remaining. He still needed to present the rest of his Kosovo defence, and start and finish the defence for both the Croatia and Bosnia indictments. On the basis of the way his trial developed, one may conclude that a defendant who is not physically fit enough to conduct their own defence on a daily basis should not be given the option of self-representation; and that a defence lawyer should be imposed by the court on any accused person who declines to engage counsel, from the outset of proceedings. Milošević's absences were a permanent threat to the trial and to his own ability to defend himself, and counsel should have been imposed much earlier – for his own sake and for the sake of justice. In order to uphold (or be seen to be upholding) judicial standards of fairness, the Trial Chamber may have inadvertently compromised justice and, thus, failed victims.

Political trials, show trials, or transformative trials?

A question that has hung over the Milošević trial – and which he actively cultivated, beginning with his Opening Statement to the court – was whether his was a political trial.[70] In 2002, his brother Borislav, former Ambassador to Russia from the FRY, said at a news conference in Moscow that it was "plainly evident" that the trial was a political trial, which he said was meant to "justify NATO's campaign in Yugoslavia."[71] When defending his right to represent himself, Milošević repeated this argument. He claimed that whether he had committed a crime was not even at issue and that certain intentions ascribed to him were "beyond the expertise of any conceivable lawyer."[72]

Scholars distinguish between political trials, which take place within the rule of law, and 'partisan trials' or 'show trials', which substitute political expediency for law.[73] Many accept, to a degree, that all trials have a political element – because in every state, the judicial system is a branch of government and thus part of a larger political system.[74] But still, there is a widespread view of the term 'political trial' as a pejorative reference to trials that use legal systems to eliminate or discredit political opponents. Ron Christenson has described political trials as "using legal procedure for political ends."[75] And Otto Kirchheimer understood political trials as those in which "the courts eliminate a political foe of the regime according to some prearranged rules."[76]

A number of scholars have posed the question of whether political trials can be fair despite a political agenda. As one legal scholar put it, fairness is the tipping point "... [and] the goal is to achieve a process that is fundamentally fair and thus predominantly legal, even if it simultaneously serves some desirable consequentialist purposes."[77] In a broad sense, all trials dealing with political violence and mass atrocities may indeed qualify as political.[78] When a regime responsible for human rights abuses or for committing mass atrocities is overthrown, a new regime must decide how to handle members of the old regime. If the choice to put them on trial is made, it is commonly understood that only a limited number of former political and military leaders can be tried; and those who are indicted are likely to be tried by their political opponents. Critics of such trials condemn them for being exercises in selective justice, while proponents praise their value in highlighting the criminality of regimes and tempering calls for vengeance. But any system of justice, whether international or domestic, is only effective if it is seen as legitimate by society.[79]

It is important, though, that political trials are not automatically equated with partisan or show trials, which are characterised as proceedings instituted by governments in order to achieve inevitable outcomes of guilt. Show trials are often associated with totalitarian ideologies and regimes – such as that of Joseph Stalin in the Soviet Union – and with the power of a singular leader to influence a trial's outcome. They are couched in the trappings of legality, but all the prosecutors, judges, and defence attorneys are controlled by the government, and the legal system is used as an instrument of politics to secure total power.[80] Preordained results can also be achieved through what are known as "structural show trials," in which it is "the structure of the proceedings that assures conviction, rather than direct control over the judges."[81]

Jeremy Peterson, a scholar and law practitioner working for the US Justice Department, analysed Saddam Hussein's trial in an attempt to determine if it qualified as a show trial. The trial, held in 2005, ended with the application of a death sentence, unleashing public debate about its fairness. Peterson defined a show trial as composed of two essential elements – certainty of the defendant's conviction and a focus on the audience outside the courtroom rather than on the defendant – and concluded that both criteria applied to the trial of Saddam Hussein.[82] Other scholars have argued that the US military commissions at Guantanamo Bay, though not show trials in the Stalinist sense, employ a system which "retains features that are fundamentally unfair" and are weighted towards conviction.[83]

The trials at the ICTY did not lead automatically to conviction, as there were regular acquittals; and in the case of Milošević, his death precluded a verdict that could have ignited debate about whether the outcome was predetermined. Still, as put forth above, one can argue that all trials held before international criminal tribunals are political trials (though not show trials), because they deal with political violence. If a "purely legal trial" is imagined to embody ideal justice – depending on fair procedure and neutral assessment only – then a "purely political trial" would be predetermined and procedure would be irrelevant.[84] Accepting, then, that the Milošević trial is by that definition a political trial, this study will draw on Leora Bilsky's definition of a 'transformative trial.' Bilsky sees transformative trials as placed somewhere between the political and the legal.[85] On the one hand, a transformative trial remains loyal to the basic liberal value of the rule of law, and on the other hand it performs a unique function as a legal forum in which society's fundamental values can be examined in the light of competing counter-narratives presented in the courtroom.[86]

Scholarly debate on the purpose of mass atrocities trials

International criminal trials represent one way of addressing the commission of crimes by past regimes, and they have been reintroduced as a transitional justice mechanism since the 1990s. But debate about the purpose of trials that deal with mass atrocities extends back to the Nuremberg and Tokyo Tribunals and is dominated by two opposing views – one, that such trials should fulfil the legal purposes of delivering justice and meting out punishment, and another that stresses the importance of their extralegal objectives to establish truth and document history.[87] Early debate was dominated by an emphasis on the exclusively legal functions of trials to "render justice."[88] Since then, a growing number of scholars have identified the distinction between legal and extralegal aims as unnecessary and limiting.

Ruti Teitel connects transitional justice with five conceptions of justice: criminal, historical, reparatory, administrative, and constitutional.[89] She equates historical truth with justice and argues that its pursuit is embedded in a framework of accountability and in the pursuit of justice more generally, to which criminal trials contribute.[90] In defining historical justice, Teitel applies the Enlightenment view, in which history is considered teacher and judge.[91] Yet Teitel cautions that 'truth' and 'history' are not universally seen as one and the same, and that when history takes an "interpretative turn" there is no single, clear lesson to draw from the past. Instead, one must recognise the degree to which historical understanding depends on political and social contingencies.[92]

Lawrence Douglas has introduced the term 'didactic legality' and argues that the trials of the Holocaust blurred the very boundary between the legal and extralegal.[93] Douglas qualifies all Holocaust trials as "orchestrations designed to show the world the facts of astonishing crime, but also to demonstrate the power of law to reintroduce order into the space evacuated of legal and moral sense."[94] He finds that insisting on the legal aspect of trials is a "needlessly restrictive vision of the trial as legal form."[95] While recognising that the primary responsibility of a criminal trial is to resolve questions of guilt in a procedurally fair manner, Douglas advocates integration of the legal and extralegal purposes of mass atrocities trials.[96]

Other proponents of recognising the extralegal value of mass atrocities trials stress that criminal trials must be conducted with a pedagogical purpose in mind. Mark Osiel asserts that, in times of democratic transition, public reckoning with how horrific events of recent history could have happened is more important for democratisation than criminal law's more traditional objectives. In his opinion, effective mass atrocities trials stimulate public discussion in ways that foster toleration, moderation, and civil respect.[97] Leora Bilsky warns against compartmentalising the discussion into the legal versus the historical. In her view, this polarisation distracts from the fact that transformative trials should "fulfil an essential function in a democratic society by exposing the hegemonic narrative of identity to critical consideration."[98] In other words, the legal and the historical do not compete with, but rather complement, each other.

A study by Jelena Subotić, aptly entitled *Hijacked Justice*, examines the fact that elites may not be motivated to agree to transitional justice mechanisms out of a desire to deal with the past, but may instrumentalise transitional justice for other reasons. Subotić identified three political aims of state-level elites in Serbia that inspired them to meet the state's obligation to cooperate with the ICTY: to get rid of domestic political opponents, to obtain international financial aid, and to gain admission to the European Union. Subotić argues that 'hijacking justice' in this way can backfire because it can "foster domestic backlash, deepen political instability, or create politicised versions of history."[99] In other words, when there is no genuine intention to deal with the past for the purposes of legal or historical justice, mass atrocities trials may fail to render justice and establish the truth.

The courtroom narrative: "two truths" about the conflict

An additional complication in trials of this nature is that they inevitably address contradictory historical interpretations. The nature of the legal system applied at international criminal courts is such that the Prosecution and Defence are likely to present competing narratives, or two truths. Each side in any conflict has its own theory as to how the conflict turned violent and who is to blame; and there is no mechanism to predict which of the narratives produced in a courtroom will prevail outside of it. Depending on how many persons are on trial, sometimes there are even more than two versions of events presented, and narratives developed in court persist regardless of the trial judgement.[100]

Kirchheimer described the polarised narratives that can be introduced in the courtroom as a gamble, asserting that the risk of subjecting every moment of traumatic history to the scrutiny of criminal legal procedure is a "double wager." Not only might a defendant prevail, but even if a trial ends in conviction it may fail in its didactic aim. He called this an "irreducible risk" and the inevitable *sine qua non* of a just trial.[101] Gerry Simpson offers an example of this legal double wager in the case of Klaus Barbie, who was tried and eventually convicted of crimes against humanity committed by Nazis in occupied France. His trial, held in 1987, became a test for the entire French nation, causing cultural upheaval and unease; for at times, France appeared to be placed alongside Barbie as a co-defendant, accused of Nazi collaboration and of having committed mass atrocities in Algeria during the colonial struggle there.[102] With the focus of public attention shifted towards French crimes in Algeria, it seemed occasionally as if Barbie was no longer the defendant at all.[103]

Milošević seemed to be very much aware of the double wager of such trials. In his Opening Statements,[104] he repeatedly addressed the responsibility of Germany, the Vatican, the European Community, and the United States as principal actors in the violent destruction of Yugoslavia. He charged that "by placing the responsibility on Yugoslavia and myself personally as aggressors, a very obvious tactic was used to ... prevent logical thinking based on empirical principles." He denied that he had been part of a joint criminal enterprise and said one had instead existed among member of the international community, which he claimed had sought to destroy Yugoslavia and then hide behind "senseless, vulgar theories about bad guys."[105] As the trial unfolded, Milošević's Defence strategy – as puzzling as it was at times from legal point of view – reflected his effort to establish a counter-narrative of what had occurred in the former Yugoslavia during the 1990s.

History in the courtroom

Research on mass atrocities trials has attempted to determine the extent that Prosecution and Defence courtroom narratives influence collective memory and interpretations of history.[106] In a trial, as in the writing of history, the judge, like the historian, aspires to produce a coherent narrative that explains, interprets, and records historical events.[107] Historians and legal scholars who have analysed the relationship between the legal and extralegal value of mass atrocities trials see no immediate contradiction between a trial's legal objectives and its extralegal effects, but they do emphasise that legal judgements should never be viewed as definitive interpretations of history. Still, Charles Maier asserts that "doing justice" and "doing history" are related activities, as a historian endeavours to "do justice" by articulating the ambitions of protagonists and exploring their choices.[108]

Michael Marrus, who studies the interplay between history and law, sees the records of mass atrocities trials as historical sources like any others. He underscores the fact that historians must evaluate every source with an eye to its provenance, since all sources are in some sense "tainted" and war crimes trial records are certainly no exception. The material used in a court is limited by legal standards and procedural rules that exclude some sources commonly depended upon by historians and which would be considered essential for shaping historical opinion. For example, although hearsay is allowed at the ICTY under certain circumstances, other materials used by historians – such as reports about the political atmosphere or general statements made by reliable commentators about the tone set by leaders – may not be allowed as evidence in the courtroom.[109]

Ruti Teitel notes that it is impossible to fix the past, which she says would "be a futile attempt to stop the state's historical accounting, to exhaust its politics and its potential for progress."[110] She stresses that any legal response to mass atrocities produces transitional historical narratives.[111] This means that a judgement, though the final stage in legal proceedings that are fixed in time, does not represent a definitive historical interpretation of the events judged.[112] Yet, there will always be history in a judgement. According to Richard Wilson, a human rights scholar, the judgements in two ICTY cases he has analysed "are characterised by detailed contextualisation of criminal acts and extensive historical interpretation."[113] He also contends that charges such as genocide, which emphasise the collective nature of the crime, compel the court "to situate individual acts within long-term, systematic policies."[114]

The Milošević trial illustrates that it is desirable, even essential, that the courtroom is a place in which history is understood, for at least two reasons. First, historical context is necessary in establishing and proving the guilty mind – *mens rea* in legal terminology – of an accused person and of fellow high-level officials involved in developing and executing a political plan that eventually led to the commission of crimes. Since a criminal plan often derives from ideological concepts conceived in the past, a proper understanding of such an ideology is best achieved, or perhaps can only be achieved, when placed in a broader historical framework. Second, historical context is necessary because it allows judges to comprehend the political dynamics that led to the occurrence of mass atrocities. In the Milošević case, a knowledge of historical political events was required if the judges were to grasp how political elites in Yugoslavia had articulated Serbian state ideology and when Milošević had embraced it as a platform for political and military action.

Awareness of these complicated and contextual dynamics on the part of judges helps deflect attempts by defendants to reframe history in support of their own narrative; for instance, Milošević's claim throughout his trial that the international community had conspired against him. "Accusations levelled against me are an unscrupulous lie," he said in his August 2004 Opening

Statement, arguing that the Tribunal itself was part of a "war which continues to be waged."[115] The two competing narratives presented in his trial are traced in this study through the oral and written argumentation by which both parties asserted their positions – in evidence tendered in court, and in indictments, briefs, opening statements, and various motions. And besides the Prosecution and Defence narratives, legal and historical narratives were also shaped during a trial. These narratives overlap, complement, and influence each other, with one distinguishing difference between the two: a historical narrative comprises material presented in and outside the courtroom, while a legal narrative is formed in the courtroom alone.

The test for the introduction of evidence in court is bound by a strict forensic process that consists of presentation by one trial party, followed by cross-examination by the opposing party, and eventually the right of re-direct by the first party. The product of this process – forensic truth – is different from historical truth in several ways. For one, a historian is not bound by the same forensic process in order to include a source in a historical account and may seek corroboration in a greater variety of sources than are admissible in a courtroom. Over the course of time, this interpretation may even be altered by other historians. For this reason, historical and legal narratives about the same topic may differ considerably; as the latter is captured in closing arguments and judgements, which are formed in the normative legal framework and in rigid court procedures, and remain fixed in time.

The trial record

Materials selected as evidence by the Prosecution and Defence in the Milošević case now constitute an unmatched historical source; and even with some gaps in the trial record, it incorporates documents from state archives that would have otherwise been unavailable to the public and to researchers for many decades. Indeed, some of the trial material would never have surfaced at all were it not for the obligation of states to cooperate with the ICTY. Still, there remains trial material that is officially available and yet inaccessible to the public, and the (in)accessibility of ICTY records by the public is an important matter. The ICTY Court Record (ICR), an electronic database, is sometimes more of a challenge than an aid to researchers because it comprises only a selection of materials, not the full record of every trial, and remains incomplete for a number of technical and other reasons.[116]

The burden of proof at the ICTY often led to the accrual of a great deal of evidence in order to prove 'the obvious' in a court bound by strict legal rules and procedures.[117] For every general allegation against Milošević, probative evidence was needed to establish that the crime actually occurred and that Milošević was criminally responsible for it. The large amount of evidence presented by the parties during the trial was also partially due to the changing world in which we live. Modern technology made the wars in the former Yugoslavia into media spectacles, watched daily on the television and captured on the Internet. Minute details of the conflicts became available and accessible to the public in nearly all the world's languages; and material from these 'open sources,' potentially relevant as evidence, was almost unlimited.[118]

Notwithstanding the huge amount of audio, video, and written material that exists about the conflicts and about the role of Slobodan Milošević in them, ICTY Prosecutors – unlike their Nuremberg counterparts – did not have full or easy access to documentary material from the archives of the former leader's country.[119] Documents from the official archives of the FRY and Serbia, considered more important from a forensic point of view than open source materials, were difficult and sometimes impossible to obtain.[120] This was in stark contrast to the experience of prosecutors in Nuremberg, for which Allied Powers had simply seized the state and Nazi Party archives of defeated Germany for use as evidence in court. Nonetheless, evidence that did come directly to the ICTY from archives in Serbia, the FRY, the RS, and the RSK makes the Milošević trial record particularly valuable, as it includes official documents that would otherwise have remained protected for untold numbers of years. Once used in court as evidence, most of these documents became public.

Extratrial material originating from the ICTY and OTP includes investigative and analytical documentation, such as reports by in-house investigators, researchers, and analysts, which were not used per se in court proceedings. Internal policy documents on topics such as indictment strategies or how to conduct the trial also fall under the designation of extratrial material. In other words, a considerable amount of this material was used for investigative and research purposes without becoming a part of the official trial record. The ICTY database contains diverse materials collected by the OTP, from demographic data on the former Yugoslavia, to media reports that may have been used to prepare for the cross-examination of Defence witnesses, to seemingly endless supporting evidence and courtroom exhibits.[121] Access to some of these materials remains limited to OTP employees until, or unless, they are made publicly available, which will depend on the conclusions of the Mechanism for International Criminal Tribunals (MICT).[122] Particular attention was paid in this research to evidence that triggered important debate after being presented in court, compelling former Yugoslav societies to face the past and deal with uncomfortable truths. Among these materials were records from meetings, which revealed Milošević's state of mind before, during, and after the armed conflicts. What makes the Milošević trial record especially interesting as a source of history is the fact that it includes responses by Milošević himself to every piece of evidence brought against him. Milošević not only represented himself in court, and therefore responded in that capacity to the evidence presented, but also made remarks throughout the trial from the standpoint of a man attempting to defend his political and private decisions.

The debate on the causes and consequences of the disintegration of Yugoslavia

The part Milošević played in events of the 1980s and 1990s has been explored in a number of political biographies and is an important sub-topic of analysis. However, the most well-known of these biographies were published before his trial or in the same year that it started.[123] Thus, few authors have presented the trail of evidence that was followed in the courtroom to determine responsibility for the break-up of Yugoslavia and, more importantly, the violence that followed.[124] The scholarly debate on the causes of Yugoslavia's dissolution offers useful insight into the complex socio-political climate in which it occurred.[125] To that end, Jasna Dragović-Soso has identified five categories of causation, focusing on: first, "ancient hatreds" and a "clash of civilisations"; second, the nineteenth-century rise of South Slav nationalist ideologies and the first Yugoslav state-building experiment; third, the Yugoslav socialist system, with its complicated federal structure, ideological delegitimation, and economic failures; fourth, Yugoslavia's breakdown in the second half of the 1980s and the actions of "political and intellectual agency"; and fifth, external factors.[126]

A majority of authors agree that Milošević played a central role in events that unfolded in the former SFRY between 1987 and 1999; and for the purposes of this study, three perspectives on this role have been identified in existing literature – those of the intentionalists, the relativists, and the apologists.[127] 'Intentionalists' see Milošević as having dictated the pace of the Yugoslav crisis through well-articulated and planned objectives that drove the other republics away.[128] According to this view, violence was used cynically and practically, and was employed against non-Serbs as part of a clear and premeditated strategy – the success of which is irrelevant – to secure Milošević's promise of "All Serbs in a Single State" at any cost.[129]

Alternative to this are authors who tend to see Milošević as an intelligent and ruthless politician whose politics were mostly reactive.[130] These 'relativists' see Milošević's policies as responses to developments that were driven by leaders of Slovenia, Croatia, BiH, and Kosovo, and by the international community. From this standpoint, Milošević genuinely wanted to preserve Yugoslavia but was unsuccessful.[131] Relativists perceive Milošević as an immensely ambitious politician who endeavoured to achieve more than he was capable of; and his rule has been cast by authors in this camp as a sequence of mistakes and failures – at the national and international levels.[132] The violence that accompanied the disintegration of Yugoslavia is thus explained as resulting from a complicated interplay of many factors, leading to an escalation of the crisis that was beyond the control of Milošević alone.

'Apologists' share the opinion held by relativists regarding the role of those republics that sought independence, and of the international community, in the disintegration of Yugoslavia. Yet they not only see Milošević's goal to preserve Yugoslavia as well-intentioned but also defend his politics and decision-making in general.[133] They downplay Milošević's calculating and ruthless side to recast him as a somewhat clumsy, wayward, and inconsistent authoritarian leader who merely failed to deliver on promises he made.[134] In fact, many apologists frame Milošević as an atypical authoritarian ruler who could have secured his power by force but was willing, instead, to compromise.[135] Apologists also dismiss arguments about the influence of Greater Serbia ideology on Milošević or on Serbia's involvement in the wars in Croatia, BiH, or Kosovo. They stress that it was NATO that committed grave crimes in Serbia and Kosovo, for which nobody has been held accountable. And, as to Milošević's domestic criminality, some apologists say that there has been no definitive proof of his personal involvement in assassinations that took place during his rule, and others go even further to absolve him by arguing that even if he did play a role in these murders, there were "not many such examples."[136]

The value of the trial record as a historical source

What can the trial record, as a historical source, contribute to the ongoing scholarly debate about Milošević? Did he genuinely try to save Yugoslavia? Did he inadvertently cause its disintegration through a series of well-intended blunders?[137] Or, did he actively work to re-draw its borders? One event in particular that has sparked contesting interpretations about Milošević's attitude toward the break-up of Yugoslavia is the 1991 meeting in Karađorđevo at which Milošević and Croatian President Franjo Tuđman allegedly discussed the partition of BiH between Serbia and Croatia. For various and sometimes contradictory reasons, scholars have described this meeting as significant; and for years, both Milošević and Tuđman managed to avoid responding to rumours about what took place. But at the trial, the meeting was addressed in detail by several witnesses with first-hand knowledge of the event.

For Milošević, the idea that he had even contemplated the partition of BiH undermined his proclaimed position as the champion of Yugoslav unity. And so, Milošević denied that he and Tuđman had *ever* discussed the partition of BiH, at Karađorđevo or elsewhere. His disavowal of the testimony of reliable witnesses was noteworthy, as it appeared designed to distance himself from what such a plan or agreement would have revealed about his state of mind. And this raised the question of whether, at the time he had claimed to be fighting for the preservation of Yugoslavia, his deeds in Karađorđevo – hidden at the time from the public – had reflected the covert objectives he truly wished to achieve.

This highlights the quandary for historians who study Milošević, that source material, including evidence given in court, exposes a discrepancy between his overt and covert agendas from his first to last days in power. Take, for instance, the long-running debate about what role the SANU Memorandum – co-authored by several prominent members of the Serbian

Academy of Sciences and Arts in 1986 – played in his policy-making. Indeed, it is hard to find any literature on the Yugoslav crisis that does not make note of connections between the SANU Memorandum and the political programme introduced by Milošević, but there are various perspectives on the nature of these connections. One view is that the Memorandum served as the "blueprint" for Milošević's war policies.[138] Another is that it more generally advocated "a reformed federation."[139] And alternative to both of these is the view that the Memorandum can be seen as an "explicit post-Yugoslav Serbian national program."[140]

Dragović-Soso argues that the Memorandum did not advocate the dissolution of Yugoslavia, the creation of a Greater Serbia, or ethnic cleansing, and that no connection has been established between the authors of the Memorandum and Milošević.[141] Contrary to this view, a number of witnesses talked about the importance of the SANU Memorandum in court, and the polarised narratives that unfolded followed the fault lines of pre-existing scholarly debate. And once again, this narrative was significantly shaped by the active participation of Milošević in courtroom discussions of his position on the SANU Memorandum with several of its authors, who appeared as Defence witnesses.

Milošević's personality was another recurring topic in the courtroom. Biographies that offer an overview of Milošević's early years often note that his life was marked by the three tragic deaths – all suicides – of his father Svetozar in 1962, his maternal uncle Milisav Koljenšić in 1963, and his mother in 1974.[142] However, no author has managed to establish any clear link between these losses and Milošević's development into the particular person and politician he became. And such loss cannot solely account for the lack of empathy that ultimately characterised Milošević. Nor can another prominent influence that was critical throughout Milošević's life and is discussed in almost every biography written about him – the close, almost pathological, relationship he had with his wife Mira. He began courting her when both were still in high school and the relationship remained strong until his death.

Milošević's relationship with his one-time political mentor and friend Ivan Stambolić also turned out to be significant, and the path it took was a reflection of the seeming incongruity of his personality. After being ushered into politics by Stambolić in 1984, Milošević turned against him in 1987 in a calculated series of political manoeuvres, and in 2000, ordered his assassination. Seeking to identify the personal pathology that might adequately describe, and perhaps even explain, Milošević's alleged ruthlessness, biographers have assigned him titles such as "Tyrant" and "Cold Narcissus,"[143] "Sociopath,"[144] and the "Butcher from the Balkans."[145] These unflattering names suggest that he was 'different' from the rest of us. But how different was he? He has been described as intelligent, charming, engaging, and attentive on one hand, and deceitful, manipulative, and forbidding on the other.[146] But duplicity and indifference do not alone make a tyrant or a mass murderer. And so, how did the trial and its record contribute – if at all – to a better understanding of Milošević, the man, the politician, the leader, and an alleged war criminal?

The transformative value of the evidence

Questions about Milošević's role in the collapse of the SFRY are most relevant where they concern how it became violent.[147] When, why, and by whom was violence unleashed, and for what purpose? In scholarly literature, the outbreak of violence has often been ascribed to Greater Serbia ideology and efforts to create a Serb state. Some authors hold that Milošević's plans corresponded with the historical goals of Greater Serbia ideologues but that his political choices actually had no basis "in any particular scheme."[148] The argument goes that despite the wealth of evidence on the part he played in Yugoslavia's dissolution – including from the ICTY – there is not one single document that "incontrovertibly implicates Milošević in a coherent, premeditated strategy of breaking up Yugoslavia in order to create a Greater Serbia."[149]

But then, in the history of mass atrocities trials, rarely has there been a single "smoking gun" document clearly ordering a war crime and signed by an indicted former leader. Historians who study the regimes of Stalin or Hitler know this all too well.[150] These historians have thus, by necessity, based their interpretations mostly on circumstantial evidence, but that has not diminished the responsibility of both leaders for the mass atrocities carried out under their rule.

The opinion of some historians is that current interpretations of the disintegration of Yugoslavia are based chiefly on "contradictory and hardly impartial evidence" such as witness accounts, personal memoirs, and Milošević's own public statements. This view is sometimes supported by the assertion that Milošević was "extremely secretive, leaving very little documentary trace," and that his strategic decisions were made in the seclusion of his home, where only his wife and a small group of advisors were party to his thoughts.[151] Among historians who take this position, there is some recognition of the necessity that new material which has emerged from the ICTY and from government archives is explored.[152] And, for good reason, because the trial record reveals a different picture – that Milošević did at times leave traces, and that audio and video records in some cases irrefutably establish the veracity of certain events or claims.

Documents tendered by the Prosecution that pertain to Milošević's state of mind before, during, and after the wars in Croatia, BiH, and Kosovo are thus vital to the developing historiography of the conflict. For the Croatia indictment, telephone intercepts, records of meetings of the Presidency of the SFRY (PSFRY), and a video known as the Kula Camp Video illustrated the evolution of Milošević's state of mind during the early years of war. For the period covered by the Bosnia indictment, the evidence again included telephone intercepts, but also records from two FRY state organs – the State Council for Harmonisation of Positions on State Policy and the Supreme Defence Council (SDC). And for the years covered by the Kosovo indictment, documents from an ad hoc body known as the Joint Command were valuable, but the key piece of evidence was undoubtedly a video that featured a Serbian-based paramilitary group, the Scorpions, executing civilians taken from Srebrenica in the summer of 1995. Although footage from the Scorpions Video was shown during the cross-examination of a Defence witness, the video was never tendered into evidence. Yet, what transpired in the courtroom caused an unprecedented uproar in the world and in the region.

It is argued in this text that evidence with transformative value has an impact on public opinion and on political processes, and contributes to shaping narratives about a conflict. In some cases, the transformative value of trial evidence is also reflected in the efforts of post-conflict elites to control or contain the damage that the exposure of incriminatory evidence in the courtroom might cause for alleged perpetrators. In the Milošević trial, early obstruction by Belgrade authorities regarding requests for certain materials added weight to the power of that evidence once it was later acquired and presented in court. And, several pieces of evidence had significant and undeniable impact on Serbian and post-Yugoslav society by laying bare the reality of wartime crimes and the degree to which state actors and institutions were linked to criminal activities. The evidence selected for examination in this study has been analysed – at least in part – according to its effect on public debate outside the courtroom and its role in:

- contributing to the existing scholarly discussion on the causes and consequences of the disintegration of Yugoslavia;
- exposing the de facto and *de jure* power of Milošević and the elites around him;
- exposing how Milošević and his associates plotted to establish and redraw Serbia's borders by force;
- exposing efforts by members of the Milošević regime to cover up their real intentions;
- exposing the extent of Milošević's criminality in the assassinations of his political opponents in Serbia;
- exposing the reluctance of post-Milošević political elites in Serbia to accept or assign responsibility for mass atrocities committed by the Milošević regime;
- triggering public revelations of crimes committed by Serb armed forces in the 1990s;
- generating public discussion about the obligation of states to cooperate or not with international courts, as well as the need for transparency in court proceedings.

What the evidence tells us about the leader, the ideology, and the plan

Who? The leader

The personal and political development of Milošević into a leader whose politics led to mass atrocities can be fully appreciated only when analysed together with concurrent political, ideological, and historical processes. An analysis of the connection between a leader and the commission of mass atrocities suggests that the attention to the 'evilness' of a leader is a concept more easily understood and accepted by the general audience than the historical and political processes that actually make the emergence of such a leader possible.[153] And, mass atrocities are indeed most likely to be unleashed by authoritarian political regimes, which by their nature rely on leadership that may be "instrumentally effective, even if morally repugnant."[154] Thus, legal and historical discourse that emerges from trials that deal with individual criminal responsibility must be careful not to neglect collective or state responsibility by overemphasising the criminality of an "evil leader."[155]

At the turn of the twentieth century, German sociologist Max Weber identified three types of authority: traditional, legal, and charismatic. Traditional authority rests on the understanding that traditional rules are to be respected and that subordinates accept the traditional right to power of a dominant and powerful individual or group. Weber classified 'patrimonialism' as a form of traditional authority that reflects the authority of fathers within families. Patrimonialism, applied more recently in an analysis of present-day regimes, is defined by Nathan Quimpo as "a type of rule in which the ruler does not distinguish between personal and public patrimony and treats matters and resources of state as his personal affair."[156] Legal authority, also known as rational authority, relies instead on enacted rules and laws. In modern societies, it is bureaucracies that largely exercise such authority.[157]

Traditional authority is seen to be preordained by status, and legal authority by policy, but charismatic authority rests on a "devotion to the exceptional sanctity, heroism, or exemplary character of an individual and of the normative patterns or order revealed or ordained by him."[158] Expanding on this concept of charismatic authority, as set out by Weber, modern-day authors describe how a charismatic leader projects onto his followers characteristics such as "self-security, a need to influence others, and a strong conviction in the moral integrity of his/her belief."[159] Most theories of charismatic leadership emphasise the attribution of extraordinary supernatural or superhuman qualities to a leader by his or her followers.[160] And so, layered atop these different types of authority, the concept of transformational leadership considers how a leader affects his or her followers. It focuses on how, when, and why followers develop trust, admiration, loyalty, and respect for a leader and it explores leadership in terms of the degree to which a leader holds influence over followers and the type of leader–follower relationship that emerges as a consequence of this interaction.[161]

Milošević understood the impact of his interaction with his followers very well, casting his political aspirations and choices as an expression of the will of Serb people everywhere and asserting that he was seen by officials at the ICTY as an agent of Serbs and Serbia. Milošević claimed it was not only he who had been accused, but all Serbs, all of Serbia, and all of his supporters around the world, remarking that Prosecutor Nice had ascribed him "superhuman powers of influencing people … outside the territory of my own country."[162] This reflected Milošević's appreciation of the important legal debate over the extent to which political and criminal responsibility can be assigned to one individual.

International criminal law does allow individuals to be held accountable for state violence committed through state structures; but a focus on individual criminal responsibility for alleged mass atrocities has a number of potential pitfalls. For one, charging a single person with extensive crimes spread over years carries the risk of 'over-prosecution,' which can distort and simplify the complex historical and political developments that provide context to a case. Before presenting the Prosecution's evidence for the Croatia and Bosnia indictments, Prosecutor Nice warned the Court to resist characterising Milošević as the sole architect of the plan and policies that led to mass atrocities. "Plans can emerge without a single originator," he said, "and this may be a reality of this Accused's personal history, he being a man to whom others committed to the plan looked for leadership that he was able to provide."[163] Because international criminal law as practised at the ICTY deals exclusively with individual criminal responsibility, the state can disappear into the background as a vague collection of institutions, disregarding the fact that every state institution is populated by individuals who run and represent it according to a prescribed hierarchy.[164] It is therefore important to address the relationship between individual, collective, and state criminal responsibility.

Recognising this, the ICTY invoked the legal doctrine of Joint Criminal Enterprise (JCE) in the Milošević case, or, very roughly, what is termed a 'conspiracy' in some national legal systems.[165] The doctrine serves to link crimes to several, at times many, individuals who participated as perpetrators of crimes, or who acted as instigators, accomplices, or planners. While connecting some individuals to the commission of actual crimes, for example the killing of civilian victims, the doctrine allows forensic consideration of the interactions between – and cooperation among – all the individuals who may be members of a group or organisation, or who may simply have acted in concert, for the purposes of the JCE.[166] The scope of the doctrine includes 'common purpose,' wherein the members of a JCE are not only involved in the perpetration of crimes but share a common understanding of its goals. At the ICTY, different levels of participation in a JCE were recognised; but each level required JCE members to have shared a common criminal purpose or to have, at minimum, knowledge that crimes were being committed by others. Critics of the doctrine point to its inability to account for "(co)responsibility in case of functional fragmentation where the lines of communication between the accomplices are diffuse or are even completely obliterated."[167]

What? The ideology and the plan

For the purpose of this study, a distinction is made – for practical and conceptual reasons – between the ideology and the plan which, together, contribute to answering that essential question of criminal investigation: *What?* The Milošević trial record contains a great deal of evidence that exposes the development and evolution of Serbian state ideology since the nineteenth century. And, whether Greater Serbia ideology is seen as the singular driving force behind Milošević's policy or not, it must be understood as a piece of the complex jigsaw puzzle of nineteenth-century South Slav nationalist movements. Originating in the mid-1800s, Greater Serbia ideology has been closely connected with the formation of a Serb state ever since, and it has been a potent political force for generations of Serb politicians. Some historians claim that Serbs abandoned the idea of a Greater Serbia when they accepted the creation of the first Yugoslav state in 1918, arguing that Serbia's genuine dedication to a common state was proven by its rejection of the London Treaty in 1915; a treaty which – if it *had* been accepted – would have created an internationally-brokered Greater Serbia.[168] Other historians disagree and see no contradiction between Greater Serbia designs and the creation of a common state, asserting that when Serb elites accepted a Yugoslav state in 1918, they envisaged it as centralised and Serb-dominated and were not prepared to treat other nations that entered the union as equals.[169] From this viewpoint, Serbian leaders made little sacrifice at all by rejecting the London Treaty, since they tried to achieve the same practical result.

Latinka Perović, a historian and former communist politician from Serbia, offers useful context for this history, explaining that two paths to a Greater Serbia have been recognised since the nineteenth century. The first, a state of South Slav peoples less the Bulgarians, was only acceptable to Serbia if it was centralised and controlled by Serbs. If such a centralised Yugoslavia was not possible, the second option was a Serb state including Serbia proper and Serb-claimed territories in Croatia and in Bosnia.[170] Still, alongside the fact that Serbian leaders turned down the London Treaty and accepted the first Yugoslavia, some Serbian historians argue that the creation of the Second Yugoslavia in 1945 further demonstrated the genuinely integrative nature of Serbian policy.[171] Not surprisingly, these topics were revisited during the trial.

Some of this evidence does not necessarily relate directly to Milošević, who occupied a position of power only between 1989 and 2000. But continuity of this ideological concept demonstrates how Milošević incorporated key elements of an already existing ideological template into his political platform, then developed it a step further by re-addressing Serbian statehood and the Serbian national question in the 1980s and 1990s. Despite differences in rhetoric, Milošević's objectives regarding borders and the geostrategic viability of a single state for Serbs overlapped significantly with long-espoused ideologies.

The Plan is conceptualised here as a separate topic, in order to mark where and when the ideology became a platform for action at the level of state policy; and this notion of the plan is very similar to the legal concept of a common purpose used to illustrate ties between the members of a JCE.[172] While the ideology is a broader concept, reflected in two centuries of evolving efforts to form a Serb state, the plan manifests the concrete objectives that Milošević and his associates strove to achieve.[173]

In order to make this distinction between the ideology and the plan even clearer, it is necessary to review several theoretical concepts that underpin ideology generally. John B. Thompson, an authority on the theory of ideology, makes a link between language and ideology, stating that language is not simply a structure employed for communication, but a social-historical phenomenon.[174] His work represents a series of attempts to explore the relationship between an ideology and the language by which it is promulgated.[175]

Thompson recognises three major conceptions of ideology – a neutral conception that denotes ideology as a "purely descriptive term," a critical conception that invests the term with a negative connotation, and a rational conception that suggests that "to study ideology is to study the ways in which meaning (or signification) serves to sustain relations of domination" through analysis of power dynamics "between actions, institutions, and socials structures."[176] Thompson writes further that if ideology is understood as a belief system, politics and ideology are inseparable because "all political action is ultimately oriented toward the preservation, reform, destruction, or reconstruction of social order, and hence all political action is necessarily guided by an ideological system of beliefs."[177] And so, adopting a combination of these conceptions, ideology can be viewed as a system of beliefs with the propensity to impose or sustain domination; and it is argued in this study that the moment at which an ideological concept becomes a dominant political force and political leaders choose to act upon it, an ideology transcends into a plan.

The Prosecution saw the plan not as a single, comprehensive political programme that had been espoused by Serbian political elites since Milošević's rise to power and could be seen as a blueprint for the events that led to war, but as something more flexible, the specifics of which changed over the course of the conflicts and were influenced by political actions and reactions from other Yugoslav republics and the international community. Thus, this study identifies five key goals that shaped the plan at different intervals, from 1987 to 1999. Analysis of these goals sheds light on how and when the plan and its implementation became criminal:

***Goal 1*, 1987 to 1990:** to centralise the Republic of Serbia by revoking the autonomy of Kosovo and Vojvodina.

***Goal 2*, 1990 to 1991:** to centralise the Yugoslav Federation with the Republic of Serbia as its dominant force.

***Goal 3*, 1991 to 1992:** to create a reduced Yugoslavia, including 'Serb-designated territories' in Croatia. For that purpose, the Republika Srpska Krajina (RSK) was established. This is the point at which the criminality of the plan and its implementation emerged in full, as the creation of the RSK was achieved through the commission of crimes.

***Goal 4*, 1992 to 1995:** to form the Federal Republic of Yugoslavia (FRY), a federation including Serbia and Montenegro, with contingencies in its Constitution for later absorption of other Serb territories. Following the model of the RSK, the Republika Srpska (RS) was created in BiH.

***Goal 5*, 1998 to 1999:** to continue efforts to dominate Kosovo (Goal 1), in the face of rising opposition from the majority ethnic Albanian population. This led to conflict between Serbia and Kosovo on the status of Kosovo, resulting in full-scale war in 1999, during which Serb forces again committed grave crimes against non-Serbs.

How? The Plan becomes criminal

At the core of every international criminal trial is evidence about the criminal nature of acts committed in the process of implementing political and military objectives – evidence from crime sites, the accounts of direct perpetrators and victims, forensic scientific evidence, eyewitness reports, and more. Of the five goals articulated above, Goal 1 was achieved primarily through political pressure from the streets, and through manoeuvring and deception that led to changes to the Serbian Constitution in 1990. Political manipulations, bullying, and eventual military intervention – in Slovenia, upon its declaration of independence – were again employed in the effort to achieve Goal 2. Yet, violence in Slovenia was short lived; the military operation there ended after ten days, and with Slovenia's secession, efforts to centralise the SFRY failed and the Federation disintegrated.

The question of *How?* becomes very important when considering Goals 3, 4, and 5 because they represent stages of planning during which mass atrocities occurred. Goal 3 led to a war in Croatia that was marked by attempts to split Croatia into two, through a strategy of 'ethnic separation' that was aimed at keeping all Serbs in a Rump Yugoslavia.[178] The goal of ethnic separation meant that crimes had to be committed against non-Serbs living in 'Serb-designated' territories. By the end of 1991, despite the failure to achieve a Rump Yugoslavia, the RSK was established; and it existed until the summer of 1995.

Goal 4 developed in response to the February 1992 vote for independence in Bosnia, which effectively ended any prospect of the Rump Yugoslavia for which Milošević had hoped. Serbia reacted by creating the Federal Republic of Yugoslavia in April 1992, as a federation between Serbia and Montenegro that was envisaged to eventually include Serb-claimed territories in Croatia and in BiH. Bosnian Serbs had refused to participate in the referendum on independence in BiH, or to accept the outcome. Applying the same methods as Croatian Serbs had, Bosnian Serbs began a military campaign of ethnic separation, seizing territories by violence and through the commission of mass atrocities from April 1992 to September 1995. The violence was most severe in areas where Bosnian Serbs did not have a majority but sought territory for its geostrategic importance. One such area was Eastern Bosnia – a region which became world renowned for the genocidal massacre that took place in the town of Srebrenica in July 1995.

Goal 5 was focused on keeping Kosovo a part of Serbia by changing its ethnic composition, and reflected efforts that began in 1990 with the introduction of various laws and decrees that encouraged the settlement of Serbs in the province. In 1998, the ineffectiveness of these policies to change the ethnic balance in Kosovo resulted in an attempt to force these demographic changes through the commission of mass atrocities against the Kosovo Albanian population. These crimes were committed under the pretext of fighting Kosovo Albanian terrorism, which led to a massive police and army deployment in the province. But in fact, violence was used indiscriminately against the entire population in some areas; and the Kosovo conflict proved to be a flagrant example by Serbia of the hostility of a state against its own citizens. The Prosecution asserted that Serbia used the 1999 NATO military intervention that was intended to end this violence as an excuse for the organised expulsion of Kosovo Albanians to neighbouring states. But Goal 5 also ended in failure for Milošević. In June 1999, Serbian and FRY forces were made to leave Kosovo, and in 2008, Kosovo proclaimed its independence.

The development of the plan parallels Milošević's development from an unremarkable politician to a criminal leader. In order to prove its case, the Prosecution highlighted events that demonstrated when and how the line was crossed between the lawful and the unlawful, and how unlawful (criminal) acts by Milošević led to the commission of particular crimes alleged in the indictments. Of all five goals outlined above, Milošević achieved only the first; and in failing to reach the others, became associated with savagery and mass atrocities not seen in Europe since the Second World War.

Notes

1 Helga Welsh, "Political Transition Processes in Central and Eastern Europe," *Comparative Politics* 26, no. 4 (July 1994): 379–394.

2 Transitional justice has been defined by the UN as "processes and mechanisms associated with a society's attempts to come to terms with a legacy of large-scale past abuses, in order to ensure accountability, serve justice, and achieve reconciliation." See: United Nations Security Council, *The Rule of Law and Transitional Justice in Conflict and Post-Conflict Societies*, No. S/2004/616, 23 August

2004, 4. Still, a universally accepted definition of the term is continues to develop, given the complexities of post-conflict societies and the creation of new mechanisms to deal with mass atrocities. For discussion, see: Neil Kritz, ed., *Transitional Justice: How Emerging Democracies Reckon with Former Regimes*, vol. 2, *Country Studies* (Washington, DC: United States Institute of Peace Press, 1995); Jon Elster, *Closing the Books: Transitional Justice in Historical Perspective* (Cambridge: Cambridge University Press, 2004); Ruti Teitel, *Transitional Justice* (New York: Oxford University Press, 2000); Melissa S. Williams, Rosemary Nagy, and Jon Elster, eds, *Transitional Justice* (New York: New York University Press, 2012); and Rachel Kerr and Eirin Mobekk, *Peace & Justice: Seeking Accountability After War* (Cambridge: Polity Press, 2007).

3 Kerr and Mobekk, *Peace & Justice*, 1–8.

4 Gerry J. Simpson, "Didactic and Dissident Histories in War Crimes Trials," *Albany Law Review* 60, no. 3 (1997): 837.

5 Michael P. Scharf, *Balkan Justice: The Story Behind the First International War Crimes Trial Since Nuremberg* (Durham, NC: University of North Carolina Academic Press, 1997), 32, 44.

6 Chris Stephen, *Judgement Day: The Trial of Slobodan Milošević* (New York: Atlantic Books, 2004), 91–92.

7 United Nations Security Council, Resolution 808, S/RES/808 (22 February 1993).

8 United Nations Security Council, Resolution 827, S/RES/827 (25 May 1993). For more on the role of the ICTY and international criminal law in international relations and in ongoing conflicts, see: Beth A. Simmons and Richard H. Steinberg, eds, *International Law and International Relations* (Cambridge: Cambridge University Press, 2007). The ICTY Statute was also adopted in UNSCR 827, and was last amended in July 2009 by Resolution 1877. See: United Nations, Updated Statute of the International Criminal Tribunal for the Former Yugoslavia (September 2009). Available at: www.icty.org/x/file/Legal%20Library/Statute/statute_sept09_en.pdf (accessed 12 December 2009).

9 United Nations, Charter of the United Nations and Statute of the International Court of Justice (October 1945), Chapter VII.

10 John Hagan, *Justice in the Balkans: Prosecuting War Crimes in the Hague Tribunal* (Chicago: University of Chicago Press: 2003), 60, 62. The term 'international community' (abbreviated IC) is used somewhat arbitrarily in different contexts, typically to connote international bodies such as the EU and the UN acting in concert with individual states such as the US, UK, and Russia in espousing joint views and undertaking multilateral action.

11 For discussion on points of criticism, see: Jovan Ćirić, ed., *Haški tribunal između prava i politike*, Institut za uporedno pravo (Beograd: Goragraf, 2013), available in B/C/S at: www.comparativelaw.info/haski-s.pdf; James Gow, Rachel Kerr, and Zoran Pajić, *Prosecuting War Crimes: Lessons and Legacies of the International Criminal Tribunal for the Former Yugoslavia* (London: Routledge, 2014); Jill A. Irvine and Patrice C. McMahon, "From International Courts to Grassroots Organizing: The Obstacles to Transitional Justice in the Balkans," in *Transitional Justice and Civil Society in the Balkans*, eds Olivera Simić and Zala Volčič (New York: Springer, 2013); Olivia Q. Swaak-Goldman, "The ICTY and the Right to a Fair Trial: A Critique of the Critics," *Leiden Journal of International Law* 10, no. 2 (June 1997): 215–221; Leila Nadya Sadat and Michael P. Scharf, eds, *The Theory and Practice of International Criminal Law: Essays in Honor of M. Cherif Bassiouni* (Leiden: Martinus Nijhoff, 2008); Bert Swart, Alexander Zahar, and Göran Sluiter, eds, *The Legacy of the International Criminal Tribunal for the Former Yugoslavia* (Oxford: Oxford University Press, 2011); Oliver Tomić, ed., *Od Nirnberga do Haga: pouke istorije* (Beograd, 2013).

12 Lilian A. Barria and Steven D. Roper, "How Effective are International Criminal Tribunals? An Analysis of the ICTY and the ICTR," *The International Journal of Human Rights* 9, no. 3 (September 2005): 356.

13 For discussion on the background of the ICTY and appraisals of its early years, see: Gary Jonathan Bass, *Stay the Hand of Vengeance: The Politics of War Crimes Tribunals* (Princeton: Princeton University Press, 2000); Hagan, *Justice in the Balkans*; Pierre Hazan, *Justice in a Time of War: The True Story Behind the International Criminal Tribunal for the Former Yugoslavia*, Eugenia & Hugh M. Stewart '26 Series on Eastern Europe (Texas A&M University Press, 2004); Mark Osiel, *Making Sense of Mass Atrocities* (Cambridge: Cambridge University Press, 2008); William A. Schabas, *Unimaginable Atrocities: Justice, Politics, and Rights at the War Crimes Tribunals* (Oxford: Oxford University Press: 2012); Scharf, *Balkan Justice*; Stephen, *Judgement Day*; Eric Stover, *The Witnesses: War Crimes and the Promise of Justice in The Hague* (Philadelphia: University of Pennsylvania Press, 2005); and Nena Tromp, "War Crimes Tribunals and The International Criminal Tribunal for Former Yugoslavia," in *15 Years of Peace Building in the Western Balkans: Lessons Learnt and Current Challenges*, eds Ernst M. Felberbauer and Predrag Jureković (Vienna, December 2010), 151–165.

14 Hagan, *Justice in the Balkans*, 3, 22, 29, 31, 105, 118, 204, and 240.

15 For more on the views of liberals and realists, see: Bass, *Stay the Hand of Vengeance*, 265, 284–286.

16 One of these studies was based on interviews with 32 Bosnian judges and prosecutors involved in prosecuting and trying war crimes, among whom there was consensus that those who commit war crimes should be held accountable; however, almost all of the interviewees of Bosnian Serb and Croat origin saw the ICTY as a political organisation that was biased and incapable of providing fair trials. See: Stover, *The Witnesses*, 37–38.

17 Scharf, *Balkan Justice*, 6–7, 67.

18 See: Vladimir Tochilovsky, "Legal Systems and Cultures in the International Criminal Court: The Experience from the International Criminal Tribunal for the Former Yugoslavia," in *International and National Prosecution of Crimes under International Law: Current Developments*, eds Horst Fischer, Claus Kress, and Sascha Rolf Lüder (Berlin: Arno Spitz GmbH, 2001), 627–644. For discussion, also see: Carrie Menkel-Meadow, "The Trouble with the Adversary System in a Postmodern, Multicultural World," *William & Mary Law Review* 38, no. 5 (1996): 5–44; Geoffrey Nice, "Trials of Imperfection," *Leiden Journal of International Law* 14, no. 2 (June 2001): 383–397; and Osiel, *Making Sense of Mass Atrocities*, 7, 63, 73, 75, 84, 92–93, 123, 134, 167, 194.

19 Geoffrey Nice, "Trials of Imperfection," 383.

20 See: Tochilovsky, "Legal Systems and Cultures in the International Criminal Court."

21 Stover, *The Witnesses*, 36–38; "Outreach Programme," ICTY: Outreach, www.icty.org/sections/Outreach/OutreachProgramme (accessed 18 April 2014).

22 See: Refik Hodzic, "Accepting a Difficult Truth: ICTY is Not Our Court," *Balkan Insight*, 6 March 2013. One interesting example of this was the ICTY's lack of outreach after the acquittals of General Momčilo Perišić, Jovica Stanišić, and Franko Simatović.

23 Lara J. Nettelfield, *Courting Democracy in Bosnia and Herzegovina: The Hague Tribunal's Impact in a Postwar State* (Cambridge: Cambridge University Press, 2010).

24 This concept is referred to by a number of similar terms, and no one term has been universalised; it may also be called 'equity of guilt,' 'equality of guilt,' and 'proportionality of guilt.' For more on the OTP's indictment policy, see (in Dutch): Frederiek de Vlaming, *De Aanklager* (Leiden: Boom, 2013). For similar

arguments in English, see: Frederiek de Vlaming, "The Yugoslavia Tribunal and the Selection of Defendants," *Amsterdam Law Forum* 4, no. 2 (2012).

25 For example, see: Ines Sabalić and Roland Kemp, "Marko Hoare: Bivši istražitelj Haškog suda," *Globus*, no. 854 (2007). In this interview, Marko Attila Hoare, a former war crimes investigator at the ICTY, claimed the Tribunal had treated war criminals less stringently than their victims.

26 For discussion, see: Kerr and Mobekk, *Peace & Justice*, 43–51. On reactions in Serbia to the acquittal of former KLA leader Ramush Hardinaj, see: Meridijana Sadović and Aleksandar Roknić, "Serbian Anger at Haradinaj Acquittal," Institute for War and Peace Reporting, 4 April 2008; Marija Ristić, "Mixed International Reactions to Haradinaj's Acquittal," *Balkan Insight*, 30 November 2012; and Edona Peci, "Kosovo and Albania Demand Inquiry Into Del Ponte," *Balkan Insight*, 3 December 2012. On reactions in Croatia to the sentences for the 'Vukovar Three,' see: Goran Jungvirth, "Croat Anger at 'Lenient' Sentences for Vukovar Three," *Tribunal Update*, no. 519, 28 September 2007; E. Radosavljević, "Oslobođeni Gotovina i Markač: Oluja iz Haškog suda oduvala pravdu," *Večernje novosti*, 16 November 2012; and "Svjetski mediji: oslobođen general Gotovina, hrvatski junak domovinskog rata," *Dnevno*, 16 November 2012.

27 See: "Sarajevo Conference: Ode to Tribunal or Requiem for Justice?" *Sense Tribunal*, 27 December 2013. Also see: "Bosnia Victims Protest Against Hague Tribunal President," *Balkan Insight*, 29 November 2013.

28 For example, see: Samantha Power, "Stopping Genocide and Securing 'Justice': Learning by Doing," *Social Research* 69, no. 4 (Winter 2002): 1093–1107.

29 For discussion, see: Diana F. Orentlicher, *That Someone Guilty Be Punished: The Impact of the ICTY in Bosnia* (Open Society Institute, 2010); Janine N. Clark, "The ICTY and Reconciliation in Croatia: A Case Study of Vukovar," *Oxford Journal of International Criminal Justice* 10, no. 2 (2012): 397–422; Nancy Amoury Combs, *Guilty Pleas in International Criminal Law: Constructing a Restorative Justice Approach* (Stanford: Stanford University Press, 2007); Roland Kostić, "Transitional Justice and Reconciliation in Bosnia-Herzegovina: Whose Memories, Whose Justice?" *Sociologija* LIV, no. 4 (2012): 649–666; Geoffrey Nice, "War Crimes Courts that Reconcile: Oxymoron or Possibility?" (lecture, Gresham College, London, 18 April 2013).

30 President Robinson's Address Before the Security Council, press release, No. VE/MOW/1353e, 18 June 2010. Available online at: www.icty.org/sid/10422 (accessed 10 August 2010).

31 Nena Tromp, "A Troubled Relationship: The ICTY and Reconciliation," in *Regional Co-operation and Reconciliation in the Aftermath of the ICTY Verdicts: Continuation or Stalemate?*, eds Ernst M. Felberbauer and Predrag Jureković (Vienna: Republic of Austria, 2013), 47–67.

32 See Article 135 of the Serbian Constitution in: Albert P. Blaustein and Eric B. Blaustein, eds, *Constitutions of Dependencies and Special Sovereignties* (Dobbs Ferry: Oceana, 1994). Also see: *Human Rights in Transition*, the Annual Report of the Helsinki Committee for Human Rights in Serbia, 2001, 41.

33 Milošević told the Court, "I consider this Tribunal a false Tribunal and the indictment a false indictment. It is illegal being not appointed by the UN General Assembly, so I have no need to appoint counsel to illegal organ [*sic*]." Trial Transcript (3 July 2001), 2. Unless otherwise noted, primary trial documents (including trial transcripts, legal filings, exhibits, motions, testimonies, etc.) refer to ICTY Trial Chamber proceedings in the case of *Prosecutor* v. *Slobodan Milošević* (No. IT-02–54).

34 For discussion, see: Preliminary Protective Motion (9 August 2001); Presentation on the Illegality of ICTY (30 August 2001); and Amici Curiae Brief on Jurisdiction

(19 October 2001) – all filed by the Accused or his representatives. Also see: the Court's Decision on Preliminary Motions (8 November 2001).

35 Decision on the Defence Motion for Interlocutory Appeal on Jurisdiction, *Prosecutor* v. *Duško Tadić*, No. IT-94–1 (2 October 1995), 16–20.

36 Michael Scharf and William Schabas, *Slobodan Milošević on Trial: A Companion* (New York: Continuum International, 2002), 99; Sharf, *Balkan Justice*, 88–89.

37 Human Rights Watch, *Weighing the Evidence: Lessons from the Slobodan Milošević Trial* (December 2006); Gideon Boas, *The Milošević Trial: Lessons for the Conduct of Complex International Criminal Proceedings* (Cambridge: Cambridge University Press, 2007); Gillian Higgins, "The Impact of the Size, Scope, and Scale of the Milošević Trial and the Development of Rule 73," *Northwestern Journal of International Human Rights* 7, no. 2 (summer 2009): 239–260; Judith Armatta, *Twilight of Impunity: The War Crimes Trial of Slobodan Milošević* (Durham, NC: Duke University Press, 2010). Timothy Waters, ed., *The Milošević Trial: An Autopsy* (New York: Oxford University Press, 2014). For a representation of the trial from the Defence point of view, see: John Laughland, *Travesty: The Trial of Slobodan Milošević and the Corruption of International Justice* (London: Pluto Press, 2007).

38 Judgement, *Prosecutor* v. *Milutinović, et al.*, No. IT-05–87-T (26 February 2009), para. 70.

39 For discussion, see: Geoffrey Nice, "Neprofesionalna Del Ponte politizirala je tužiteljstvo," *Jutarnji list*, 16 September 2007; and Merita Arslani and Snježana Pavić "Haaški istražitelji nisu htjeli tražiti dokaze protiv Miloševića," *Jutarnji list*, 10 September 2007.

40 Nice, "Neprofesionalna Del Ponte politizirala je tužiteljstvo."

41 For example, see: Michael Farquhar and Janet Anderson, "Serb Leader's Death 'Tragic for Victims'," *Tribunal Update*, no. 444, 11 March 2006; Gwyn MacCarrick, "Lessons from the Milošević Trial," *On Line Opinion*, 26 April 2006, www.onlineopinion.com.au/view.asp?article=4394&page=1 (accessed 4 May 2014).

42 For comparison, see the original Kosovo indictment from 24 May 1999 and the amended indictment from 19 June 2001; the original Croatia indictment from 1 October 2001 and the amended indictment from 23 October 2002; and the original Bosnia indictment from 22 November 2001 and the amended indictment from 22 November 2002.

43 Amici Curiae Motion for Judgement of Acquittal (3 March 2004).

44 Decision on Motion for Judgement of Acquittal (16 June 2004), Schedules A through F. The Decision is hereinafter referred to as the Half-Time Judgement. Also see: Boas, *The Milošević Trial*, 80. The Decision on Motion for Judgement of Acquittal is the only document akin to a judgement offered by the Chamber regarding those counts that the *amici curiae* claimed were inadequately established. The test applied by the judges at that stage was not whether they were satisfied beyond a reasonable doubt that the offence(s) had been committed but whether there was sufficient evidence for the case on that count to continue and whether there was enough evidence to convict.

45 For discussion, see: Prosecution's Position in Relation to Management of Trial Proceedings and the Regime for Presentation and Admission of Evidence with Comments on Issues Concerning the Accused's Health (5 April 2002).

46

> If you only prove one spot in Bosnia or one spot in Croatia, you never prove the widespread and systematic nature of the campaign, which is what this trial is about. We have recently, and quite specifically, effectively invited the judges to look at this and indicate have we got enough. Because there's no test. Is it ten villages? Is it four municipalities? Or is it one? I don't know. And if I put on too little, then the case fails.

Statement by Prosecutor Geoffrey Nice, as recorded in *Milošević on Trial*, directed by Michael Christofferson (Copenhagen: Team Productions, 2007).

47 'Viva voce' is live evidence given by a witness in court.

48 For discussion, see: Order Rescheduling and Setting Time Available to Present Defence Case (25 February 2004); Order Concerning the Time Available to Present the Defence Case (10 February 2005); Order Recording Use of Time Used in the Defence Case (1 March 2005); and Human Rights Watch, *Weighing the Evidence*, 61.

49 Scheduling Order for a Hearing (22 November 2005), 3.

50 Trial Transcript, Pre-Trial Status Conference (30 August 2001), 18. Status conferences are held before a trial starts so that the Prosecution and Defence can discuss practical issues concerning the preparation and conduct of the upcoming trial. Also see: ICTY Statute, Article 21, section 4(d).

51 Order Inviting Designation of *Amicus Curiae* (30 August 2001). The following tasks were assigned to the *amicus*:

> (a) making any submissions properly open to the accused by way of preliminary or other pre-trial motion; (b) making any submissions or objections to evidence properly open to the accused during the trial proceedings and cross-examining witnesses as appropriate; (c) drawing to the attention of the Trial Chamber any exculpatory or mitigating evidence; and (d) acting in any other way which designated counsel considers appropriate in order to secure a fair trial.

Their tasks were expanded by the Order Concerning *Amici Curiae* (11 January 2002).

52 Human Rights Watch, *Weighing the Evidence*, 72.

53 Milošević's legal advisors were Zdenko Tomanović, Dragoslav Ognjanović, and Branko Rakić.

54 For example, see the reactions of the judges in the courtroom: Trial Transcript (15 March 2002), 2461; Trial Transcript (12 June 2002), 6824–6889 and 6895; and Trial Transcript (10 April 2003), 18933.

55 Procedural Hearing (11 November 2002), 12835.

56 Prosecution's Submission on the Implications of the Accused's Recurring Ill-health and the Future Conduct of the Case (Corrected Version) (30 September 2003), 2.

57 Scheduling Order for Hearing (22 December 2005), 3.

58 Reasons for Decision on Assigned Counsel (22 September 2004).

59 Ibid., para. 65.

60 Ibid., para. 69.

61 Decision on Interlocutory Appeal of the Trial Chamber's Decision on the Assignment of Defence Counsel (1 November 2004), para. 20.

62 Testimony of Kosta Bulatović (19 April 2005), 38591–38592.

63 Decision on Contempt of the Tribunal (13 May 2005).

64 Motion on Joinder (27 November 2001); Reasons for Decision on Prosecution Interlocutory Appeal from Refusal to Order Joinder (18 April 2002), para. 26.

65 Further Order on Future Conduct of the Trial Relating to Severance of One or More Indictments (21 July 2004).

66 Prosecution's Submission in Response to Trial Chamber's Decision (19 July 2004).

67 See: Scheduling Order for a Hearing (22 November 2005).

68 Trial Transcript, Procedural Hearing (29 November 2005), 46695.

69 Prosecution Submission in Response to the Trial Chamber's 22 November 2005 "Scheduling Order for a Hearing" on Severing the Kosovo Indictment (28 November 2005), para. 53.

70 Trial Transcript, Defence Opening Statement (15 February 2002), 352.
71 "Slobodan Milošević's Trial is a Political Case," *The Voice of Russia*, 3 January 2002.
72 Trial Transcript, Appeals Hearing (21 October 2004), 53.
73 See: Leora Bilsky, *Transformative Justice: Israeli Identity on Trial* (Ann Arbor: University of Michigan Press, 2004); Ron Christenson, *Political Trials: Gordian Knots in the Law* (New Brunswick: Transaction, 1999); Gerry J. Simpson, *Law, War & Crime: War Crimes, Trials and the Reinvention of International Law* (Cambridge: Polity Press, 2007); Otto Kirchheimer, *Political Justice: The Use of Legal Procedure for Political Ends* (Princeton: Princeton University Press, 1961); and Judith Shklar, *Law, Morals and Political Trials* (Cambridge, MA: Harvard University Press, 1964).
74 Schabas, *Unimaginable Atrocities*, 23. Schabas writes that the political dimension of mass atrocities trials is inescapable.
75 Ibid., xiii.
76 Kirchheimer, *Political Justice*, 6.
77 Stuart Ford, "Fairness and Politics at the ICTY: Evidence from the Indictments," *North Carolina Journal of International Law and Commercial Regulation* 39 (2013): 57–58.
78 Simpson, *Law, War & Crime*, 14.
79 Ibid., 16.
80 Christenson, *Political Trials*, xv. Also see: Ford, "Fairness and Politics at the ICTY," 53–54.
81 Ford, "Fairness and Politics at the ICTY," 53.
82 Jeremy D. Peterson, "Unpacking Show Trials: Situating the Trial of Saddam Hussein," *Harvard International Law Journal* 48, no. 1 (2007): 257–259, 260–265.
83 Mary M. Cheh, "Should Lawyers Participate in Rigged Systems: The Case of the Military Commissions," *Journal of National Security Law and Policy* 1 (2005): 408.
84 Ford, "Fairness and Politics at the ICTY," 56.
85 Bilsky, *Transformative Justice*, 7.
86 Ibid., 8.
87 For discussion on this debate in general, see: ibid.; Lawrence Douglas, *The Memory of Judgment: Making Law and History in the Trials of the Holocaust* (New Haven: Yale University Press, 2001); Michael R. Marrus, "History and the Holocaust in the Courtroom," in *Lessons and Legacies*, ed. Ronald M. Smelser, vol. 5, *The Holocaust and Justice* (Evanston: Northwestern University Press, 2002), 215–239; Osiel, *Mass Atrocities*; Gerry Simpson, "Didactic and Dissident Histories in War Crimes Trials"; Teitel, *Transitional Justice*; and Hannah Arendt, *Eichmann in Jerusalem: A Report on the Banality of Evil* (New York: Penguin, 1963), 233. Also see: Ian Buruma, *Wages of Guilt: Memories of War in Germany and Japan* (Plume, 1995), in which Buruma wrote: "When the court of law is used for history lessons, then the risk of show trials cannot be far off." On the view that trials have extralegal purposes, see: Marrus, "History and the Holocaust," 215–216.
88 Arendt, *Eichmann in Jerusalem*, 233.
89 Teitel, *Transitional Justice*.
90 Ibid., 72.
91 Ibid., 69.
92 Ibid., 70.
93 Douglas, *The Memory of Judgment*, 3.
94 Ibid.
95 Ibid., 2.
96 Ibid., 3.

97 Osiel, *Mass Atrocities*, 1–2.
98 Bilsky, *Transformative Justice*, 7.
99 Jelena Subotić, *Hijacked Justice* (Ithaca: Cornell University Press, 2009).
100

> At Nuremberg, with twenty-two defendants, including Martin Bormann who was tried *in absentia*, the accused often disagreed among themselves in describing what had happened in Nazi Germany and reacted quite differently to accounts of the persecution and murder of European Jews.
>
> From: Marrus, "History and the Holocaust," 229

101 See for discussion: Douglas, *The Memory of Judgment*, 5. Kirchheimer, *Political Justice*, 339.
102 Simpson, "Didactic and Dissident Histories," 802–803.
103 Ibid., 834.
104 In ICTY trials, both parties have the right to make an Opening Statement at the start of each part of the trial; thus, Milošević gave an Opening Statement in both February 2002, at the start of the Prosecution part of the trial, and again in August 2004, at the start of the Defence part of the trial.
105 Trial Transcript, Defence Opening Statement (31 August 2004), 32173–32174.
106 See: Bilsky, *Transformative Justice*, 3, 7; and Charles S. Maier, "Doing History, Doing Justice: The Narrative of the Historian and of the Truth Commission," in *Truth v. Justice: The Morality of Truth Commissions*, eds R.I. Rotberg and D. Thompson (Princeton: Princeton University Press: 2000), 271.
107 Maier, "Doing History, Doing Justice," 271.
108 Ibid., 270.
109 Marrus, "History and the Holocaust," 228.
110 Teitel, *Transitional Justice*, 117.
111 Ibid.
112 Fergal Gaynor, "Uneasy Partners: Evidence, Truth and History in International Trials," *Journal of International Criminal Justice* 10, no. 5 (2012): 1257–1275.
113 Richard Wilson, "Judging History: The Historical Record of the International Criminal Tribunal of the Former Yugoslavia," *Human Rights Quarterly* 27, no. 3 (2005): 908.
114 Ibid.
115 Trial Transcript, Defence Opening Statement (31 August 2004), 32158.
116 There are more than 190,000 public records on the ICTY website as of mid-2014, and it is updated daily. These records range from arrest warrants, to motions and trial evidence, to final appeal judgements.
117 Louise Arbour, former ICTY Chief Prosecutor, said that "general knowledge" was the ICTY's worst enemy:

> I am told all the time, "Why didn't you indict this man or that man? Everybody knows he is guilty." It is long way from what everybody ostensibly knows to an indictment for crimes listed in the Statute of the Tribunal that will withstand the test before the court. When the accused are not famous personalities nobody asks us, "Why haven't you indicted them?"

As quoted in: "Why Did Prosecution Fail to Prove What 'Everybody Knows'," *Sense Tribunal*, 7 April 2008.
118 'Open Sources' is the term used at the ICTY to denote media and other publicly accessible information such as scholarly research.
119 See the sections titled "State Cooperation" or "Cooperation" in the Annual Reports submitted by the ICTY President to the UN Security Council from 2000 to 2006. Available at: www.icty.org/en/node/8121 (accessed 18 January 2016).
120 The FRY, or the Federal Republic of Yugoslavia, existed from 1992 to 2003 as a federation of the republics of Serbia and Montenegro. In 2003, it became

known as Serbia and Montenegro, until Montenegro chose independence in 2006. In the text of ICTY documents, it is difficult to discern the FRY and Serbia and Montenegro from the Republic of Serbia, given the political dominance of Serbia in each incarnation of the federation.

121 By mid-2011, the OTP's database included 8.5 million items (each item representing one page of documentation).

122 The Mechanism for International Criminal Tribunals (MICT) was created by UNSC Resolution 1966 on 22 December 2010 in order to maintain the legacy of the ad hoc UN Tribunals – the ICTR and ICTY – and the ICTY branch of the Mechanism will hear any appeals that may follow the few cases that are still in process.

123 For discussion on this topic in English, see: Lenard J. Cohen, *Serpent in the Bosom: The Rise and Fall of Slobodan Milošević* (Boulder: Westview Press,2002); Slavoljub Đukić, *Milošević and Marković: A Lust for Power* (Montreal: McGill-Queen's University Press, 2001); Duško Doder and Louise Branson, *Milošević: Portrait of a Tyrant* (New York: The Free Press, 1999); Adam LeBor, *Milošević: A Biography* (London: Bloomsbury, 2002); Louise Sell, *Slobodan Milošević and the Destruction of Yugoslavia* (Durham, NC: Duke University Press, 2002); and Vidoslav Stevanović, *Milošević: People's Tyrant* (London: I.B. Tauris, 2002). And, in B/C/S, see: Borisav Jović, *Knjiga o Miloševiću* (Belgrade: IKP Nikola Pašić, 2001); *Knjiga o Miloševiću* has been translated in English and exhibited in English and the original Serbian version under exhibit number P596.3. Ivan Stambolić, *Put u bespuće* (Belgrade: B92, 1995). The following chapters of *Put u bespuće* were used as exhibits in the Milošević case: Chapter VI, "The Memorandum, In Memoriam to Yugoslavia," was Exhibit P800a; Chapters VII, VIII, IX, X, and XI, "My Biggest Mistake," "The Schism," "It Started in Kosovo," "The Fateful Shots in Paraćin," and "A Prelude to the Eighth Session," respectively, were presented collectively as Exhibit P811a. These Exhibits comprise English translations of the book, originally published in B/C/S. In the text, the references from both books will correspond to their original Serbian editions.

124 For discussion on the causes and consequences of the disintegration of the SFRY, see: Christopher Bennett, *Yugoslavia's Bloody Collapse: Causes, Course and Consequences* (London: Hurst, 1995); Lenard J. Cohen, *Broken Bonds: Yugoslavia's Disintegration and Balkan Politics in Transition* (Boulder: Westview Press, 1995); Misha Glenny, *The Fall of Yugoslavia: The Third Balkan War* (London: Penguin, 1992); Branka Magaš, *The Destruction of Yugoslavia: Tracking the Break-Up, 1980–92* (London: Verso, 1993); Victor Meier, *Yugoslavia: A History of Demise* (London: Routledge, 1999); Catharine Samary, *Yugoslavia Dismembered* (New York: Monthly Review Press, 1995); Laura Silber and Alan Little, *Yugoslavia: Death of a Nation* (London: Penguin, 1995); Jasminka Udovički and James Ridgeway, eds, *Burn This House: The Making and Unmaking of Yugoslavia* (Durham, NC: Duke University Press, 1997); Susan L. Woodward, *Balkan Tragedy: Chaos and Dissolution after the Cold War* (Washington, DC: Brookings Institution, 1995).

125 For discussion, see: Jasna Dragović-Soso "Why did Yugoslavia Disintegrate? An Overview of Contending Explanations," in *State Collapse in South-Eastern Europe: New Perspectives on Yugoslavia's Disintegration*, eds Lenard J. Cohen and J. Dragović-Soso (Indiana: Purdue University Press, 2008), 1–39; Nena Tromp, *The Background of the Yugoslav Crisis: A Survey of the Literature*, Appendix VI, in NIOD, *Srebrenica: A "Safe" Area*, (Amsterdam: Boom Uitgeverij, 2002).

126 Dragović-Soso, "Why did Yugoslavia Disintegrate?" 1–2.

127 Ibid., 14.

128 Sell, *Slobodan Milošević and the Destruction of Yugoslavia*, 4–5.

129 For example, see: Sonja Biserko, *Yugoslavia's Implosion: The Fatal Attraction of Serb Nationalism* (Oslo: Norwegian Helsinki Committee, 2012); Sell, *Slobodan Milošević and the Destruction of Yugoslavia*; Norman Cigar and Paul Williams, *Indictment in The Hague: The Milošević Regime and Crimes of the Balkan Wars* (New York: New York University Press, 2002).

130 For example, see: Cohen, *Broken Bonds*, 130 and 265.

131 See: Cohen, *Broken Bonds*; Cohen, *Serpent in the Bosom*; Aleksandar Pavković, *The Fragmentation of Yugoslavia: Nationalism and War in the Balkans* (London: Macmillan, 1997); Woodward, *Balkan Tragedy;* and, in B/C/S, Dejan Jović, *Jugoslavija: država koja je odumrla* (Zagreb: Prometej, 2003).

132 Jović, *Jugoslavija: država koja je odumrla*, 491–492; Woodward, *Balkan Tragedy*, 80 and 94.

133 For example, see: Slobodan Antonić, *Slobodan Milošević: još nije gotovo* ["Slobodan Milošević: It's Not Over Yet"] (Belgrade: Vukotić medija, 2015); Jović, *Od Gazimestana do Haga: vreme Slobodana Miloševića* (Belgrade: Metaphysica, 2009), 200. Jović emerged as an apologist in *Od Gazimestana do Haga*, especially in his evaluation of Milošević's conduct at his trial in The Hague, which Jović characterises as a heroic defence of Serbia.

134 Antonić, *Slobodan Milošević*, 478. Some former admirers have more recently referred to Milošević as no more than a "smalltime banker." See: "Kusturica: Milošević je bio mali bankar, a ne Hitler," *Kurir*, 19 August 2011, www.kurir-info.rs/kusturica-Milošević-je-bio-mali-bankar-a-ne-hitler-clanak-106097 (accessed 20 September 2014). Also see: Milica Jovanović, "Srećko Horvat: intervju," 13 January 2014, *Peščanik*, http://pescanik.net/srecko-horvat-intervju/ (accessed 25 September 2014).

135 Antonić, *Slobodan Milošević*, 478–479.

136 Ibid., 479.

137 See: Jović, *Knjiga o Miloševiću*, 52–56 and 59–61. Jović described Milošević as an able politician who was a true democrat at the beginning of his political career, but who nevertheless made several significant tactical mistakes – notably his contribution to the dissolution of the League of Communists (LC) of Yugoslavia in January 1990. Milošević also postponed multi-party elections in Serbia long as he possibly could, miscalculating the disadvantage this would create for Serbia in relation to the other republics.

138 For example, see: Sell, *Slobodan Milošević and the Destruction of Yugoslavia*, 46; Dragović-Soso, "Why did Yugoslavia Disintegrate?" 18.

139 Dragović-Soso, "Why did Yugoslavia Disintegrate?" 18.

140 Ibid., 19.

141 Ibid.

142 Doder and Branson, *Milošević: Portrait of a Tyrant*, 15–16, 24, 26.

143 Ibid., 11.

144 Betty Nguyen, interview with Richard Holbrooke, *Saturday Morning News*, CNN, 11 March 2006.

145 James L. Graff, "Butcher of the Balkans," *Time*, 8 June 1992.

146 See for example: Stambolić, *Put u bespuće*, 133–180.

147 For example, see: James Gow, *The Serbian Project and its Adversaries: A Strategy of War Crimes* (London: Hurst, 2003), 8–9.

148 Cohen, *Serpent in the Bosom*, 142.

149 Dragović-Soso, "Why did Yugoslavia Disintegrate?" 16. For discussion, also see: Eric Gordy, "Destruction of the Yugoslav Federation: Policy of Confluence of Tactics," in Cohen and Dragovic-Soso, *State Collapse in South-Eastern Europe*, 281–301, 292.

150 For example, on Hitler, see: Ian Kershaw, *Hitler: Profiles in Power* (New York: Routledge, 2013). Kershaw argues that a vague doctrine, open-ended decrees, and

a complex system of bureaucracy within the Third Reich helped obscure Hitler's direct responsibility for the Holocaust. And, on Stalin, see: Johnathan Brent, *Inside the Stalin Archives: Discovering the New Russia* (New York: Atlas & Co., 2008). Brent writes that even when evidentiary documents emerge about historical events, it is often "only researchers with encyclopaedic knowledge of their subject" who can glean meaning from them because there are "no smoking guns as such, documents that could stand alone and tell the 'whole' story." However, he says, there may be "many guns with the smell of smoke in their barrels," 92.

151 Dragović-Soso, "Why did Yugoslavia Disintegrate?" 16.

152 Ibid., 27.

153 Angelo Izama: "Kony is Not the Problem," *International Herald Tribune*, 21 March 2012. The author argues that: "While the evil methods of men like Kony are easily understood by millions, the politics so crucial to sustaining their brutal campaigns are harder to grasp."

154 Joseph Masciulli, Mikhail A. Molchanov and W. Andy Knight, eds, *The Ashgate Research Companion to Political Leadership* (Surrey: Ashgate, 2009), 10.

155 Izama, "Kony is Not the Problem."

156 Nathan Quimpo, "Trapo Parties and Corruption," *KASAMA* 21, no. 1 (January–February–March 2007).

157 For discussion, see: Max Weber, *The Theory of Social and Economic Organizations* (New York: The Free Press, 1947); Gary Yukl, "An Evaluation of Conceptual Weaknesses in Transformational and Charismatic Leadership Theories," *The Leadership Quarterly* 10, no. 2 (summer 1999): 285–305; Michael Hechter and Christine Horne, eds, *Theories of Social Order: A Reader* (Stanford: Stanford University Press, 2003); and Ingo Winkler, *Contemporary Leadership Theories: Enhancing the Understanding of the Complexity, Subjectivity and Dynamics of Leadership* (Berlin: Verlag, 2010).

158 Weber, *The Theory of Social and Economic Organizations*, 215; Hechter and Horne, *Theories of Social Order*, 104.

159 Winkler, *Contemporary Leadership Theories*, 32–33.

160 Yukl, "An Evaluation of Conceptual Weaknesses," 285–286.

161 Ibid., 286–287.

162 Trial Transcript, Defence Opening Statement (14 February 2002), 248.

163 Trial Transcript, Prosecution Opening Statement (26 September 2002), 10187.

164 The ICTY Statute allows for two types of criminal liability, as defined by Articles 7(1) and 7(3). Article 7(1) reads: "A person who planned, instigated, ordered, committed or otherwise aided and abetted in the planning, preparation or execution of a crime referred to in articles 2 to 5 of the present Statute, shall be individually responsible for the crime." And Article 7(3) reads:

> The fact that any of the acts referred to in articles 2 to 5 of the present Statute was committed by a subordinate does not relieve his superior of criminal responsibility if he knew or had reason to know that the subordinate was about to commit such acts or had done so and the superior failed to take the necessary and reasonable measures to prevent such acts or to punish the perpetrators thereof.

For discussion on the criminal responsibility of states, see: Osiel, *Making Sense of Mass Atrocities*, 189–194; and Schabas, *Unimaginable Atrocities*, 125–153.

165 "The notion of Joint Criminal Enterprise denotes a mode of criminal liability of all participants in a common criminal plan." See: Antonio Cassese, "The Proper Limits of Individual Responsibility under Doctrine of Joint Criminal Enterprise," *Journal of International Criminal Justice* 5 (2007): 110–111.

166 For discussion, see: Harmen van der Wilt, "Joint Criminal Enterprise: Possibilities and Limitations," *Journal of International Criminal Justice* 5, no. 1 (2007):

91–108; Allison M. Danner and Jenny S. Martinez, "Guilty Associations: Joint Criminal Enterprise, Command Responsibility and the Development of International Criminal Law," *California Law Review* 93, no. 1 (2005): 75–169.

167 Van der Wilt, "Joint Criminal Enterprise," 92.

168 Dragović-Soso, "Why did Yugoslavia Disintegrate?" 7.

169 Ibid., 6.

170 Latinka Perović, interview (11 August 2004). Perović was approached by the OTP as a potential rebuttal witness regarding topics brought up by Defence expert witnesses Čedomir Popov, Kosta Mihailović, and Slavenko Terzić.

171 Dragović-Soso, "Why did Yugoslavia Disintegrate?" 6.

172 For example, see: Judgement, *Prosecutor* v. *Milutinović et al.*, No. IT-05–87-T (26 February 2009), para. 97 and 103.

173 Serbs lived across the SFRY in the republics of Croatia, BiH, Montenegro, and Macedonia; and a Serb state was envisioned to encompass Serbs across the Federation. But, Greater Serbia ideology and Serbian state ideology pre-date Yugoslavia, extending back to the Ottoman era.

174 John B. Thompson, *Studies in the Theory of the Ideology* (Berkeley: California University Press, 1984), 2.

175 Ibid., 3.

176 Ibid., 3–4.

177 Ibid., 78–79.

178 The term 'ethnic separation' refers to the physical segregation of ethnicities; but if this segregation is not self-imposed, ethnic separation requires the forced movement of people – in other words, ethnic cleansing. Ethnic cleansing can refer to a range of ways through which population transfer or demographics shifts are manufactured, from deportation to mass murder.

2 The leader and the ideology

The evolution of Milošević as a leader was entwined with his adoption and promotion of Serb nationalism. However it is impossible to fully appreciate his rise to power without contextualising his political career against the various social and political processes that reignited nationalistic movements that had been relatively dormant for decades until the 1980s and which have marked the breakup of the SFRY. Upon his death, some attributed the wars in the former Yugoslavia exclusively to Milošević's "embrace of Serbian nationalism,"[1] implying that the ideology had driven his behaviour; and others framed him as a "ruthless manipulator of Serbian nationalism,"[2] suggesting instead that he had instrumentalised the ideology for his own ends. But a study of the trial record reveals that in fact both of these assessments were true at different times, and that the dynamics between his power and Serbian nationalism were more nuanced.

The leader

Any evaluation of Milošević's leadership must weigh the degree to which his leadership style and charisma constituted a 'game changer' in Yugoslav politics in the late 1980s. Drawing on the definition of transformational leadership and the effect a leader has on his or her followers, the questions to be answered are: How, when, and why did followers develop trust, loyalty, and respect for Milošević and make him the leader of all Serbs? Was he a charismatic leader who triggered a revival of the post-communist nationalist movement and its populist appeal, or had Serbian nationalists kept their agenda alive during the communist period, waiting for the right moment to act and the right man to lead them? Also, to what extent was Milošević a product of the dominant political culture in which a single leader was the state's most powerful political institution? Was he a dreary and predictable bureaucrat who found himself suddenly in the eye of a spiral of violence that he had triggered but was unable to stop, or was he a calculating autocrat prepared to use every means at his disposal to attain and maintain his grip on power?[3]

The making of a leader

Until 1987, Slobodan Milošević's biography was typical of a professional communist functionary, with nothing to distinguish him from many others who had also loyally served the party, the political system, and the state. Born in the small Serbian town of Požarevac in 1941, Milošević left home at the age of 18 to study law at the University of Belgrade. Although the Prosecution did not dwell on his youth and the trial record does not contain material about those years, a number of authors have explored Milošević's childhood, searching for clues that explain his later behaviour and political conduct.[4] His parents' ideological differences – his mother an orthodox communist and his father an Orthodox priest – could certainly have created confusion for a young boy. But it was not until he was much older that he faced the oft-cited tragedy of both of his parents committing suicide. His father killed himself when Milošević was a 21-year old student in Belgrade, and ten years later, his mother also took her own life. It was an extraordinary start to his adulthood, and in part why his relationship with his wife Mira Marković would turn out to be the most important relationship of his life. In fact, she has been regarded by many of their contemporaries as the driving force behind Milošević's political ambitions. They met in high school before going together to Belgrade to study, and both were devoted communists.[5]

A firsthand account of Milošević's early years in politics can be found in a book written by his former political mentor, Ivan Stambolić, who detailed his dealings with Milošević during the 1980s power struggle in Serbia, in *Put u bespuće* ("Road to Nowhere").[6] Stambolić was President of the Presidency of the LC of Serbia in the mid-1980s and President of the Presidency of the Republic of Serbia from 1986 to 1987.[7] In his book, he described the political culture in which the post-Second World War generation of communists in Serbia was raised and cultivated. They studied, worked, and socialised together, and considered each other friends. And so, when Stambolić entered politics, his friends naturally followed.[8]

Stambolić saw the younger generation of communist politicians as more innovative and less bureaucratic, and Milošević held a special place in this group as a political protégé and favourite of Stambolić.[9] Their friendship had started when they were both law students at the University of Belgrade and Stambolić, several years his senior, became Milošević's mentor.[10] The relationship defined Milošević's career path. Tragically, in the end, it also defined Stambolić's path as well. They parted ways bitterly in 1987, never to mend their friendship; and in 2000, while Milošević was still in power, Stambolić was assassinated – leaving his 1995 book as a testimonial against his former protégé.

Although Milošević had earned a law degree, he initially chose a career in management and banking. His entrance into politics came relatively late in life, at the age of 43. It was then, in 1984, four years after the death of the communist leader Josip Broz Tito, that Milošević became Chairman of the

City Committee of the LC of Belgrade – one of the top four political positions in Serbia.[11] In 1986, as Stambolić rose through the ranks, becoming the President of the Presidency of the Republic of Serbia, Milošević succeeded him, becoming the President of the Presidency of the Central Committee of the LC of Serbia.[12] In those early years, Milošević was remembered as a supporter, to some degree, of market-oriented reform; and in 1984, he called on Serbian Communists to support a stronger Yugoslavia, which was very much in the line with "the usual communist rhetoric."[13]

Stambolić's appointment of Milošević as his successor in 1986 marked a decisive turn in Milošević's political career.[14] In retrospect, Stambolić recognised that the unwritten rule which had allowed departing party leaders to determine their successors was in error. He grew to believe that if Milošević had been elected on a broader, more democratic platform, "he would have been under greater control and subject to a more direct review" by his peers.[15] Indeed, Stambolić would later reflect on his choice to appoint Milošević as one of the worst he had ever made.[16] He had initially viewed Milošević as representing an ideal politician – young, ambitious, and unburdened by the past. In the course of time he became aware of Milošević's shortcomings.[17] He noticed that Milošević was unable to cope with criticism, that he could be rash, and that he was prone to draw superficial conclusions and judge too harshly.[18]

Still, without the lens of time, Stambolić had viewed Milošević as a man who was decisive and dynamic – qualities he thought were required in a leader faced with implementing economic and political reforms. He had disregarded scepticism, expressed to him in person and in writing, about his faith in Milošević. Vladimir Jovičić, a writer and active party functionary, left a letter on Stambolić's desk one year before Milošević's appointment, stating his reservations that Milošević was "arrogant, haughty, [and] craving power."[19] Cvijetin Mijatović, a member of the PSFRY in the early 1980s, told Stambolić that certain forces were uniting against him.[20] Even Draža Marković, Mira Marković's uncle and a member of the communist elite, warned Stambolić that history and the Serbian people would never forgive him for having pulled Milošević along, because Milošević "would destroy everything."[21]

But aware as he was of Milošević's personal deficiencies, Stambolić never expected them to become political drawbacks. When he read in the newspapers that Milošević was appointing candidates to the Central Committee of the LC of Serbia and the City Committee of Belgrade whom he had not managed to push through as members of the Presidency of the LC of Serbia, Stambolić ascribed it to Milošević's need to demonstrate independence. Eventually, though, Stambolić was forced to admit that he had underestimated Milošević's cunning character and political (mis)conduct. Milošević's long-term plan to take power in Serbia became clear to Stambolić when the candidates with whom Milošević had populated the LC voted Stambolić out of office in favour of Milošević. Yet, for Stambolić, the realisation that his protégé had played a successful game of deception came too late.[22] The committees in which Milošević installed his loyalists became important centres of his personal power, where he successfully advanced policies on which he and Stambolić disagreed.[23]

Despite Milošević's political manipulation, Stambolić still recalled him many years later as an amiable companion who radiated optimism and energy.[24] Indeed, Milošević's deceitful side seems to have been well hidden by his charming façade; and according to Stambolić, Milošević skilfully won the allegiance of people when it suited him. For example, he made a point of ingratiating himself to the older generation of communists by remembering their birthdays and visiting them in hospital, securing their support and sympathy.[25] He also hid behind his charm when faced with his own blunders – usually responding to confrontation with a large dose of self-criticism, matched with a sudden warmth and indulgence. Although he sometimes overused this tactic, it often succeeded in bringing him back into favour.[26]

The leader made in Kosovo

Milošević's entry into politics in the 1980s was tightly connected to the revival of Serb nationalism that was fomented by ethnic clashes in Kosovo. Ethnic Albanians had taken their grievances to the streets in April 1981, only one year after the death of Tito, and federal authorities saw them as a very serious threat to the stability of the SFRY. The 1974 Federal Constitution had created ambiguity about the status of Kosovo and Vojvodina – Serbia's two autonomous provinces – by making them territorial parts of the Republic of Serbia and, at the same time, federal units with representation equal to that of the six constituent republics. Both provinces had representatives in the PSFRY, with voting powers. While many praised the 1974 Constitution as a model for a functioning decentralised federation, nationalists in Serbian intellectual circles saw it as a threat to Serbian territorial integrity.[27] Critics claimed, *inter alia*, that it divided Serbia into three territories, thereby weakening it economically and politically relative to the other five republics; none of which had autonomous provinces within their borders.[28]

Riots on Kosovo streets in the spring of 1981 were followed by political manoeuvring. Kosovo Serbs – encouraged by intellectual elites from Belgrade, the Serbian Academy of Sciences and Arts (*Srpska akademija nauka i umetnosti*, or SANU), and the Serbian Writers Association – formed the Serbian Resistance Movement of Kosovo (*Srpski pokret otpora Kosova*, or SPOK) in 1982. According to Miroslav Šolević,[29] one of the founders, the driving forces behind the SPOK were writer and eventual President of the FRY Dobrica Ćosić and Dušan Ristić. Ristić, a former professional politician from Kosovo, had held various party and state positions, including President of the Kosovo Provincial Assembly, before he was expelled from the party in 1981. He had inside knowledge of communist political culture and suggested that the demands of the SPOK should be addressed to existing political and state institutions, because he felt that if the communist establishment was approached first, the movement would be less likely to be labelled as nationalist, anti-Yugoslav, or anti-communist.[30] For the SPOK to be efficient in pursuing its still developing political agenda through the LC, it needed a leader who was already respected in Serbian party and republican structures.[31]

Kosta Bulatović, another of the founding members of the SPOK, testified as a Defence witness that in 1986, after consulting Ćosić, he and other Kosovo Serbs had drafted a petition to the authorities calling for changes they claimed were necessary in order to stop alleged terror by Kosovo Albanians against Kosovo Serbs.[32] According to Bulatović, he was arrested by Kosovo authorities on 2 April 1986 simply because he had a text of this petition on his person. When asked by Judge Robinson about the arrest, which seemed puzzling given that this text had been published in the press, Bulatović answered that he had been arrested so that "nobody else would dare speak the truth."[33]

Subsequent to Bulatović's arrest, the SPOK leadership invited Stambolić to visit Kosovo. Stambolić accepted, apparently unaware that Bulatović was in custody.[34] The SPOK organised public protests, demanding the immediate release of Bulatović, and when Stambolić realised how precarious the situation was, he gave a reconciliatory speech – sending a signal to Kosovo Serb activists that he would not advance their agenda.[35] With Bulatović still in prison, where he spent three days, his fellow activists threatened to bring their protest to the streets of Belgrade.[36]

Communist leaders in Kosovo started their own inquiry and found that no order had been issued by the Kosovo police to arrest Bulatović; the police, it seemed, did not know, or could not say, on whose authority he had been detained. It eventually emerged that he had been arrested on the orders of someone from Belgrade, and Kosovo communists realised that the arrest and the protests may have been staged. Bulatović was released and communists in Kosovo, including top leaders like Azem Vllasi, began to understand that they were pawns in a game much bigger than they could appreciate from Priština or Prizren.[37]

On his return from Kosovo, Stambolić told members of the Serbian Central Committee that the situation in Kosovo was so unstable that one bloodthirsty slogan yelled by a prominent Serbian nationalist at a rally would bring the Serbs to rebellion.[38] One year later, in the spring of 1987, another high-level visit from Belgrade to Kosovo was scheduled. Originally, Stambolić was expected to go; but he felt it was time for another Serbian leader to become acquainted with the political problems of the province. Some senior functionaries disagreed Stambolić's choice to delegate such an important function, but he held firm and chose his protégé Milošević, the second highest-ranking official in Serbia.[39] Before his departure, Milošević sought advice from Stambolić about how to approach the visit. Stambolić recalled advising Milošević not to succumb to emotions, telling him that the tense and passionate atmosphere could easily explode and unleash violence. He told Milošević to "be careful and keep a cool head."[40]

Milošević's visit to Kosovo took place on 17 April 1987 and followed usual party protocol. At the end of the visit, Kosovo Serb activist Miroslav Šolević confronted Milošević, saying they had not wanted a monologue, they wanted dialogue. "When are you coming back?" he asked.[41] Milošević replied that he would return the following Friday; and the week between these two visits would prove to be crucial to Milošević's political rise. The trial record does not reveal what happened in that week, or with whom Milošević consulted, but his return visit to Kosovo appeared meticulously orchestrated and was organised through his own channels, bypassing the LC of Kosovo.[42]

The political leadership in Kosovo resolved to confront Milošević upon his arrival for this second visit, over his disregard of official protocol; but they waited for him in Priština in vain.[43] Just one hour before the meeting was to start, he landed, leading Kosovo communists to think that he was deliberately avoiding an encounter with them. Azem Vllasi insisted on meeting immediately, arguing that Milošević was to blame for any delay, but Milošević, visibly upset, said the public event should not be delayed and was adamant that they meet afterward.[44]

The entire group went to Kosovo Polje, only to discover that there had been substantial changes in the organisation of the event. Vllasi and the LC of Kosovo had planned for the meeting to take place in a Railway Company Hall that could accommodate only a limited number of people and where attendance would have had to be controlled by invitation. When they arrived, they saw that the Railway Company Hall was empty and they were told that a parallel meeting had been arranged in the nearby Cultural Hall.[45] According to Vllasi, the leadership of the LC of Kosovo learned through an informer that Milošević had already sent his own Chef de Cabinet to the province to coordinate directly with members of the SPOK. Further, local Serbs had been encouraged to prepare speeches in advance, to share their plight and request constitutional changes for Kosovo, and every word was set to be broadcast on television.[46] Miroslav Šolević later explained that the SPOK had been given only three days to re-organise the event, which he admitted had been changed without informing Kosovo's communist leaders. And part of the plan, he explained, was to park roadwork trucks in front of the Cultural Hall, loaded with stones to be thrown at the local police in order to start a riot if Kosovo Serbs were not allowed inside.[47]

As originally envisioned, 300 people were to attend the event, but many more turned up.[48] Even with the venue change, not everyone could fit; and indeed, as expected, many of those without invitations were kept outside, giving the SPOK activists an excuse to spark unrest. Mitar Balević was with the local LC at the time, in charge of organising the meeting, and appeared as a Defence witness. He explained that he had been informed at the start of the meeting that a crowd of some 15,000 had gathered, and that police were holding them back by violent means. "I asked you to go outside the building and to address the citizens, and I asked Azem Vllasi to do the same," he told

Milošević in court, "and the first people who came up to you said 'We are being beaten, President.'" According to Balević, Milošević told them, "They must not beat you," but the commotion made it difficult to hear, and so loudspeakers were mounted at the window to allow him to address the citizenry from there.[49]

This second visit to Kosovo by Milošević led to his meteoric rise to power and has been regarded as a turning point in Yugoslavia's history as well as the beginning of the process of disintegration and war. The debate among scholars over the historical meaning of the words ascribed to Milošević on that day – "No one is allowed to beat you"[50] – is still ongoing, with some claiming he made the statement on the spur of the moment and others arguing that it was part of a premeditated plan. Nonetheless, these words were attributed to Milošević in heroic terms even though they did not reflect any real brutality in the moment or any real heroic poise on his part. The meeting ended up taking place as planned, and when local Serbs were allowed inside, they spoke in front of the cameras from prepared speeches about the personal suffering they claimed to endure in Kosovo just because of their ethnicity.[51] These testimonies dragged on for hours, and a total of 76 people spoke.[52]

The events of 24 April 1987 were aired live on Serbian television and Milošević's utterance of "No one is allowed to beat you" was taken out of context and instrumentalised by Kosovo Serb activists and the intellectual establishment in Serbia to forge a new leader. The footage was rerun endlessly and the visit became a major topic in the written press as well, presenting Milošević to Serbs outside of Kosovo as a saviour and unifier of the Serb people and placing the Kosovo issue solidly on the federal (and later, state) political agenda. Years afterward, Šolević summarised this interlude aptly, remarking that it would be wrong to say the SPOK had put Milošević in power, for he already had it; but what they did was make a leader out of him.[53]

The Eighth Session: Milošević seizes power in Serbia

The Kosovo Serbs may, indeed, have played a vital role in making Milošević a leader, but he had yet to win power in Serbia at the republic level. As his public profile rose and he started to enjoy support from influential Serbian elites, he soon became a threat to the communist establishment that gravitated around Stambolić – who persisted in underestimating Milošević's craving for power until he was confronted with it in a very public and humiliating way. Only three months after Milošević's visit to Kosovo Polje, a showdown occurred between the two at the Eighth Session of the Central Committee of the LC of Serbia, held in September 1987, with Milošević presiding. Milošević attacked Stambolić indirectly, by targeting Dragiša Pavlović, another of Stambolić's protégés, who held an influential position as Chairman of the LC of Belgrade and who had criticised Milošević's nationalistic rhetoric.[54] Everyone in attendance understood that Milošević was also assailing Stambolić and the policies he represented.

Borisav Jović, a close ally and advisor to Milošević, recalled the atmosphere of the meeting, explaining that the media broadcast every word and that citizens, while watching, began sending telegrams of support to Milošević. These telegrams were read aloud at the session, to the dissatisfaction of Stambolić supporters, encouraging further telegrams. As the pressure increased, only seven voices opposed Milošević's policy and the vote led to Pavlović's dismissal.[55]

To viewers, Milošević appeared resolute and self-assured – a person determined to win even at the cost of publicly humiliating his political mentor and former friend. Stambolić, on other hand, looked totally unprepared to respond to an attack against his politics and leadership. It seemed he did not comprehend the consequences of shifts in Serbian politics, for himself or for the future of Serbia and the SFRY.[56]

Prosecution Expert Witness on history, Audrey Budding, summarised the importance of these events in 1987, noting that Milošević had targeted those who opposed his Kosovo policies or criticised his inflammatory portrayal of the Albanian population there.[57] Budding – like many other historians, political commentators, and political opponents of Milošević – views the changes to Serbian political leadership that followed, and the unorthodox manner in which it happened, as a putsch.[58] Indeed, in the aftermath of the Eighth Session, the LC of Serbia was purged of those who were not aligned with Milošević. Objections to or questions about what happened to these members were met with the simple explanation that they exhibited "professional incompetence."[59]

In May 1989, Milošević became President of the Presidency of the Republic of Serbia, the position previously occupied by Stambolić. Commenting later on his own role in Milošević's rise to power in Serbia, Stambolić explained that it had been more than his influence and Milošević's election as President of the Presidency of the Central Committee that had pushed Milošević to new heights. It had also taken well-coordinated efforts to make a cult figure out of Milošević; for which songs were written about him, paintings painted, and his photographs printed in great numbers for public display. And, adding further to this persona, academicians competed in their praise of him, comparing Milošević to French President Charles de Gaulle and American President Theodore Roosevelt.[60]

Empowered by a legacy of authoritarian political culture

While the veneration for Milošević that emerged after his appearances in Kosovo had certainly helped make him the leader of all Serbs, as Šolević noted, it was the system that had given him authority. The political system of the former Yugoslavia developed from a monarchy before the Second World

War into a communist federation after it, always with power concentrated in the hands of a single leader.

The first Yugoslav state existed from 1918 to 1941 as a parliamentary monarchy that was strongly influenced by the king. In 1941, the Communist Revolution started; but drastic modifications to the political system that were introduced after the Partisan victory in 1945 brought little change to a political culture that had long accepted strong leadership.[61] As in other communist regimes, the Yugoslav government revolved around the personality cult of its leader, Josip Broz Tito (1892–1980), who would rule the country for 35 years. And despite Tito's determination that a single person would not succeed him as head of state and Chairman of the Party (he had laid out plans for his successors to rule through a collective presidency), his will alone could not change political culture overnight. So, although it was not officially possible for another politician to succeed Tito and carry out all his functions after his death in 1980, there was a general expectation among the public that another strong leader would emerge.

It was in this historical and political context, and in the tradition of political patrimonialism, that Milošević was able to assume a position that gave him power beyond his formal political entitlement.[62] It had been his ambition to impose himself as the leader of Yugoslavia through the LC; but, with the end of the communism in 1990, state structures changed and so did Milošević's ambitions. He would have to secure his place as leader of Serbia through democratic elections.

Milošević's first term as the President of Serbia, still in a one-party system, lasted only one year.[63] Then, in 1990, Serbia was the last of all six SFRY republics to organise multi-party elections. In July of that year, Milošević and his allies formed a new political party with a socialist orientation. The Socialist Party of Serbia (*Socijalistička partija Srbije*, or SPS) was constituted by merging two existing organisations, the Socialist Union of the Working People of Serbia and the LC of Serbia.[64] It inherited a legacy of one-party politics that its leaders sought to replicate despite the ostensibly multi-party environment in which they now operated. The SPS embraced and tried to unite various ideologies, from left to right, and Milošević's role in forming the SPS – a party based on socialist principles at least in name – conflicted with the doctrine of his nationalist supporters. But in reality, he wasn't driven by either ideology, beyond their instrumental benefit, and was thus well placed to embrace both at the same time.

Winning political power in Serbia, with a mandate from the Serbian people themselves, Milošević entered a new stage in his political career. Latinka Perović described Milošević as a "consensual autocrat" because he came to power with considerable public support but then used the electoral mandate of Serbian voters as a platform to rule autocratically. According to Perović, Milošević was not an authentic nationalist but someone who simply rode the wave of nationalism that was put into motion by the Serbian intellectual elite.[65]

As Chairman of the SPS, Milošević controlled the federal government as well as republic-level governments and assemblies, through party loyalists, much as he had under communism. This secured the next phase of his political agenda; namely, imposing the SPS Party Programme – which had been legitimised by Serbian voters – as the dominant state policy in Serbia. Zoran Lilić, a former prominent SPS official and President of the FRY from 1993 to 1997, testified as a Prosecution witness about how the SPS became the power base through which Milošević influenced legislation that was eventually passed at all levels of government.[66] Lilić said that important decisions were first reviewed by Milošević's family (alluding to his wife Mira Marković), then by an inner circle of close associates from the SPS. The Executive Committee of the SPS's Main Board subsequently confirmed decisions made by the inner circle, and trusted leaders of municipal and regional boards implemented those decisions without question.[67]

The SPS participated in every federal government in the decade between 1990 and 2000, extending the reach of Milošević to all federal institutions.[68] The party also won majorities in republic-level parliamentary elections in 1990, 1992, and 1996, giving opposition parties no chance to shape legislation.[69] And it was clear that Milošević understood just how much political control resulted from his position in the SPS. Upon his election as President of Serbia in 1990, he ceded the position of SPS chairman to Borisav Jović for a short time because the Serbian Constitution prohibited the President from engaging in other public duties; but, several months later, disregarding the Constitution, Milošević reclaimed his chairmanship.[70]

In 1992, Milošević was re-elected President of Serbia and, in 1997, he was appointed President of the FRY – moving his power to the federal level. With his departure from the office, the position of President of Serbia suddenly lost all influence. Milošević's successor, Milan Milutinović, settled comfortably into the role of a lapdog.

Power for the sake of power

Milošević's taste for power developed quickly. While his leadership had been attained with the support of Serbian intellectuals and Serbs from Kosovo – who were determined to re-define Serbian statehood via nationalism – evidence presented at the ICTY revealed that Milošević's central motivation over ten years as the leader of Serbs was his desire to have and hold onto power. And when faced with choices between the welfare of Serbia and his own political power, Milošević chose the latter.

Surviving mass protests

The first serious threat to Milošević's authority and regime came in demonstrations that were organised by his political opposition on 9 March 1991 in central Belgrade. They were massive but peaceful; and yet, Milošević knew they could bring his leadership to an end. Alarmed by the prospect, he called PSFRY President Borisav Jović to request military intervention. Jović, who was not in Belgrade at the time and was reliant on Milošević's assessment of the security risk, began contacting the other seven PSFRY representatives to garner support for deployment of the Army on Belgrade streets.

Vasil Tupurkovski, the Macedonian representative, recalled later that Jović had told him in a midday conversation that the demonstrations were peaceful; but by that evening, television reports of violence having broken out among the protestors began to air. Whether or not it was provoked by Serbian police in order to create the necessary conditions to declare a state of emergency has never been established with certainty, but after seeing the violence on the streets of Belgrade Tupurkovski eventually gave his consent.[71] Even JNA Chief of Staff General Veljko Kadijević was apparently reluctant to involve the Army, and only changed his mind when demonstrators neared JNA Headquarters.[72] And so, since Milošević had managed, through Jović, to secure a favourable majority, the JNA did intervene – dispersing demonstrators by using tanks, water cannons, and tear gas.[73]

It wasn't just Tupurkovski who wondered if manoeuvring had taken place to justify use of the JNA; and Milošević and his associates heard enough rumblings of distrust from other PSFRY members in the immediate aftermath of these events to understand that they could no longer rely on the PSFRY for a majority vote the next time they felt the need to deploy armed forces. Indeed, the test came just days later when the JNA proposed introducing extraordinary measures that would have allowed the Army to take action against the Croatian government for its noncompliance with orders the PSFRY had given earlier that year. Five votes were needed to enact the measures, only seven members were present, and BiH representative Bogić Bogićević, an ethnic Serb, voted against. Sensing that there was indeed a growing schism, the Serbian Bloc – consisting of the four members of the PSFRY who were compliant with Milošević's demands; namely Borisav Jović from Serbia, Branko Kostić from Montenegro, Jugoslav Kostić from Vojvodina, and Sejdo Bajramović from Kosovo and Metohija[74] – realised that the PSFRY could be an obstacle as far as use of the JNA was concerned. And so, the day after the session, Milošević gave a rare public address in which he announced the formation of special police forces in the Republic of Serbia.[75]

Defying political opponents

The next challenge to Milošević's power followed the formation of the Federal Republic of Yugoslavia in 1992, and came from Milan Panić, a successful US businessman with dual citizenship who FRY President Dobrica Ćosić had put forth as Prime Minister. According to Borisav Jović, Panić approached him in May 1992 with intelligence that the United States was willing to help lift UN sanctions against the FRY if Milošević would step down. When Jović brought this to the attention of Milošević, he was dismissive and avoidant, leading Jović to believe that Milošević feared the intelligence could lead to his forced resignation.[76] Although Milošević had initially been in favour of Panić's appointment, their relationship very quickly cooled, and Milošević began to do all he could to sideline Panić. He even banned Panić from attending sessions of the Supreme Defence Council, the collective commader-in-chief of the FRY.[77]

But Panić was allowed to participate in meetings of the State Council for Harmonisation of Positions on State Policy (*Savet za usaglašavanje stavova o državnoj politici*) because this ad hoc body had been brought to life by his close political ally Ćosić. Zoran Lilić, who succeeded Ćosić as President, explained that the Council for Harmonisation had been created to provide a forum for the political leaders of the FRY, Serbia, Montenegro, and occasionally the RSK and the RS to discuss issues of vital importance to their common political future.[78] Records of the eight sessions of the Council for Harmonisation, held between July 1992 and April 1993, were discovered by the Prosecution by chance in 2001. They reveal a great deal about Milošević's politics, but also the resentment and even open hostility he directed towards Panić, who was willing to contradict Milošević. Although Ćosić and Panić were both federal leaders and therefore his superiors, Milošević did not tolerate their criticism or entertain the political course they advocated – instead, contradicting, obstructing, and marginalising them.

A showdown between Milošević and Panić was developing in the weeks before the London peace conference held on 26 and 27 August 1992, which was called by the international community after information emerged about Serb-run detention camps in Northern Bosnia and ethnic cleansing of the non-Serb population. At the Council of Harmonisation meeting on 18 August, a stern Milan Panić found little support among Milošević and his followers, and the delegation went to London several days later without a unified position.[79] According to Jović, Panić had requested that Milošević withdraw from politics and that he announce it in London. Apparently Ćosić had supported Panić in asking Milošević to step down; only, he thought that the announcement should not take place in London, but in Belgrade at the Serbian Parliament.[80] Milošević was incensed. Upon returning to Belgrade from London, he pressured his party to initiate a motion of distrust in the FRY Parliament against Panić as Prime Minister.[81] In the unfolding power struggle, Panić – who had no party base in Serbia – took a risk and challenged Milošević in the December 1992 elections. He lost. He left Serbia and returned to his career in business, abandoning politics after only several months. Milošević won and remained in power for the next eight years.

After London, Milošević also turned against Ćosić, and the depth of the rift between them became apparent at the Council of Harmonisation session held on 2 November 1992.[82] The immediate cause of a heated debate that polarised Serbian and FRY representatives at the meeting was a raid that had been executed by the Serbian Ministry of Internal Affairs (MUP) on the Federal Ministry of Internal Affairs. Pavle Bulatović, Minister of the Federal

MUP at the time and one of Milošević's closest associates, was blindsided. He complained that when Serbian MUP officers took the building – purportedly in response to a dispute over its ownership – they also took over its communication system, cryptographic equipment, devices, documentation, registries, and cars from the car pool.[83]

The Prosecution considered this event a turning point, for the Serbian MUP had usurped the Federal MUP to become the most powerful security service in the country. By taking over sophisticated intercepting and cryptographic equipment and seizing intelligence files on many prominent political, military, and intellectual figures, Milošević could control his political opponents. He had also succeeded in diminishing federal authority and humiliating President Ćosić and Prime Minister Panić, who were both out of the country at the time. Ćosić – livid about the takeover – noted in his diary that he was "astounded by Milošević's act." He could not believe that Federal MUP officers had been disarmed and that the state had been left without its constitutionally mandated Security Service. He went on to call the raid a "coup" and Milošević "the Požarevac despot."[84] The Serbian takeover of the Federal MUP was an important part of the Prosecution's theory as to how Milošević's de facto power was tied to the Serbian MUP, which implemented his policies inside and outside Serbia from April 1991 until the end of his mandate.[85]

In mid-1993, not long after Panić's withdrawal from politics, Milošević finally managed to force Ćosić out of his position as President. With the elimination of Ćosić, Milošević successfully initiated changes to the federal leadership that further tightened his grip on power by appointing only those most loyal to him. And despite losing some support from Serbian nationalist circles loyal to Ćosić, Milošević was firmly in control.

Keeping it in the family

When Milošević's charismatic authority began to fade in the mid-1990s, it was largely due to the economic disaster that had been set off by the high price of Serbia's involvement in war. Milošević's war politics had been criticised by the international community and international sanctions and UN sanctions, along with widespread corruption among elites close to Milošević and his wife, had left Serbia impoverished.[86] Milošević's political tenure was marked by a huge gap between a small group of excessively rich elites – including his family – and a large group of excessively poor citizens. According to Borisav Jović, Milošević was not actually committed to the principles of social justice he had claimed to espouse at the formation of the SPS in 1990, and he began to lose the support of many who had believed he held socialist convictions.[87]

Milošević's early supporters also could not possibly have envisaged the degree to which his leadership would be influenced by his wife. Milošević's political alliance with Mira Marković strained the relationships he had with many close associates; and indeed, Milošević was defined by Marković and was uxoriously deaf to the opinions of others. In 1991, for example, Jović advised Milošević to remove a photograph of his wife from the wall of his presidential office. It was the same size as the portrait of Tito that hung next to it; and this was not something that would pass unnoticed by visitors. Milošević replied that he would rather remove Tito's photograph than his wife's, so this is what he did – and thus it would remain until the end of his time in office.[88]

Jović and Lilić both witnessed first-hand the influence Mira Marković had on her husband and, through him, on Serbian politics generally, and they both testified about how Milošević and his wife engaged in a destructive political game that led to irrational and inexplicable decisions. Jović recalled how Marković began writing published articles in the form of diary, recording her thoughts and ideas for the biweekly magazine *Duga*. The articles fascinated the public. Once, she attacked the SPS, asserting that it was not a socialist but a nationalist party and claiming that some party members did not want a peaceful solution to the Yugoslav crisis. The fact that Marković attacked her husband's party led to rumours that they were about to divorce, but this turned out to be far from the truth.

Mihailo Marković (no relation to Mira) was known worldwide for his role in introducing the Praxis School into Marxist philosophy, and he was one of the founders of the SPS and its principal ideologue. He responded in the media to Mira's accusations only to see Milošević come to her rescue when, through an intermediary, he demanded that Mihailo stop arguing with Mira in public.[89] Shortly after their clash, Mira Marković founded her own political party, the Yugoslav United Left (*Jugoslavenska ujedinjena levica*, or JUL). Notwithstanding that this new party would directly compete for votes with the SPS – another leftist party at least in name – Milošević more or less ordered SPS leadership to attend the JUL party gathering. Those who refused, as Jović did, became outcasts from the SPS leadership, essentially writing off their political futures.[90]

Jović later discovered, apparently by accident, that Milošević had personally taken part in the foundation of the JUL – supposedly to help him remove warmongers, criminals, and thieves from his own SPS ranks. But Jović was sceptical of this reasoning; he felt Milošević could have dealt with this problem without founding a new party.[91] Lilić also testified about Milošević's involvement in the foundation of the JUL, and said the influence exercised by the SPS and JUL was indistinguishable. He explained that the JUL had taken over some of the most important functions in the Republic of Serbia and in the FRY, including controlling financial affairs as well as media, and concluded that both parties were under Milošević's authority.[92]

These testimonies supported the Prosecution's characterisation of Milošević as a man without personal conviction or honour, motivated only by power.[93] But does that sufficiently explain his political conduct and the violence that resulted? Arguably, the ideological platform from which he acted must also be taken into account. But does it matter if he adopted an ideology out of conviction or out of political opportunism? An exploration of the relationship between Milošević's leadership and Serbian state ideology begins to tackle these questions.

The ideology

Throughout the Milošević trial, witnesses who were once close to him – or had engaged in political negotiations with him – testified about discrepancies between Milošević's words and deeds. So, what were Milošević's true intentions? And why would he try to obscure his political goals? Was it because he knew that the creation of an expanded Greater Serbia could only be achieved through violence against non-Serbs? In establishing *mens rea*, it was essential for the Prosecution to present evidence on Milošević's adoption of this ideology and his knowledge that it has long inspired efforts by Serbian political elites to create an ethnically-defined Serbian state, frequently through violent means.[94]

Since the nineteenth century, Greater Serbia ideology has been associated with territorial expansionism, advocating that the Serbian state be enlarged to the south (into Macedonia and Kosovo) and to the west (into BiH and Croatia). Early proponents sought to expand Serbian borders into Ottoman and then Habsburg territories – which had ethnically mixed populations with large numbers of non-Serbs – and the Prosecution argued that this history of efforts to enlarge Serbian territory was one of mass atrocities against those non-Serb populations.

Greater Serbia ideology and a history of violence: from terrorism to mass atrocities

Expert witnesses for both the Prosecution and Defence addressed the history of the concept of Greater Serbia. Prosecution expert Audrey Budding credited the term to Serbian politician Ilija Garašanin (1812–1874), who wrote a short nationalistic manifesto in 1844 known as *Načertanije* ("The Outline"), which identified the borders of a future Serbian state.[95] The document was kept secret until it was finally published in 1906.[96] Since Garašanin's time, there has been much debate over his ideology and what the notion of Greater Serbia implies. Is it a unified South Slavic state incorporating a large number of non-Serbs, or a Serbian national state meant to unite Serbs and connect all Serb-majority territories? In other words, does it reflect Yugoslavism or Serb nationalism?

In his Opening Statement, Milošević asserted that the idea of a Greater Serbia had been invented for a propaganda campaign launched by the Austro-Hungarian Empire. When Ottoman territory conquered by Christian powers was redistributed in 1878 by the Congress of Berlin, BiH became an Austro-Hungarian protectorate, to the great consternation of the adjacent emerging Kingdom of Serbia.[97] Between 1878 and 1914, the relationship between the Kingdom of Serbia and the Austro-Hungarian Empire was dominated by a rivalry over BiH territory, which worsened when Austro-Hungary annexed BiH in 1908. Milošević cited that rivalry as the reason the Austro-Hungarian Empire had devised the Greater Serbia concept, in order to accuse the Kingdom of Serbia of expansionism.[98]

Čedomir Popov, a Defence witness on the topic, made similar claims, testifying that the "myth" of Greater Serbia had been fostered as a scare tactic meant to

> prevent the creation of a Serbian state within its national borders, to conceal the fact that Austria possessed some of the Serbian and Balkan territories and aspired to others, and to open the routes to a Catholic missionary campaign among the Orthodox population of Southeastern Europe.[99]

A number of other Defence witnesses repeated this explanation, calling the notion of Greater Serbia a foreign invention meant to discredit the increasingly powerful Kingdom of Serbia and prevent its westward expansion.[100] Defence expert Kosta Mihailović also claimed that two well-known Serbian socialists – Dimitrije Tucović (1881–1914) and Svetozar Marković (1846–1876) – had contributed to a negative appraisal of the term "Greater Serbia" by applying it to Serbian expansionist policies in the second half of the nineteenth and beginning of the twentieth centuries, and whose views he said were due to "unyielding" ideological positions that were "one-sided."[101]

Čedomir Popov addressed the content of *Načertanije*, saying it had not advocated aggression and should not be seen as having instigated violence.[102] Instead, Popov argued, Garašanin's plan focused on integrating lands claimed by Serbia on linguistic and religious grounds – BiH, Northern Albania (specifically Kosovo and Metohija), and Montenegro – allowing Serbia to unite all Serbs while leaving the door open to other South Slavic nations, including Bulgarians as well as Croats from Slavonia, Croatia, and Dalmatia. According to Popov, Garašanin's primary aim was to liberate Serbs in the Balkans from Ottoman rule, invoking their "sacred historical right" based on the pre-Ottoman legacy of the fourteenth-century Serbian state under Tsar Dušan the Mighty.[103]

Asked by the Prosecution to comment on the proposition that such a Serbian state would have been based on historic, ethnic, religious, linguistic, and geostrategic criteria and be led by a Serb dynasty, Popov replied that *Načertanije* had indeed advocated the national interest of Serbs, but he said that similar nationalist[104] conceptions "prevailed throughout Europe in the 19th century" and that "Serbs also had the right to espouse such an idea."[105] In his Expert Report, Popov characterised Greater Serbia ideology as having been "nourished, fostered, and spread" to destabilise Serbia by enforcing a stereotype against Serbs as hegemonic. When Milošević asked if he in fact saw Serbia as a "victim nation and a victim state," Popov said that he did.[106] His answer reflected the ideological framework of Serb victimhood by which Serb nationalist elites had mobilised social action in Kosovo in the 1980s.

A history of expansion of the Serbian state by force, 1912–1941

The Balkan Wars, 1912–1913

Serbian state borders were re-drawn twice during the Balkan Wars, waged in 1912 and 1913, in which emerging Balkan states fought the Ottoman Empire. Serbia extended its borders south, to Vardar Macedonia (a region also known as Old Serbia because it was part of the medieval Kingdom of Tsar Dušan) and into Kosovo and parts of Sandžak. These conquests meant that the Kingdom of Serbia incorporated large numbers of non-Serbs.[107]

In his Expert Report, Defence witness Kosta Mihailović wrote that Serbian socialist Dimitrije Tucović asserted at the time of the Balkan Wars that Serbia's 1912 military incursion into northern Albania proved it was trying to conquer that territory as well, with aspirations to gain an outlet to the Adriatic Sea. Mihailović contested this, saying that it was in fact the threat of the creation of a Greater Albania that had spurred the start of the Balkan Wars in the first place.[108] But it wasn't just the Albanians who had expansionist ideas; and the danger of competing territorial claims had been recognised several decades earlier by another Serbian socialist, Svetozar Marković, who drew attention to the hypocrisy of Serbia for asserting the right to an exclusive state in the Balkans but denying that right to others. In his Report, Mihailović dismissed Marković's concerns, saying, "it can be reasonably assumed that he did not know the real intentions of [Serbian] policy."[109]

The Serbian conquest of territory in Kosovo during the Balkan Wars involved atrocities committed by Serbian and Montenegrin soldiers, which some observers saw as a systematic attempt to alter the demographic balance of the region in order to justify the incorporation of Kosovo into the Serbian state.[110] On this issue, Prosecution expert Budding referred to the Carnegie Endowment's 1914 *Report of the International Commission to Inquire into the Causes and Conduct of the Balkan Wars*, which chronicled these atrocities. It described the total destruction of villages and populations and "incredible acts of violence" by soldiers who desired "the entire transformation of the ethnic character of regions inhabited exclusively by Albanians."[111] Defence witness Popov acknowledged that atrocities had been committed by Serbian forces; but he contended that they came only in response to attacks by Albanian units, which he claimed refused to accept Serbian authority.[112]

Slavenko Terzić, who was called by the Defence to testify on the history of Kosovo, notably omitted any reference to the Balkan Wars in his Expert Report. Yet, the significance of this particular episode in the history of Kosovo and Serbia is undeniable because, in 1913 – after almost 500 years – Serbia repossessed Kosovo from the retreating Ottoman Army and incorporated its territory into the expanding Kingdom of Serbia. In the Prosecution's cross-examination, Terzić was asked why he hadn't mentioned these events, including mass atrocities committed against Kosovo Albanians by Serb soldiers, in his Report. Terzić accepted that the Carnegie Endowment's accounting of the extent of the atrocities was probably accurate, but called them expected consequences of war. He rejected the Prosecution's suggestion that these atrocities resulted from a Serbian government plan to ethnically cleanse that territory, concluding that such a plan would have been implemented had it existed.[113]

Terzić also failed to mention in his Report that the Serbian government had offered certain economic privileges to Serbs who were willing to settle in Kosovo after 1913 as part of a colonisation programme. As Audrey Budding explained, the purpose of the programme was to change the ethnic composition of Kosovo in favour of Serbs. But the scheme never really worked and Kosovo Albanians maintained a majority.[114]

The First World War, the London Treaty of 1915, and a Greater Serbia

The Prosecution pressed Čedomir Popov during cross-examination on the fact that some of the first Greater Serbia ideologues had advocated violence in order to unify Serb-claimed territories. When asked about the early twentieth-century organisation known both as "Unification or Death" (*Ujedinjenje ili smrt*) and the "Black Hand" (*Crna ruka*), Popov corroborated that, indeed, a member of the organisation had assassinated Aleksandar Obrenović – the last king of the Obrenović Dynasty – in 1903. Obrenović was known for having cultivated a good relationship with Austro-Hungary, then seen by Serb nationalists as the major obstacle to territorial expansion, especially into BiH. This same group was also implicated in the assassination of Franz Ferdinand in Sarajevo in 1914.[115]

Popov, who had initially rejected the Prosecution's proposition that Greater Serbia ideology was linked to violence, eventually admitted that terrorism had indeed marked early attempts of Serbian expansionism. He agreed that the assassinations of King Aleksandar and Archduke Franz Ferdinand represented a shift towards support for a more violent approach by the Black Hand, which he described as a paramilitary organisation comprised of active army officers of the Serbian Royal Army. The objective of the group, he said, was Serbia's unification with Serbs from Bosnia – an aim he claimed was fully supported by Bosnian Serbs.[116] But Popov denied that the assassination of Archduke Ferdinand in 1914 was an expression of broader Greater Serbia ambitions, asserting that Bosnian Croats and Bosnian Muslims were members alongside Bosnian Serbs of Young Bosnia (*Mlada Bosna*), the organisation that actually carried out the assassination. According to Popov, Young Bosnia representatives sought support from the Black Hand only after they were refused assistance from the Serbian government.[117] The assassination was seen as triggering the outbreak of the First World War, during which the Austro-Hungarian Empire disintegrated and after which BiH became part of a newly formed Kingdom of Yugoslavia.

The Defence position was that Serbs had never aspired to form a Greater Serbia, and had even rejected an enlarged state when it was offered to them in the 1915 London Treaty, preferring instead to form a joint state with the Slovenes and Croats. In his Opening Statement in August 2004, Milošević stressed that the Serbs had rejected the London Treaty despite promises by the Allies to enlarge Serbia to include BiH and territories in Croatia. He said that "Serbia instead embraced and espoused Serbs, Croats, and Slovenes alike from the former territories of the Austro-Hungarian Empire, and this is how the Kingdom of Croats, Serbs and Slovenes was created."[118] According to Milošević, the choice by Serbia to create the common state of Yugoslavia most served the interests of the Croatians and Slovenians, who he claimed were protected from "territorial fragmentation" by becoming "part of the winning camp."[119]

Čedomir Popov contextualised the London Treaty historically, explaining that the territory of Austro-Hungary – the enemy state – had been offered to Italy by the British if Italy got involved in the war on the side of the Allies. According to Popov, Serbia was not part of these secret negotiations; but the British had apparently agreed to award a considerable part of the Austro-Hungarian Empire with Italy, and designated the rest as either a Serbian or a common Serb, Croat, and Slovene state.[120] He testified that there were actually two London Treaty maps, the second of which dealt specifically with Serbia and captured changes made to the first, marking territories offered up

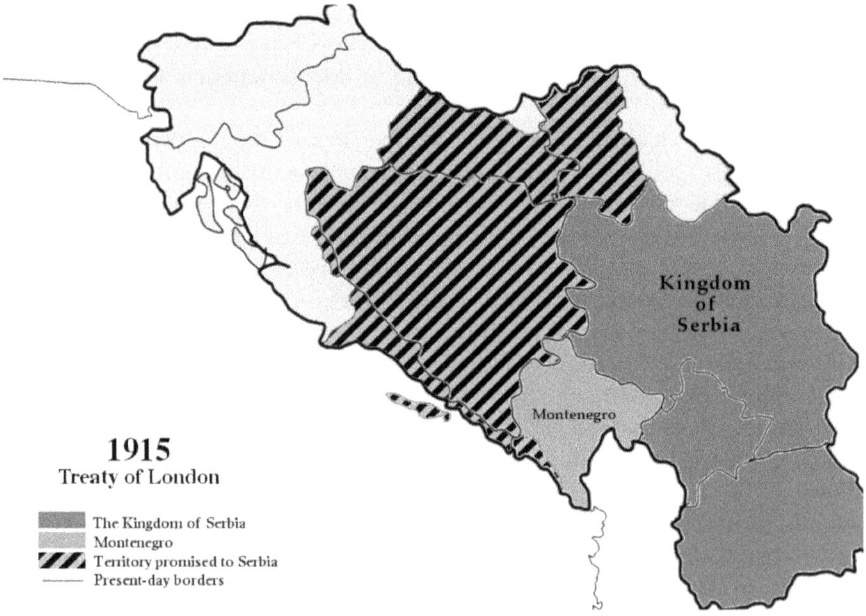

Map 2.1 Land offered to Serbia by the Allied Forces in the London Treaty of 1915 (adapted from Exhibit D267).

to Serbia, including in Macedonia, as compensation for the fact that Serbia lost much of Dalmatia to Italy.[121] In fact, Popov said that Serbia was offered more territory than it ever considered rightfully due, including Bosnia, Eastern Slavonia, Bačka, Syrmia, and part of Dalmatia.[122]

The First Yugoslavia or Greater Serbia?

Popov testified that Serbia's war aims had been laid out in the 1914 Niš Declaration, which had prioritised the creation of a common Yugoslav state.[123] This was the basis of the Defence argument that, despite the fact that the London Treaty would have secured what was in effect a Greater Serbia, the Kingdom of Serbia rejected it, choosing instead to liberate other South Slavs living under Austro-Hungarian rule. However, Prosecution expert Budding offered a different view, explaining that Serbian political elites in fact saw a common state as an expanded Serbian state and not as a Yugoslav state, which was then a fundamentally new concept. According to Budding, the notions of Greater Serbia and Yugoslavia were synonymous at the time, at least in the minds of political decision makers. From this perspective, the Niš Declaration supported Serbia's pursuit to unify all Serbs.[124]

Croat representatives involved in negotiations that preceded the creation of the first Yugoslav state advocated for a confederation; though they eventually compromised with the Serbs and established the Kingdom of Serbs, Croats, and Slovenes under the Serb royal dynasty of Karađorđević.[125] Some Serbian intellectuals recognised the importance of making a distinction between a common state and the expansion of Serbian domination, and pushed for a federal model that would decentralise power.[126] In 1929, the Kingdom changed its name, becoming the Kingdom of Yugoslavia, or the First Yugoslavia. The state was troubled by inter-ethnic relations and growing Serbo-Croatian conflict; still, Serbia did engage politically with Croats and Slovenes and treated them as nations. Its relationship with other ethnic groups, however – the Bosnian Muslims, the Macedonians, and the Kosovo Albanians – was problematic.

An extreme example of how some Serbs felt towards the non-Serb population can be seen in yet another document that remained hidden away from the public for years, at the Institute for Military History in Belgrade, titled "The Resettlement of the Arnauts" (*Iseljavanje Arnauta*).[127] The term 'Arnauts' was used to denote ethnic Albanians, and the document recommended moving the Albanian population to Turkey and paying the Turkish government for resettlement costs. The proposal was written by Vasa Čubrilović, then a junior historian and Assistant Professor at the University of Belgrade who was known for his Young Bosnia membership at the time of the assassination of Franz Ferdinand. He presented it in 1937 at the Serbian Cultural Club – an establishment for the elite, including prominent Serb politicians, high-ranking military personnel, and intellectuals with considerable influence over politics and public opinion.[128] It was eventually never implemented, but it did reveal the pattern of thought in which the change of the ethnic composition of Kosovo was seen as the solution for keeping Kosovo under Serb control.[129]

The Second World War and the historical legacy of Moljević's "Homogeneous Serbia"

The disintegration of the First Yugoslavia in 1941 and its partition among the Third Reich, Italy, and neighbouring Nazi satellite states – such as Hungary and Bulgaria – re-drew the map of Yugoslavia considerably. Croatia was rewarded with more territory for its alliance with the Third Reich, extending its borders to the east by annexing BiH and Syrmia and reaching as far as the suburban town of Zemun in the vicinity of Belgrade. The Serbs, on the other hand, were left by Nazi Germany with a state that was much smaller than the new, neighbouring Independent State of Croatia (*Nezavasina država Hrvatska*, or NDH). Led by the extreme right Ustasha movement, the NDH began exterminating Serbs, Roma, Jews, and communists in the Jasenovac concentration camp, attempting to change the state's ethnic composition in favour of Croats.

In both Nazi Serbia and the NDH, several Serb Chetnik guerrilla units were active. Under the command of Colonel Draža Mihailović, they were considered by Allied Forces to be a royal army and were seen as an official resistance movement until 1943, when Tito's victorious communist guerrillas – the Partisans – became the only recognised resistance force in the former Kingdom of Yugoslavia. One of the ideologues of the Chetnik movement was Stevan Moljević (1888–1959), a lawyer from Banja Luka and a member of the Serbian Cultural Club who authored a 1941 pamphlet titled "Homogeneous Serbia" (*Homogena Serbia*). It revitalised Greater Serbia ideology in the political and military context of the Second World War and the changing European state system.

Commenting on Moljević's contribution to the Chetnik movement and Greater Serbia ideology, Čedomir Popov described the Chetniks as an incoherent group; though, he admitted that Draža Mihailović, the Chetnik war time commander, indeed seemed to have adopted some of Moljević's ideas. According to Popov, Moljević had envisaged Greater Serbia to encompass even more territory than the London Treaty offered, and had also outlined a programme of population exchange – non-Serbs from Serb territory for Serbs outside of it. Even the Chetniks rejected this idea, which was apparently later revised under pressure from the Allies to the federative Yugoslav model, which Popov claimed was designed "with Serbia at its centre."[130]

The importance of the Moljević map in the development of the Greater Serbia creed is its demarcation of a western border running through Croatia – from the northern town of Virovitica, through Karlovac to Karlobag in the south. Asked by the Prosecution to address the boundary proposed by Moljević, which would have left Croatia with a very narrow strip of territory

Map 2.2 Moljević's Greater Serbia (adapted from *Izvori Velikosrpske Agresije*, p. 146, Exhibit P807).

squeezed between Slovenia and Greater Serbia, Popov said the border was not accepted by all advocates of a Serb state.[131] And indeed, that's possible; but the Virovitica–Karlovac–Karlobag (V–K–K) line grew to be seen by many as a potent and enduring symbol of Greater Serbia aspirations, and proved relevant to the war in Croatia in 1991.

The Serb national question in the SFRY, 1945–1985

The Serb national question was not entirely resolved by the creation of communist Yugoslavia, resurfacing periodically, as Audrey Budding explained in her Expert Report.[132] Serbia had dominated the Kosovo political scene in the 1950s and 1960s, when Aleksandar Ranković, an influential Serbian communist functionary, had made the centralisation of the Federation a key political goal. Ranković had risen to the highest political ranks by serving as the first Head of the Communist State Security Service (UDBA); and even when he moved on to more visible political functions – making an impressive career in post-Second World War Yugoslavia by becoming Vice-President of the Federation – he continued to control the Secret Service. In 1966, Ranković was dismissed from the party for disloyalty to Tito and for espousing Serbian unitarism. He was also accused of abusing his power over the security services, including by allegedly putting Tito himself under surveillance, as well as for unlawful use of the police in Kosovo. Later, some of his contemporaries claimed that Ranković had actually been loyal to Tito, but he was nonetheless labelled a Stalinist, a centralist, and a Serb nationalist, and the post-Ranković period brought democratisation and decentralisation of the party and the state.[133]

Audrey Budding testified that changes to the status of the provinces began much earlier – in three sets of constitutional amendments that were passed from 1968 to 1971 and which gave the provinces greater independence from Serbia and greater decision-making power at the federal level. The most radical of these were passed in 1971 when a 23-member collective federal presidency was introduced, with three representatives from each republic and two from each province, and Tito as the twenty-third member. The 1974 Constitution then reduced that number to nine, with one representative from each republic and province, and Tito as the ninth member.[134] This represented a shift towards equal representation for the republics and provinces alike.

Serbian communist liberals led by Marko Nikezić and Latinka Perović, who were in power until 1972, welcomed decentralisation. But many Serbian intellectuals and sitting communist politicians resisted reforms. According to Budding, there were two groups of opponents to decentralisation: Yugoslav unitarists were ardent Yugoslavists who saw decentralisation as weakening the original Yugoslav ideal, and the 'particularists' were early proponents of Yugoslavism who sought unity in Serbdom when they felt a common state was being undermined. This latter group remained preoccupied with the unity of Serbs and resisted their division among different federal units, eventually raising concerns about the rights of Serbs outside Serbia.[135]

The most serious and explicitly political condemnation of decentralisation efforts came from the Law Faculty of the University of Belgrade in March 1971, when Serbia's most authoritative legal experts concluded that Yugoslavia would no longer exist as a state after adoption of the proposed amendments. Some of them called on Serbs, in Serbia and beyond, to protect their own interests and alluded to a post-Yugoslav era.[136] Philosopher Mihailo Đurić went so far as to claim that "in the name of national equality several independent and even opposing national states had already been established on Yugoslavia's territory."[137] Federal authorities responded repressively without addressing the issue, which Budding called a missed opportunity.[138]

The 1974 Constitution was widely criticised by Serbian intellectuals for granting autonomy to Kosovo and Vojvodina. In 1977, the Serbian Presidency commissioned an analysis of the 1974 Constitution and its impact on

Serbia. The results were never officially discussed by the party or made public, due to explicit criticism of the Constitution, but were presented in March of that year in what was dubbed the Blue Book (*Plava knjiga*) because of its blue cover page.[139] The Blue Book stated that Serbia had been divided into three separate political, legal, and economic entities since each province, like all the republics, had its own constitution, presidency, government, and supreme court. The authors emphasised the procedural difficulties of passing or implementing laws that applied to the whole republic, and drew attention to the political asymmetry resulting from the fact that republic-level organs were theoretically empowered to enact measures for the entire republic but were limited in practice to sovereignty over Serbia proper, i.e. excluding the provinces. Further, representatives of the two provinces took part in decision-making processes and bodies of the republic, while there were no representatives of the republic in the decision-making organs of the provinces.[140]

The authors of the Blue Book avoided nationalist language and saved their most extreme statements for its conclusion, where a lack of cooperation between Serbia's republican and provincial bodies was said to be adversely affecting the unity of Serbian national culture and identity. The question was also raised as to whether Serbs were being allowed to fully exercise their right to a national state in the Yugoslav framework.[141] Budding noted that similar rhetoric cropped up in the 1980s among activists, creating common ground for cooperation between Serbia's politicians and opposition intellectuals.[142] And indeed, contrary to the culture of a one-party system, several petitions in the 1980s demanded protection of the rights of Serbs in Kosovo.[143]

One petition, made public in January 1986 and signed by over 200 Belgrade intellectuals, promoted the idea that Serbs had long been victimised.[144] Among other things, it claimed that Kosovo Albanians had been driving Serbs from Kosovo for three centuries. Although the ethnic composition in Kosovo did change over that time, the number of migrations in the twentieth century was exaggerated in the petition text, as were their causes; but these claims portended the economic and political arguments that would be expressed in the SANU Memorandum, published later that year.

The petition's core assertion was rooted in the fact that the percentage of Serbs and Montenegrins in Kosovo had fallen from 27 per cent in the four censuses after the Second World War to just under 15 per cent in 1981.[145] Serb nationalists saw this emigration pattern as proof of a federal policy that favoured Kosovo Albanians and discriminated against Serbs in the province; and they cited high birth rates among Kosovo Albanians as evidence of a 'special war' waged against Serbs. But this argument failed to account for significant demographic, social, and cultural differences between Kosovo Albanians and Kosovo Serbs. For example, Kosovo Albanians were the majority population in rural areas, where women generally did not work, leading somewhat automatically to higher birth rates than among Serbs, who lived predominantly in towns.[146] Nevertheless, the petition asserted that emigrations of Serbs and Montenegrins had been due to intimidation and violence that was being used to create an "ethnically pure" Kosovo. The word "genocide" was also deployed, alongside the claim that it could not be stopped unless profound social and political changes were made throughout the country.[147] These views were echoed in court by Defence expert and SANU member Slavenko Terzić.[148]

The SANU Memorandum and Serbian state ideology

So, what were the ideological underpinnings of Milošević's policies and when did he begin his turn from communism to nationalism? Did it all start in 1986 with the SANU Memorandum? The scholarly debate on the place of the Memorandum in Milošević's political paradigm qualifies it as everything from a "blueprint for war" to merely an indicator of "a change in attitude toward the common state."[149] Mainstream views of the historiography of the Yugoslav conflict once held that there was no connection between Milošević and the authors of the Memorandum at the time it was written, and it was assumed that Milošević – like the rest of the Serbian leadership – had condemned it. But the trial record includes material that has shed more light on this issue.

In court, the Prosecution underlined that Milošević had been careful not to commit himself publicly to any ideological concept, including ideas laid out in the Memorandum, but argued that the SANU Memorandum had in fact been the roadmap for Milošević's Kosovo politics. His tacit adoption of the goals of the Memorandum was in part confirmed by Milošević himself, who spoke highly of the SANU and invited some of the Memorandum's authors to appear on behalf of the Defence. When its two principle authors – Mihailo Marković and Kosta Mihailović – were called to the witness stand, they repeated the same arguments by which they had legitimised the wars in the 1990s, namely that the Serbs needed their own state as a safeguard against inevitable genocide and physical annihilation where they lived intermingled with non-Serbs. They rejected any suggestion that Milošević had carried out a nationalist agenda; however, they acknowledged a connection between the Memorandum and the views he held. Still, they asserted that the Memorandum had not introduced the Serbian crisis to Milošević but had probably confirmed his own observations.[150]

In 1985, Serbian leaders approved the proposal of members of the Serbian Academy of Sciences and Arts (SANU) that they contribute to solving the profound social, economic, and political crises that faced both Yugoslavia and the Republic of Serbia. Stambolić firmly believed that science should be part of such efforts and invited the SANU leadership to organise several expert teams to analyse different aspects of the crisis and submit proposals for how to resolve them.[151] Yet the product of this work – the SANU Memorandum – took Stambolić by surprise. When its "leaked version" appeared in 1986, he qualified it as an "obituary for Yugoslavia" and felt that the recommendations it advanced ran contrary to the interests of Serbs in Yugoslavia, whom he felt were best served by a common state.[152] Stambolić warned against the dangers of attempts to unite Serbs on the ruins of Yugoslavia, and saying presciently that this would lead to conflict with other Yugoslav nations and the rest of the world.[153]

In the months following a 'leaked' disclosure of the Memorandum, it was a hot topic at all party forums. But unlike his fellow high-ranking politicians Stambolić and Dragiša Pavlović, Milošević was diligent about not speaking against the Memorandum in public.[154] Still, while he never commented openly about the contents of the Memorandum, Milošević defended the Academy on a number of occasions, saying that it was only natural that an institution of the highest intellectual and moral standards would deal with solving complex domestic issues.[155]

The Prosecution mentioned the SANU Memorandum only briefly in its Opening Statement, referring to the threats it had alleged were faced by Serbs in Kosovo and Croatia and the fear this rhetoric had instilled in Serbs.[156] But as the trial went on, the Memorandum kept cropping up in evidence, progressively revealing its significance as an apparent blueprint for the political programme implemented by Milošević. The central arguments in the Memorandum were based on the view that economic and political systems had suffered negative consequences as a result of the 1974 Yugoslav Constitution, which had made the SFRY a confederation. According to the Memorandum's authors, this had turned the Yugoslav political system into "a textbook case of inefficiency" that could only be corrected by abandoning systems based on that Constitution.[157] They also identified three additional issues confronting Serbia in the Federation: its economic underdevelopment, its unresolved relationship with the state and the provinces, and "genocide in Kosovo."[158]

These and other very serious charges painted a dim picture of life for Serbs, especially in Kosovo and Croatia, where the authors alleged "physical, political, legal, and cultural" threats had affected the ethnic balance in Yugoslavia.[159] Their conclusion was that the root of both the Yugoslav crisis and the Serbian crisis lay in the Federation's decentralisation. They called for Yugoslavia to be transformed; and they referred – though only in passing – to the possibility of its collapse.[160] In her testimony, Audrey Budding drew attention to this fact, noting that unlike previous critics of the 1974 Constitution, the authors of the SANU Memorandum had not only catalogued old grievances but had paired them with the groundbreaking new inference that Serbs might be able to do without Yugoslavia.[161]

Authors of the Memorandum appear as Defence witnesses

In his Opening Statement in February 2002, Milošević said that the indictments against him accused not just him but all Serbs, including the Serbian intelligentsia and members of the SANU. He defended the SANU and the Memorandum, saying that Serbian academics had responsibly and authoritatively described the situation in Kosovo.[162] And while his reticence on the topic meant it was difficult to prove that Milošević had even read the Memorandum, its role in shaping his ideology emerged when he called some of its most prominent authors to the stand for his Defence – a choice which spoke volumes.[163] Professor Kosta Mihailović, an economist who was among the Memorandum's authors, was an advisor to Milošević at all major negotiations in the early 1990s. He testified about Serbia's economic sluggishness in the First Yugoslavia (1918–1941), but was also cross-examined about the Memorandum and Milošević's attitude towards it.

In 1995, Mihailović co-authored a book titled *Memorandum of the Serbian Academy of Sciences and Arts: Answers to Criticisms* in which he and Vasilije Krestić – a Professor of History and a fellow SANU member, who was responsible for the part of the Memorandum addressing the history of genocide against Serbs – explained why and how the Memorandum was written. Mihailović confirmed in his testimony that there was indeed a link between the ideas in the Memorandum and the views of Milošević on legal, political, and economic aspects of the crisis; but in the book, he and Krestić denied that this was anything but coincidental, calling it a "pure fabrication" that Milošević had activated a plan laid out in the Memorandum. They characterised such claims as "anti-Serbian propaganda" and said that it was only natural that Milošević "may have seen some of the problems and solutions in the same or similar light."[164] Mihailović and Krestić went on to excuse the few criticisms Milošević had expressed about the Memorandum, which they described as "rare and relatively mild," as a function of party compliance. In fact, they gave him credit for stopping attacks against the Academy and bringing a "change of heart toward the intelligentsia" as a part of democratic reforms.[165]

Mihailović testified that uproar over the Memorandum was unjustified because the version that was leaked was unauthorised.[166] In response, the Prosecution produced an analysis that compared the leaked "unauthorised" version from 1986 with the official version published nine years later in Mihailović and Krestić's book. Only six small differences existed between the two, and mostly in language not in substance. Even Mihailović admitted that any differences could be only minor; a concession that somewhat undermined his argument that the leaked draft did not contain the official text. Still, he insisted that the document was never meant to be made public.[167]

Mihailović attributed the leak to Professor Jovan Đorđević's son-in-law, a journalist at the daily *Večernje Novosti* who allegedly spotted the draft text at Đorđević's house and published it in the newspaper.[168] Such an explanation seemed unlikely, because it was quite improbable in the communist system for any journalist to publish such an explosive text without the consent of their editor-in-chief and the backing of at least a handful of politicians. After all, the media were tightly controlled by the LC. The Prosecution saw the Memorandum's wide distribution as a deliberate act that had been aimed at stirring up interest among the masses, and contended that the secrecy associated with the document until its publication actually served at least two specific purposes by design. First, it generated public appeal beyond what the contents really merited and, second, the 'leak' of the unfinished report allowed the authors to deny its contents on the convenient grounds that it was never finished or officially adopted.

The Prosecution compared the clandestine nature of the Memorandum to the treatment of *Načertanije* – which was written in 1844 but kept secret until it was published in 1906. Mihailović rejected the suggestion that secrecy had helped generate popular interest in either of those documents and insisted the Memorandum was intended only to animate the political establishment.[169] But, its publication led to a buying frenzy among Serbian citizens, with photocopies sold at every street corner in Belgrade.

In his Expert Report, Prosecution witness on propaganda Renaud de la Brosse qualified the public release of the Memorandum as a "deliberate leak" and said that its appearance in a daily newspaper in several instalments would not have been possible without approval from members of the LC.[170] Just how broad support for the Memorandum was in Serbia became apparent at the Eighth Session of the Central Committee, held in September 1987, when it divided Serbian leadership into Stambolić and Milošević blocs. A majority of delegates supported Milošević against Stambolić and Pavlović – the two most vocal critics of the Memorandum – and the ensuing standoff exposed proponents and opponents of a new policy course.[171]

The influence of the SANU Memorandum on post-Communist Serbian state ideology

Serbia is a good example how in post-Cold War transformations, post-communist elites did not seek to develop democracy but concerned themselves first with 'self-determination' – or the establishment of nation states based on an ethnic principle.[172] Yet, with all attention given to the state and the collective rights of nations, there was hardly any regard for the development of civil society and the rights of individuals.[173] The authors of the SANU Memorandum had effectively synthesised and aggregated several strains of grievances, criticisms, and arguments that stemmed from the adoption of the 1974 Constitution, and had given them new legitimacy in the post-Tito era. Its authors were tasked with responding to deep political, economic, inter-ethnic, and social crises that had been unfolding in the Federation since the late 1970s; yet, their primary focus was the status of Serbia and of Serbs in other republics, and their proposed solution was revocation of the autonomy of the two Serbian provinces.[174] Even Vasa Čubrilović – who authored "The Resettlement of the Arnauts" in 1937 and was himself a member of the SANU – reportedly criticised the recommendations of the Memorandum, accusing its authors of having spent years analysing maps of Bosnia, looking for ways to connect Serb territories from Belgrade to the Croatian town of Karlovac.[175]

The principle of self-determination as an element of Milošević's Greater Serbia designs

Still, while Greater Serbia ideology has been cast in different forms by elites in Serbia throughout the twentieth century – and at times denied altogether – repeated failures to realise an expanded Serb state have never led to an abandonment of the underlying ideology. On the contrary, after each failure, new opportunities to reinvent the ideology have always been based on the same or similar principles but adapted to new political circumstances.

Milošević's vocal advocacy of the principle of self-determination was seen by the Prosecution as a variation of this same ideology. In court, the debate over self-determination developed on two tracks, based on different applications of the term in the post-Yugoslav space. Serbs and Serbia had applied the right of self-determination to *peoples*, or the right of a nation of people to territorial autonomy. Slovenia and Croatia – along with the international community – had instead applied the self-determination principle to *republics*, meaning in practical terms that the republics would become independent within existing borders after disintegration of the SFRY.

The Prosecution argued that Serbian insistence on self-determination of peoples over republics was inherently tied to aspirations for an enlarged Serbia, and that attempts to unify all Serbs by forcibly re-drawing republican borders amounted to the creation of a "de facto Greater Serbia." Since there was no evidence that Milošević had ever actually expressed his political aims or war goals by using the term 'Greater Serbia' – which lacks a universally agreed definition anyway – the Prosecution exercised caution and spoke only of this "de facto Greater Serbia" when describing Milošević's objectives. Still, intercepted telephone conversations involving Milošević and Karadžić in 1991 showed they were both aware of negative connotations surrounding the term. Karadžić, for instance, complained to a fellow Bosnian Serb that Croatian Serbs needed to be more careful about explicitly stating their desire to join Serbia because it might sound too much like they were talking about a Greater Serbia.[176] And Milošević warned Karadžić to avoid reminding the public of historical efforts to achieve a Serb state, instructing him in September 1991 to remove a reference to Serbia's 1914 borders from a speech.[177]

But Greater Serbia designs were clearly at the heart of Serb territorial designs in the 1990s. Discussing a common political future and the "regionalisation" or "cantonisation" of BiH, Karadžić told Milošević about a conversation he had with a French official, who had remarked that compromise wasn't being reached on the issue of Bosnia. Karadžić had informed him that anything but a Greater Serbia would be a compromise for Serbs.[178] And in a 1992 discussion with a Serbian politician, Karadžić said that the goal was not Greater Serbia per se, but that existing borders were unacceptable because they divided Serbs.[179]

Milošević's particular interpretation of Greater Serbia ideology was analysed in court, and an important question for the Prosecution was to what extent the more euphemistic terms used by Milošević and his associates – such as "All Serbs in a Single State" or "the right of the Serb people to self-determination" – referenced something akin to the historical concept of Greater Serbia. Arguing that the application of a self-determination principal to Serbs (as opposed to Serbia) would inevitably expand Serbian territory, the Prosecution used the term "de facto Greater Serbia" to describe the ideology espoused by Milošević, but also stressed that this ideology had not manifested in a single, fully articulated and overarching plan from the very start. Though the size and shape of a future Serb state – regardless of its designated name – was always at the core of his politics, Milošević's strategy had changed with circumstances, affected by the actions of other SFRY republics and the international community.[180]

When the Prosecution questioned Defence expert Čedomir Popov on whether violent connotations associated with Greater Serbia ideology had prevented people from espousing it publicly, he continued to deny that the ideology had ever been anything more than a fabrication. But as the Prosecution pressed, Popov asked agitatedly just how small Serbia would have to be to avoid being called Greater Serbia.[181]

Notes

1 Marlise Simons and Alison Smale, "Slobodan Milosevic, 64, Former Yugoslav Leader, Accused of War Crimes, Dies," *New York Times*, 12 March 2006.
2 Ian Traynor, "Slobodan Milosevic," *Guardian*, 12 March 2006.
3 For discussion of the motivations of someone accused of mass crimes, see: Bettina Stangneth, *Eichmann Before Jerusalem: The Unexamined Life of a Mass Murderer* (New York: Alfred A. Knopf, 2014). Also see: Jennifer Schuessler "Book Portrays Eichmann as Evil, Not Banal," *International New York Times*, 4 September 2014.
4 For example, see more on his early life: Sell, *Slobodan Milošević and the Destruction of Yugoslavia* (Durham, NC: Duke University Press, 2002), 16; and Stevanović, *Milošević: People's Tyrant* (London: I.B. Tauris, 2002), 3.
5 Stevanović, *Slobodan Milošević*, 3–5.
6 Stambolić, *Put u bespuće*.
7 In Communist Yugoslavia, the structures of the party and the state were parallel but technically separate; but positions in each were named so similarly as to create confusion. The party was known as the LC beginning in 1952, and had a federal-level body with lower-level branches at the republic, provincial, and municipal levels. Communist functionaries from some cities, especially Belgrade – which was an economic and political centre for the SFRY – held significant power. The party's Central Committees (CC), at the federal and republic levels, were consensus decision-making bodies, each with a Chairman as well as a collective Presidency led by a President of the Presidency of the Committee. The state structure also employed a collective Presidency at the federal and republic levels, also led by a President of the Presidency (the executive branch); along with federal- and republic-level Assemblies (the legislative branch) that each had an internal hierarchy similar to that of a parliament or congress. Thus, there was a President of the Presidency of each LC Central Committee and a President of the Presidency of each republic and of the federal state, as well as a Chairman of each LC Central Committee (and of provincial or municipal committees) and a

President of each legislative Assembly. Due to the convoluted nature of these titles, they are spelled out in this text to provide as much clarity as possible.
8 Stambolić, "My Biggest Mistake," in *Put u bespuće*, 133–134.
9 Ibid., 134.
10 Audrey H. Budding, *Serbian Nationalism in the Twentieth Century: Historical Background and Context*, Expert Report, 11 April 2003, Exhibit P508, 58.
11 The three more powerful positions were: President of the Presidency of the Central Committee of the LC of Serbia, President of the Presidency of the Republic of Serbia, and Representative of the Republic of Serbia in the PSFRY. For details of Milošević's career, see: Second Amended Indictment, 27 July 2004. Hereinafter, the Croatia Indictment.
12 Budding, *Serbian Nationalism in the Twentieth Century*, 59. Stambolić, "My Biggest Mistake," in *Put u bespuće*, 135–136.
13 Budding, *Serbian Nationalism in the Twentieth Century*, 59.
14 Stambolić, "My Biggest Mistake," in *Put u bespuće*, 133–134.
15 Ibid., 134–135.
16 Ibid., 133.
17 Ibid., 135.
18 Ibid., 136–137.
19 Ibid., 138–139.
20 Ibid., 139–140.
21 Ibid., 148–151.
22 Ibid., 149.
23 Ibid., 158–161.
24 *Cutting Edge*, "Sloba and Mira: Their World," directed by Frank Smith, presented by Phil Rees, BBC, 1999.
25 Stambolić, "My Biggest Mistake," in *Put u bespuće*, 147.
26 Ibid., 140–141.
27 Budding, *Serbian Nationalism in the Twentieth Century*, 44, 48–49, and 53–55.
28 Kosta Mihailović and Vasilije Krestić, *Memorandum of the Serbian Academy of Sciences and Arts: Answers to Criticisms* (Belgrade: SANU, 1995), Exhibit D250a.
29 Miroslav Šolević, interview (16 April 2005). Šolević did not testify, though he was approached by the Prosecution in 2005 as a possible rebuttal witness to be called at the end of the trial.
30 Ibid.
31 Ibid.
32 Testimony of Kosta Bulatović (14 April 2005), 38525–38526. The petition was thought of as a particular success at the time, given that only 78 people signed a petition of similar substance in 1984.
33 Ibid.
34 Stambolić, "It Started in Kosovo," in *Put u bespuće*, 165–166.
35 Miroslav Šolević, interview.
36 Azem Vllasi, interview (17 April 2005).
37 Ibid.
38 Stambolić, "It Started in Kosovo," in *Put u bespuće*, 166.
39 Ibid.
40 Ibid., 167.
41 Miroslav Šolević, interview. Also see: *Death of Yugoslavia*, "Enter Nationalism," Part I, produced by Brian Lapping Associates, BBC, 1995. The *Death of Yugoslavia* documentary series detailed the violent dissolution of Yugoslavia and relevant portions of the film were shown in court by the Prosecution on numerous occasions.
42 Azem Vllasi, interview.
43 Ibid.
44 Ibid.

45 Miroslav Šolević, interview.
46 Azem Vllasi, interview.
47 See statement by Miroslav Šolević in *Death of Yugoslavia*, Part I.
48 Testimony of Mitar Balević (25 January 2005), 35660.
49 Ibid., 35653–35654.
50 The sentence "*Niko ne sme da vas bije*" has been seen colloquially as a symbol of his ascent to power. In reality, the words were uttered in a different order: "Ne sme niko da vas bije." This has been translated in a number of ways, for example, as "Nobody will be allowed to beat you" and "No one shall beat you."
51 Testimony of Mitar Balević (25 January 2005), 35661–35680.
52 Ibid., 35689.
53 Statement by Miroslav Šolević in *Death of Yugoslavia*, Part I.
54 Budding, *Serbian Nationalism in the Twentieth Century*, 58.
55 Borisav Jović, *Knjiga o Miloševiću* (Belgrade: Nikola Pašić, 2001), 39.
56 Stambolić, "A Prelude to the Eighth Session," in *Put u bespuće*, 201–203.
57 Budding, *Serbian Nationalism in the Twentieth Century*, 61.
58 Ibid., 58.
59 Jović, *Knjiga o Miloševiću*, 17–18, 24–27.
60 Stambolić, "My Biggest Mistake," in *Put u bespuće*, 144.
61 For discussion, see: Nora Beloff, *Tito's Flawed Legacy: Yugoslavia and the West since 1939* (London: Westview, 1985); Vladimir Dedijer, *Novi prilozi za biografiju Josipa Broza Tita* (Rijeka: Liburnija, 1981); Stevan K. Pavlowitch, *Tito: Yugoslavia's Great Dictator – A Reassessment* (Columbus: Ohio State University Press, 1992); Stevan K. Pavlowitch, *The Improbable Survivor: Yugoslavia and its Problems, 1918–1988* (London: C. Hurst & Company, 1988); Jasper Ridley, *Tito* (London: Constable, 1994); and Richard West, *Tito and the Rise and Fall of Yugoslavia* (New York: Carroll & Graf, 1995).
62 See: Nathan Quimpo, "Trapo Parties and Corruption," *KASAMA* 21, no. 1 (January–February–March 2007).
63 Until January 1991, his official title was President of the Presidency of the Republic of Serbia; then, after multi-party elections, his title was simply President of Serbia.
64 "Programme of the Socialist Party of Serbia from the First Congress," 16–18 July 1990, Exhibit P469.3a.
65 Latinka Perović, interview (11 August 2005).
66 Testimony of Zoran Lilić (17 June 2003), 22551–22552.
67 Ibid., 22557–22558.
68 Ibid., 25551.
69 Ibid., 25552.
70 Ibid., 25555.
71 According to Tupurkovski:

> Finally at about six o'clock in the evening, when Jović called me for seventh or eighth time, I told him, 'OK I will vote Yes,' because I saw that there were casualties. . . . Everything was getting out control, it was obvious.
>
> See: Death of Yugoslavia, Part II

72 Jović, *Knjiga o Miloševiću*, 65–67.
73 See: Testimony of Branko Kostić (7 February 2006), 48174; Testimony of Major General Aleksandar Vasiljević (13 February 2003), 16045–16046.
74 See: Croatia Indictment, para. 30.
75 See: Slobodan Milošević, public address, 16 March 1991, Exhibit P328.29.
76 Jović, *Knjiga o Miloševiću*, 34.
77 Ibid., 33–34. He prevented Panić from attending SDC meetings by using Panić's dual citizenship – Serbian and American – as justification, and asserted that

Panić's presence was not necessary. See: "Minutes from the 3rd Session of the Supreme Defence Council," 23 July 1992, Exhibit P667.3.2a, 2–4.

78 Testimony of Zoran Lilić (18 June 2003), 22745–22746.

79 "Stenographic Notes from the Council for the Co-ordination of Positions of State Policy," 18 August 1992, Exhibit P469.42.

80 Jović, *Knjiga o Miloševiću*, 102–103.

81 Ibid.

82 For this session, only minutes were provided. "Minutes from the Council for the Co-ordination of Positions of State Policy," 2 November 1992, Exhibit 469.45.

83 Ibid., 2.

84 Dobrica Ćosić, *Piščevi zapisi: 1992–1993* (Belgrade: Filip Višnjić, 2004), 183.

85 By late 1992, an internal document actually stated explicitly that the Serbian MUP was to take over security tasks on behalf of the FRY. See: "Rules Governing the Amendments to the Rules on the Internal Organisation of the State Security Department in the Ministry of the Interior," 13 November 1992, 1. However, this document reached the OTP after the trial was over and thus did not shape (but did validate) the Prosecution's theory.

86 Jović, *Knjiga o Miloševiću*, 18–20.

87 Ibid., 20.

88 Ibid.

89 Ibid., 21–22.

90 Ibid., 22.

91 Ibid., 23.

92 Testimony of Zoran Lilić (17 June 2003), 22555–22557.

93 Trial Transcript, Prosecution Opening Statement (11 February 2002), 9.

94 A number of witnesses testified to this history. The Prosecution called Audrey Budding as an expert witness on history, Renaud de la Brosse on political propaganda, and Ton Zwaan as an expert on genocide. The Defence called Slavenko Terzić on the history of the Kosovo conflict, Kosta Mihailović on Serbia's economic disadvantages in Yugoslavia from 1918 to 1991, and Čedomir Popov on Greater Serbia. The Defence also called other expert witnesses, such as historian Vasilije Krestić, who was set to testify on the history of genocide against Serbs in Croatia; and Kosta Čavoški, who wrote a report called "Budding vs. Budding" in direct response to the expert testimony of Audrey Budding. They did not testify in the end, due to the premature conclusion of the trial.

95 Budding, *Serbian Nationalism in the Twentieth Century*, 3.

96 For example, see: Dušan T. Bataković "Ilija Garasanin's Nacertanije: A Reassessment," *Balkanica* XXV, no. 1 (1994): 157–183. The article was tendered into evidence as Exhibit P805.

97 The Principality of Serbia existed from 1812 to 1878 under nominal Ottoman rule. It gained full independence after formal recognition by the Berlin Congress in 1878, and was thereafter known as the Kingdom of Serbia until it joined a pan-Slavic state in 1918 at the end of the First World War.

98 Trial Transcript, Defence Opening Statement (31 August 2004), 32193.

99 Testimony of Čedomir Popov (9 December 2004), 34457. Popov also wrote an Expert Report that was later published as a book in 2007, in B/C/S. See: Čedomir Popov, *Velika Srbija: Stvarnost i Mit* (Novi Sad: Sremski Karlovci, 2007). For the text in English, see: Čedomir Popov, *Greater Serbia – Reality and Myth*, Expert Report, Exhibit D263a.

100 For example, see: Testimony of Mihailo Marković (17 November 2004), 33541.

101 Kosta Mihailović, *Economic Aspects of the "Greater Serbian Policy"*, Expert Report, Exhibit D265a, 12–13. Although Professor Mihailović was officially listed as an expert witness, the Prosecution considered him to be more of a fact witness, for Mihailović participated in events of significant relevance to the planning and

strategy of the conflicts. See: Testimony of Mihailo Marković (17 November 2004), 33541.

102 Testimony of Čedomir Popov (16 December 2004), 34590–34591. Also see: Bataković, "Ilija Garasanin's Nacertanije: A Reassessment."

103 Budding, *Serbian Nationalism in the Twentieth Century*, 12–13.

104 In Yugoslav political rhetoric, the Serbian nationalism has been referred to as *hegemonism*, denoting the aspiration to rule over the territories claimed by Serbs. the term *irredentism* was distinguished from *separatism*. Irredentism has been associated with Kosovo Albanian nationalism and their alleged attempts to join Albania; separatism has been associated with Slovenia, Croatia, and BiH and their attemps to break away from Yugoslavia.

105 Testimony of Čedomir Popov (15 December 2004), 34586.

106 Testimony of Čedomir Popov (16 December 2004), 34565–34566.

107 Budding, *Serbian Nationalism in the Twentieth Century*, 3–5.

108 Mihailović, *Economic Aspects of the "Greater Serbian Policy"*, 13–14.

109 Ibid., 13.

110 Budding, *Serbian Nationalism in the Twentieth Century*, 5.

111 George F. Kennan, *The Other Balkan Wars: A 1913 Carnegie Endowment Inquiry in Retrospect* (Washington, DC: Carnegie Endowment, 1993), 151, quoted in Budding, *Serbian Nationalism in the Twentieth Century*, footnote 21.

112 Testimony of Čedomir Popov (16 December 2004), 34601–34602.

113 Testimony of Slavenko Terzić (9 December 2004), 34374–34376. Also see: Slavenko Terzić, *Kosovo and Metohija in the 20th Century*, Expert Report, Exhibit D259a.

114 Budding, *Serbian Nationalism in the Twentieth Century*, 5.

115 Testimony of Čedomir Popov (16 December 2004), 34592–34593.

116 Ibid., 34593–34594.

117 Ibid.

118 Opening Address of Slobodna Milošević, 31 August 2004, T 32193

119 Trial Transcript, Defence Opening Statement (31 August 2004), 32193.

120 Testimony of Čedomir Popov (15 December 2004), 34507–34508.

121 Ibid., 34511–34512.

122 Ibid., 34513.

123 Ibid., 34514.

124 Testimony of Audrey Budding (24 July 2003), 24930.

125 For discussion on the creation of the First Yugoslavia, see: Dragnich, *The First Yugoslavia*; and Dimitrije Đorđević, ed., *The Creation of Yugoslavia, 1914–1918* (Santa Barbara: Clio Books, 1980).

126 Budding, *Serbian Nationalism in the Twentieth Century*, 9.

127 Vasa Čubrilović, "The Resettlement of Arnauts," Exhibit P799a.

128 Testimony of Slavenko Terzić (7 December 2004), 34345.

129 See for discussion: Testimony of Slavenko Terzić (7 December 2004) T34355–34356.

130 Testimony of Čedomir Popov (15 December 2004), 34524–34525.

131 Testimony of Čedomir Popov (16 December 2004), 34609–34610.

132 Budding, *Serbian Nationalism in the Twentieth Century*, 55–56, 21.

133 Ibid.

134 Ibid., 21–22. In 1980, after Tito's death, no one replaced him as a singular head of state and the Presidency became an eight-member body.

135 Ibid., 32–33.

136 Ibid.

137 Ibid.

138 Ibid., 39.

139 Ibid., 44.

140 Ibid., 44–45.
141 Ibid., 45–46.
142 Ibid.
143 Ibid., 50–51. There were three important petitions that mobilised public opinion in Serbia in favour of Serbs in Kosovo, issued in 1983 and 1986.
144 Ibid.
145 Ibid.
146 Ibid. 51–52.
147 Ibid., 50.
148 See for example: Testimony of Slavenko Terzić (6, 7, and 9 December 2004, 34206-34207, 34237-34249, 34270-34271, 34358, 34295, 34300, 34316).
149 Dragović-Soso, "Why did Yugoslavia disintegrate?..." 18–19.
150 Mihailović and Krestić, 81.
151 Stambolić, "The Memorandum, In Memoriam to Yugoslavia," in *Put u bespuće*, 118–119.
152 Ibid., 120.
153 Ibid.
154 Budding, *Serbian Nationalism in the Twentieth Century*, 58.
155 Ibid., 37.
156 Trial Transcript, Prosecution Opening Statement (12 February 2002), 17.
157 Budding, *Serbian Nationalism in the Twentieth Century*, 54.
158 Mihailović and Krestić, *Memorandum of the Serbian Academy of Sciences and Arts*, 119.
159 Ibid., 128.
160 Budding, *Serbian Nationalism in the Twentieth Century*, 55–56.
161 Ibid., 58.
162 Defence Opening Statement (14 February 2002), 247–248.
163 SANU Members and Memorandum authors Mihailo Marković and Kosta Mihailović both appeared, as well as Slavenko Terzić, Smilja Avramov, and Čedomir Popov. Vasilije Krstić was scheduled to testify and his Expert Report was already filed before Milošević died.
164 Mihailović and Krestić, *Memorandum of the Serbian Academy of Sciences and Arts*, 80–81.
165 Ibid., 81.
166 Testimony of Kosta Mihailović (17 December 2004), 34748–34749.
167 Ibid., 34751–34753.
168 Ibid., 34751–34752.
169 Ibid., 34758–34759.
170 Renaud de la Brosse, *Political Propaganda and the Plan to Create a "State for all Serbs": Consequences of Using the Media for Ultra-Nationalist Ends*, Expert Report, January 2003, Exhibit P446.2, 34 and 38.
171 Jović, *Knjiga o Miloševiću*, 37–40.
172 For example, see: Dov Ronen, "End the Campaign to Spread Democracy," *The New York Times*, 30 April 2013, 8. Ronen discusses the tension between self-determination and democracy. In his view, what people have aspired to a number of contexts is self-determination, not democracy. Also see: Dov Ronen, *The Quest for Self-Determination* (New Haven: Yale University Press, 1979).
173 For discussion on the history of the Yugoslav state from 1918 to 1991, see: Dušan Bilandžić, *Historija SFRJ: glavni procesi, 1918–1985* (Zagreb, 1985); Vladimir Dedijer, Ivan Božić, Sima Ćirković, and Milorad Ekmečić, *History of Yugoslavia* (New York: McGraw-Hill, 1974); Bogdan Denitch, *Legitimation of a Revolution: The Yugoslav Case* (New Haven: Yale University Press, 1975); Alex Dragnich, *The First Yugoslavia: Search for a Viable Political System* (Stanford: Hoover Press, 1983); John R. Lampe, *Yugoslavia as History: Twice There Was a*

Country, 2nd edn (Cambridge: Cambridge University Press, 2000); Branko Petranović, *Istorija Jugoslavije, 1918–1988*, 3 vols (Belgrade, 1988); and Sabrina Petra Ramet, *The Three Yugoslavias: State-Building and Legitimation, 1918–2005* (Bloomington: Indiana University Press, 2006).

174 Budding, *Serbian Nationalism in the Twentieth Century*, 55.

175 Stambolić, "The Memorandum, In Memoriam to Yugoslavia," in *Put u bespuće*, 125. Vasa Čubrilović died in 1990. His mention of Karlovac infers the V–K–K line.

176 Intercept of Conversation between Radovan Karadžić and Anđelko Grahovac, 24 June 1991, Exhibit P613.12a, 4.

177 Intercept of Conversation between Slobodan Milošević and Radovan Karadžić, 20 September 1991, Exhibit P613.70a, 1.

178 Intercept of Conversation between Slobodan Milošević and Radovan Karadžić, 19 September 1991, Exhibit P613.67a, 5.

179 Intercept of Conversation between Radovan Karadžić and Budimir Košutić, 7 February 1992, Exhibit P613.171a.

180 Prosecution Response to Amici Curiae Motion for Judgment of Acquittal Pursuant to Rule 98 *bis*, 4 May 2002, para.262.

181 Testimony of Čedomir Popov (16 December 2004), 34595.

3 A centralised Yugoslavia as a solution to the Serb national question

In 2004, while preparing to cross-examine Ratko Marković, the Prosecution stumbled upon a 1992 article he had authored in the law journal *Pravni život* ("Legal Life") on the unresolved question of Serbian statehood. If not for Marković's political engagement on the side of Milošević, his article would probably have been lost in oblivion given the limited audience such specialist journals typically enjoy. But Marković appeared as a Defence witness, and the Prosecution thus saw the article as evidence of advanced planning by Serbian political and intellectual elites under Milošević's leadership.[1]

The article, "The Constitutional Status of Serbia and her Choice for a Joint State with Montenegro," was published in early 1992, coinciding with the establishment of the FRY. It gave a comprehensive account of the history of the Serb national question, unveiling the two principal alternatives for statehood that were pursued by Serbian leadership under Milošević: a centralised Yugoslav federation or an ethnically-defined state that would unite all Serbs.[2] Marković preferred a federation because of the ethnically-mixed population of the former Yugoslavia. He acknowledged that there were enclaves populated by one nation and surrounded on all sides by other nations, and recognised, too, that in some territories, no nation had a majority. Marković advocated a federation with non-Serbs and rejected a confederation, calling it a historically outdated model.[3] The alternative he outlined was an enlarged, independent, and sovereign Serbia consisting of all territories with a Serb majority, which would need to be connected. He conceded that connecting Serb territories with Serbia would necessitate the inclusion of intermediate territories with a non-Serb majority, bringing a risk and high probability of war; and he appreciated that this would expose Serbia to condemnation and sanctions by the international community.[4]

Marković's article was significant not only because he was an academic and constitutional expert, but because he was also an active politician and SPS member who served from 1994 to 2000 as Deputy Prime Minister of Serbia. When the Prosecution suggested to Marković that the introductory footnote accompanying his article – which referred to him as someone who could "inspire [Serbia's] wise constitutional thinkers" to consider the "perspective of gradual unification" of all Serb territories and people[5] – had implied that he advocated an enlarged Serbia, Marković protested that it had been the journal's editorial board, not he, who wrote the note. He insisted that Serbia had done everything possible to remain within Yugoslavia, but also said that Serbs did not wish to be absorbed into a Croatian or Bosnian state and preferred to "remain in the state they had lived in."[6] Yet, other Serbian elites had in fact already expressed indifference toward Yugoslavia by the time Marković published his article. Dobrica Ćosić, for example, explained to Karadžić in 1991 that attempts to unify the South Slavs had failed and he identified the unification of Serbs as the next goal.[7]

This chapter explores the period during which Serb leadership under Milošević tried to centralise Yugoslavia; a process which encompassed two key goals. Milošević achieved the first goal – to centralise Serbia – by instrumentalising the grievances of Kosovo Serbs in order to politically mobilise Serbs and justify changes to the status of Kosovo and Vojvodina. After Milošević had successfully centralised Serbia, he also sought to centralise the SFRY, with the Republic of Serbia as its dominant force. This coincided with fall of communism in 1990 and the introduction of multi-party systems in the republics, after which a debate ensued among the republics on reform of the SFRY.

The centralisation of Serbia, 1987–1990

The implementation of SANU Memorandum goals by mob rule, 1988–1989

Although the SANU Memorandum was never explicitly invoked by Kosovo Serb activists, its narrative supported theirs and was echoed in the rhetoric they used at public rallies to advocate that the provinces "become genuinely integral parts of the Republic of Serbia."[8] And these cries for change legitimised later constitutional reforms as expressions of the will of the people. The first step in achieving the reintegration of Kosovo and Vojvodina through modifications to the 1974 Serbian Constitution was to change the sitting leadership in the provinces. Milošević needed guaranteed support from provincial leaders to pass constitutional amendments in the provincial Assemblies. And so, in 1988, the street was mobilised in mass protests led by the same activists who made a leader out of Milošević in 1987.

This unorthodox method of bottom-up political activism through public pressure was dubbed a 'happening of the people.'[9] At demonstrations, Kosovo Serbs claimed that Serb women had been raped, that the graves of their ancestors had been desecrated, and that Serbs and Montenegrins from Kosovo had been bullied and expelled by ethnic Albanians. And the strategy was effective; after protests that took place in Vojvodina's capital of Novi Sad in October 1988 – known as the 'yoghurt revolution' because demonstrators came from factories with prepared lunches that included yoghurt – provincial and party leadership withdrew and handed over control to Milošević's supporters.[10]

Defence witness Kosta Bulatović, a Kosovo Serb activist, testified that the goal of these rallies had been to inform the public of various issues but especially of how much Serbs were suffering in Kosovo.[11] Still, while many Kosovo Serbs insisted they deserved redress and demanded changes to the Constitution, there was no reason to ensnare Vojvodina in an identical process; nobody there had expressed similar suffering or demands. In fact, Vojvodina was among the most multiethnic places in Yugoslavia and took pride in the tolerance and peaceful coexistence of its inhabitants. According to Bulatović, Kosovo Serb activists took demonstrations to Vojvodina on their own initiative, because they estimated that the leadership there presented "quite a hindrance."[12] For the amendments to be passed, Serbia needed votes in favour from *both* the Kosovo and Vojvodina Assemblies, as the 1974 SFRY Constitution stated explicitly that the border of an autonomous province could not be altered without the consent of that province.[13]

Street protests did not come to an end upon the installation of new leadership in the two provinces, though. In Montenegro, the smallest of the republics and the one most historically and culturally similar to Serbia (indeed, the ethnic distinction between a Serb and Montenegrin is sometimes quite arbitrary[14]), a January 1989 'happening of the people' replaced sitting leaders. The protests were labelled an "anti-bureaucratic" revolution, suggesting that the old leadership was too stuffy and inert and more youthful and dynamic politicians were needed. Like their predecessors in Vojvodina, the leaders of the Montenegro protests looked to Milošević for direction; and he subsequently rewarded their loyalty with impressive political careers.[15] Montenegro thus became an important ally of Serbia, giving Milošević effective control over four votes in the eight-member PSFRY – those of Serbia, Kosovo, Vojvodina, and Montenegro. Revoking the autonomous status of the provinces had actually brought their representation in the PSFRY into question from a legal standpoint; but with control of four votes, Milošević no longer seemed concerned that the two provinces he had fought to disempower enjoyed representation equal to the six republics.

Adoption of amendments to the Serbian Constitution, 1989

Over time, federal support became decreasingly important to those determined to press for constitutional changes in Serbia. In a speech given at the Serbian Assembly in January 1989, Milošević openly criticised federal institutions as ineffective and accused federal leadership of "a lack of readiness and capability." He went so far as to characterise the new political landscape as a "conflict between the people and its many representatives" and said of recent protests that "things that cannot be changed institutionally … will be changed un-institutionally." He added that if Serbia could not count on support from others in the Federation, it was prepared to do without Yugoslavia, marking the first time a politician in the SFRY had said this publicly.[16]

Kosovo Albanians were equally determined not to accept the constitutional reforms advocated by Belgrade. The social and political protests that unfolded in the province in 1988 had culminated with strikes at the Stari Trg mine in February 1989.[17] Striking Kosovo Albanian miners, opposed to Milošević's imposition of new leadership in the Kosovo Assembly, gathered in the thousands.[18] Kosovo Serbs were concerned that the strikes could obstruct the Assembly's 23 March vote on the amendments, so on 27 February, they headed to Belgrade and gathered in front of the Federal Assembly to demand that federal authorities proclaim a state of emergency in Kosovo. A nervous Raif Dizdarević, the President of the PSFRY and its representative from BiH, addressed them, calling for "brotherhood and unity." But the crowd hadn't come to see Dizdarević. They demanded Milošević, who kept them waiting all day.[19]

Though Milošević seemed genuinely reluctant to address the crowd, his closest associates urged him on, saying that if he did not, the rally would never end.[20] Eventually he appeared, giving one of his most memorable public performances. The crowd greeted him by demanding the arrest of ousted Kosovo leader Azem Vllasi, and Milošević responded theatrically, vowing that "those who deceive the people ... those who are plotting against Yugoslavia ... will be arrested and punished!"[21] To the astonishment of the rest of Yugoslavia, Vllasi was subsequently detained on charges of organising the strike and engineering social unrest in Kosovo, and though he was ultimately released, he had lost all of his power.[22]

On 10 March 1989, the constitutional amendments Milošević sought were passed by the Vojvodina Assembly, and on 23 March, by the Kosovo Assembly – which was effectively eliminated by its own vote. Milošević's supporters saw enactment of the amendments as a triumph. And for Milošević, the episode was an important demonstration of his influence and a chance to show the public that he was capable of manipulating the federal authorities. Due to the PSFRY's declaration of a partial state of emergency in Kosovo, the vote there occurred amid a climate of tension. The Prosecution introduced evidence depicting the atmosphere of fear and intimidation that was created by the presence of tanks on Kosovo streets, columns of which started moving towards the province in the days before the vote. Further, military and secret service officials were present in the Kosovo Assembly Hall during the voting; and delegates who voted seemed to have been given advance directives by their local committees to agree to the changes.[23] In the end, the official result showed only ten out of 187 delegates voting not to surrender the province's autonomy.[24]

Prosecution witness Adnan Merovci, a Kosovo Albanian politician, testified that many Assembly members had in fact opposed the amendments during public debates that preceded the vote. And according to Merovci, people who were not members of the Assembly were allowed to vote.[25] Nonetheless, Milošević repeatedly pressed Defence witnesses to attest to the legitimacy of the overwhelmingly one-sided results, and they all claimed that the Kosovo Assembly session at which the amendments passed had been truly democratic.

But the Prosecution was not alone in wondering why a political body would so easily give up its autonomy; and when Mihailo Marković testified, he was asked by the judges to explain why the Kosovo Assembly would abolish itself. He was evasive, dodging the essence of the question by insisting that the vote had not been on the revocation of autonomy and admitting only that "elements of the sovereignty of the provinces were removed."[26] Indeed, it was technically true that members had not voted explicitly to revoke Kosovo's autonomy, but they had implicitly understood that measures introduced by the amendments would lead to a new constitution, in which centralising reforms would be codified – and that is what happened when the Serbian Assembly adopted a new constitution in September 1990. Veton Surroi, a Kosovo Albanian politician and publisher who testified as a Prosecution witness, described the constitutional changes as an *Anschluss*, or an annexation of Kosovo, by Serbia.[27]

A victory for Milošević

The reactions of the Serbian elite, as well as of ordinary Serbs, were unreservedly supportive of the 1990 Constitution. The political opposition was left without any real challenge to Milošević's popularity, and he easily won Serbia's first multi-party elections in December 1990. Still, between the vote on the amendments on 23 March 1989 and the adoption of the Constitution in September 1990, unrest and violence in Kosovo – including deadly encounters between police and protesters – had continued unabated.[28] Defence witnesses were adamant that this was not due to the constitutional changes, though. Kosta Bulatović asserted, for example, that adverse reactions on the part of Kosovo Albanians had not immediately followed the passage of the amendments but had only later been encouraged and funded by foreign influences. When Judge Robinson asked Bulatović how he knew about this funding, he replied that the newspapers had written of Kosovo Albanians "being funded from the Middle East through drug trafficking channels and arms trade."[29]

The Gazimestan speech: celebration of a political triumph in Kosovo

Milošević had scored a victory with the adoption of the amendments and public celebrations of the constitutional changes that resulted were held on 28 June 1989, with an event at the Gazimestan memorial in Kosovo, erected to commemorate the 600th anniversary of the battle of Kosovo Polje. A confident and exultant Milošević was the keynote speaker. Addressing domestic and foreign dignitaries and an audience of almost one million Serb supporters, he delivered a speech that made this one of the most significant public appearances of his career.

Prosecution expert Renaud de la Brosse testified about the different ways the speech was viewed by Serbs and non-Serbs. Milošević's political opponents and many non-Serbs saw it as an exercise in sabre-rattling, and most non-Serbian media coverage of the speech emphasised Milošević's budding determination to achieve his goals by violence. On the other hand, Serbian media – and in particular Serbian television – cast Milošević as a saviour who had restored Serbs' collective dignity.[30]

Calling Kosovo "the heart of Serbia" and invoking the legend of the Battle of Kosovo, Milošević told the crowd that "Kosovo heroism" had inspired Serbs for six centuries. "At one time," he said, "we were an army great, brave, and proud; one of the few that remained undefeated when losing." But it was the next sentences that most concerned some non-Serbs; for Milošević claimed that Serbs were

> again engaged in battles.... They are not armed battles, although such things cannot be excluded yet. However, regardless of what kind of battles they are, they cannot be won without resolve, bravery, and sacrifice; without the noble qualities that were present here on Kosovo Polje.[31]

The late President of SFRY, who later also served two terms as President of Croatia, Stjepan Mesić, testified that "the possibility of an armed struggle was intimated," and that this "was the first time that anybody in Yugoslavia had ever mentioned ... the possibility of actually going to war." For Mesić and many others, the speech was a signal "that a restructuring of Yugoslavia was being prepared which would no longer be a federal one and which would no longer be the one prescribed by the 1974 Constitution."[32] And according to Mesić, Milošević's assertion that the possibility of armed struggle could not be excluded had "mobilised the masses," who realised that the Yugoslavia they knew could cease to exist. He told the Prosecution that Yugoslavia was best

> thought of as a chain, a chain in which the republics and provinces were the links.... Now, if you do away with one of the links, the chain is no longer able to function. In other words, the Federation ceases to function.[33]

Analysis of the Gazimestan speech in the courtroom – and questioning of some key Defence witnesses – revealed significant connections between the topics addressed in the speech and in the SANU Memorandum. For instance, the speech strongly reflected rhetoric in the Memorandum about concerns over Serbia's administrative borders and its integrity as a state.[34] Indeed, Milošević had declared triumphantly at Gazimestan that Serbia had "regained its state and its dignity."[35] The Memorandum and the speech also both referred to the betrayal of the Serbian people by their leaders, including Serbian communists, who the Memorandum criticised for having allowed

Serbia to stagnate economically in the post-Second World War period and for their inadequate response to the 1974 Constitution and the Kosovo issue.[36] At Gazimestan, Milošević accused Serbian leaders of making concessions "at the expense of their people" that he said "could not be accepted historically and ethically by any nation in the world."[37]

In court, Milošević dismissed the Prosecution's narrative about his speech, rejecting any suggestion that it had included content which could have fanned the flames of nationalism among Serbs in the audience. He said he was proud of the speech, maintained that the Prosecution's interpretation of it was politically motivated.[38] He also argued that the attitudes of Western media and politicians had been fickle, depending on the political context, and noted that a contemporaneous article in the *Independent* had praised his Gazimestan speech for its language of tolerance and had even cheered him for "assuming the mantle of a statesman and Yugoslavia's natural leader."[39] Yet, ten years later, Milošević noted, British Foreign Secretary Robin Cook said instead that the speech had not delivered a message of hope and reform, but had threatened the use of force.[40]

The 1990 Serbian Constitution

At the time of its adoption, the 1990 Serbian Constitution was seen as an endorsement of Milošević's three years of domination over Serbian politics. During the trial, discussion about the March 1989 amendments and the 1990 Constitution was partly focused on technical legal issues, which were addressed in great detail by Prosecution expert Ivan Kristan. Kristan – a former judge and constitutional law specialist – analysed the amendments and singled out several that had most impacted Serbian policy towards Kosovo. He concluded that revocation of the autonomy of the provinces by the Republic of Serbia was a contravention of the SFRY Constitution because it required Serbia to assume powers it was not constitutionally granted.[41] Kristan's position was that the 1990 Serbian Constitution had "abolished crucial elements of the autonomous provinces" in a manner that was inconsistent with the rule of law.[42] The provinces had ceased to be federal entities and, though they retained a form of territorial autonomy, lost their statehood attributes, placing them "in an inferior position to the one they had under the SFRY Constitution and the one they had previously had under SR Serbia's Constitution."[43]

Defence witness Ratko Marković, who was involved in drafting the 1990 Constitution, was questioned by the Prosecution in cross-examination about Article 135, which stipulated that the Serbian Constitution would be enforced in accordance with the SFRY Constitution but also, somewhat incompatibly, that

> if acts of the agencies of the Federation or acts of the agencies of another republic … violate the equality of the Republic of Serbia or in any other

> way threaten its interests without providing for compensation, the republican agencies shall issue acts to protect the interests of the Republic of Serbia.

Asked to comment on the content of the Article, Marković denied that it gave Serbia primacy over federal agencies or laws and called it a "defensive clause" meant to protect Serbia from the acts of other republics. He pointed out that similar amendments had been made to the Slovenian Constitution in 1989, which according to him, had announced Slovenia's secession.[44]

Another important change brought about by Serbia's 1990 Constitution was an expansion of the *de jure* executive powers of the President of Serbia, who was designated as head of the armed forces in both times of peace and war and was granted the power to order general or partial mobilisations in preparation for defence.[45] This capacity would prove vital to Milošević, who had been careful – at least ostensibly – to observe constitutional and legal requirements, even when organising the kind of public intimidation and pressure that had been on display in Kosovo during the March 1989 Assembly vote. The question of Kosovo and the activism of Kosovo Serbs had been an early key to Milošević's ability to exercise his political will at the provincial, republic, and federal levels; but after achieving the constitutional changes he sought, he distanced himself from Kosovo Serb leaders and moved on to the next stage of the plan – the centralisation of the Federation.[46]

From the SANU Memorandum to the SPS party programme

Pressured by the introduction of multi-party systems in the other republics, Milošević eventually had to follow suit; but Serbia was the last to do so, with elections held in December 1990. Less than six months before this, in July, Milošević and his political allies had founded the Socialist Party of Serbia, or the SPS. Borisav Jović recalled that Milošević had originally rejected the introduction of political pluralism in Serbia because he was anxious that Kosovo Albanians would gain control of Kosovo and Serbia would lose the province. Jović said Milošević was not similarly concerned about Vojvodina because "no one there could do anything to us, regardless of multiple parties, because of the ethnic composition."[47]

Four of the 16 contributors to the SANU Memorandum – Miloš Macura, Antonije Isaković, Dušan Kanazir, and Mihailo Marković – became members of the Main Board of the SPS.[48] This meant the party base was a curious ideological mix of communists and Serb nationalists, which broadened their electoral appeal and facilitated a win of the popular vote. And not surprisingly, the 1990 SPS party platform had much in common with the SANU Memorandum.

The SPS focused special attention on the position of Serbs outside Serbia, promising to

> regularly monitor the living conditions and development of Serbs living in the other republics and abroad, and maintain intensive relations … believing it to be only natural for other nations to maintain such relations with their fellow countrymen living in Serbia.[49]

Additionally, the platform stated that Serbia would "extend material and moral assistance to [Serbs], help improve their living conditions, preserve their national identity and cultural traditions and ensure more intensive cultural development."[50] So, upon winning the December 1990 election and forming the first post-communist Serbian government in February 1991, the SPS established the Ministry for Serbs Outside of Serbia.[51] Concern for the status of Serbs living outside the Republic had been expressed in the SANU Memorandum, too, and the establishment of a Ministry to address the issue renewed it as a pragmatic political question in the months before the outbreak of war.[52]

The SPS also called for a new federal constitution that would allow the formation of autonomous provinces "on the basis of the expressed will of the population and national, historical, cultural and other specificities."[53] This seemed inconsistent with the political efforts of Milošević before 1990, when his top agenda item for years had been to revoke the autonomous status of Kosovo and Vojvodina. So, the Prosecution asked Defence witness Mihailo Marković, a leading SPS ideologue, whether the ability to create new autonomous provinces had been intended to legalise the establishment of Serb territories in Croatia and Bosnia. He answered that indeed, this was the intent, meant to correct perceived historic injustices in places like the Krajina – where he claimed Serbs had lived for many years "enjoying separate rights," but that those rights had been abolished and could now be restored.[54]

The SPS viewed the Kosovo problem as strictly ethnic and proposed dealing with it through policies that would reverse demographic shifts in the province, repopulating it with Serbs and Montenegrins. Party ideologues suggested that this would require a multifaceted approach, including "determined efforts to stop Serbs and Montenegrins from moving out of the province and secure their return," matched by a campaign that would "tell the world the full truth about Kosovo and … about the causes and grave consequences of the actions of Albanians, chauvinists, and separatists."[55] Following their December 1990 electoral victory, the SPS had a decade to test this strategy, remaining in power at the republic and federal levels until October 2000.

A failure to centralise the SFRY, 1990–1991

As the SFRY dissolved, the former republics emerged as nascent states, and courtroom narratives on the causes and consequences of Slovenia's and Croatia's proclamations of independence raised a number of questions. The Prosecution asserted that the violent disintegration of Yugoslavia had been the result of Serbia's rejection of a confederation and the preconceived plans of its leaders for a Rump Yugoslav state incorporating parts of other republics. But the Defence argued that Yugoslavia's collapse was triggered by "unilateral" declarations of independence by Slovenia and Croatia. So, why did the SFRY fragment? And moreover, how did the outbreak of the war in June 1991 and the ensuing Hague Peace Conference – seen by many as the European Community's last attempt to preserve the common Yugoslav state – impact geopolitical realities on the ground?

A failed attempt by Serbia to control the SFRY through the League of Communists

Slovenia had been the first republic to publicly raise concerns about Serbian efforts to revoke Kosovo's autonomy, straining Slovenian–Serbian relations on the eve of the break-up of the SFRY. In court, this period was explored during the testimony of Milan Kučan, Slovenia's former President, who explained that Slovenian leadership had organised a public event in late 1989 in Ljubljana to show support for striking Kosovo Albanian miners. This generated a wave of negative reactions from Serbian leaders and from Kosovo Serbs – who quickly announced their intention to organise their own public rally in Ljubljana, following the example of similar successful events in Vojvodina and Montenegro. But the gathering, which organisers called the 'Rally of Truth,' never took place.[56] Kučan testified that Slovenian authorities had assessed the situation and had decided that a rally was not the best way for Kosovo Serbs to share their message with the Slovenian public. They were concerned that large numbers of Serb demonstrators on the streets of the capitol could threaten public security. Milošević accused Slovenian leaders of bias and alleged that, by banning the rally, they had disregarded Kosovo Serb victims of Albanian terrorism.[57]

The cancellation of the Rally of Truth forced Milošević to find other ways to influence Slovenia. Emphasising that an atmosphere of emergency and crisis faced the Federation, he called for an early Congress of the LC of Yugoslavia, which became known as the 14th Extraordinary Congress. It took place in January 1990 as division and animosity between Serbian and Slovenian leaders heightened, but Slovenian delegates saw the Congress as a real chance for progress and, believing solutions to the crisis lay in reforms, they prepared a series of proposed federal amendments – ranging from an endorsement of political pluralism, to abolition of the crime of "verbal offence," to a proposal to release all political prisoners.[58] Yet, when votes were called on the Slovenian proposals, Milošević led with one of the very first negative responses; and others followed. In the end, every Slovenian amendment was rejected without any discussion on its substance. The Slovenian delegates concluded that Milošević had never actually been interested in reform, but in trying to use the Congress to impose Serbian control over the LC of Yugoslavia.[59]

The power monopoly inherent in a one-party political system made the LC a chief instrument of political control. It was governed by a doctrine of "democratic centralism," according to which delegates were free to have and express their own opinions, but were expected to uphold any decision once it was made.[60] Thus, by controlling the decision-making processes within the LC of Yugoslavia, Milošević was positioned to influence the transformation of the Federation so that, in the end, delegates with minority opinions had to accept majority decisions. But the 14th Extraordinary Congress backfired. Instead of putting the Federal League of Communists under his control, Milošević triggered its disintegration. Slovenian and Croatian delegates, disgusted by his tactics, walked out while the Congress was still in session, and both republics held multi-party elections shortly thereafter, breaking the monopoly of the LC and changing the political landscape forever. By the end of 1990, all six republics had held multi-party elections and the LC of Yugoslavia ceased to exist.

The Defence narrative was that Milošević had acted to preserve Yugoslavia at the 14th Extraordinary Congress – in part because this would have kept Serbs in a single state – and it was Slovenia that played the leading role in, and bore responsibility for, the dissolution of the LC and subsequently of the SFRY. Defence witnesses asserted that Slovenian leaders had used their delegates' failure at the Congress to justify leaving the Federation but claimed that Slovenia's decision to secede from the SFRY had actually been made prior to the Congress.[61] The Defence even claimed that Serbian delegates had voted against the Slovenian proposals in order to block disingenuous reform efforts.[62]

But the Prosecution argued that Milošević's public statements in support of the SFRY had not been matched by his deeds. By obstructing the Slovenian amendments at the Congress, Milošević had rejected a reformed Federation and had provided legitimacy for the introduction of multi-party systems in the republics. Even his trusted ally at the time of the Congress, Borisav Jović, testified that Milošević's conduct at the Congress contributed to the collapse of the Federation. "One could say that although he firmly advocated Yugoslavia and its unity," explained Jović, "at this Congress he did not work for the unity of Yugoslavia but, rather, toward its break-up."[63]

Serbia's obstruction of federal reforms, 1989–1990

The Prosecution's line of reasoning was based partly on evidence that, under Milošević's leadership, Serbia had opposed essential economic, financial, and political reforms proposed by the federal government of SFRY Prime Minister Ante Marković at the end of 1989. This uncooperative and sometimes obstructive behaviour undercut federal authority and Prosecution witnesses claimed that this eventually led to the dissolution of the SFRY.[64] Marković testified that Milošević had acted in direct opposition to his expressed goal to preserve Yugoslavia, commenting that he "always came out in favour of Yugoslavia. However, at the same time what he was doing was undermining Yugoslavia."[65]

According to Marković, when he had presented his reform programme for a vote in the Federal Assembly, deputies loyal to Milošević – from Serbia, Kosovo, Vojvodina, and Montenegro – had been instructed to vote against it. When Marković's reforms were adopted by the Assembly anyway, Serbia orchestrated an obstruction, objecting to the reforms because they would allegedly enrich the wealthier parts of the SFRY but further impoverish the poorer parts.[66] Borisav Jović insisted that Serbia had opposed the reforms for economic, not political, reasons.[67] Still, Ante Marković was resolute that Serbia's response to his programme had been strongly motivated by politics; for while the package did include some economic reforms, other political, legal, and social reforms would have made it impossible for one leader to usurp power, as Milošević aimed to do.[68]

In December 1990, Serbian opposition to the Marković reforms reached a critical threshold when the republic managed to illegally transfer 18.2 billion dinars (at the time worth over US$1.3 billion) from the National Bank of Yugoslavia to the National Bank of Serbia. In his testimony, Marković called the transfer "daylight robbery, pure and simple" and said it "shook the very foundations of Yugoslavia."[69] After Marković intervened, Milošević repaid about 10 billion dinars; however, the balance of the money was never returned and the federal government was left weakened and humiliated by Serbia's brazen appropriation of federal financial authority and control.[70]

As 1990 passed into 1991, the federal government became almost completely dysfunctional and the republics became increasingly noncompliant with federal law. Slovenia and Croatia had already opted for independence and, as a consequence, allocated to their states the funds that would normally have been directed to the federal budget – such as customs revenues and taxes. Serbia had stopped paying its dues altogether. By 1991, only Macedonia and BiH, the poorest republics, continued contributing; and what they paid was insufficient to meet the needs of the Federation. More money needed to be printed, and while the amount was initially limited by regulations, when governors from Slovenia and Croatia left the Council of the National Bank of Yugoslavia in the second half of 1991, it was no longer possible to regulate the emission of currency.[71] Over the course of 1991, the federal government slowly surrendered all its authority to republic-level leaders who dictated the pace and shape of developments from then on.

Serbia's rejection of a confederation

Discussion among the republics from January to June 1991 was focused on the structure of a common state. The question was: Should the Federation become centralised as Serbia and Montenegro preferred, or become a confederation as Slovenia and Croatia proposed? While a majority – Slovenia, Croatia, BiH, and Macedonia – favoured a confederation, Serbia and

Montenegro demanded a more centralised model. Croatian and Slovenian leaders argued that the republics should either form a confederation or opt for independence, while Serbian leaders asserted that Serbs should be able to remain in a single state even if the SFRY disintegrated. According to Croatian Serb politician Milan Babić, Milošević said that Serbs could neither live across four different states nor consider a confederation a single state.[72]

By the summer of 1990, the PSFRY had invited Slovenian and Croatian leaders to elaborate in writing on their concept of a modern confederation, but in its January 1991 session, the PSFRY rejected the model they proposed.[73] Before that session, in early January, Jović noted in his diary that he and Milošević had already agreed that Serbs in Croatia would have the right to self-determination if Croatia were to secede. In court, Jović was pressed by the Prosecution to explain how Serbs living in other republics would be incorporated into a Serb state, which he was adamant would not involve "taking over anybody's territory."[74] Instead, he said the Serbs envisioned that new borders would be drawn based on ethnic distribution, not on already exiting republican borders that encompassed multiple ethnic groups.

Between March and June 1991, the Presidents of all six republics negotiated the future of the SFRY at five inter-republic meetings.[75] No federal representatives were included, reflecting the Federation's loss of power as the republics gained it.[76] The most significant development of these meetings was the May 1991 Izetbegović-Gligorov Proposal for a confederation, put forth by the leaders of BiH and Macedonia. These two republics had every reason to remain in a common state – whether a federation or a confederation – but only as long as all of the other republics also stayed, and Bosnian President Izetbegović had been vocal that BiH would only remain in a Yugoslav federation if Croatia and Slovenia did.

Milošević had accepted the Izetbegović-Gligorov Proposal at the inter-republic meeting held in June 1991 in Stojčevac, near Sarajevo, and he repeatedly emphasised this in court.[77] But it is impossible to know whether Milošević underwent a genuine change of heart from his insistence on strong centralisation or had simply been shrewd enough to recognise that Croatia would never accept the Proposal. Prosecution witness Stjepan Kljuić, a Bosnian Croat politician, testified that Milošević had in fact only agreed to the Proposal because the Croats were sure to oppose it.[78] Armed conflict was already unfolding in Croatia and the Yugoslav People's Army (JNA) had sided with the rebelling Croatian in carving out the Croatian territory. Accepting the Proposal Serbia appeared cooperative with no risk of having to commit to its principles.

Milošević's intentions in Stojčevac were further brought into question by an intercepted telephone conversation he had with Bosnian Serb leader Radovan Karadžić in June 1991, only days before the meeting, when the two had discussed and rejected the Izetbegović–Gligorov Proposal.[79] Milan Babić testified that he had also discussed the Proposal with Milošević, and had asked him if perhaps just Serbia and Croatia could form a confederation. According to Babić, a Croatian Serb, Milošević said of Croatia, "Let them go. I don't want them." And then, "I'll join with Greece."[80] Babić concluded that despite Milošević's public advocacy for a federation, he wanted to create something based more on the self-determination principle than on republican sovereignty; in other words, a state that "could be composed not only of republics but also of parts ... from other republics."[81]

Indeed, earlier that year, Milošević had suggested in a PSFRY session that "Yugoslavia was created only by Yugoslavs and not republics." He argued that the borders of republics could not constitute state borders because "they do not represent boundaries within which Yugoslav nations [of people] live."[82] Rejecting a confederate model and arguing that a confederation is not a state, Milošević said that each nation had an "equal right to decide freely about its destiny" and that Serbs wanted "to live in one state." He called any division of the Federation – and the Serb population – into several states "out of the question" but said that "every nation wanting to live with the Serbian people in the same state on an equal basis is welcome."[83] This invitation was an empty gesture and other republics were left seeking solutions that did not depend on Serbia's political participation, including gaining recognition as independent and sovereign states.

The debate over responsibility for the disintegration of the SFRY

Milošević had alluded to the possibility of a political future for Serbia outside of Yugoslavia as early as 25 June 1990, in a speech before the Serbian Assembly. Recognising that other republics were leaning towards a confederation, he suggested that Serbia could become an independent state, perhaps with new borders, and said that the republic's draft constitution accounted for this possibility. He framed the passage of a new constitution as an opportunity to "make clear that Serbia's current administrative borders are linked exclusively to the federative state system in Yugoslavia." Stressing again that a confederation is not a state, but only "a union of independent states," he declared that "all constitutional issues would be opened", including the question of Serbian borders, if a confederal model for Yugoslavia was adopted.[84]

The Prosecution viewed this speech as evidence that the 1990 Serbian Constitution had been designed to allow for an independent Serbia, and argued that it had set the tone for the debate over federal reforms by creating uncertainty and concern in other republics – especially in the parts of Croatia and BiH where Serbs had a majority – over whether borders could become an "open political issue." Slovenian Milan Kučan recalled the anxiety that was stimulated by Milošević's speech, which Kučan had interpreted as an inference that borders might be re-drawn by force.[85] Kučan also testified about the meeting of republic presidents held in Brdo kod Kranja in Slovenia, in April 1991, where Milošević had remained steadfast that Serbia would never agree to a confederation.[86] Given the results of the December 1990 referendum on independence held in Slovenia, Kučan had insisted that it was time to discuss the issue more concretely; and Croatian President Tuđman said that if Slovenia declared independence, Croatia would have no choice but to do the same.[87] According to Kučan, Milošević told him during a private walk that he would not oppose Slovenia's departure from the SFRY but that Croatia was another story. He could not let it go without re-drawing its borders, because too many Serbs lived there.[88]

The transformative value of the evidence: what telephone intercepts revealed

To help illustrate the contradiction between Milošević's overt and covert political and military aims from May 1991 to February 1992, the Prosecution relied on recordings of intercepted telephone conversations he held with other leaders during this time. Relatively free of caution, these power brokers discussed plans for dealing with former Yugoslav republics after the disintegration of the SFRY, revealing gaps between their real and proclaimed objectives. By the time they were used in court, the existence of these audio intercepts had been known for quite a while. They were first revealed at a meeting of the Federal Executive Council (*Savezno izvršno veće*, or SIV) of the FRY on 19 September 1991, after which selected parts became available to the public through the media and in several books.[89] Like so much of the Milošević trial record, these materials are important historical documents that are readily available on the ICTY's website; yet scholars have not explored their full potential.[90]

The Prosecution tendered 245 telephone intercepts into evidence, all of which were authenticated by an expert who worked for the BiH State Security Service and had been directly involved in the wire-tapping project. They offered a glimpse into conversations Milošević had with Karadžić and with other Serbian, Croatian Serb, and Bosnian Serb officials, and the Prosecution reconstructed the circumstances in which these conversations took place by situating them within political, diplomatic, and military contexts that added to their evidentiary value. This was done first by discussing them in court with witnesses such as Milan Babić, the former President of the RSK, and General Aleksandar Vasiljević, the former head of the Military Counterintelligence Service (*Kontraobveštajna služba*, or KOS) – both of whom were participants in the conversations or were mentioned in them, and were thus well placed to explain and deconstruct the intercepts.

Conversations recorded between June and October 1991 particularly revealed how Milošević had insisted on portraying Yugoslav unity to the outside world while simultaneously counting on the independence of Slovenia and Croatia to bring an inevitable end to the Federation.[91] In late June, an exchange between he and Karadžić reflected the development of Milošević's rhetoric on Croatian independence specifically, when both leaders were adamant that 'Serb-designated territories' in Croatia must be kept in Yugoslavia should Croatia secede. Their formulation was that these territories were not separating from Croatia, but that Croatia was separating from a reduced Yugoslavia in which Serb territories remained.[92] That summer, Karadžić and Milošević also discussed the various initiatives put forward to preserve Yugoslavia, including the confederal proposal of Croatian President Tuđman. When Karadžić worried that Serb plans would be spoiled if Tuđman agreed to stay in a Yugoslav state, Milošević exclaimed, "How could Franjo stay in Yugoslavia?!"[93]

In court, however, Milošević blamed Tuđman and his fellow Croatian Stjepan Mesić for engineering the collapse of Yugoslavia, and claimed that they had worked to pin the Federation's downfall on Serbian leaders. Milošević suggested to Mesić, who testified as a Prosecution witness, that he had planned all along for the dissolution of the Federation, accusing him of betraying Yugoslavia and contributing to its break up. It was true that Mesić had said in May 1991 that he would be the last President of Yugoslavia; but when asked by the Trial Chamber to clarify this statement, Mesić explained that he believed at the time that the Yugoslav crisis would be solved by political means, and almost surely by moving to a confederal model – meaning that the Federation would cease to exist. "Everyone was dissatisfied with Yugoslavia!" he told the Court. "Serbia claimed that it was being exploited.... Croatia was saying that its hard currency was being siphoned off to Belgrade. If everybody was dissatisfied, why not adopt a new model?" According to Mesić, Milošević's obstinacy regarding a strong federation had been foreshadowed by events in Kosovo and Vojvodina, pushing the other republics towards negotiations, out of fear that this pattern could be repeated elsewhere. "I thought that it was better to negotiate for ten years rather than to wage war for ten days," he said, but "some people were in favour of the war option, and Slobodan Milošević was certainly one of those."[94]

Croatia's proclamation of independence on 25 June 1991 was identified by the Defence as the start of armed conflict with the former republic. In court, Milošević quoted US Secretary of State James Baker, who had said at the time that Slovenian and Croatian independence had been declared despite a warning from the United States that this could trigger war.[95] Milošević also highlighted the role of Germany, asserting that its "premature" recognition of these new states had led to violence.[96] But what Milošević failed to acknowledge was that violence in Croatia had actually begun in August 1990 – with a rebellion of Croatian Serbs in the Knin Krajina – and had then intensified by April 1991 in the Plitvice region before spreading to both Western and Eastern Slavonia in May. By June, the conflict had become a full-scale war.

Violence and the disintegration of the SFRY

Milošević's fixation on Croatia as Yugoslavia dissolved was linked to the fact that a significant number of Serbs lived there, but he had readily agreed to

Slovenia's departure from the SFRY because the ethnic composition was overwhelmingly Slovene and Serbia had no territorial aspirations there. Still, in the night following the Slovenian declaration of independence, federal armed forces – consisting of JNA units and Federal MUP officers – intervened to prevent Slovenia's secession. For the PSFRY to have issued such an order, the consent of both the Slovenian and Croatian representatives would have been required, and so the question was on whose orders, and for what purpose, these forces were called up; a question that was asked in court by both the Prosecution and the Defence.

Milošević claimed that the federal government of Ante Marković was responsible for the decision to intervene militarily in Slovenia and accused him of having directly ordered the JNA to act, without informing the PSFRY.[97] Marković rejected this proposition as preposterous, saying that only the PSFRY had the authority to deploy the JNA. He acknowledged that federal police units had been sent to Slovenia on his authority, to supervise federal facilities there, and that they were to be assisted by JNA units already deployed along the border.[98] But, according to Marković, cooperation between the federal police and the JNA border units never happened because the JNA had been given separate orders to invade Slovenia by Milošević, who he said had de facto control of the Army.[99]

Yet, if Milošević had no attachment to Slovenia, why would he encourage – or even order – JNA intervention there, as suggested by Marković? What would Milošević gain through military action that could lead to lost lives, would meet no strategic objective, and risked inviting negative reactions from the West? One theory is that he was manoeuvring to appease JNA leaders, who represented the only surviving federal institution and one that could not be preserved without the continued existence of the SFRY. Yet, if Milošević's claims that he sought to preserve Yugoslavia were true, both Ante Marković and the JNA would have been his natural allies, especially since he was aware that JNA leadership viewed Marković and his government as potential partners in ensuring the continued existence of some form of Yugoslavia and, thereby, of the Army.[100]

Constitutionally, the JNA was obliged to preserve the external borders of the SFRY as well as the socio-political order of the Federation.[101] And so, when Ante Marković could not secure reforms that would have saved the SFRY, he lost his political authority and the JNA was left in hands of Milošević. But by mid-1991, the composition of the formerly multiethnic army had drastically changed so that it was an increasingly Serb force; and non-Serb officers were encouraged to leave in light of new political realities that followed the Slovenian and Croatian declarations of independence.

Despite the accusations he levelled against Mesić and Marković regarding the conflict in Slovenia, Milošević also suggested in his cross-examination of Milan Kučan that the Slovenians themselves had started the war by declaring independence without first making efforts to negotiate.[102] Kučan firmly rejected the assertion that Slovenia had not engaged in negotiations, explaining that the Slovenian Assembly had adopted a Declaration on Disassociation in February 1991 only after multiple failed attempts to achieve an agreement on the restructuring of the Federation. He said the Assembly had sought consensus from other republics but only received a response from Croatia.[103] Kučan also denied Milošević's proposition that the war in Slovenia was waged over customs revenues. According to Milošević, by taking control of the border crossings between the West and the SFRY, Slovenia had appropriated revenues from custom taxes, which he claimed made up 75 per cent of the federal budget.[104] Kučan replied that the Slovenian government had actually deposited income from customs taxes into a special holding fund as it awaited a definitive outcome on the future of Yugoslavia or a decision on the matter from the Slovenian Assembly.[105]

The end of Yugoslavia

The Brioni Declaration

The war in Slovenia was short-lived, lasting just ten days before it was brought to an end on 7 July 1991 by a European Community (EC) brokered truce, signed at an international peace conference held on the Croatian island of Brioni. The signatories agreed to a ceasefire, to be monitored by an EC Monitor Mission, along with a three-month moratorium on the independence of Slovenia and Croatia and talks on a political solution for Yugoslavia.[106] Ante Marković, who represented the Federation at the talks, originally proposed a six-month moratorium. He felt that three months would not offer enough time to achieve a compromise of two extremes – Slovenia's call for a loose confederation on one hand and Serbia's call for a centralised federation on the other.[107] But three months was decided upon; during which the principles of a reformed common state were to be negotiated.

Branko Kostić, a close Montenegrin ally of Milošević, was involved in the negotiations in Brioni as well as in talks held later in The Hague, when he was Vice President of the PSFRY. In his testimony, he asserted that the Prosecution either failed to understand, or had deliberately misportrayed, the essence of the Brioni Declaration. According to him, its key aims were to establish peace and to stipulate that a political solution be sought within three months; but Kostić denied any agreement on a moratorium that only temporarily suspended the independence of Slovenia and Croatia.[108] The Prosecution showed Kostić the text of a Memorandum of Understanding attached to the Brioni Declaration that referred to the moratorium, which indeed permitted Slovenia and Croatia to declare independence as of 8 October 1991 if a political solution had not been reached. In fact, it was the "implementation of the declarations of independence" that were explicitly suspended "for the period of three months."[109] Nonetheless, Kostić insisted that the agreement made by all parties had been to resolve just "the situation along the borders" within that time.[110]

Kostić also testified that negotiators did not intend for that part of the Declaration to apply to Croatia, the leadership of which he said had "interpreted in their own way everything that was mutually agreed upon" in order to achieve independence. And this characterisation was reflected by Milošević, who spent much time and effort challenging the factual basis of the Declaration, in part to contest the date of Croatian independence. This was significant from a legal standpoint because it was linked to when the war in Croatia became an international armed conflict.[111]

The Hague Conference and Milošević's rejection of the Carrington Plan

Following July's Brioni Declaration, negotiations on the future of Yugoslavia were held in The Hague under the leadership of the EC, chaired by British politician and diplomat Lord Peter Carrington within the framework of a newly formed International Conference on the Former Yugoslavia (ICFY).[112] The Hague Peace Conference, held from September to December 1991, effectively failed by 18 October – an outcome that was not entirely unpredictable given the "legalistic and inflexible" attitude of Serbia from the start.[113] In a speech at the opening of the Conference on 7 September, Milošević blamed "unilateral secessionist policy, first of Slovenia and then of Croatia," as the cause of the crisis and alleged that these republics had "jeopardised the Yugoslav constitutional order."[114] He also insisted that existing republican borders could not be seen as inter-state boundaries, qualifying them as merely administrative and arguing that the independence of former SFRY republics was thus illegal.[115]

Still, when negotiators met alone with Milošević and his Croatian counterpart Tuđman on 4 October, both consented to three fundamental components for a general agreement to be presented at a plenary session two weeks later:

1. a loose association or alliance of sovereign or independent republics;
2. adequate arrangements for the protection of minorities, including human rights guarantees and possible special status for certain territories; and
3. no unilateral changes to borders.[116]

This meant that a loose federation of sovereign states would be formed by allowing all the republics to first declare independence, as Slovenia and Croatia did on 8 October, and then build political, economic, and other ties from there.[117] But the plenary session at which this proposal was presented ended without an agreement.

Attempting to depict what occurred between 4 October and 18 October and led to Milošević's eventual rejection of the Carrington Plan, the Prosecution presented a revealing courtroom reconstruction of behind-the-scenes dynamics in the days before the critical plenary session. Along with the testimony of witnesses, a memoir by Momir Bulatović – who was President of the Republic of Montenegro at the time of the Conference – helped the Prosecution piece together the details. In *Pravila ćutanja* ("Rules of Silence"), Bulatović offered valuable insight into this period. The Prosecution had planned to introduce the book when he appeared as a Defence witness, but an opportunity to present excerpts of it arose earlier when Bulatović's former colleague Branko Kostić testified in February 2006. And so, the Prosecution referred to parts of Bulatović's book in its cross-examination of Kostić as a jumping-off point for discussion of the Hague Conference, calculating that even if Bulatović did not end up testifying, the most valuable parts of his book would still be tendered into evidence through Kostić's testimony.

According to the Prosecution narrative that developed, events directly leading to Milošević's reversal regarding the Carrington Plan began in Belgrade on 14 October, when he called a meeting with his allies and Serbian and Montenegrin leaders all agreed to accept the plan.[118] Two days later, Carrington sent a draft proposal for final consideration to all parties, based on the three components that had been agreed upon by Milošević and Tuđman. The next day, 17 October, Milošević met with the JNA while Bulatović led the Montenegrin Assembly in a vote on whether to accept the plan.[119] But Milošević's meeting, which he expected to be routine, took an unexpected turn; and Bulatović, who had fought hard to persuade Montenegro Assembly members to vote in favour, received a call from Milošević during the Assembly session with surprising instructions *not* to accept the plan. Milošević said that Serbia would reject the proposal and advised Montenegrin leaders do the same, with no explanation as to why.

Bulatović agreed to convey Milošević's message to members of the Montenegrin ruling party, the DPS, after which Milošević reckoned that the DPS majority would vote against the plan; but the Montenegrin Assembly voted in favour of it.[120] On his flight to The Hague, Bulatović was torn – still undecided about whether he should accept Carrington's proposal. But in the end, he voted in favour, prompting an angry reaction from Milošević.[121]

In his book, written years later, Bulatović explained why Milošević had backpeddled from his original consent. Apparently, JNA leadership, headed by Veljko Kadijević, had rejected the plan because it would abolish the SFRY and thereby the Army. Arguing that the Federal Constitution explicitly forbade such action, JNA leaders told Milošević that they would challenge civil leadership in the event of a breach of the Constitution – a statement that some interpreted as a threat of a *coup d'état*.[122] This had swayed Milošević because he knew he could not risk disobeying the JNA hierarchy without putting his power at stake; and he needed the Army to implement the next stage of his plan.

Smilja Avramov had given a similar account of these events in her book, published before Bulatović's, in 1997. She described the arrival of the draft Carrington Plan in Belgrade on 16 October as having been received as "lightening from the blue sky." Avramov agreed that it was the meeting on

17 October between Serbian and JNA leadership that had prompted Milošević to change his mind, and she asserted that the speech Milošević gave at the plenary session on 18 October in The Hague was a synthesis of the opinions expressed the night before in Belgrade.[123]

Milošević's rejection of the Carrington Plan at the plenary session effectively ended the talks; and while negotiators still aimed to reach an agreement by November, Milošević worked actively against this in the two weeks from 18 October to 1 November. Serb leaders such as Milan Babić, President of the self-proclaimed Republika Srpska Krajina (in Croatia) at the time, testified that Milošević had lobbied on behalf of the plan before the plenary session, and in particular the component that granted "special status" to Serbs in Croatia – a feature Babić was not enthusiastic about because he worried that Serbia would get its state and leave "the Croats to take revenge" on Croatian Serbs who had established separate entities within Croatia.[124] But after Milošević's sudden change of heart, Babić was summoned by Milošević, along with Karadžić, to a meeting in Bosnia where they were both instructed to reject the plan. Babić deduced that this directive was linked to the fact that the plan awarded special status to *all* minorities, which would have restored the rights of Kosovo Albanians and reversed years of work by Milošević as the champion of Serbs in Kosovo.[125]

In a dramatic epilogue to events in The Hague, Momir Bulatović ended up changing his position on the Carrington Plan as soon as he returned to Montenegro, reportedly under the threat of removal from office.[126] In his book, Bulatović described the harassment he endured, from intimidation, to accusations that he was a traitor, to rumours that he had sold his vote to the Italians – who were said to have committed themselves to financial aid for Montenegro in exchange for a favourable vote on the plan.[127] Under pressure from the public and Milošević, Bulatović co-signed an amendment to the plan, jointly filed by Serbia and Montenegro, which proposed that the rights of those who wished to continue living in a joint state also be recognised.[128] But Milošević presented a different version of this history, suggesting during his examination of Defence witness Vojislav Šešelj that Bulatović's initial decision to sign the Carrington Plan was proof that Milošević had not controlled Montenegrin leaders. Šešelj agreed and added that Bulatović had eventually changed his mind because of pressure from Montenegrin citizens, not Milošević.[129] But this claim was incompatible with Šešelj's own reference to Milošević as "political figure number one."[130]

Establishing the nature of Yugoslavia's disintegration

One important corollary of the Hague Peace Conference was a list of Opinions formulated by the Badinter Arbitration Commission. The Commission had been formed to assist Lord Carrington in addressing issues raised by the parties to the talks. Named for Chairman Robert Badinter, a Constitutional Judge from France, the Commission issued 11 Opinions over the course of the Conference.

The Commission's first Opinion addressed opposing interpretations of the declarations of independence that were made by former SFRY republics. Serbia assumed that the SFRY would continue to exist despite what it saw as the secession of some republics; but the other republics didn't view their proclamations of independence as secession because they felt that the SFRY had functionally disintegrated when several constituent units decided to leave the Federation. The Badinter Commission responded, *inter alia*, that upon four republics having expressed a desire to become independent, the SFRY was indeed in a process of dissolution. Both Slovenia and Croatia had declared independence on 25 June 1991, after referendums held in December 1990 and May 1991 respectively. Macedonia had voted in favour of independence in a referendum held in September 1991, and the BiH Assembly adopted a resolution on sovereignty on 14 October 1991 – though its validity was contested by the Bosnian Serb community.[131] The Commission stated that the question of state succession was for the republics to settle according to the principles and rules of international law, and that it was up to any republics that wished to do so to work together to form new institutions.[132]

Opinion No. 3 answered the question of whether internal boundaries between Croatia and Serbia and between Serbia and BiH could be regarded as external borders under international law. In an elaborate response, one of the points made by the Commission was that these boundaries "may not be altered except by agreement freely arrived at." The Opinion also stated that, where existing boundaries became frontiers in the international legal sense through political processes, those borders must be respected per the principles of the United Nations Charter; and further that "the alteration of existing frontiers or boundaries by force is not capable of producing any legal effect."[133]

The Commission's last Opinion, No. 11, was issued on 16 July 1993 and responded to questions about the precise dates that SFRY successor states achieved independence. The findings of the Commission were that: Croatia and Slovenia became independent on 8 October 1991, in accordance with the Brioni Declaration; Macedonia officially became a sovereign state on 17 November 1991; and BiH attained independence on 6 April 1992. Regarding BiH, the Commission cited its own Opinion No. 4, issued on 11 January 1992, which had stipulated that BiH independence ought to be contingent on a referendum, and noted that one had been held on 29 February and 1 March 1992.[134]

Milošević did not accept the authority accorded to the Badinter Commission by the Prosecution and the Trial Chamber, referring to the logic of its Opinions as "legal metaphysics."[135] In his August 2004 Opening Statement, he harshly criticised the international community for recognising the independence of secessionist states, which he said had destroyed not just the SFRY but the "United Nations system ... [and] the corpus of principles upon which world civilisation was based."[136] Milošević felt the international community had played a two-faced game and that the Serbian delegation had been betrayed at the Hague Peace Conference.

To support his assertion that there had been "a great deal of rhetoric involved in the destruction of Yugoslavia," Milošević asked Defence witness Vladislav Jovanović to recount a meeting held on the initiative of French President François Mitterand on 29 August 1991, designed to convince Serbia to agree to the principles of the Conference. Jovanović, who had accompanied Milošević in his capacity as Minister of Foreign Affairs, testified that Mitterand informed the Serbian delegation then of the appointment of Robert Badinter as head of the Arbitration Commission. Mitterand reportedly told them that he considered Badinter his personal friend and therefore Serbia's friend, too; and he assured Milošević that members of the Commission would be presidents of the constitutional courts of Greece, France, Britain, and Germany – suggesting that there would be at least three members sympathetic to the Serb cause.[137] According to Jovanović, Mitterrand had acknowledged Serbia's "strong political and historical arguments" and said there was no reason to worry that Serb interests would be overlooked at the Conference.[138]

Expecting the international support they believed had been assured in Paris, the Serbian delegation was unpleasantly surprised by what they encountered at the Hague Conference, where they felt the republics that had chosen independence were favoured from the very first days. Their perspective was that the Conference had ended with a take-it-or-leave-it diktat and that republics which did not accept the Carrington Plan were punished through sanctions.[139] But as a backdrop to talks, armed conflict in Croatia had continued, practically unabated. A ceasefire had been reached on 17 September in Igalo, Montenegro, when Milošević, Tuđman, and JNA General Kadijević met with Lord Carrington and agreed to an immediate end to hostilities. However, the JNA began a large-scale operation in Croatia just two days later, and the fighting went on as negotiations in The Hague – which had come in response to JNA operations in Croatia – failed.[140] Milošević's rejection of the Carrington Plan was the effective end to any possibility that Slovenia and Croatia would remain in a Yugoslav state, making his plan to centralise the SFRY futile. But Milošević moved on to the third of his goals, and his attempts to create a reduced Yugoslavia that would incorporate 'Serb-designated territories' in Croatia is examined in the next chapter.

Notes

1 Marković was a Professor of Constitutional Law who was involved in drafting amendments to the Serbian Constitution in 1990, the RSK Statute in 1991, and the FRY Constitution in 1992. He was an active SPS politician and became Deputy Prime Minister of Serbia in 1998 – a critical time in the Kosovo crisis – and was a principle negotiator at the failed Rambouillet talks in February 1999. Marković's academic work and his involvement in the drafting of important constitutional texts, together with journal articles he wrote in the 1990s, proved to be of significant probative value for establishing the real goals of Serbian political and military leadership at that time, notwithstanding his attempts in court to minimise the importance of the role he played.

2 For the article as written in B/C/S, see: Ratko Marković, "Državnopravni Položaj Srbije i Njeno Opredelenje za Zajedničku Državu sa Crnom Gorom," *Pravni život* 42, no. 3–4 (1992). For the English translation, see: Ratko Marković, "Constitutional Status of Serbia and Her Choice for Joint State with Montenegro," Exhibit P824a.
3 Ratko Marković, "Constitutional Status of Serbia..." Exhibit P824a, 3–4.
4 Ibid., 4.
5 Ibid., 1.
6 Testimony of Ratko Marković (24 January 2005), 35526–35527.
7 Intercept of Conversation between Radovan Karadžić and Dobrica Ćosić, 11 November 1991, Exhibit P613.113a.
8 Mihailović and Krestić, *Memorandum of the Serbian Academy of Sciences and Arts*, 139.
9 Testimony of Branko Kostić (25 January 2006), 47607–47608.
10 Boško Krunić, interview (17 April 2005).
11 Testimony of Kosta Bulatović (14 April 2005), 38561.
12 Ibid., 38560–385601.
13 Testimony of Ratko Marković (19 January 2005), 35339–35341.
14 For example, Milošević had roots in Montenegro but identified himself as a Serb, while his brother made a career in Yugoslav diplomacy as a Montenegrin.
15 Testimony of Nikola Samardžić (8 October 2002), 11160–11162. Montenegrin Pavle Bulatović was the Federal Minister of Internal Affairs of the FRY and later the Defence Minister (until his assassination in 2000, which remains unsolved), and Momir Bulatović and Milo Đukanović both started impressive political careers as well, becoming the President and Prime Minister of Montenegro respectively.
16 Slobodan Milošević, speech as recorded in "Unauthorised Transcript of the 2nd Session of the Central Committee of the League of Communists of Yugoslavia," 30 January 1989, Exhibit P447.2a.
17 Testimony of Dr. Vukašin Andrić (23 February 2005), 36556; Testimony of Vukašin Jokanović (2 December 2004), 34130.
18 The new leadership consisted of Rahman Morina, Ali Shukri, and Sinan Hasani. See: Testimony of Vukašin Jokanović (2 December 2004), 34130–34131.
19 *Death of Yugoslavia*, "Enter Nationalism," Part I, produced by Brian Lapping Associates, BBC, 1995.
20 Borisav Jović, *Knjiga o Miloševiću* (Belgrade: Nikola Pašić, 2001), 15–16.
21 *Death of Yugoslavia*, Part I.
22 Testimony of Vukašin Jokanović (2 December 2004), 34141.
23 Testimony of Ibrahim Rugova (3 May 2002), 4190–4191; and (6 May 2002), 4330–4331.
24 Testimony of Vukašin Jokanović (1 December 2004), 34063–34064.
25 Testimony of Adnan Merovci (24 May 2002), 5479–5480.
26 Testimony of Mihailo Marković (17 November 2004), 33503.
27 Testimony of Veton Surroi (18 April 2002), 3467–3468.
28 Testimony of Halit Barani (27 February 2002), 1173–1174; and (28 February 2002), 1277–1279 and 1306–1307.
29 Testimony of Kosta Bulatović (14 April 2005), 38554–38556.
30 Renaud de la Brosse, *Political Propaganda and the Plan to Create a "State for all Serbs": Consequences of Using the Media for Ultra-Nationalist Ends*, Expert Report, January 2003, Exhibit P446.2, 45.
31 "Speech, Gazimestan," 28 June 1989, Exhibit D251.1A, 2–3.
32 Testimony of Stjepan Mesić (1 October 2002), 10517–10518.
33 Ibid., 10518.
34 Mihailović and Krestić, *Memorandum of the Serbian Academy of Sciences and Arts*, 125–127 and 139.

35 "Speech, Gazimestan," 1. Also see: Testimony of Mihailo Marković (17 November 2004), 33503–33505.
36 Mihailović and Krestić, *Memorandum of the Serbian Academy of Sciences and Arts*, 124–127.
37 Ibid.
38 Trial Transcript, Defence Opening Statement (1 September 2004), 32291.
39 Ibid., 32291–32294. Also see: "Milošević Carries Off the Battle Honours," *Independent*, 29 June 1989.
40 Trial Transcript, Defence Opening Statement (1 September 2004), 32291–32294.
41 Ivan Kristan, *Report on Constitutional and Legal Issues in the Case Against Slobodan Milošević*, 4 April 2003, Expert Report, Exhibit P524a, 84.
42 Ibid., 85.
43 Ibid.
44 Testimony of Ratko Marković (24 January 2005), 35529–35530. Also see: "Federal Republic of Yugoslavia, Republic of Serbia," in *Constitutions of Dependencies and Special Sovereignties*, eds Albert P. Blaustein and Eric B. Blaustein (Dobbs Ferry: Oceana, 1994). This book was tendered into evidence as Exhibit P319.1a.
45 Kristan, *Constitutional and Legal Issues in the Case Against Slobodan Milošević*, 57.
46 Miroslav Šolević, interview.
47 Borisav Jović, Rule 89 (F) Witness Statement, 18 November 2003, Exhibit P596.1a, para. 13. His book, *Poslednji dani SFRJ* ("Last Days of the SFRY"), was tendered into evidence in English as Exhibit P596.2a.
48 Testimony of Mihailo Marković (17 November 2004), 33489.
49 Ibid., 33560. Also see: "Programme of the Socialist Party of Serbia from the First Congress," 16–18 July 1990, Exhibit P469.3a.
50 "Programme of the Socialist Party of Serbia from the First Congress," 16–18 July 1990, Exhibit P469.3a.
51 The Ministry for Relations with Serbs Outside of Serbia was established on 5 February 1991. The Ministry existed until 1998 and was led by three Ministers, all SPS members: Stanko Cvijan (1991–1993); Bogoljub Bjelica (1993–1994); and Radovan Pankov (1994–1998).
52 Mihailović and Krestić, *Memorandum of the Serbian Academy of Sciences and Arts*, 133.
53 Testimony of Mihailo Marković (17 November 2004), 33560.
54 Ibid., 33561.
55 See: "Programme of the Socialist Party of Serbia from the First Congress," 10–11.
56 Testimony of Milan Kučan (21 May 2003), 20970.
57 Ibid., 20973.
58 Ibid., 20874–20875. The crime of 'verbal offence' refers to public expressions in opposition to the political system or state, which were treated as criminal offences under communism.
59 Ibid., 20875.
60 Testimony of General Imra Agotić (30 June 2003), 23417–23418.
61 Testimony of Mihailo Marković (17 November 2004), 33493–33495. Also see: Testimony of Marko Atlagić (22 February 2006), 48665–48666.
62 Testimony of Marko Atlagić (22 February 2006), 48667.
63 Testimony of Borisav Jović (19 November 2003), 29199. Also see: Borisav Jović, Witness Statement, para. 159.
64 Testimony of Ante Marković (15 January 2004), 30920–30921.
65 Testimony of Ante Marković (23 October 2003), 28023.
66 Ibid., 28003–28008.
67 Testimony of Borisav Jović (20 November 2003), 29359–29365.
68 Testimony of Ante Marković (23 October 2003), 28007–28008.

69 Ibid., 28011–28012.
70 Ibid., 28013–28014.
71 Ibid., 28015.
72 Testimony of Milan Babić (19 November 2002), 13011–13012.
73 Testimony of Milan Kučan (21 May 2003), 20890–20891.
74 Testimony of Borisav Jović (20 November 2003), 29443.
75 The first meeting was held in Split (Croatia) on 28 March 1991, then others followed in Brdo kod Kranja (Slovenia) on 11 April 1991, Ohrid (Macedonia) on 18 April 1991, Cetinje (Montenegro) on 29 April 1991, and Stojčevac (BiH) on 6 June 1991.
76 On this, Marković remarked in court: "You excluded the rest of us from these discussions because you were the actual people in power. That is, the republics rather than the federal institutions." Testimony of Ante Marković (15 January 2004), 30885–30886.
77 For discussion on the Izetbegović-Gligorov Proposal, see: Testimony of Audrey Budding (24 July 2003), 24947–24948; Testimony of Milan Milanović (15 October 2003), 27625–27626; Testimony of General Milosav Đorđević (11 March 2003), 17618–17619; Testimony of Nikola Samardžić (10 October 2002), 11429–11430; Testimony of Ibro Osmančević (24 November 2003), 29528.
78 Testimony of Stjepan Kljuić (15 July 2003), 24480–24481.
79 Intercept of Conversation between Radovan Karadžić, Slobodan Milošević, and Nikola Koljević, 4 June 1991, Exhibit P613.5a.
80 Testimony of Milan Babić (3 December 2002), 13805.
81 Ibid.
82 BBC Summary of World Broadcasts (17 January 1991), "Other Reports on SFRY Presidency Session," Exhibit P469.5.
83 Ibid.
84 "Transcript of Speech by Slobodan Milošević in the Serbian Parliament regarding the New Constitution of Serbia," 25 June 1990, Exhibit P447.6a.
85 Testimony of Milan Kučan (21 May 2003), 20887–20889.
86 Ibid., 20893.
87 Ibid., 20894.
88 Ibid.
89 For example, see: Stipe Mesić, *Kako smo srušili Jugoslaviju* ("How We Destroyed Yugoslavia") (Zagreb: Globus International, 1992), 236; Duško Doder and Louise Branson, *Milošević: Portrait of a Tyrant* (New York: The Free Press, 1999), 95–96; and Paul Williams and Norman L. Cigar, *A Prima Facie Case for the Indictment of Slobodan Milošević* (Washington, DC: Alliance to Defend Bosnia-Herzegovina, 1996), 20–21. Parts of the conversations were also published in the Serbian daily *Vreme* on 30 September 1991, and two years later in *Politika Ekspres* and *Srpska reč* on 24 May 1993.
90 An important step was taken in this direction by Josip Glaurdić in: "Inside the Serbian War Machine: The Telephone Intercepts, 1991–1992," *East European Politics and Societies* 23, no. 1 (February 2009): 84–104.
91 For example, see: Intercept of Conversation between Radovan Karadžić and Slobodan Milošević, 17 June 1991, Exhibit P613.9a.
92 Intercept of Conversation between Radovan Karadžić and Slobodan Milošević, 24 June 1991, Exhibit P613.13a.
93 Intercept of Conversation between Radovan Karadžić and Slobodan Milošević, 9 August 1991, Exhibit P613.30a.
94 Testimony of Stjepan Mesić (2 October 2002), 10669–10671.
95 Trial Transcript, Defence Opening Statement (18 February 2002), 456–458.
96 Ibid., 482.
97 Testimony of Ante Marković (15 January 2004), 30830–30831.

98 Ibid., 30832.
99 Ibid.
100 Intercept of Conversation between Radovan Karadžić and Slobodan Milošević, 17 June 1991, Exhibit P613.9a.
101 See: "The Socialist Federal Republic of Yugoslavia Constitution (1974)," Exhibit P131a.
102 Testimony of Milan Kučan (21 May 2003), 20910–20911.
103 Ibid., 20912–20913.
104 Trial Transcript (21 May 2003), 20910–20911.
105 Testimony of Milan Kučan (21 May 2003), 20913–20925. Also see: Testimony of Ante Marković (15 January 2004), 30899–30900.
106 "Brioni Joint Declaration," 7 July 1991, Exhibit P330.35a. The text of the Declaration is also available in Exhibit D333.63e, excerpted from Branko Kostić, *Lest We Forget* (Beograd: Obodsko Skivo, 1996).
107 Testimony of Ante Marković (23 October 2003), 28049–28050; and (15 January 2004), 30848.
108 Testimony of Branko Kostić (1 February 2006), 32168–32170. Kostić also argued that there were inconsistencies in the text and that "the dissolution of Yugoslavia is being linked to two different dates." Also see: Testimony of Ratko Marković (18 January 2005), 35171–35172.
109 "Documents of the European Communities, including the 'Memorandum of Understanding on the Monitor Mission to Yugoslavia'" (13 July 1991), Exhibit P946a, 3.
110 Testimony of Branko Kostić (13 February 2006), 48312–48317.
111 The distinction between internal and international armed conflict is important in international criminal law. In this case, once Croatia or Bosnia became recognised as independent, military action by Serbian-controlled forces exposed Serbian leaders to investigation as possible war criminals.
112 The ICFY would become the forum for peace negotiations until the end of the conflict in BiH in 1995. The Hague Peace Conference marked the first of many ICFY negotiations, which moved to Geneva throughout the war.
113 "Official Report on Conference of Yugoslavia," No. hagc895/cpeu1020, 20 September 1991, Exhibit P777.
114 Testimony of Vladislav Jovanović (14 February 2005), 36048–36051.
115 Testimony of Herbert Okun (28 February 2003), 17084–17085.
116 Testimony of Kosta Mihailović (17 December 2005), 34767–34768. Also see: "Official Report on Conference on Yugoslavia," No. hagc1224/cpeu137, 18 October 1991, Exhibit P778.
117 See: "Joint Session of all Chambers of the Parliament of the Republic of Croatia," 8 October 1991, Exhibit P641.22a. It states that, following the end of the three-month moratorium agreed to in the Brioni Declaration, "the Republic of Croatia severs all state/legal ties … [with] the previous SFRY and disavows the legitimacy and legality of all borders of the former federation."
118 Momir Bulatović, *Pravila ćutanja* (Belgrade: Narodna knjiga, 2004), 66–69. An English translation of an excerpt of the book was tendered into evidence. See: "Momir Bulatović's Book Rules of Silence," Excerpt of pages 65–77 and 93, Exhibit P942a. Also see: Testimony of Branko Kostić (8 February 2006), 48204–48207; and (13 February 2006), 48382–48383.
119 Testimony of Nikola Samardžić (10 October 2002), 11434.
120 Bulatović, *Pravila ćutanja*, 69–73.
121 Testimony of Nikola Samardžić (8 October 2002), 11225.
122 Bulatović, *Pravila ćutanja*, 85.
123 Smilja Avramov, *Postherojski rat Zapada protiv Jugoslavije* (Belgrade: Akademija za diplomatiju i bezbednost, 1997), 274.

124 Testimony of Milan Babić (21 November 2002), 13197.
125 Ibid., 13199–13201.
126 Testimony of Nikola Samardžić (8 October 2002), 11227–11229.
127 Testimony of Smilja Avramov (8 September 2004), 32543.
128 Testimony of Branko Kostić (2 February 2006), 15863–15864.
129 Testimony of Vojislav Šešelj (1 September 2005), 43617–43618. Šešelj claimed it had been "impossible" for Milošević to gain control over Montenegro and that leaders there had espoused positions close to his only to gain power.
130 Ibid., 43619.
131 "Conference on Yugoslavia Arbitration Commission (Badinter Commission): Opinions on Questions Arising from the Dissolution of Yugoslavia (Nos. 1,3,5,8,11)," Exhibit P641.32.2–5a. Opinion No. 1 was published 27 November 1991.
132 Ibid.
133 Ibid. Opinion No. 3 was published 11 January 1992.
134 Ibid. Opinion No. 11 was published 16 July 1993.
135 Trial Transcript, Defence Opening Statement (31 August 2004), 32159.
136 Ibid.
137 Testimony of Vladislav Jovanović (14 February 2005), 36048.
138 Ibid., 36050–36051.
139 Ibid., 36051.
140 The Security Council passed Resolution 713 on 25 September 1991, noting its alarm about "violations of the cease-fire and the continuation of fighting."

4 The formation of the Republika Srpska Krajina (RSK) and the policy of ethnic separation in Croatia

Following the failure to centralise Yugoslavia, Slobodan Milošević and the political and military circles he controlled, instructed and supported Serbs in Croatia to create self-declared "Serb Autonomous Regions" (*Srpska autonomna oblast*, or SAO) along the projected western borders of a future Serb state. The creation of the SAOs in Croatia marked the point at which criminality entered the conflict, and according to the indictment, Milošević – who was President of the Republic of Serbia at the time – exercised considerable control over other JCE participants and, through the PSFRY, over Serb-controlled forces in Croatia. These forces allegedly attacked and took control of Serb-claimed territories and then created a climate of persecution and destruction to drive out non-Serbs.

The indictment also alleged the murder of hundreds of non-Serb civilians and the forcible transfer of at least 170,000, as well as the imprisonment of thousands more in deplorable and inhumane conditions.[1] The Prosecution argued that ethnic violence in Croatia had resulted from the Serb policy of ethnic separation. But the Defence asserted that the creation of the RSK was a legitimate right of Serbs who wanted to remain living in Yugoslavia and did not want to live in a newly independent Croatia.

Milošević's *de jure* position was different in each of the three indictment periods for which he was charged; but in the period relevant to the Croatia indictment, as President of Serbia, he had no direct political authority at the federal level. Yet, by gaining indirect control of the PSFRY, he effectively gained control of federal armed forces. Thus, charges against Milošević for crimes allegedly committed in Croatia were based on his de facto power, exercised at various levels of government through a number of proxies – members of the PSFRY, commanders of the JNA, individuals in the Serbian Ministry of Internal Affairs, leaders of para-state special operations units, and Croatian Serb politicians.

Evidence on Milošević's responsibility for the violence in Croatia, both de facto and *de jure*, included transcripts from PSFRY sessions that were crucially important to understanding the degree to which Milošević had cooperated with the PSFRY and JNA to establish the western borders of a Rump Yugoslavia through a policy of ethnic separation.[2] His role as the de facto leader of all Serbs was also exposed in telephone intercepts between him, Radovan Karadžić, and other Serb politicians. Further, these intercepts showed the extent of their joint planning, which had undermined the SFRY while Serbian authorities simultaneously claimed they were working to preserve it. Some evidence presented in the courtroom had unexpected impact. Video evidence revealing Milošević's role in creating a para-state unit designed to operate covertly outside of Serbia during the wars of the 1990s played a transformative role in the courtroom and in Serbian society.

The armed rebellion of Serbs in Croatia, 1990

In the 1986 SANU Memorandum, Serbian intellectual elites had dramatically expressed concerns about the position of Serbs in Croatia, writing that they were facing their biggest existential threat since the Second World War, when the extremist Ustasha movement had been in power. The Memorandum called for an immediate solution and warned that the failure to find one would be disastrous, not only for Croatia but for Yugoslavia as well.[3] Belgrade's position regarding the status of Croatian Serbs was solidified when the Croatian Democratic Union (*Hrvatska demokratska zajednica*, or HDZ), a nationalist party led by Franjo Tuđman, won and formed a government after elections in early 1990. Inter-ethnic relations were strained by the ideological confusion of Tuđman's post-communist government, which alienated both former Croatian communists and Croatian Serbs, who made up 12 per cent of the population.[4] During election campaigning, the HDZ had distanced itself from the region's communist past and, by uniting the Croatian anti-communist opposition, had opened its doors to political emigrants with sympathies towards the Ustasha movement and the Ustasha-led Independent Croatian State (NDH) of the Second World War.[5]

It was understandable that the political revival of NDH symbolism alarmed Croatian Serbs, who had faced a policy of genocide by NDH leaders during the Second World War. Former Croatian Serb politician Marko Atlagić testified for the Defence that a hostile atmosphere had been created by the newly installed Croatian government, which he alleged aimed to establish an independent Croatia devoid of Serbs. To illustrate this point, he referred to "purges" of Serbs from sectors such as the police and Territorial Defence Units.[6] And, although Serb parties were represented in the Croatian Parliament, the *Sabor*, the most successful of them – the Serb Democratic Party (*Srpska Demokratska Stranka*, or SDS)[7] – left the body by July of 1990.

In response to the HDZ win, Croatian Serbs from the Knin region made it a top priority to gain autonomy in the areas where they constituted a majority. The starting point for the creation of the Serb Autonomous Region of Krajina, with Knin as its administrative centre, was the Declaration of the Sovereignty and Autonomy of Serbian people in Croatia, adopted by the Serbian Assembly on 25 July 1990.[8] The Declaration stipulated that Serbs from the Republic of Croatia were fully entitled to opt for a federal or confederal system, either jointly with Croatia or independently. It also declared that the Serb National Council, a self-proclaimed assembly of Croatian Serbs, had the right to hold referendums on all issues relevant to the status of Serbs in Croatia and Yugoslavia, including regarding the establishment of autonomy.[9]

The formation of this first SAO in Croatia came at the hands of Milan Babić, a dentist by profession and a communist who, after the fall of communism, became active in the SDS. A one-time political ally of Milošević, Babić appeared as a Prosecution witness in 2002, offering a comprehensive testimony. What emerged was that Croatian Serb leaders had sought to resolve the Serb question in Croatia via Belgrade, where Babić himself turned for support and advice in the summer of 1990. On 13 August, Babić and a group of leaders from Knin met PSFRY President Borisav Jović to discuss problems that Serbs in Croatia faced since the new Croatian government had come to power in May. Jović promised them political support in his capacity as the Serbian representative to the PSFRY and also told them that a law was being prepared on the right of peoples to self-determination, advising that a referendum be held.[10] Less than a week later, on 18 August, a referendum in the SAO of Krajina – comprised of 11 municipalities with a Serb majority – invited Croatian Serbs to vote on sovereignty and the autonomy of Serbs.

Leaders in Knin, worried that Croatian authorities may try to prevent the referendum by force, armed Croatian Serbs. According to Babić, the first supply of weapons came from Serbs in Bosnia.[11] On 17 August, one day before the referendum, demonstrations that became known as the "Log Revolution" – because logs were used to blockade roads – were held in Knin, marking the start of a long-term rebellion by Croatian Serbs. Knin was at the centre of Croatian territory and barricades that blocked access to the region effectively cut Croatia in two, with the capital Zagreb in the north and the Adriatic coast in the south. As the first log barriers were erected in the summer of 1990, Croatian Serb authorities in Knin proclaimed a state of war, which lasted until the April 1992 arrival of UN peacekeepers.[12]

In court, Milošević denied having had anything to do with the Log Revolution, noting that he was on vacation in Dubrovnik when the rebellion began. Moreover, he asserted that no Serbian leaders had known about it.[13] But Babić's testimony painted a different picture. He explained that in the summer of 1990, Croatian Serb leader Dr Jovan Rašković – the founding father of the Croatian SDS – had conducted negotiations with Croatian President Franjo Tuđman, after which Rašković told Babić that there was a "third element, wishing [for] a conflict" – which Babić understood referred to Milošević and the JNA.[14] But the talks between Rašković and Tuđman had been secretly taped and were leaked by a Croatian official, discrediting the entire process; and with little faith that the Croatian government could be trusted, SDS members sought an altogether new approach.[15] Hence, the Log Revolution marked a strategic shift.

With the start of the Log Revolution, Croatian Serbs announced that they were prepared to achieve their strategic objectives in Croatia by military means, and with support of the JNA. According to Stjepan Mesić, who was the Croatian representative in the PSFRY at the time, the Croatian government only became aware that the JNA had taken the Serb side when Army forces prevented Croatian police from dismantling the log barriers that were blocking vital north-south transport routes.[16] And the JNA was not the only federal institution that supported the rebellion; the Federal and Serbian Ministries of Internal Affairs (MUP) also assisted the Croatian Serbs, with support directed through individuals loyal to Milošević, such as Federal MUP Minister Petar Gračanin – who boasted before television cameras that Federal MUP troops had helped Croatian Serbs erect barricades.[17]

These actions in the summer of 1990 represented a turning point at which political conflict became military conflict, and this was reflected in the personnel files of JNA officers who served in Croatia at the time. The Law on the Yugoslav Army allowed double counting of pensionable service during periods of armed activity, and officers received double pensions for service from 17 August 1990 to 14 December 1995.[18] And by this measure, the JNA marked the start of the war as 17 August 1990, one day before the referendum. On 18 August, only Croatian citizens of Serb ethnicity were allowed to vote, despite the fact that about 40 per cent of the population on the territories in question was non-Serb, mostly Croat.[19] Not surprisingly, the results indicated an overwhelming majority in favour of autonomy.[20]

Babić's testimony offered a first-hand account of Milošević's de facto control over both the JNA and Serb leaders outside Serbia. Serbs in Croatia and Bosnia had turned to Belgrade for political patronage and protection and, at the time, considered the JNA to be *their* army; yet in hindsight, Babić saw how Serbian leaders had instrumentalised Serbs in the other republics for their own political goals.[21] In a telephone conversation in July 1991, Karadžić instructed a fellow Bosnian Serb that they must not form a "Serb army" openly because the JNA would become the de facto Serb army in due course, since no non-Serb conscripts would respond to the call to mobilise.[22] But Belgrade was giving orders not just to JNA forces in Croatia, but also to Serbian MUP forces. The first MUP training camp in Croatia was established in April 1991 in the village of Golubić, near Knin, and was run by Serbian State Security (*Državne bezbednost*, or DB) officers led by DB official Franko Simatović – an ethnic Croat who was sent by Milošević to the Krajina in response to Babić's request for a local police force.[23]

On 29 May 1991, Croatian Serbs – anticipating Croatia's proclamation of independence – declared the establishment of the SAO of Krajina, an "autonomous political-territorial region" within the SFRY.[24] That same day, a Decision was adopted to apply the legal regulations of the Republic of Serbia in the SAO.[25] This was the first step towards formation of the Republika Srpska Krajina, which was an important precondition for plans conceived in Belgrade to solve the Serb national question by forming a reduced Yugoslavia that would result from the secession of Slovenia and the non-Serb parts of Croatia. Military conquests eventually led to the official formation of the RSK on 19 December 1991, and two other SAOs were also formed that year, in Western and Eastern Slavonia.

The Belgrade Initiative and the partition of Croatia, 1991

The Belgrade Initiative was launched in August 1991, following Croatia's 25 June proclamation of independence.[26] A short document, it offered an alternative for those who did not want independence, but wished to remain in a common state. Although it was developed under Milošević's political patronage, it was purported to be a proposal of the speakers of the assemblies in the Republics of Serbia, Montenegro, and BiH. The earliest evidence of the Initiative came from an intercepted telephone conversation between Milošević and Karadžić in which they discussed setting a meeting of those assembly speakers, as well as the presidents of the republics, with the goal of declaring their intention to continue living in the existing Yugoslav state.[27] Indeed, in light of Croatia's independence and the approaching Hague Peace Conference, the common political future of all Serbs from the former Yugoslav republics became a top priority for leaders in Belgrade; and Milošević was dissatisfied with the loose federation advocated by federal Prime Minister Ante Marković and Bosnian President Alija Izetbegović.[28] In his opening speech at the Conference, Milošević said the Belgrade Initiative offered a political alternative for republics that chose not to secede, so that they could remain together in a reduced Yugoslavia.[29]

On 22 October 1991, only four days after the Hague Conference failed, an article entitled "How We Shall Redraw the Borders" appeared in *Epoha* magazine, published by Milošević's SPS. The article included several maps illustrating potential Yugoslav states without Slovenia and parts of Croatia.[30] The most significant of these showed an 'Optimal Western Border' and included detailed territorial demarcations between Yugoslavia and Croatia. This was important corroborating evidence that the war violence in Croatia did not happen randomly but was planned in advance by Serb political leaders; for the border identified on the map marked the very areas where mass atrocities against Croats were committed in 1991 and 1992.[31] Further, this 'optimal' western border roughly matched the V–K–K line, inxtricably tied to Greater Serbia ideology since the publication of Moljević's "Homogeneous Serbia" pamphlet in 1941. Even the author of the *Epoha* article, a demographer, recognised that this proposed border was not viable because it would require the inclusion of 1.5 million Croats in a "Third Yugoslavia" and he did not envisage that Serb majority areas in Croatia could be ethnically cleansed of non-Serb populations.[32] However, in the unfolding crisis, this was exactly what Serb ideologues and politicians eventually sought to achieve.

Map 4.1 The 'Optimal Western Border' (adapted from *Epoha*, 22 October 1991, Exhibit P786).

Similarities between the 22 October *Epoha* map and Greater Serbia designs from the past now seem obvious. Yet, the Prosecution discovered the link by chance during the cross-examination of Professor Smilja Avramov, who appeared as the very first Defence witness. An international law scholar, she had served as an advisor to Milošević on issues related to international public law and was a member of an expert working group during the Hague Peace Conference in 1991. When shown the *Epoha* map in court, Avramov mistook it for the London Treaty Map of 1915. Informed that the map was in fact drawn in 1991, she steadfastly asserted that it was a

> projection of the offer to Serbia in 1915 to give up Yugoslavia and to stay as the Kingdom of Serbia. This was in … the London Treaty, which the allies offered to Serbia. So this was the basis for this particular map.[33]

The Prosecution reminded the judges of a 29 October 1991 telephone intercept, tendered into evidence during the Prosecution part of the trial, in which Milošević and Karadžić had considered the possibility of reviving the Yugoslav state according to the London Treaty.[34] Karadžić had suggested reactivating discussions about the London Treaty and Milošević said he would make further inquiries. In another conversation a few days later, Karadžić asked if Milošević and Avramov had discussed the Treaty's revival.[35]

In his Opening Statement before the start of his Defence case in August 2004, Milošević highlighted Serbia's rejection of the London Treaty as an example of how Serbia had refused a Greater Serbia in favour of a common South Slav state.[36]

The Prosecution asked Defence witness Čedomir Popov if he thought that contemporary discussions of Serb borders which roughly aligned with those in the London Treaty revealed the influence or adoption of Greater Serbia ideology. Declining initially to answer, Popov eventually confirmed that this would indeed reflect that ideology. But, apparently unaware of the intercepted telephone conversation in which Milošević and Karadžić had discussed the London Treaty, Popov denied that any such plan had existed among Serbian leaders.[37]

The re-organisation of the JNA, de facto Greater Serbia borders, and the RAM plan

The London Treaty Map of 1915, Moljević's "Homogeneous Serbia" pamphlet of 1941, and the 22 October *Epoha* map all projected the demarcation between Serb territory and the rest of Croatia as running generally along the V–K–K line. Milošević never spoke in public of a Greater Serbia or of the V–K–K line, but his strategy in response to Croatian independence and his attempts to re-draw Croatia's borders were consistent with these pre-existing historical and political notions. According to former JNA General Imra Agotić, the JNA had actually sought to bring the whole of Croatia under the control of a centralised SFRY in 1991; but when that proved impossible, the plan was made to cut Croatian territory into two at the V–K–K line and retain most of the 'Serb-designated territories' in a reduced Yugoslavia. Eventually, that plan also had to be modified to reflect more realistic territorial objectives, according to which the JNA, along with Serb insurgents, would take only those territories where Serbs were the majority.[38]

The goal to sever Croatia along the V–K–K line was supported by changes that had been made to the organisation of the Army several years earlier. Witness B-1493, a former JNA officer with first-hand knowledge about JNA war planning, testified that SFRY political and military leadership had re-organised the structure of military districts in 1988, so that they no longer corresponded with republican borders. The Seventh Army in BiH and the Ninth Army in Slovenia were both disbanded and the First and Fifth Military Districts were formed, with headquarters in Belgrade and Zagreb respectively. The new distribution of territories was such that the First Military District's Novi Sad Corps covered a huge territory between the Drava and Sava rivers, right up to Virovitica.[39]

Witness B-1493 also confirmed the existence of a plan known as "RAM," discussed by Milošević and Karadžić in an intercepted July 1991 telephone conversation in relation to the mobilisation of troops from various Territorial Defence units and JNA battalions.[40] The name RAM first appeared in the media after an audiotape of that conversation was played at a meeting of federal government representatives in September 1991.[41] The acronym has never been definitively decoded, and while different authors have ascribed different meanings to the name, none has been confirmed through documentary evidence and the Prosecution never found an official text.[42] Still, Witness B-1493 testified that he believed the RAM plan existed and that it was a factor in the 1988 restructuring of the JNA.[43]

Ante Marković testified that Alija Izetbegović had informed him of the taped discussion between Milošević and Karadžić about the RAM plan that was later made public. Izetbegović had said that "it was evident that Serbian paramilitary units in Bosnia and Herzegovina were being armed." Marković testified that he "clearly recognised the voices" of Milošević and Karadžić, who, he said, discussed "the organisation of armies, the arrival of helicopters, the arrival of a colonel, a RAM programme which I was not aware of ... [and] the handover of weapons and the places where weapons could be acquired."[44]

Witness B-1493 linked the concrete military implications of the 1988 re-organisation of the JNA, known as the S2 Plan, and elements of the RAM plan, noting that the creation of the First Military District – the Belgrade District – coincided fully with the RAM plan, as did deployment strategies for the District's units.[45] Milošević attempted to minimise the testimony of Witness B-1493 by calling the information he presented about S2 "common knowledge," and by denying the existence of the RAM plan and its connection to the 1988 JNA re-organisation or plans for a Greater Serbia. But Witness B-1493 insisted that there were clear links and that the First Military District in fact operated within the boundaries of an imagined Greater Serbia.[46] Later, when the Prosecution cross-examined General Geza Farkaš, an ethnic Hungarian who remained loyal to Milošević throughout his active military career and beyond, he corroborated that the newly-formed First Military District had included parts of Serbia, Kosovo, BiH, and Croatia, with its western borders stretching from the area near Virovitica all the way to the sea via Karlobag.[47]

Milošević asserted in court that the term "RAM" had not referred to a plan but had been used as a code word to indicate the need to use encrypted language.[48] Yet, in an exchange between him and Bosnian Croat politician Stjepan Kljujić, Kljujić claimed he had actually heard Milošević and Karadžić discussing an operation named RAM. Milošević tried to move quickly past the topic, saying "let's leave that alone," but Kljuić spoke up, addressing the judges: "Your Honours, may I clarify and make matters simpler? The army was supposed to take the lines, take up positions along the lines to which Belgrade had territorial pretensions."[49] The Defence narrative – that Milošević had never worked to achieve a Greater Serbia – dictated that he not only deny the RAM plan, but it's purported aims; and he told the court that Kljuić knew "full well" that Belgrade never had "any territorial pretensions whatsoever." Milošević's explanation did not sound convincing; for if "RAM" was really the code word he claimed it was, why had Milošević and Karadžić not switched into encrypted language after the word was mentioned in the midst of their discussion of the arming of Bosnian Serbs by the JNA?

JNA plans and strategies, no matter what they were called, were also detailed in *My View of the Break-Up: An Army Without a State*, written by General Veljko Kadijević – the SFRY Minister of Defence in its last years – in which he revealed that the strategic objectives of the Army had indeed overlapped with those of Serb nationalist leaders in 1991 and early 1992.[50] According to Kadijević, the basic aims of the JNA deployment were to first defeat the Croatian Army to a degree that that would enable "full coordination with Serb insurgents in the Serbian Krajina" and allow JNA forces remaining in Slovenia to pull out, and second, to achieve a complete air and sea blockade in order to "liberate" Serb-claimed territories and JNA garrisons deeper inside Croatia. To realise this second goal, he said, the Army would need to "cut Croatia along the following lines: Gradiška-Virovitica; Bihać-Karlovac-Zagreb; Knin-Zadar; Mostar-Split."[51]

The strategy outlined by Kadijević was confirmed by other witnesses, for both the Prosecution and the Defence. General Nojko Marinović was a former JNA Deputy Commander of the Trebinje Brigade who walked over to the Croatian side in 1991 and commanded Croatian forces defending Dubrovnik. He testified that when he was still stationed in Trebinje – a town in Eastern Herzegovina not far from the Croatian border – the JNA formed an Operational Group for Southeast Herzegovina that consisted of land, air, and marine units from Herzegovina and Montenegro. These forces had the joint task of launching an attack along several axes to reach the Neretva River as soon as possible and connect up with the 10th Brigade from Mostar. They were to continue to advance across Croatian territory in the direction of the Croatian town of Sinj, to link up with the Knin Corps. The plan was to reach the Neretva valley in seven days and advance from there in two weeks to Sinj, from where they would proceed to the V–K–K line.[52]

Dubrovnik, like Vukovar, was attacked for geostrategic reasons and not because of ethnic territorial entitlement. In fact, only approximately 7 per cent of the population in the larger Dubrovnik area were Serbs and they faced no threat.[53] But coastal Dubrovnik was desired in a reduced Yugoslavia and the prospects of establishing a provisional government there were discussed between Serb leaders as early as October 1991.[54] Then, in November, Karadžić referred to "the further cleansing" of Dubrovnik in a conversation with Božidar Vučurević, a Serb leader from Eastern Herzegovina.[55] Karadžić, already thinking ahead about territories that could be Bosnian Serb, was interested in acquiring the Croatian harbour of Ploče, south of Dubrovnik – which he knew would require the use of force since the populations in both towns were overwhelmingly Croat.[56]

In court, the siege of Dubrovnik was tied to Greater Serbia designs by a number of Prosecution witnesses who described Dubrovnik as a key location in Serb plans to establish a new eastern border and then incorporate much of the Croatian coast, including towns such as Split, Šibenik, and Zadar.[57] But attacking Serb forces had apparently not anticipated the robust defence they would encounter in Dubrovnik. According to General Marinović, the JNA had expected to walk right into the city and face no resistance, because it was a demilitarised area. But under Marinović's leadership, citizens of Dubrovnik joined together to oppose these forces; and when the JNA responded by shelling the Old Town, the international community reacted strongly, compelling a shift in JNA strategy.[58]

Defence witness General Božidar Delić, a former JNA and VJ officer with a war career that spanned the battlefields of Dubrovnik, BiH, and Kosovo, denied the existence of any strategic plans for Dubrovnik and asserted that the JNA could have taken the city in one day if it had really wanted to.[59] Delić maintained that the Army's only interest was to preserve the integrity of Yugoslavia, and that this happened to coincide with the interests of Serbs who were scattered over several SFRY republics and preferred to remain in a single state.[60] Some months after General Delić, former RSK Minister of Foreign Affairs Slobodan Jarčević also testified for the Defence, repeating the same narrative as if rehearsed. Jarčević did concede that many politicians had been in favour of taking Dubrovnik at the time of the siege, but he claimed that this was because "from the earliest times," it had been a "Serbian town."[61]

The distinction between Greater Serbia and "all Serbs in a single state"

The Prosecution argued that in order to understand Milošević's motivation in pursuit of his political goals, the court would need to be able to distinguish between the historical concept of a Greater Serbia – from Garašanin to Moljević – and the version of it that was advocated by Milošević in the 1990s.[62] In the Prosecution's view, the concept of a Greater Serbia was expressed under Milošević's leadership through the rhetoric of "All Serbs in a Single State," and there was in fact little variation between the two concepts or between their practical goals; they were simply two different expressions of Serbian state ideology as it had developed over time. And so, efforts by Milošević to ensure that Serbs who lived in the former Yugoslavia could continue living on 'Serb-designated territories' in a single state led the Prosecution to qualify his political goal as a "de facto Greater Serbia."[63]

The Prosecution had the unique opportunity to revisit the topic of Greater Serbia ideology, and with a man who has openly and proudly espoused it, when Milošević called extreme-right Serbian politician Vojislav Šešelj to the stand as a Defence witness.[64] Šešelj's Serbian Radical Party (SRS) had been explicit in its support for a Greater Serbia, which he testified was envisaged as extending to a western border running along the Virovitica-Karlovac-Ogulin-Karlobag line. Šešelj added Ogulin, a small Croatian town between Karlovac and Karlobag, making the curve of the border run even more westerly than the V–K–K line.[65] In an interview given to the German weekly *Der Spiegel* in 1991, Šešelj had revealed his ambitions to expand Serbia westward by mobilising Serbs to "amputate Croatia in a quick war" so that the Serb parts of Croatia could be joined with the provinces of Vojvodina and Kosovo, and the republics of Bosnia and Herzegovina, Macedonia, and Montenegro.[66]

Šešelj's 2005 testimony indicated that he continued to hold his wartime views on Greater Serbia, and on how to achieve it. His political party had advocated the elimination of Croatia in 1991 and, in court, he blamed the Serbian government for failing to establish the western borders of Greater Serbia.[67] He referred to the Krajina as being "under Croatian occupation" and expressed his determination that it would be "liberated and returned to Serb hands."[68] Indeed, despite the lost wars in the 1990s, Šešelj adhered to notion that the Virovitica-Karlovac-Ogulin-Karlobag line was a territorial aim, insisting in the courtroom that it should become the Serbian state border yet.[69]

Šešelj rejected any suggestion that his notion of Greater Serbia had any influence over – or link to – an alleged Serbian Joint Criminal Enterprise, and he insisted that Milošević was his ideological opponent. To illustrate this point, Šešelj said that he was the only Serbian politician who had not favoured preservation of the Federation when faced with Slovenian independence, and that he was happy to let them go because he did not think of the Slovenes as Serbs "in disguise" as he thought of the Croat Catholics and Bosnian Muslims.[70] Yet, the Prosecution had already presented telephone intercepts that revealed that Milošević's position on the independence of Slovenia had overlapped with Šešelj's. On 17 June 1991, just a week before the Slovenian and Croatian declarations of independence, Milošević told Karadžić that things were going "exactly the way we planned it."[71] The conversation indicated that Milošević and Karadžić favoured disintegration but did not want to be seen as the parties responsible for it, determined instead to ascribe the blame for Yugoslavia's dissolution to the leaders of Slovenia and Croatia.[72]

In another intercepted conversation one week later, Milošević and Karadžić agreed to avoid advocating openly for the unification of all Serb territories, aware that it could trigger negative reactions from the outside world; and instead decided that their purported goal must be the preservation of a common Yugoslav state. Karadžić criticised the wording used by Croatian Serb leadership in the referendum they had held on the political future of Serb-claimed territories, which asked voters whether or not they wanted "to join with Serbia." Karadžić was displeased with the formulation, saying the question should have been cast as whether or not "to stay in Yugoslavia." He was concerned that the referendum would appear to be an attempt to create a Greater Serbia – a goal which he said they should work to achieve in secret.[73]

The Defence dismissed Šešelj as an agitator who had used extremist rhetoric to win votes.[74] But the Prosecution saw the rocky political relationship between him and Milošević as having strategically served Milošević, who had controlled Šešelj's access to the media and, in times of political cooperation, could use his extreme views to attract voters on the far right – who preferred Šešelj's blunt nationalism to Milošević's controlled discourse and communist background.[75] Šešelj did at times react fiercely when Milošević appeared to give up on the creation of a Serb state, as he did in August 1994 after Milošević threatened to abandon RS leadership.[76] Still, the two continued to cooperate at the state level and in 1999, during the Kosovo indictment period, Šešelj was a Deputy Prime Minister of Serbia.

The creation of the Republika Srpska Krajina

Armed engagement by Croatian Serbs was presented by the Defence as a self-organised resistance to the aggressive policies of a nationalist Croatian government.[77] But in mid-August 1991, just one month after the Brioni Peace Agreement, an attack was launched on the small village of Kijevo by a joint force made up of police from the SAO of Krajina and troops from the Yugoslav Army. The village, which had a Croatian majority, was a military target not because Serbs living there were threatened, but because it was situated on an important route to Knin and had to be taken for geostrategic reasons.[78] The operation in Kijevo, in Krajina, was not included in the Croatia indictment, which concentrated instead on crimes committed in the region where the western borders of the RSK had been established, through fighting in the vicinity of Benkovac, Škabrnja, Nadin, and Bruška.

In his testimony, Milan Babić emphasised that these villages had posed no threat to the JNA or to Serbs, but said that one JNA officer had told him that the JNA needed to "even out" or "ethnically homogenise" certain regions with mixed Serb and Croat populations so that the partition line was straightened by the beginning of winter. The involvement of the JNA in atrocities committed in this area was linked particularly to JNA officer Tripko Čečović, who was promoted in 1995 for his war record in Croatia, where he was Commander of the Benkovac Brigade.[79] At the trial, an eyewitness to the crimes committed in Škabrnja identified Čečović as a direct perpetrator.[80]

The village of Voćin, near Virovitica – the town in central Slavonia that features in the V–K–K line – was also one of the crime sites featured in the indictment. Serb armed forces, including volunteers from Serbia, committed atrocities in the predominantly Croat village, killing 32 people before withdrawing from the area on 13 December 1991.[81] But Voćin was never taken by the Serbs because of difficulties they had in conquering the surrounding villages and towns as they tried to move toward Virovitica. The failure by Serbs to secure that part of Croatia left the SAO of Western Slavonia smaller than originally planned, encompassing only the Okučani area along the border with BiH. Still, between May and November 1991, the SAO of

Eastern Slavonia had also been established after months of intense fighting that ended with the fall of Vukovar – another central crime site in the Croatia indictment.

Formation of the RSK, international negotiations, and the strategy of ethnic separation

After the failure of the Hague Peace Conference and the Carrington Plan in October 1991, international mediators grasped once again for how to achieve peace in Croatia. Cyrus Vance, a veteran US diplomat, was appointed UN Secretary-General Special Envoy to Yugoslavia in early November and the so-called Vance Peace Plan was presented within months, in January 1992. The Plan led to the cessation of hostilities and the deployment of UN peace-keeping forces in Croatia, but also enforced ethnic separation through the establishment of United Nations Protection Areas (UNPAs) that secured the territory held by Serbs, the SAOs.[82] The UNPAs were to be demilitarised and their inhabitants, by then almost exclusively Serbs, secured by UN infantry units and UN civilian police monitors.[83]

According to the Defence narrative, Serbia's support for the Vance Peace Plan was evidence of its genuine dedication to the politics of peace, and

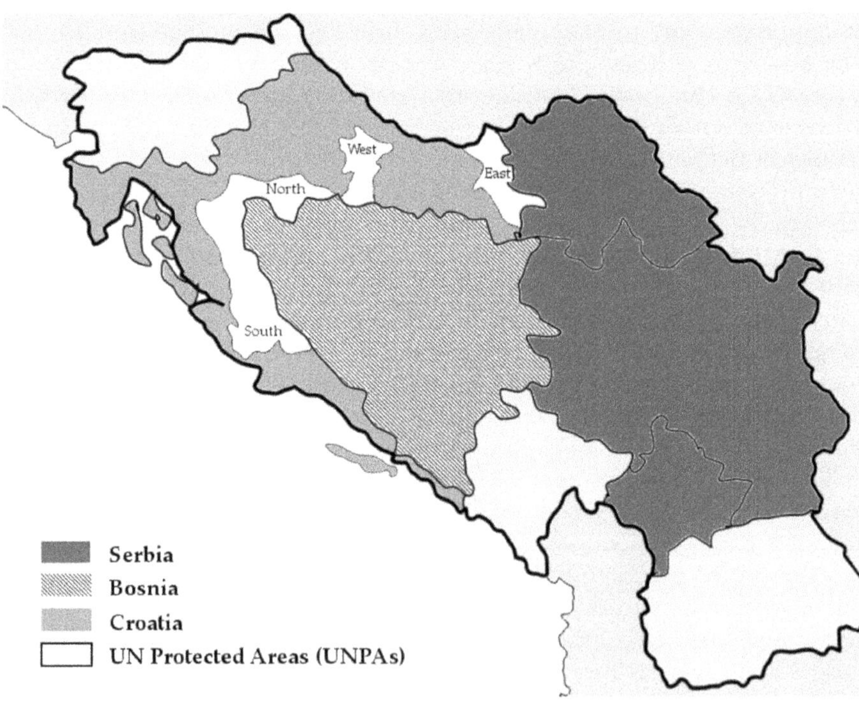

Map 4.2 The Vance Peace Plan (source: data from the Geographic Information Systems Unit of the ICTY).

concerns expressed by Croatian leaders that the plan could make ethnic separation permanent was evidence of their unwillingness to accept a truce. The Defence also stressed that the original request for the deployment of UN troops came from the Rump PSFRY at its 9 November 1991 session, motivated by a desire to protect Serbs living in Krajina.[84] But the Prosecution argued that, against the backdrop of unsuccessful negotiations in The Hague and the expectation that the European Community would be moving forward in recognising the independent Yugoslav republics, Serb leaders saw the UN peacekeeping mission as an opportunity to consolidate territorial gains and formalise ethnic separation with international backing. Further, reservations that had been voiced by Croatian leaders about the Vance Plan were seen by the Prosecution to have reflected valid uncertainties about the long-term territorial integrity of the Croatian state.[85]

Croatian Serb leaders initially refused to accept the Vance Plan, spurring Milošević to engage in a public debate with RSK President Milan Babić – who opposed the arrival of UN forces – accusing Babić of rejecting peace. Milošević also published a letter to Babić in which he argued that the Vance Peace Plan would not prejudice a political solution, but would enable the citizens of Krajina to lead normal lives again.[86] In reply to Milošević's letter, Babić clarified his position regarding the deployment of UN troops, saying he was against their deployment in the RSK but favoured it along the division line between Croatian and RSK forces.[87] Finally, after months of negotiations conducted between New York, Zagreb, and Belgrade, an agreement was reached. The Vance Peace Plan would be implemented in its original form without revision.

On 21 February 1992, UN Security Council Resolution 743 established a United Nations Protection Force (UNPROFOR) of 13,000 troops for an initial period of 12 months, clearly stipulating that recognised Croatian borders would be respected.[88] Still, Defence witness Mihailo Marković testified that Serb acceptance of UNPROFOR in Croatia had been based on the expectation that, after the war, people living in the RSK under UN protection would be able to decide in which state they wanted to live; and he suggested that Serbs would have chosen to join other Serbs in a single state.[89] To that end, on 26 February 1992, the Assembly of the RSK amended its Constitution – which defined the territory as the "state of the Serb people and of all citizens living therein" – in order to incorporate the SAOs of Slavonia, Baranja, and Western Syrmia (SBWS) and the SAO of Western Slavonia, all of which were UNPAs.[90] Ultimately, this plan failed to materialise because the RSK was retaken by Croatian armed forces, and UN troops left, by the end of 1995.

The transformative value of evidence on Milošević's *de jure* and de facto power during the conflict in Croatia

The ICTY Statute allows only for allegations of individual criminal liability; thus, to prove its case against Milošević, the Prosecution's focus was on evidence of his personal responsibility. The core of this evidence was related to Milošević's use of armed forces across the three different indictment periods – and arguably to his criminal state of mind – and was found in the records of the three political bodies with the power to command armies and other forces during his tenure. Documentation from the PSFRY was mostly, though not exclusively, relevant to the Croatia indictment; that from the Supreme Defence Council (SDC) was mostly, though not exclusively, relevant to the Bosnia indictment; and that from the Joint Command was relevant to the Kosovo indictment. The stenographic notes, decisions, and communiqués of these bodies revealed the extent of Milošević's *de jure* and de facto powers, as well as his specific knowledge of political and military events in territories over which he had no *de jure* sovereignty.

The Presidency of the SFRY

The PSFRY, with authority under the 1974 Constitution to deploy SFRY armed forces as the Commander-in-Chief, took over the leadership of the Federation in 1980 on the death of Josip Broz Tito.[91] The PSFRY therefore had *de jure* command of Yugoslav armed forces. It was a collective body meant to provide for power sharing and balance among the national and ethnic diversity of the former Yugoslavia, and consisted of eight members – one for each of the six Yugoslav republics and for each of the two autonomous provinces. In this way, the Serbian provinces of Kosovo and Vojvodina were granted federal status equal to that of the republics, something that was never accepted by the Serbian nationalist-minded political and intellectual elite.

The most powerful person in the Presidency was the President of the PSFRY, whose tenure was rotational, so that the office passed from the designated representative of one republic or autonomous province to the next, each year. The rotating President was in charge of the armed forces in accordance with decisions of the PSFRY and had to ensure implementation of the collective body's acts and declarations. In the absence of a President, or in the event of their prolonged inability to be effective, the Vice President of the Presidency would take over.[92]

Records of PSFRY meetings from October 1991 to April 1992 provided valuable evidence of Serbia's involvement in the war in Croatia through Milošević's de facto takeover of the PSFRY and thereby of the Army. As President of Serbia, Milošević was technically junior to members of the PSFRY, but he managed to impose his political authority through the compliance of the four Presidency members that made up the Serbian Bloc.[93] Still, Milošević's de facto power during the war in Croatia was not easy for the

Prosecution to deconstruct or prove because it was always someone else who held *de jure* power over the armed forces in the years covered by the indictment.

To establish the real extent of the control Milošević had over the Croatian conflict, the Prosecution depended on witnesses who had observed his close cooperation with the PSFRY at that time. For example, Borisav Jović testified that Milošević's considerable de facto power extended over more than a decade and that, as the key political figure in Serbia, he held absolute authority with the people and within his party, taking a crucial role in all decision-making. According to Jović, Milošević was a main actor in everything that came to pass during that period.[94] In his testimony, Jović referred to the "Group of Six" – which comprised Slobodan Milošević, then the President of Serbia; Jović and Branko Kostić, members of the PSFRY; General Veljko Kadijević, then the Federal Minister of Defence and Chief of Staff of the JNA; General Blagoje Adžić, Kadijević's Deputy; and Momir Bulatović, then the President of Montenegro.[95] Jović described the Group as an informal cadre of highly-ranked officials who were instrumental in planning and implementing Serbian policies from 1990 into 1992. By Jović's estimate, he met or consulted with Milošević literally hundreds of times between 15 May 1989 and July 1992, often with representatives from the JNA, the PSFRY, and Montenegro.[96] The Prosecution contended that the Group of Six had existed because of the overlapping political and military goals of its members and their acceptance of Milošević as the de facto leader of all Serbs.[97]

The PSFRY sessions

Initially, some records of PSFRY sessions reached the OTP through individual witnesses, most of them through Stjepan Mesić. But records of sessions that took place after the Serbian Bloc managed to take exclusive control of the Presidency (when Mesić was no longer attending) were requested by the OTP in both 2005 and 2006 but were never received in full, even with several follow-up requests. For some of these sessions, held between October 1991 and April 1992, no records of any kind were provided; for others, either minutes or stenographic notes were provided, but not both. Because most of the records from the periods covered in the Croatia and Bosnia indictments were thus not received until 2005 – when the trial was already in the Defence stage – the Prosecution was unable to tender all relevant PSFRY records into evidence. And while the February 2006 testimony of Branko Kostić offered the Prosecution an opportunity to present some additional records, many are simply not part of the trial record.[98]

Stjepan Mesić testified about the pressure the Serbian Bloc had exercised to prevent his appointment as President of the PSFRY in the run-up to their takeover. Although the rotation of the presiding member should have been routine, Mesić's appointment was obstructed for months. He became President on 15 May, but only presided over meetings until October, when he no longer attended because he did not feel safe in Belgrade.[99] Serb leaders – who understood the importance of the PSFRY as a powerful political instrument that provided access to the JNA – sought to ensure that the PSFRY would function without Mesić, and so Mesić's own Vice President, Branko Kostić, amended the rules of procedure to legalise their takeover without the consent of other republics.[100]

PSFRY records show that the Serbian Bloc took power over the Presidency as of October 1991, when representatives from Croatia, Slovenia, Macedonia, and BiH stopped attending meetings as the result of growing political and military tensions and the full-scale war being waged in Croatia. The Serbian Bloc continued to meet, forming a Rump Presidency and assuming all powers, including that of collective Commander-in-Chief.[101] The first incomplete session of the Rump Presidency, on 1 October, included Bosnian Bogić Bogićević and Macedonian Vasil Turpukovski – although it was to be their last meeting.[102] When they followed the lead of Mesić and Slovenian representative Janez Drnovšek and did not attend subsequent PSFRY meetings, the legality and legitimacy of the PSFRY was brought into question.[103]

The Rump PSFRY and evidence on planning

Milošević's instrumentalisation of the PSFRY had reached a defining moment at the 143rd session, on 1 October. In the Croatia indictment, it was at this session that a blueprint for the disintegration of the SFRY and the use of the JNA to achieve Milošević's political and military goals was said to have been developed. The session, presided over by PSFRY Vice President Kostić, was attended by several high-level federal functionaries – including the Ministers of Defence and Internal Affairs – and the central topics of discussion were the political situation in general and the danger of a full-scale civil war in particular.[104]

Still, despite Kostić's attempt to legitimise the Serbian Bloc's takeover by amending procedural rules, the legal and constitutional basis of the Rump Presidency was uncertain.[105] Predictably, Kostić testified that the formation and operation of the Rump Presidency had met all legal conditions; but a central issue that emerged in court was whether or not the PSFRY had proclaimed an imminent threat of war on 1 October, and if so, whether it had done so within the confines of the law.[106] Only if such a proclamation was made legally would subsequent deployment of the JNA also have been legal.

The Prosecution argued that the proclamation and all ensuing PSFRY decisions on the use of federal armed forces – including the decision that led to JNA attacks on the Croatian towns of Dubrovnik and Vukovar – were in fact illegal. In response, Kostić insisted that an imminent threat of war had been agreed upon by the required majority, with six members voting in favour. But the Prosecution produced a copy of the official statement released after the 1 October session, and it did not entirely fit with Kostić's account;

for the text referred to a state of emergency as being only "evaluated" and not proclaimed.[107] Further – and embarrassingly for Kostić – an interview he had given for the documentary *The Death of Yugoslavia* confirmed the Prosecution's contention that a vote had not been held specifically on the question of an imminent threat of war.[108] In the interview, played in the courtroom, Kostić admitted that the only mention of this imminent threat had been "sneaked in" to a larger document. He testified that the Serbian Bloc had been aware that Macedonian and Bosnian representatives Tupurkovski and Bogićević would object to "some provocative stands" and had thus covertly added this text.[109] According to Kostić, when Tupurkovski and Bogićević did not attend the next session on 3 October, that document "empowered [the PSFRY] to work and make decisions with as many members that were present ... one, three, or all five." He conceded that they had used a "small political trick," but said "that wasn't the first or the last time such methods were resorted to."[110]

In his testimony, Stjepan Mesić also qualified the use of Yugoslav armed forces after 1 October 1991 as illegal. He placed responsibility for the crimes committed by the JNA not only on JNA leadership, but also on the Rump Presidency and Milošević.[111] Indeed, aware of the potential consequences of the Serbian Bloc's full control over Yugoslav armed forces, Mesić had sent letters to the international community in the immediate aftermath of their takeover, warning of Serbia's hold over the PSFRY and the "Serbianisation" of the JNA.[112] In the courtroom, Mesić asserted that the Rump Presidency had been established expressly to advance Milošević's policy goals.[113]

Based on Mesić's testimony and the interview Kostić had recorded for *The Death of Yugoslavia*, the Prosecution argued strongly that the Rump Presidency had in fact been unlawfully formed and had thus acted illegally in all decisions taken after 1 October 1991, including those relating to the JNA. Indeed, the Prosecution suggested to Kostić that Tupurkovski and Bogićević surely would have voted against a proclamation of an imminent threat of war, asking, "that's why you tricked them, right?"[114] Kostić replied quite candidly, denying nothing and remarking only that "there were moments of honesty"; but also insisting that the actions of other representatives, who he said "boycotted" the PSFRY, had forced the Bloc to act deviously.[115] Kostić rejected the Prosecution's proposition that, given the situation on the ground, it had been difficult – if not impossible – for some members of the Presidency to travel to Belgrade to attend the 3 October meeting. Instead, he framed the absence of the four non-Serbian Bloc members as a conscious effort to obstruct the work of the PSFRY.[116]

And so, the Rump Presidency cleared the way to take decisions with its reduced composition, eliminating the constitutional requirement for a quorum of six members, and the Serbian Bloc's strategy unfolded in subsequent meetings. On 4 October, the Presidency adopted an Order on Partial Mobilisation to strengthen commands, staffs, units, and institutions of the armed forces in order to ensure their combat readiness.[117] On 6 October – with Hague

Conference negotiations still ongoing – Minister of Defence General Veljko Kadijević's Deputy, Admiral Stane Brovet, identified the Croatian cities of Vukovar, Zadar, Dubrovnik, and Karlovac as the focus of military action.[118] The immediate issue of unblocking JNA barracks in Croatia that had been cut off by Croatian forces was also addressed, and Serbian member Borisav Jović, who was among Milošević's closest associates at the time, took the strong position that the JNA must remain deployed in Serb territories in Croatia.[119] One month later, at the 6 November session, Admiral Brovet explained that the JNA's goals were to protect the population from genocide and to secure the safety of all citizens who wanted to stay in a Yugoslav state, pending an adequate political solution.[120]

Occasionally, PSFRY sessions included non-member officials from Serbia, Montenegro, the Republika Srpska, and the Republika Srpska Krajina, along with Milošević himself. Records of those meetings made especially clear that Serb leadership in Croatia and BiH shared the political and military goals of the Rump Presidency and that they had discussed and aligned these goals as part of a single overarching strategy. For instance, at a joint meeting with Serb representatives from Croatia and BiH held on 9 and 12 December 1991, territories claimed by the Serbs were discussed in detail. Serb representatives from Western Slavonia insisted on the inclusion of several villages in plans to carve out Serb municipalities there, naming towns very near Virovitica – the starting point of the V–K–K line – which would turn out to be the area where some of the gravest crimes were committed against civilians in the village of Voćin.[121] Milošević was present on the second day of this meeting and he participated actively in dialog about common objectives.[122] He also expanded Serbian political goals to include the preservation of a Serb ethnic space within Croatia, and expressed his view that UN protection of certain areas was an important precondition for the development of economic and cultural ties between those areas and Serbia – which he predicted would also lead to a loss of ties between those areas and Croatia.

In the meeting, Milošević described Serb military conquests as "armed resistance" and emphasised that political recognition of Serb-claimed territories could be achieved only through political means.[123] Records of meetings such as this one, in combination with intercepted telephone conversations, laid bare the de facto power Milošević held over federal institutions that were technically superior to him, such as the PSFRY and the JNA. Indeed, Milošević had acted as a trusted intermediary between Croatian and Bosnian Serb leadership and the Army.[124] Further, the Serbian MUP had been a channel for communication between Milošević and Serb leadership in the republics, and an important facilitator of provisions of aid from Serbia to the Bosnian and Croatian Serbs.[125] By early 1992, acting JNA Chief of Staff General Blagoje Adžić told the PSFRY that a civil war in BiH would need to develop similarly to the conflict in Croatia, through the seizure of Serb territories and the facilitation of Serb resistance.[126] And in the weeks between 27 April and 2 June 1992, the agenda of the Rump Presidency was dominated by the war in BiH and the transformation of the JNA into three Serb armies – the Army of Yugoslavia (*Vojska Jugoslavije*, or VJ), the Army of Republika Srpska (VRS), and the Serbian Army of Krajina (*Srpska Vojska Krajine*, or SVK).[127]

The importance of video evidence: the Kula Camp Video and the formation of the JSO

Milošević had announced the formation of special police forces in March 1991, after demonstrations against his regime in Belgrade. Later, he would admit that the arming of Serbs in Croatia had intensified after a failed attempt to enact extraordinary measures at the PSFRY session that had followed, held from 12 to 15 March 1991.[128] But the full extent of the role these special police forces played in that process was not uncovered until the discovery of a 1997 video recording of an award ceremony for the Serbian MUP's Unit for Special Operations (*Jedinica za specijalne operacije*, or JSO).

The recording, which became known as the Kula Camp Video, provided proof that Milošević had established a para-state military unit in 1991 that was designed to operate in the other republics.[129] He and his associates had tried to obscure the existence of the JSO, and so the Prosecution sought to ascertain what the unit's formal status had been within the Serbian MUP. And a speech that opened the award ceremony, given by the Commander of these forces, Franko "Frenki" Simatović, made a powerful connection between Milošević's March 1991 reference to special police forces and his actions thereafter.[130] Simatović offered a comprehensive account of the unit's war record, including that it had been constituted on 4 May 1991. Since then, he said, it had "constantly worked to protect national security in circumstances where the existence of the Serbian people was directly jeopardised throughout its entire ethnic area." He characterised the unit's operations as anti-terrorist and compared the unit's history to a heroic epic, explaining that, "due to the international circumstances familiar [to us all], we were forced to operate in complete secrecy."[131] Simatović also confirmed that the JSO had been active on territories outside Serbia's borders, in Croatia and BiH.

The speech by Simatović stood alone as compelling evidence, but Milošević's reaction to the video in court was just as telling. He insisted the JSO had been established after the war, in 1996, and tried to dismiss the video altogether. To the Prosecution, this denial of the unit's wartime existence and operations revealed a guilty mind. The Prosecution's own investigation into the unit uncovered that its official name had been changed at least once. From 1991 to 1996, the unit was referred to in official documents as the Unit for Anti-Terrorist Operations (*Jedinica za anti-teroristička dejstva*, or JATD), before it was renamed in 1996 to the JSO. But it was always best known as the Red Berets (*Crvene beretke*), which is a confusing term given that various combat groups wore red berets but did not belong to this special unit. However, the defining feature of the unit was not its name but its core group of commanders and soldiers – who were featured in the video, and whose names were mentioned regularly in evidence during the trial.

Evidence of a criminal state of mind

The Kula Camp Video not only showed Milošević listening to Simatović's speech but subsequently touring the JSO compound, guided by Milorad 'Legija' Luković who was later charged and sentenced as the central figure responsible for the murders of both former Serbian President Ivan Stambolić in 2000 and Serbian Prime Minister Zoran Đinđić in 2003. Introduced to veterans of the unit, Milošević shook hands with several notorious combatants as well as with Zvezdan Jovanović, alias Zmija, who was also found guilty in 2007 of the murder of Prime Minister Đinđić.[132] When introduced to Radojica Božović, one of the unit's commanders, Milošević revealed his familiarity with JSO activities, telling Božović that he had read his reports.[133]

The fact that the ceremony depicted in the Kula Camp Video took place a year and a half after the end of the war in Bosnia did not diminish its evidentiary value. On the contrary, it was one of the most convincing pieces of evidence presented during the trial on the criminal state of mind of Milošević. What's more, the video clearly showed the faces of a number of other top-level officials, from both republican and federal institutions, who had attended the ceremony; and their presence indicated that they, too, had knowledge of the unit's existence and of its combat activities. These guests included Života Panić, VJ Chief of Staff from May 1992 to May 1993; General Aleksandar Dimitrijević, head of the VJ's Military Counterintelligence (KOS), later renamed the Security Directory (*Uprava Bezbednosti*, or UB), from 1993 to 1999; Vlastimir Đorđević, head of the Public Security Service from 1997 to 2000 and an ICTY indictee; Mihalj Kertes, Head of the Federal Customs Office from 1994 to 2000; and Milorad Vučelić, Head of Serbian Radio Television between 1993 and 1995 and a member of the SPS Main Board from 1990 to 1995.

The video was also important for establishing links between perpetrators on the ground, many of whom received awards during the ceremony for bravery on the battlefields of Croatia and BiH. According to Simatović, the war record of the JSO had begun with fighting in the RSK, and Milan Babić corroborated this, testifying that he had personally contacted Milošević to request assistance in forming an MUP in the RSK. In response, Simatović – along with Dragan Vasiljković, alias Kapetan Dragan – had arrived in Krajina in April 1991 to establish a military camp in Golubić.[134] The first generation of Golubić trainees were referred to as the *Knindžas* and a number of very notorious combatants came from this original group of 52.[135] Veljko Milanović, for example, became the leader of the Wolves from Vučjak, a paramilitary group that operated during the war in Bosnia; and Goran 'Klempo' Opačić, a Serb from Croatia, was identified during the Milošević trial as one of the perpetrators of crimes committed against Croatian civilians in the Benkovac area, where he was the head of the special police.[136] And, shortly after the formation of the Golubić camp, a second training camp was set up in Erdut, in Eastern Croatia, under the direction of Željko 'Arkan' Ražnatović, who would become among the most infamous figures in the conflicts of the 1990s as Commander of the Serbian paramilitary unit known as the Tigers.[137]

The Prosecution tendered the Kula Camp Video into evidence though Dragan Vasiljković, who almost irreparably discredited himself in court and, by doing so, nearly compromised this crucial piece of *mens rea* evidence. Vasiljković had been cultivated as a Prosecution witness in great secrecy over several years by a handful of investigators and lawyers responsible for the Bosnia indictment. His testimony in chief started as rehearsed, but as it progressed, he began to colour events quite differently than he had in his signed statement. When questioned about the Kula Camp Video, he readily admitted that he had been present at the ceremony and even helped improve the original transcript of the tape, correcting the names of participants that had been transcribed incorrectly.[138] But he soon became a hostile witness, taking the Prosecution by surprise. Asked a routine question about the secretive nature of the JSO, Vasiljković became agitated and short tempered. He claimed that Simatović's speech had been a "staged performance" meant to impress Milošević and that numbers of troops and their activities had been embellished and exaggerated.[139]

In contrast, the cross-examination conducted by Milošević of Vasiljković found the two of them in perfect harmony, and they both placed responsibility for all troop activities in Krajina at the feet of Milan Babić.[140] But the Prosecution had an opportunity to re-examine Vasiljković and address the inconsistencies between his signed statement and the account he gave in court. This led to some dramatic courtroom scenes when the witness, looking at the statement he had initialled and signed, declared that he never stated what was written.[141] Growing increasingly frustrated when confronted with particular passages and claiming that the Prosecution had used its own "wording," Vasiljković insisted that his statement "had been twisted around" and that his bad memory of "exact happenings" was the cause of many errors. "I honestly don't accept that this is what I have signed," he told the court.[142]

The Prosecution then asked Vasiljković if he had made contact with Frenki Simatović since he had arrived in The Hague and if they had discussed the Kula Camp Video, and his answer was as conflicted as the rest of his testimony. He admitted that he had spoken one time with Simatović, but claimed they had talked about his courtroom appearance in only the most general terms and only very briefly, before discussing dinner plans for when they were both back home. But Vasiljković had testified earlier that day that he and Simatović had discussed the video. When pressed by the Prosecution on this point, he said that, no, they had not; and moreover, that they had spoken for just "fifteen seconds."[143]

Judge Richard May, the British presiding judge, intervened to warn the Prosecution that cross-examining its own witness in this way could destroy his credibility.[144] As the contradictions piled up, it became increasingly difficult – if not impossible – for the judges to decide which parts of his testimony were reliable. And, the fact that he made contact with Simatović in the middle of giving sworn testimony added further to the question of his credibility. The Prosecution was left with the dilemma of how to reintroduce the Kula Camp Video two years later through other witnesses, and in the end, it was Defence witness Obrad Stevanović who contributed most substantially to establishing its evidentiary value. At the time of the Bosnian conflict, he was the commander of Special Police Units (*Posebne jedinice policije*, or PJP) in the Public Security Sector of the Serbian MUP, a post he held between 1994 and 1996.

The impact of the Kula Camp Video in Serbia

In the summer of 2001, the OTP began questioning individuals identified in the Kula Camp Video. Word of the existence of the video spread in JSO and MUP circles, causing anxiety among attendees of the ceremony, who knew the recording exposed them to the risk of ICTY prosecution and would lead to questions about Serbia's role in cross-border combat. Revelations from the video started a process that challenged the impunity JSO members had enjoyed, protected until then by the Milošević regime and its legacy. Indeed, many JSO officers had survived Milošević's fall from power and continued to hold positions of authority that allowed them to shield each other from ICTY and domestic investigations; but the emergence of the video threatened their careers.

After the indictment and arrest of two former JSO members, the Banović brothers, and alarmed by the commitment of post-Milošević leadership led by Prime Minister Zoran Đinđić to cooperate with the Tribunal, the most prominent JSO officers mutinied in November 2001.[145] This was their first attempt to obstruct or end cooperation between Serbia and the ICTY, and it threatened to overthrow the Đinđić government and bring about a political U-turn.[146] The mutiny was successfully brought to an end, and its instigators, Milorad 'Legija' Luković, Zvezdan Jovanović, Dušan Maričić, and others were arrested. But, "lacking the capability to stand up to the JSO," the Đinđić government released them soon afterward.[147]

The same group made a second attempt to end cooperation with the ICTY in March 2003. In February of that year, the Kula Camp Video had been shown in the courtroom, and about two weeks later, on 12 March, Prime Minister Đinđić was assassinated. In the aftermath of the assassination, Serbia declared a state of emergency and initiated a massive sweep-up operation, known as 'Sabre' – the goal of which was to identify the direct perpetrators and organisers of the assassination and prevent further destabilisation of the state and the sitting government. Ensuing investigations confirmed the existence of close ties between organised crime, state institutions, and the political and military establishment in Serbia that was still loyal to Milošević.[148]

The state of emergency lasted 42 days. Eventually, 13 individuals were indicted and tried for Đinđić's assassination in a trial that began in December 2003 and ended in May 2007, when 12 of the accused were found guilty. Legija and Jovanović were sentenced to 40 years each, and the rest of the perpetrators received sentences from eight to 35 years. Jovanović – who had actually pulled the trigger – was reported to have said in his written statement that he did not kill Đinđić for money, but to prevent the extradition of "our people" to The Hague.[149] In November 2011, precisely ten years after the mutiny and eight years after Đinđić's assassination, Serbia's Special Prosecutor's Office for Organized Crime finally completed its investigation, qualifying the mutiny as a critical feature of the political background to Đinđić's murder and filing an indictment in March 2012 against its organisers.[150]

The investigation into Đinđić's murder also led to important information about the assassination of former Serbian President Ivan Stambolić in 2000. It was Legija's bodyguard who revealed the details of that murder as well as the location of Stambolić's remains; and in September 2003, the Special Court in Belgrade issued an indictment charging a conspiracy that involved direct perpetrators as well as former head of the State Security Service Radomir Marković, former VJ Chief of Staff General Nebojša Pavković, and Slobodan Milošević.[151] In the Stambolić murder trial, Marković testified that Milošević had told him that members of the opposition in Serbia were bandits who needed to be liquidated, suggesting they should be targeted by explosives at a public gathering. Marković said further that, on one occasion, Milošević told him that Stambolić should be "removed" because he was a direct threat to the country. According to Marković, Milošević himself had suggested engaging Legija to do the job, and had met shortly afterward with him to discuss the murder of Stambolić as well as of Vuk Drašković, a fellow Serb politician and severe critic of Milošević and his wife.[152] In the Stambolić Judgement, delivered in 2005, the Court concluded that Milošević had ordered the killing of his political rival in order to retain power.[153] Tens of unsolved murders committed between 1991 and 2003 in Serbia were arguably politically motivated.[154]

Notes

1 Second Amended Indictment, 27 July 2004. Hereinafter, the Croatia Indictment.
2 It is important to stress that not all the PSFRY transcripts analysed in this chapter were tendered into evidence due to the delayed procurement of some of them.
3 Kosta Mihailović and Vasilije Krestić, *Memorandum of the Serbian Academy of Sciences and Arts: Answers to Criticisms* (Belgrade: SANU, 1995), Exhibit D250a, 130–133.
4 The official 1991 census for Croatia showed that 12.2 per cent of its population was of Serb ethnic origin. Some Defence witnesses inflated this figure, claiming that Serbs constituted 18–20 per cent of the Croatian population before the war. For example, see: Testimony of Zoran Lilić (18 June 2003), 22691.

5 Testimony of Marko Atlagić (15 February 2006), 48558.
6 Ibid., 48554–48556 and 48569.
7 The Croatian SDS existed only from 1990 to 1995. However, the Bosnian SDS – also founded in 1990, by Radovan Karadžić – remains a leading Serb political party in BiH.
8 Testimony of Milan Babić (25 November 2002), 13481.
9 "The Declaration of the Sovereignty and Autonomy of Serbian People in Croatia," 25 July 1990, Exhibit P351.10a, para. 1.
10 Testimony of Milan Babić (18 November 2002), 12921; (26 November 2002), 13608–13609; (2 December 2002), 13669; and (4 December 2002), 13932.
11 Testimony of Milan Babić (18 November 2002), 12910.
12 Testimony of Milan Babić.
13 Trial Transcript (22 January 2004), 32324–32325. Milošević's account was contrary to those given by Milan Babić and Borisav Jović in their testimonies.
14 Jovan Rašković (1945–1992) was a psychiatrist and a member of the Serbian Academy of the Sciences and Arts (SANU) who came into politics on the initiative of Dobrica Ćosić. He was also a former professor and political mentor of Radovan Karadžić, and inspired and encouraged Karadžić's political career, which started with the founding of the SDS in BiH. Rašković left politics in April 1991 following armed clashes between Croatian and Croatian Serb police units. See: Testimony of Milan Babić (25 November 2002), 13436–13438; (26 November 2002), 13544.
15 Testimony of Milan Babić (18 November 2002), 12894–12896; (26 November 2002), 13561–13565.
16 Testimony of Stjepan Mesić (1 October 2002), 10524–10525 and 10532–10536; (2 October 2002), 10706.
17 Petar Gračanin, interview, in *Death of Yugoslavia*, "The Road to War," Part II, produced by Brian Lapping Associates, BBC, 1995. In 1989, negotiations over Gračanin's appointment delayed the formation of Ante Marković's federal government for three months because Milošević would have no one else in the position. Gračanin's alliance with Milošević was beyond dispute, even if, formally, Marković was his boss. See: Testimony of Milan Babić (18 November 2002), 12923–12931.
18 For example, see: "JNA/VJ Personnel File of General Zdravko Tolimir," 11–14.
19 Testimony of Milan Babić (18 November 2002), 12908–12910; and (26 November 2002), 13543–13545.
20 "A report on the referendum conducted among the Serbian people in the Republic of Croatia on the Serbian autonomy submitted by the Central Commission for Referendum," 30 September 1990, Exhibit P351.11a. The reported results of the referendum were: 567,127 in favour, 144 against, and 46 invalid.
21 Testimony of Milan Babić (25 November 2002), 13472–13472.
22 Intercept of Conversation between Radovan Karadžić, Radoslav Brđanin, and Miloslav Mičević, 2 July 1991, Exhibit P613.16a. Radoslav Brđanin was indicted, tried, and eventually convicted at the ICTY of crimes against humanity and war crimes. He is currently serving a 30-year sentence in Denmark. Brđanin was the first Vice President of the ARK, formed in the summer and fall of 1991 and also known as the SAO of Bosanska Krajina. Like the RSK in Croatia, it was created by joining a number of self-proclaimed 'Serb regions' in Bosnia. Banja Luka was its administrative capital.
23 Testimony of Milan Babić (20 November 2002), 13106, 13117–13121, 13064, and 13121–13123.
24 "A decision on the proclamation of the Statute of the Serbian Autonomous Region of Krajina [as] the Constitutional Law of the Serbian Autonomous Region

of Krajina," 29 May 1991, Exhibit P351.36a; "The Constitutional Law of the Serbian Autonomous Region of Krajina," 29 May 1991, Exhibit P351.37.1a.

25 "The Law on Application of Legal Regulations of the Republic of Serbia in the Territory of the Serbian Autonmous Region of Krajina," 29 May 1991, Exhibit P351.43a.

26 The original title of the document, dated 12 August 1991, is: Inicijativa za mirno i demokratsko rješenje i dodnošenje novog Ustava Jugoslavije (Initiative for a Peaceful and Democratic Resolution of the Yugoslav Crisis and for Adoption of a New Constitution of Yugoslavia). The full text has been published in: Branko Kostić, *1991 – da se ne zaboravi* ("1991 – Not to be Forgotten") (Belgrade: Filip Višnjić, 1996), 422–423.

27 The Belgrade Initiative was a major topic of conversation in the summer of 1991 and was a reflection of the common plan of Serb leaders. See: Intercept of Conversation between Slobodan Milošević and Radovan Karadžić, 7 August 1991, Exhibit P613.27a; 4 September 1991, Exhibit P613.34; 13 September 1991, Exhibit P613.63a; 19 September 1991, Exhibit P613.67a; and 20 December 1991, Exhibit P613.37a and Exhibit P613.60a.

28 Intercept of Conversation between Radovan Karadžić and Slobodan Milošević, 4 September 1991, Exhibit P613.34.

29 "Draft of Treaty Provisions for the Convention," 4 November 1991, Exhibit P780; "Official Report on Conference on Yugoslavia," No. hagc1224/cpeu137, 18 October 1991, Exhibit P778.

30 "How We Will Draw New Borders," in "Article from Epoha issue 1," 22 October 1991, Exhibit P786a, 12–20.

31 Ibid., 13. The following areas were listed: 1. The Serbian Autonomous Region of Krajina; 2. Western Slavonia; 3. The Serbian Autonomous Region of Slavonia, Baranja, and Western Syrmia; 4. Western Herzegovina; 5. Šamac Posavina; 6. Dubrovnik Republic; and 7. Western border of Serbian countries. Two of those areas, Western Herzegovina and Šamac Posavina, were in BiH. Also see: Testimony of Mihailo Marković (17 November 2004), 35553.

32 Jovan Ilić, "Kako ćemo se razgraničavati," *Epoha*, 22 October 1991, 12–20. Defence Witness Čedomir Popov testified that Dr Ilić was a demographer. See: Testimony of Čedomir Popov (15 December 2004), 34538. Slobodan Antonić dealt recently with the *Epoha* map and related article. He calls the evidence erronous and claims the author of the article provided an educated discussion in the spirit of equality and tolerance. See: Slobodan Antonić, *Slobodan Milošević: još nije gotovo* ("Slobodan Milošević: It's Not Over Yet") (Belgrade: Vukotić medija, 2014), 450.

33 Testimony of Smilja Avramov (8 September 2004), 32556.

34 Ibid. Also see: Intercept of Conversation between Radovan Karadžić and Slobodan Milošević, 26 October 1991, Exhibit P613.101a.

35 Intercept of Conversation between Radovan Karadžić and Slobodan Milošević, 29 October 1991, Exhibit P613.103a.

36 Trial Transcript, Defence Opening Statement (31 August 2004), 32193.

37 Testimony of Čedomir Popov (16 December 2004), 34604–34605.

38 Testimony of General Imra Agotić (27 June 2003), 23287–23289.

39 Testimony of Witness B-1493 (10 April 2003), 18964–18965.

40 Intercept of Conversation between Radovan Karadžić and Slobodan Milošević, 8 July 1991, Exhibit P613.17a.

41 For example, see: Stipe Mesić, *Kako smo srušili Jugoslaviju* ("How We Destroyed Yugoslavia") (Zagreb: Globus International, 1992), 236; Doder and Branson, *Milošević: Portrait of a Tyrant*, 95–96; Paul Williams and Norman L. Cigar, *A Prima Facie Case for the Indictment of Slobodan Milošević* (Washington, DC: Alliance to Defend Bosnia-Herzegovina, 1996), 20–21. Parts of the conversations were

also published in the Serbian daily *Vreme* on 30 September 1991, and two years later in *Politika Ekspres* and *Srpska reč* on 24 May 1993.

42 The Prosecution never acquired any documents on the origin of the RAM plan; it remains a mystery that may yet be solved. Authors such as Sonja Biserko, a human rights activist, have written with authority that the RAM plan existed, as she did in her 2012 book, *Yugoslavia's Implosion: The Fatal Attraction of Serbian Nationalism*. Her sources included books by General Ilija Radaković (*Besmislena Yu-ratovanja*, 1997) and Stjepan Mesić (*Kako je srušena Jugoslavija*, 1994), but these sources did not produce actual documentation on the origins of the RAM, nor did they detail its purpose.

43 Testimony of Witness B-1493 (10 April 2003), 18964.

44 Testimony of Ante Marković (23 October 2003), 28030.

45 Testimony of Witness B-1493 (10 April 2003), 18966.

46 Ibid., 18968–18969.

47 Testimony of General Geza Farkaš (10 November 2005), 46466.

48 The RAM plan was discussed in cross-examinations of Prosecution witnesses on 6 December 2002, 10 April 2003, and 15 July 2003.

49 Testimony of Stjepan Kljujić (15 July 2003), 24449.

50 Kadijević's book was published in B/C/S: Veljko Kadijević, *Moje Vidjenje Raspada: Vojska Bez Države* (Belgrade: Politika, 1993). Excerpts of the book were submitted in English as Exhibit P449a.

51 Veljko Kadijević, *My View of the Break-Up: An Army Without a State*, Excerpt, Exhibit P449a, 73.

52 Testimony of General Nojko Marinović (3 April 2003), 18516–18517. Also see: "Statement of General Nojko Marinović," 8 August 2000, Exhibit P374a, 16–17.

53 According to the 1991 Census, there were 58,836 Croats living in Dubrovnik and 4,765 Serbs. The total population of Dubrovnik was 71,419.

54 Intercept of Conversation between Radovan Karadžić and Slobodan Milošević, 7 October 1991, Exhibit P613.83a.

55 Intercept of Conversation between Radovan Karadžić and Božidar Vučurević, 14 November 1991, Exhibit P613.116a.

56 Intercept of Conversation between Radovan Karadžić and Branko Kostić, 26 November 1991, Exhibit P613.128a.

57 For example, see: Testimony of Petar Kriste (27 January 2003), 14853; Testimony of Pero Poljanić (11 December 2002), 14422–14423.

58 For discussion, see: Testimony of General Nojko Marinović (3 April 2003), 18522.

59 Testimony of General Božidar Delić (20 July 2005), 42578.

60 Ibid., 42579.

61 Testimony of Slobodan Jarčević (28 February 2006), 48991–48992. Jarčević even asserted that the Croatian language was not spoken in Dubrovnik at the time of the trial. Yet, records from every era contradict his claims. In 1689, Count Tolstoy wrote that "Ragusans ... call themselves Croats" and noted that they spoke the Dalmation language. And, since 1948, censuses show that no more than 12 per cent of the population has identified as Serb; indeed, in 2011, over 90 per cent of the population identified as Croat and over 95 per cent listed their mother tongue as Croatian. Results of the 2011 census are available from the Croatian Bureau of Statistics, at: www.dzs.hr/default_e.htm (accessed 3 October 2014).

62 Testimony of Vojislav Šešelj (25 August 2005), 43225.

63 Ibid., 43218–43219.

64 In November 2014, Šešelj was granted a temporary release from custody to return to Serbia for cancer treatment. See: Order on the Provisional Release of the Accused *Proprio Motu*, *Prosecutor* v. *Šešelj*, No. IT-03-67-T, 6 November

2014. A judgement in his trial – which has been called "a series of unfolding disasters" – has not been decided as of this writing, and Šešelj has declared that he will not honour a summons to return to The Hague for the verdict. Questions have been raised about his release because Šešelj himself refused a provisional release in June 2014 due to the fact that it stipulated that he avoid politics, but the Court then took the "unprecedented step" of releasing him *proprio motu* with very few stipulations. For more on this, see: Daisy Sindelar, "In Releasing Šešelj, ICTY Solves One Problem – But Creates Many Others," *Radio Free Europe*, 20 November 2014, www.rferl.org/content/balkans-seselj-hague-release-creates-problems/26702184.html (accessed 20 November 2014).

65 Testimony of Vojislav Šešelj (15 September 2005), 44104.
66 Testimony of Vojislav Šešelj (6 September 2005), 43813.
67 Ibid., 43814.
68 Testimony of Vojislav Šešelj (14 September 2005), 43987–43989.
69 Testimony of Vojislav Šešelj (6 September 2005), 43814.
70 Ibid., 43223.
71 Intercept of Conversation between Radovan Karadžić and Slobodan Milošević, 17 June 1991, Exhibit P613.9a.
72 Ibid.
73 Intercept of Conversation between Radovan Karadžić and Anđelko Grahovac, 24 June 1991, Exhibit P613.12a.
74 See: Testimony of Čedomir Popov (16 December 2004), 34604.
75 Testimony of Vojislav Šešelj (16 September 2005), 44295–44298; Testimony of Dejan Anastazijević (10 October 2002), 11477–11478.
76 Testimony of Dejan Anastazijević (10 October 2002), 11478–11479.
77 Smilja Avramov, *Postherojski rat Zapada protiv Jugoslavije* (Belgrade: Akademija za diplomatiju i bezbednost, 1997), 137.
78 *Death of Yugoslavia*, "Wars of Independence," Part III, produced by Brian Lapping Associates, BBC, 1995. Also see: "Minutes of the 16th Session of the Assembly of the Serbian People in BiH," 12 May 1992, Exhibit P463.49a. In this session, Mladić praised the joint action in Kijevo. Milošević had also been made aware of the operation, when Babić visited him on the eve of the attack. See: Testimony of Milan Babić (2 December 2002), 13650–13651.
79 ečović was promoted to VJ Commander of the Podgorica Corps in 1995.
80 Testimony of Marko Miljanić (14 July 2003), 24317–24318; 24320–24322; 24363. Also see: Marko Miljanić, Rule 92 *bis* Witness Statement, Exhibit P501a, para. 24–27.
81 See: Croatia Indictment.
82 "The Vance Plan" in *The International Conference on the Former Yugoslavia: Official Papers*, vol. 1, ed. B.G. Ramcharan (The Hague: Kluwer Law, 1997), 447–453. The Plan was submitted into evidence as Exhibit P355.
83 Ibid., 451. Also see: "Concept for a UN Peace-Keeping Operation in Yugoslavia," Annex III in *Report of the Secretary-General Pursuant to Security Council Resolution 721*, No. S/23280, 11 December 1991.
84 Testimony of Branko Kostić (6 February 2006), 47996–47997.
85 Ibid., 47999–48000.
86 "Open Letter from Slobodan Milošević to Milan Babić and Milan Babić's Response," 9 and 12 January 1992, Exhibit P352.79a. Milošević attacked Babić, saying:

> citizens of Krajina should know that because of what you have done, you have lost all the trust we had in you, and for future relations with the authorities of the Republic of Serbia they have to delegate persons who will hold the interests of their people above personal political prestige.

87 Ibid.
88 United Nation Security Council, Resolution 743, No. S/RES/743, 21 February 1992.
89 Testimony of Mihailo Marković (17 November 2004), 33554.
90 "The Constitution of the Republic of Serbian Krajina," 1991, Exhibit P351.68a, 2; "The Amendments to the Constitution of the Republic of Serbian Krajina...," 26 February 1992, Exhibit P351.74a.
91 See: "The Socialist Federal Republic of Yugoslavia Constitution (1974)," Exhibit P131a, Article 313; "The Law on All People's Defence adopted by the SFRY Assembly," 13 April 1982, Exhibit P352.21a, Article 106.
92 "The Socialist Federal Republic of Yugoslavia Constitution (1974)," Article 328.
93 Croatia Indictment, para. 30.
94 Testimony of Borisav Jović (18 November 2003), 29131. Also see: Jović, Rule 89(F) Witness Statement, para. 7.
95 Ibid., 29128–29129.
96 Jović, Rule 89(F) Witness Statement, para. 5.
97 Croatia Indictment.
98 Any sessions that were tendered into evidence are cited with an exhibit number; when no such number is cited, the session was not in evidence.
99 Testimony of Stjepan Mesić (1 October 2002), 10563–10564.
100 For example, see: the notice of the 1 October 1991 PSFRY Session Agenda in Exhibit P328.20a; the notice of Decisions from the 3 October 1991 PSFRY Session in Exhibit P328.23a; a letter from Stipe Mesić "...regarding the illegal convocation of the SFRJ Presidency informing those invited to the meeting of his objection," Exhibit P328.19a; "...proposal for the Change and Amendment of the Rules of Procedure of the Work of the SFRJ Presidency," Exhibit P328.12a. Also see: Testimony of Stjepan Mesić (1 October 2002), 10569–10570.
101 Croatia Indictment, para. 30.
102 Testimony of Stjepan Mesić (2 October 2002), 10582.
103 Ibid.
104 "Draft Minutes from the 143th sitting of the PSFRY," 1 October 1991, Exhibit P328.28a.
105 Testimony of Stjepan Mesić (1 October 2000), 10570.
106 Testimony of Branko Kostić (13 February 2006), 48335.
107 Ibid., 48318–48321 and 48336–48337. Also see: "Public Notice regarding the PSFRY meeting 1 October 1991...," Exhibit P328.6a; and "Draft Minutes from the 143rd sitting of the PSFRY."
108 The documentary featured interviews of a number of the main protagonists of the Yugoslav crisis. Eventually, the OTP requested the complete interview tapes for many of the military and political leaders interviewed, including Branko Kostić. His interview was recorded on seven videotapes, all in B/C/S, which served as very valuable contemporaneous documentation, as most of the material had been recorded in 1994 and 1995 when the war still ongoing.
109 Testimony of Branko Kostić (13 February 2006), 48318–48319.
110 Ibid., 48319–48320.
111 Testimony of Stjepan Mesić (2 October 2002), 10582–10584.
112 Testimony of Stjepan Mesić (1 October 2002), 10582–10584. Also see a letter from President Mesić to the UN Secretary General: "Letter originating from the SFRY Presidency ... addressed to Javier Pérez de Cuéller," Exhibit P329.12a.
113 Testimony of Stjepan Mesić (1 October 2002), 10593–10594; and (3 October 2002), 10753.
114 Testimony of Branko Kostić (13 February 2006), 48320.
115 Ibid.
116 Ibid., 48337–48340.

117 "Draft Minutes marked Strictly Confidential of the 145th sitting of the PSFRY...," 4 October 1991, Exhibit P328.11a; Testimony of Branko Kostić (13 February 2006), 48343–48345.
118 Notes of the 147th PSFRY Session, 6 October 1991, 5.
119 Ibid., 16.
120 Notes from the 159th PSFRY Session, 6 November 1991, 14–15.
121 Notes from PSFRY Session, 12 December 1991, 136. The municipalities mentioned were: Grubišno Polje, Novska, Podravska Slatina, Slavonska Požega, Orahovica and Virovitica.
122 Ibid., 172.
123 Ibid., 178.
124 For example, see: Intercept of Conversation between Radovan Karadžić and Slobodan Milošević, 8 July 1991, Exhibit P613.17a; 9 August 1991, Exhibit P613.30a; and 9 September 1991, Exhibit P613.48a.
125 For example, see: Intercept of Conversation between Radovan Karadžić and Mihalj Kertes, 24 June 1991, Exhibit P613.10a and Exhibit P613.11a; Intercept of Conversation between Radovan Karadžić and Jovica Stanišić, 8 August 1991, Exhibit P613.28a; 8 September 1991, Exhibit P613.44a; 21 December 1991, Exhibit P613.144a; 6 January 1992, Exhibit P613.157a; and 28 January 1992, Exhibit P613.169a; and Intercept of Conversation between Radovan Karadžić and Milan Babić, 8 September 1991, Exhibit P613.46a.
126 Notes from the 191st PSFRY Session, 3 April 1992, 14.
127 Notes from the 197th, 199th, 200th, 201st, and 202nd PSFRY Sessions, held respectively on 4 May 1992, 8 May 1992, 19 May 1992, 20 May 1992, and 21 May 1992. The Presidency continued to meet after the formation of the FRY on 27 April 1992, until the FRY Supreme Defence Council took control of all issues relating to war and peace in June.
128 Trial Transcript (14 February 2003), 16167.
129 The ceremony took place at JSO headquarters, located in Kula, Serbia, at a former JNA garrison.
130 Franko Simatović was indicted and tried at the ICTY along with former head of the DB Jovica Stanišić (Case No. IT-03–69). The Kula Camp Video was a key piece of evidence against the two. Still, they were both acquitted in May 2013 in first instance judgements. In June 2013, the Prosecutor filed its notice of appeal and an Appeals Hearing took place on 6 July 2015.
131 "Video showing an Award Ceremony with members of the Red Berets, political leaders and military leaders..." Exibit P390.1. Also see: "Corrected Transcript of Video (V000–3533)," Exhibit 390.3a.
132 Ibid.
133 Ibid.
134 Testimony of Milan Babić (20 November 2002), 13106, 13117–13118, and 13163–13164.
135 The name *Knindža* was a play on the words Knin and ninja (*nindža* in B/C/S).
136 Testimony of Milan Babić (25 November 2002), 13400–13402. These perpetrators are idolised by some in Serbia. For instance, in 2007, the Serbian Radical Party proposed renaming a Novi Sad street after Milanović, for his "contribution to the liberation of Western Slavonia, Modriča and Derventa." See: *HINA News*, 4 April 2007.
137 Testimony of Dobrila Gajić-Glišić (21 October 2003), 27849–27852. Also see: Testimony of Milan Milanović (8 October 2003), 27264–27265.
138 Testimony of Dragan Vasiljković (19 February 2003), 16451.
139 Ibid., 16558–16560.
140 Ibid., 16593.
141 Testimony of Dragan Vasiljković (21 February 2003), 16735.

142 Ibid., 16736.
143 Ibid., 16747.
144 Judge Richard May presided over the Trial Chamber until February 2004, when he resigned due to ill health. Judge Iain Bonomy from Scotland then joined the two other judges for the trial – Judge Robinson from Jamaica and Judge Kwon from South Korea – and Judge Robinson became the Chamber's presiding judge.
145 "JSO Mutiny Probe 'Almost Complete'," B92.net, 4 January 2011, www.b92.net/eng/news/crimes-article.php?yyyy=2011&mm=01&dd=04&nav_id=71918 (accessed 3 October 2014).
146 Testimony of General Obrad Stevanović (31 May 2005), 40158.
147 James Gow and Ivan Zverzhanovski, *Security, Democracy and War Crimes: Security Sector Transformation in Serbia* (London: Palgrave Macmillan, 2013), 133.
148 Srđa Popović, "Proposal for Supplementing of Evidence Presentation Proceedings," *Helsinki Bulletin* 11 (March 2007). Available at: www.helsinki.org.rs/doc/HB-No11.pdf (accessed 25 May 2008).
149 For example, see: "Twelve Guilty of Đinđić Murder," *BBC News*, 23 May 2007, http://news.bbc.co.uk/2/hi/6683463.stm (accessed 3 October 2014).
150 "Former JSO Members to be Questioned," B92, 22 September 2011, www.b92.net/eng/news/crimes-article.php?yyyy=2011&mm=09&dd=22&nav_id=76512 (accessed 3 October 2014). Also see: "Trial for JSO Mutiny Begins in Belgrade," B92, 3 October 2012, www.b92.net/eng/news/crimes.php?yyyy=2012&mm=10&dd=03&nav_id=82465 (accessed 3 October 2014).
151 Testimony of General Obrad Stevanović (31 May 2005), 40158. Pavković and Milošević were not actually tried for the crime.
152 The Stambolić Judgement is available in Cyrillic at: www.reportingproject.net/peopleofinterest/profil.php?profil=21 (accessed 18 January 2016).
153 Ibid.
154 The following is a list of only some of the unsolved assassinations in Serbia during that period: Milan Todorović Kundak, a businessman and JUL member who was close to Mira Marković, was killed in 1997; Assistant Minister of the MUP Radovan Stojičić Badža, who had a war history in Eastern Slavonia and had been close to Milošević, was killed in 1997; Slavko Ćuruvija, a publisher and journalist with long time ties to Mira Marković, was killed in 1999; paramilitary leader Željko 'Arkan' Ražnatović, infamous for his wartime activities in Croatia, BiH, and Kosovo, was killed in 2000; and Pavle Bulatović, former FRY Minister of the MUP and later FRY Minister of Defence, was also killed in 2000.

5 The formation of the Republika Srpska and the policy of ethnic separation in Bosnia and Herzegovina

This chapter examines the war in BiH, the crimes committed there against non-Serbs as part of the Serb strategy of ethnic separation, and the creation of the Serb-controlled territory that became known as the Republika Srpska (RS). Implementation of the fourth goal in Milošević's planning manifested in the creation of the RS. The Prosecution cited parallels between the establishment of the RSK in Croatia and that of the RS in BiH, where ethnic separation of Serb-claimed territories again led to crimes against non-Serbs, mostly Bosnian Muslims. According to this narrative, ethnic separation and the subsequent creation of the RS were necessary to insure the contiguity of Serb territories in Croatia and BiH in order to link them up with Serbia and Montenegro. And for that purpose, Milošević had initiated the formation of the Federal Republic of Yugoslavia (FRY) – a federation comprised of Serbia and Montenegro – with contingencies in its Constitution for later absorption of other Serb territories. The Defence asserted that Serbs had waged a defensive war because they faced threats to their physical survival in a unitary and Muslim-dominated independent BiH.

The Bosnia indictment alleged that Milošević had participated in a Joint Criminal Enterprise (JCE) from at least 1 August 1991 to at least 31 December 1995, which had worked to forcibly remove the majority of non-Serbs from large areas of BiH and had "planned, instigated, ordered, committed or otherwise aided and abetted the planning, preparation and execution of the destruction" of thousands of Bosnian Muslims beginning on or about 1 March 1992. In some places, the JCE was said to have specifically targeted "educated and leading members" of the Bosnian Muslim community for extermination. Further, it was alleged that thousands more had been detained in the most inhumane conditions, "calculated to bring about [their] partial physical destruction," and had been tortured, raped, and starved as part of a genocidal process. Milošević was said to have effectively controlled other members of the JCE as well as various armed forces – including paramilitary groups – and was therefore responsible for the murder and forced transfer of non-Serbs in Bosnia, as well as for the intentional destruction of large numbers of cultural and religious institutions, historical monuments, and sacred sites.[1]

Milošević's role in the commission of these crimes as well as the unofficial but de facto links that existed between himself and other leaders were discovered when communications that had been ostensibly confidential were brought to light. For instance, intercepts of telephone conversations he had in 1991 and 1992 with Serb politicians from Serbia, BiH, and Croatia exposed his role in planning the post-Yugoslav political future of BiH and demonstrated the power he held over Bosnian Serb leaders. Important evidence about his de facto power also came from the records of the State Council for Harmonisation of Positions on State Policy (*Savet za usaglašavanje stavova o državnoj politici*), which existed from August 1992 to April 1993. A number of strategic questions relating to BiH were discussed in these sessions and, at times, heated debate between high-level officials forced meeting participants to further clarify their positions, making these records particularly valuable.

However, to make its case, the Prosecution also needed to present evidence of the *de jure* and de facto power Milošević had in commanding armed forces during the Bosnian conflict. His *de jure* position was linked to his role on the Supreme Defence Council (SDC), and the Prosecution tendered many records of the Council's sessions into evidence. The SDC – which first met in June 1992 – was the joint Commander-in-Chief of FRY armed forces as stipulated in the 1992 FRY Constitution, and it included the Presidents of the FRY and of the Republics of Serbia and Montenegro. As President of Serbia, Milošević sat on the SDC throughout the war years in BiH. Thus, the Prosecution approached the evidence with an eye for proof of the *de jure* links between the Yugoslav Army and Serb forces in Croatia and BiH. With the disintegration of the SFRY, the JNA had also ceased to exist, and its personnel and equipment were divided into three separate but connected Serb armies – the Army of Yugoslavia (VJ), the official army of the newly formed FRY; the Serbian Army of Krajina (SVK), formed in the RSK; and the Army of Republika Srpska (VRS), formed in the RS. Because parallel political and military structures co-existed in the FRY and the Serb entities, the Prosecution also had to prove the de facto line of control and influence Milošević had exercised over the RS political and military establishment. And this added to the significance that Milošević and his collaborators had made special efforts to try and keep materials such as the SDC records from public view.

Pre-war plans for Bosnia and Herzegovina

Courtroom reconstruction of the Karađorđevo meeting and the agreement to partition BiH

At the PSFRY session held on 9 January 1991, Croatia had been called on to disarm its police forces and punish those responsible for illegally importing arms to the republic. When no action had been taken by the time of the March session, JNA Chief of Staff and Federal Minister of Defence General Veljko Kadijević proposed that extraordinary measures be introduced in response to Croatia's noncompliance. These measures – legally required in order to activate the armed forces in times of peace – were intended to allow use of the JNA against the legitimately elected Croatian government. Of eight PSFRY votes, five were needed; and only seven members were present. So, when BiH representative Bogić Bogićević – an ethnic Serb – voted against the proposal, he surprised his fellow Serbs by preventing passage of the measures.[2]

This failure by Serbian and JNA leaders to impose their will led to a dramatic walkout by Borisav Jović, the Serbian representative and President of the PSFRY at the time. In a televised address that followed, Milošević declared that Yugoslavia was finished and that Serbia would no longer be bound by decisions of the federal Presidency.[3] He quickly reversed his position and brought Jović back into the PSFRY; for, in truth, Serbia could not afford to give up its share of the power afforded by the Presidency and the access it provided to the JNA.[4]

After these events in March, relations between Serbia and Croatia worsened by the day. At a meeting with Jović, Croatian PSFRY representative Stjepan Mesić complained about what he saw as concerted efforts by local Serbs and the JNA to destabilise Croatia. According to Mesić, Jović told him that Serbia was not interested in Croatia, but in BiH, and particularly in the 66 per cent of BiH territory that they felt was, and should remain, Serb. Mesić proposed a meeting to identify and resolve these issues through political means – in particular concerning BiH – and a meeting between Presidents Milošević and Tuđman was set.[5]

Tuđman arranged a *tête-à-tête* with Milošević at Karađorđevo. He invited no one to join him, nor did he later disclose the content or outcome of the meeting.[6] But Tuđman's view on BiH changed so completely after the meeting in Karađorđevo that Mesić described it in his testimony as an "about turn."[7] Mesić said that Tuđman had been in favour of maintaining the territorial integrity of BiH; but after the meeting, advocated for dividing BiH between Serbia and Croatia in order to restore Croatia to its historical glory and re-establish the borders of the Croatian Banovina that had existed from 1939 to 1941. Indeed, Milošević had allegedly promised Tuđman the Muslim majority towns of Cazin, Kladuša, and Bihać in the Bosnian Krajina – once known as Turkish Croatia.[8] Prosecution witness Stjepan Kljuić, the leader of the HDZ in BiH, which was affiliated in the 1990s with Tuđman's Croatian HDZ, gave a similar account of assurances between Milošević and Tuđman over future territories. Kljuić, who was known for his vocal opposition to the division of BiH, testified that Tuđman had also told him about the pledge Milošević made to hand over Turkish Croatia. Kljuić recalled telling Tuđman that such a pledge was akin to Milošević offering Sardinia or Sicily as a gift, saying "it doesn't belong to you and it doesn't belong to Mr. Milošević."[9]

Prosecution witness Hrvoje Šarinić, Tuđman's Chef de Cabinet before and during the wars in Croatia and BiH, met as a special envoy with Milošević many times. He testified that the Karađorđevo meeting took place on 26 March 1991 and said that it had not led to any firm agreements, but to the establishment of two working groups that were tasked with expanding on the principles agreed upon at the meeting.[10] Yet, despite three working group sessions held over a week-and-a-half, nothing concrete was achieved.[11]

Dušan Bilandžić, of the Croatian working group, wrote on various occasions of his account of these sessions. In an October 1996 article, he claimed Tuđman told the Croatian working group that an agreement on partition had been made with Milošević in principle, for which the working groups were to develop concrete maps.[12] During its cross-examination of Serbian working group member Ratko Marković, the Prosecution presented him with a passage from this article. He denied that any secret agreement for partition had been reached in Karađorđevo or elsewhere, or that a division was ever discussed at working group sessions he attended.[13] He did allow, however, that the maps Bilandžić referred to might have been discussed at the third session held in Zagreb, which Marković claimed he had not attended.[14]

Smilja Avramov, another member of the Serbian working group, wrote in her book that the major issues to emerge in working group discussions were the problems of borders and the continuity of public law.[15] At the sessions she attended, she recalled that there had been discussion about whether existing republican borders could be the basis for drawing new state borders. According to Avramov, the Croatians had insisted that Serbs give up the Krajina in Croatia, which the Serbian delegation rejected.[16]

Still, former SFRY Prime Minister Ante Marković testified that Milošević and Tuđman were indeed planning for the dissolution of Yugoslavia at Karađorđevo and asserted that they had discussed two key topics – the partitioning of BiH between Serbia and Croatia, and how to get rid of Marković. He claimed that Milošević and Tuđman had confirmed this to him personally when he confronted them both on separate occasions.[17] According to Marković, Milošević told him that BiH was an artificial and unsustainable entity created by Tito, claiming that most Bosnian Muslims had been Orthodox before they were forced to convert. When Marković warned that partitioning BiH could bring bloodshed, Milošević seemed confident it wouldn't because, together, Serbs and Croats made up a majority of the Bosnian population and because an enclave for Muslims was planned.[18]

Tuđman had apparently echoed Milošević's rhetoric; only, Tuđman claimed that Muslims in Bosnia had been Catholics who converted to Islam. He also did not believe a partitioning would lead to a war, because he thought Europeans wouldn't support a Muslim state in the heart of Europe.[19] Šarinić testified that Tuđman felt Tito had erred by not making BiH an autonomous province of Croatia. Tuđman saw BiH as a historical anomaly that had resulted from Turkish conquests in the fifteenth century and proposed broadening the thin strip of land in the south of Croatia by integrating it with a part of BiH that the Croatians could claim on the basis of ethnicity.[20] Indeed, during his first election campaign in 1990, Tuđman had complained about the shape of Croatia, saying disparagingly that it looked like a *kifla* – a crescent-shaped roll popular in Central and Eastern Europe.[21]

Valuable testimony about the plans discussed at Karađorđevo also came from Milan Babić, who testified that Milošević had showed him a map on which the division of BiH, as agreed between he and Tuđman, was marked.[22] But Milošević worked hard in the courtroom to downplay the Karađorđevo meeting and any evidence of plans to carve up BiH. Unable to refute or seriously challenge the evidence given by Prosecution witnesses, he brought up the meeting with Defence witness Vojislav Šešelj, who alleged that its details had been invented in order to upset Alija Izetbegović and other Bosnian Muslim politicians so that they would turn against Serbia and Croatia. Yet, when asked by the Chamber to elaborate on who had invented the story, Šešelj responded vaguely. First, he alluded to the *Borba* newspaper, a pro-communist newspaper that he said had sided with the federal government of Ante Marković and Western powers. The Chamber then asked him to explain why Marković might spread false rumours, and Šešelj postulated rather unconvincingly that he may have feared that a possible agreement between Milošević and Tuđman would sustain Yugoslavia but eliminate him as its leader.[23]

Milošević himself confirmed in court that he and Tuđman had met in Karađorđevo, and said they shared an understanding that the future of the SFRY rested on the relationship between Serbs and Croats or, rather, between Serbia and Croatia. But he denied any discussion of partitioning BiH or of removing Ante Marković, suggesting that Marković had accorded himself too much importance and asking during cross-examination why they would have considered him at all.[24] Marković replied that Serbia, Croatia, and Slovenia had all embraced the idea of independence by 1991, and that they had schemed about his dismissal because they perceived the reforms he advocated – which were aimed at preserving Yugoslavia – as a threat. As Marković saw it, a common state was no longer an option for Milošević or Tuđman and he stood in the way of their plans to establish their respective states within ethnically-defined borders, each incorporating territories in BiH.[25]

Milošević also challenged Hrvoje Šarinić over his testimony on Karađorđevo, claiming that the topic of conversation had been the influence of Islamic fundamentalism in BiH. Šarinić corrected Milošević, saying that this particular issue had not been discussed in Karađorđevo but at the follow-up meeting in Tikveš, which Šarinić had attended.[26] He went on to testify that, at that meeting, Milošević had given Tuđman a handwritten note detailing a supposed Muslim axis, which he referred to as the 'Green Transversal.' Milošević had asserted that this axis ran through Turkey, Bulgaria, Western Macedonia, Sandžak, and Kosovo, and that Muslims sought a unitary state which would include BiH – where Serbs and Croats would be a minority. According to Šarinić, after this meeting in Tikveš, Tuđman grew less optimistic about cooperating with Milošević.[27]

Šarinić also testified that Tuđman had brought attention in Tikveš to the Croatian Serbs' Log Revolution, protesting the fact that it had cut off a large part of Croatian territory from its central authority in Zagreb. When Milošević denied any involvement, Tuđman challenged him, calling Krajina the Trojan horse of Serbian politics in Croatia and implying that Milošević stood behind RSK leadership. Milošević continued to deny the role he played, but granted that he could help solve the Croatian problem; leaving Šarinić wondering how this could be if he really had nothing to do with the Log Revolution in the first place.[28] But what Šarinić eventually learned was that, for Serbia, the Serb national question in BiH was of far greater importance than the Serb national question in Croatia. In 1995, Milošević himself told Šarinić that the creation of the RS had resolved 90 per cent of the Serb national question just as President Tuđman had resolved the Croat national question with the establishment of Herceg-Bosna, a territory in BiH claimed by Bosnian Croat leadership as of November 1991.[29]

Although there has been no official and final resolution to the question of whether a partition of BiH was agreed to by Milošević and Tuđman, the spirit of such a plan was manifested in efforts by both Serbia and Croatia to encourage population transfers within BiH; and these efforts were at least somewhat coordinated. In fact, on 8 January 1992, Nikola Koljević, a politician in the Serb Democratic Party of Bosnia (*Srpska Demokratska Stranka*, or SDS), had informed Tuđman that Bosnia must be re-organised and had stressed the need for ethnic homogenisation of certain areas through the transfer of property and populations.[30] But, even if the Croatian and Serbian leaders thought a civilised and mutually agreed transfer was possible and preferable, it was something the Bosnian Muslims never accepted. Muslims in BiH understood that 'homogenisation' would amount to ethnically uniform Serb and Croat territories, at the expense of the Muslim population.

In September 1992 Tuđman again discussed a transfer of populations in BiH, with then FRY President Dobrica Ćosić, in Geneva.[31] Yet, despite attempts by both Serbia and Croatia to partition BiH, Hrvoje Šarinić insisted that the Croatian approach to BiH was less straightforward than that of Serbia given that Bosnian Croats, unlike Bosnian Serbs, had supported the February 1992 referendum on the independence of BiH.[32] And indeed, in support of this position, Croatia was among the first countries to recognise BiH after its declaration of independence in April 1992.[33] Serbia, conversely, withheld its recognition until after the RS borders, achieved by war, were cemented in the 1995 peace agreement that brought an end to the war.

Milošević's pre-war plans to keep BiH in Yugoslavia

Intercepted telephone conversations between Milošević and Karadžić held significant evidentiary value in establishing their coordinated and premeditated plans for BiH. Introducing the Belgrade Initiative to Karadžić on 12 June 1991, for instance, Milošević instructed him to tell the deputies of the SDS – Karadžić's party – that BiH should remain in Yugoslavia, and to stress that the interests of the SDS and Serbia were identical.[34] But if BiH were to be incorporated into Rump Yugoslavia peacefully, success was crucially linked to securing the support of leading Bosnian Muslim politicians. After Izetbegović refused to cooperate, Serb leaders had turned to his rival Adil Zufilkarpašić, reaching a so-called "historical agreement" that supposedly ensured the support of Muslims in BiH.[35] In reality, Zufilkarpašić did not speak for the Bosnian Muslim population and could not deliver. After initial enthusiasm on the part of Serbs, it quickly became evident that any settlement on the future of BiH would need the endorsement of Izetbegović; but it was unrealistic to think he would even consider the plan advocated by Milošević, which he had qualified as "a capitulation."[36] The positions of Izetbegović and Milošević grew increasingly incompatible as Izetbegović pushed for Bosnian sovereignty while Milošević asserted that BiH could be sovereign within a new Yugoslavia.[37]

When the BiH Assembly announced on 3 October 1991 that it would organise a referendum on independence, Serb concerns intensified. Milošević told Karadžić that Izetbegović would request international recognition – which he considered a catastrophe – and he insisted that Yugoslavia had to be preserved with Serbia as its central pillar.[38] Still, although Karadžić was happy to carve out Serb-populated territories in BiH with no concern for the fate of Bosnian Muslims, Milošević remained keen to keep the Muslims on his side. On at least one occasion, telephone intercepts revealed Karadžić disagreeing loudly and emotionally to this approach, and rejecting the idea that Serbs live in the same state with Muslims. His vision was that Serbs should gain control of 60 per cent of Bosnian territory and establish parallel state organisations.[39] In late December 1991, in a conversation with Jovica Stanišić – who would head the State Security Department (the DB) in the MUP of Serbia from 1992 to 1998 – Karadžić brought up the possibility of a confederal BiH, which reflected a modified partition of the sort allegedly discussed in Karađorđevo, whereby the Serb part would maintain ties with Serbia and the Croat part with Croatia, provided that Croatia would recognise the RSK.[40] Of course, Croatia would not give up a third of its territory to Croatian Serbs for the RSK and so this never materialised. The Serbian leadership and its supporters launched in January 1992 one last attempt to keep BiH in Yugoslavia.

Serbia's failure to keep BiH in Yugoslavia

Milošević's attempts to preserve a reduced Yugoslavia that included the whole of BiH persisted until January 1992. In the background Karadžić had been working on an alternative plan since September 1991, for ethnic and territorial separation within BiH. On 7 September, the very day the Hague Peace Conference began, the SDS issued a "Decision on the Promulgation of Autonomous Regions."[41] The formation of Serb Autonomous Regions (SAOs) in Bosnia was to adhere to the example set by Croatian Serbs and, to that end, a "regionalisation policy" was announced to establish regions in which Serbs were an absolute or relative majority.[42] Three days later, on 10 September, Karadžić spoke with Milošević about the possibility of the "regionalisation" or "cantonisation" of BiH.[43]

The next milestone in the ethnic separation project undertaken by the SDS was the establishment of the Assembly of the Serb People in BiH (later known as the RS Assembly) on 24 October 1991 by a majority vote of Bosnian Serb deputies in the BiH Assembly. The RS Assembly then adopted a "Decision on the Serb People of BiH Remaining in the Joint State of Yugoslavia," which formed a basis for the referendum put to Bosnian Serbs on 9 and 10 November, in which an overwhelming majority voted in favour of staying in a Yugoslav state.[44] On 21 November 1991, the Bosnian Serb Assembly passed a decision declaring that all places in which over 50 per cent of Serbs had voted in the November referendum should pronounce that they were still a part of Yugoslavia. The Assembly also proclaimed the establishment of five SAOs, describing them as federal units of the SFRY.[45]

Notwithstanding these developments or Karadžić's protests, Milošević was resolute that all of BiH had to remain in Yugoslavia. After the European Community invited the SFRY Republics to apply for independence in December 1991, the Rump PSFRY launched an initiative on 3 January 1992 called the Convention for a Third Yugoslavia.[46] Defence witness Branko Kostić, who officially presided over the Convention in his capacity as President of the Rump PSFRY, described it as a joint effort by nine political parties from BiH.[47] But, while the Convention was presented as the brainchild of Presidency members, intercepted telephone conversations between Milošević and Karadžić revealed that it was actually Milošević's idea. At the end of 1991, Milošević and Karadžić had discussed a draft of the Convention, agreeing that it should stress the continuation of the old Yugoslavia. Their concern was to avoid giving the impression that a new state was to be constituted.[48]

The Convention for a Third Yugoslavia was ultimately of little significance. Only Serb political parties from BiH were in attendance; and the event might have passed unnoticed were it not for an article in *Epoha* magazine on 7 January 1992.[49] The *Epoha* article presented the stated principles upon which a new Yugoslavia and parts of the old Yugoslavia were to separate in a "just territorial and material manner." According to Kostić, this referred to drawing new borders between the newly independent states and a new Yugoslavia, not to a partitioning of BiH, and was intended in the first place as a solution for Serbs in Croatia.[50] He testified that, at the time, he did not expect war to break out in BiH.[51] Still, accompanying the *Epoha* article was a detailed map showing Serb majority municipalities in BiH and Croatia, with the BiH municipalities that had opted in the November 1991 referendum to remain in Yugoslavia highlighted. This map became important to the Prosecution as evidence of pre-planning for a partition of BiH that corresponded with Serb territorial designs.

Formation of the RS, ethnic separation, and the commission of crimes in BiH

On 19 December 1991, Karadžić's SDS had issued "Instructions for the Organisation and Activity of the Organs of the Serb People in Bosnia and Herzegovina in Extraordinary Circumstances."[52] Prosecution witness Miroslav Deronjić, who was a high school teacher before the war and who served as the mayor of Bratunac between 1990 and 1992, participated in a meeting convened in Sarajevo and presided over by Karadžić, where the Instructions were conveyed.[53] The meeting brought together Serb mayors and deputies of the Bosnian Serb Assembly to discuss the establishment of Bosnian Serb governmental bodies in Serb-claimed municipalities. The Instructions laid out two variants: Variant A dealt with municipalities where Bosnian Serbs comprised a majority of the population and Variant B addressed municipalities where the Serb population was a minority. Karadžić explained the precise steps to be taken in order to establish Bosnian Serb control, in two phases of action described in the Instructions. The first required municipalities with a Serb minority to form Crisis Staffs and Serb Assemblies, after which a written order would be conveyed to implement the second phase. Deronjić testified that implementation of the second phase involved several steps, all of which were clearly taken to prepare for the use of force against non-Serbs in Variant B municipalities.[54]

The arming of Serbs in BiH by the JNA had begun as early as the spring of 1991, as intercepted telephone conversations between Milošević and Karadžić would later bring to light. And by early 1992, Milošević started to modify his position on BiH as it became clear that Bosnian Muslims could not be enticed into joining a new Yugoslav state. Discussing future strategy with Karadžić in the aftermath of the failed Convention for a Third Yugoslavia, in a conversation on 15 January 1992, Milošević instructed him to tell US Ambassador Warren Zimmerman that the Serbs still favoured keeping the whole of BiH in Yugoslavia, but with "an internal transformation."[55] What this meant was clarified in a call a few days later between Karadžić and Budimir Košutić, a law professor at the University of Belgrade and the Deputy Prime Minister of Serbia at the time. Discussing the political implications of the Vance Peace Plan for Serbs in Croatia and Bosnia, and for the future of Yugoslavia, Košutić emphasised that the talks should not establish permanent state borders or divide Serbs between Croatia and Bosnia, saying "we must not in any way deliver Krajina to Croatia."[56]

Though they interpreted responsibility for events differently, both the Prosecution and Defence contended that the war in BiH was triggered by fallout from the referendum on independence held in February 1992, which the vast majority of Bosnian Serbs boycotted and in which Bosnian Muslims and Bosnian Croats overwhelmingly voted for independence.[57] Based on those results, BiH had officially proclaimed its independence; but Bosnian Serbs treated the referendum and that proclamation as unconstitutional, arguing that they were one of the three constituent peoples of BiH and had not agreed to leave Yugoslavia.

The Defence contended that the war was triggered by ethnic violence against Serbs, and cited a killing at a Serb wedding party in the centre of Sarajevo in April 1992 as the spark that lit the fire. In fact, Milošević rejected the notion that Bosnian Serbs or Serbia had played any role in starting the conflict, laying all blame on Bosnian Croats, Bosnian Muslims, and the international community and saying it was "nonsensical to accuse the wrong side." The voice of Serbs in BiH had been ignored in breach of the tripartite "formula upon which Bosnia rests," he argued, claiming that Serbs had actually comprised more than a third of the population and had owned more than a third of the land, and yet had been dismissed.[58] Branko Kostić underlined this argument, pointing out that an overwhelming majority of Bosnian Serbs had voted in November 1991 to remain in Yugoslavia, before the Muslims and Croats decided to hold a referendum on independence.[59] He saw the referendum as a violation of the SFRY Constitution because Bosnian Serbs were constituent peoples of BiH and had not participated.[60] Nonetheless, the referendum legitimised the Bosnian application for independence and the EU and United States recognised BiH as an independent state in April 1992, with UN recognition following in May.[61] The Prosecution asserted that war broke out because Bosnian Serbs did not accept the results of the referendum and the independence of BiH but sought to seize Serb-claimed territories by force.

The Six Strategic Objectives and the war in BiH

Bosnian Serb protestations over the inequity of the February referendum ignored the organised boycott that had led to their abstention as well as the one-sidedness of their own 1991 November referendum, after which Bosnian Serb leaders had laid out plans for ethnic separation – well in advance of the vote for independence. According to Miroslav Deronjić, Karadžić's Instructions envisaged ethnic separation in non-Serb majority municipalities to follow a pattern in which irregular or "volunteer" units, such as Arkan's Tigers, for example, would enter a territory and instil fear in the population through the "killings of innocent people, widespread looting, robbing of private property, mainly from people of Muslim faith, resulting in the intimidation of the Muslim community and their fleeing from the area." Deronjić said some people initially saw the arrival of the JNA in Bosnia as positive and assumed that their presence would put a stop to the criminal activities of irregular units, but it soon became clear that the Army had "sided with the Serbs." He claimed that that JNA had even directly taken part in offensive actions in and around Bratunac, where he was mayor.[62]

Ethnic separation as an official policy of Bosnian Serb leadership was reinforced in a second key document adopted by the RS Assembly in May 1992 and known as the Six Strategic Objectives. It listed the following aims:

1 Establish state borders separating Serb people from the other two ethnic communities.
2 Set up a corridor between Semberija and Krajina.
3 Establish a corridor in the Drina river valley, that is, eliminate the Drina as a border separating Serb states.
4 Establish a border on the Una and Neretva rivers.
5 Divide the city of Sarajevo into Serb and Muslim parts and establish effective state authorities in both parts.
6 Ensure access to the sea for the Republika Srpska.[63]

The corridors referred to in the Six Strategic Objectives were where the gravest crimes occurred during the war. Their qualification as 'Serb-designated territories' on the basis of strategic significance and not ethnic makeup meant that these areas often had large non-Serb populations. Defence witnesses varied in their explanations for why territories without a Serb majority were included in Bosnian Serb plans and the suggestion that all three ethnic groups were simply engaged in a civil war failed to explain why the Bosnian government and its forces would need to fight for Bosnian territory at all.[64] BiH was an internationally-recognised sovereign state and its only credible motivation was to fight to preserve its integrity. Unlike the Serbs, the BiH government and its army were defending BiH, not fighting to claim any parts of it.

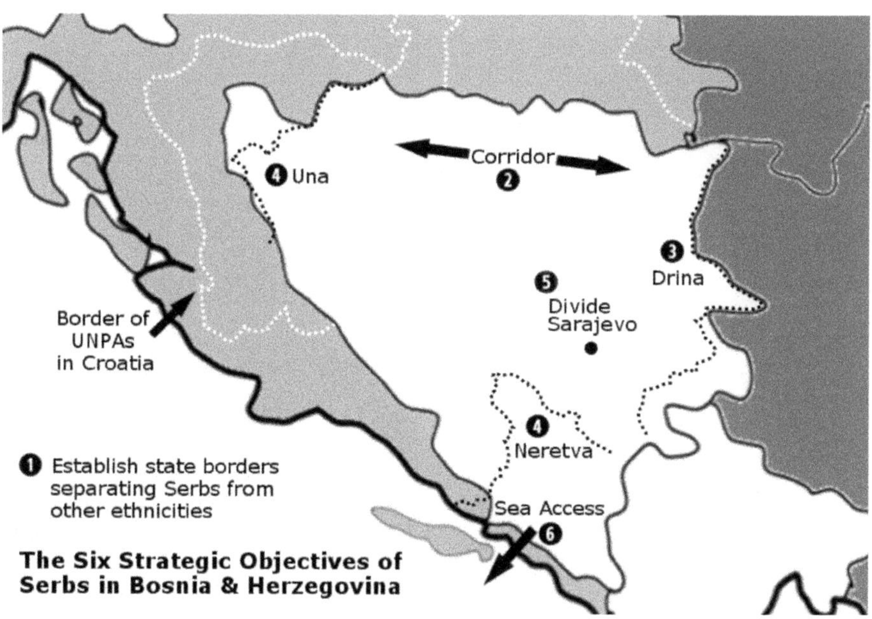

Map 5.1 The six strategic objectives of Serbs in Bosnia and Herzegovina (source: Data from "Decision on Strategic Objectives of the Serbian People in Bosnia and Herzegovina," 12 May 1992, Exhibit P451.12a).

In December 1992, UNPROFOR produced a map marking the de facto front line between Serb and BiH government forces after eight months of war.[65] This map strongly resembled the map that had accompanied the *Epoha* article in January of that year, and both maps were used by the Prosecution as evidence of a premeditated plan to capture large parts of BiH territory by force. The war, of course, continued beyond December 1992, but Serb forces had more or less achieved ethnic separation by that time, with approximately 70 per cent of BiH territory under their control. A comparison of the map depicting the Six Strategic Objectives (above) and the UNPROFOR map (below, with Serb-controlled areas marked in light grey) reveals why the Serbs pressed on with war even after taking so much territory; because several strategic objectives had yet to be achieved.

As 1993 began, the town of Brčko and the Bihać pocket still had to be captured in the Posavina corridor; the Drina corridor – Srebrenica, Žepa, and Goražde – was not yet taken; and the besieged BiH capital of Sarajevo was not yet divided. And the most important feature of each of these territories was their strategic value as corridors that would secure the contiguity of Serb territories, from Croatia through BiH to Serbia. Efforts to secure these corridors accounted for nearly four, deadly years of sieges – of Sarajevo, the Eastern Bosnian enclaves, and the Bihać pocket – by Bosnian Serb forces.[66]

Although Milošević never talked specifically about the Six Strategic Objectives, recordings of his participation at high-level meetings – including

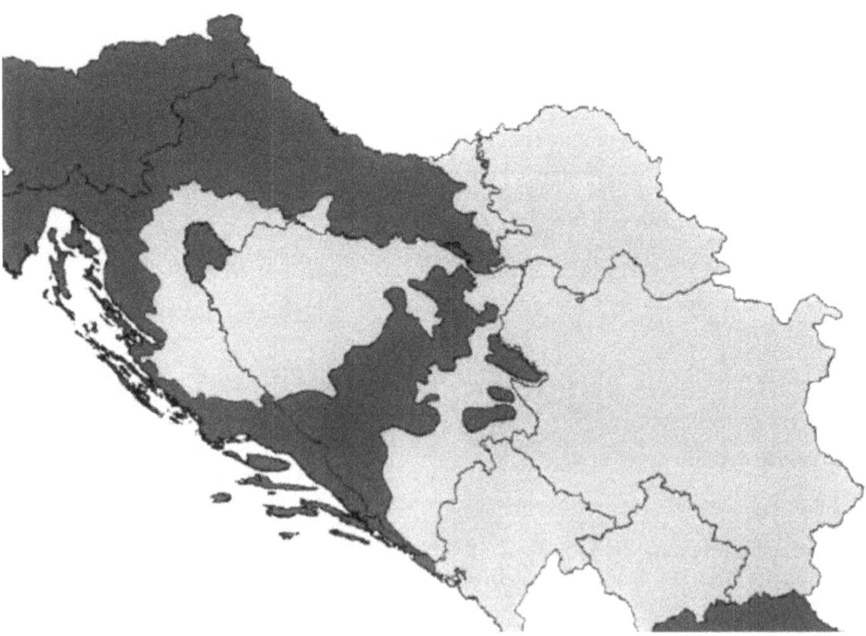

Map 5.2 Serb-controlled areas (light grey), per UNPROFOR, as of 30 December 1992 (adapted from Exhibit P809).

of the State Council for Harmonisation of Positions on State Policy – revealed his contributions to Serb policy in BiH and showed that he fully understood and supported Bosnian Serb strategic objectives. The Council for Harmonisation was formed by then FRY President Dobrica Ćosić in August 1992 and met until April 1993, one month before Ćosić's ouster from power, after which his successor Zoran Lilić ceased convening the Council.[67] But the Council met eight times and had included participants from the FRY and sometimes the RS and the RSK. Milošević, as President of Serbia, and Momir Bulatović, the President of Montenegro, were present at every meeting.[68]

Vladislav Jovanović, the Minister of Foreign Affairs for Serbia and later for the FRY, testified that the Council had been founded in order to harmonise the viewpoints of republic and federal organs in response to the performance of Prime Minister Milan Panić, who Jovanović claimed had acted independently and without understanding the issues.[69] Although Milošević had initially supported the appointment of Panić – a successful businessman who held both American and Serbian citizenship – their relationship cooled quickly; and as early as July 1992, Milošević banned Panić from attending sessions of the Supreme Defence Council.[70] But Panić remained in attendance at meetings of the Council for Harmonisation until he lost the December 1992 elections and returned to the United States. He was one of the few people willing to contradict Milošević, and his vocal challenges exposed discrepancies between the overt and covert plans of Serb leadership and shed light on Milošević's political designs.

Various strategic objectives of Serbs in BiH were discussed in Council for Harmonisation meetings in 1992. At the first session of the Council, held on 11 August, General Života Panić, Chief of Staff of the VJ, offered an assessment of the ongoing war in BiH, explaining that Serbia and the FRY were seen by the international community as the main culprits behind the conflict. He noted difficulties in controlling the Bosnian Serbs and expressed his disapproval over their choice of strategic goals, particularly their insistence on taking Sarajevo – to which Milošević expressed surprise that the capture of Sarajevo had not yet been renounced.[71] One week later, President Ćosić's political advisor Svetozar Stojanović criticised the Bosnian Serbs for not keeping only the parts of Sarajevo where they were a majority, as put forth in the fifth strategic objective, and instead besieging the entire city.[72] But Sarajevo, without qualification, played a central role in a number of documents that outlined designs for a future Republika Srpska. The RS Constitution of February 1992, for example, stated that RS territory consisted not only of Serb ethnic regions but also of territories where genocide had historically been committed against Serbs, and identified Sarajevo as the RS capital. The significance of this was obvious in retrospect, given that Sarajevo was under siege by Serb forces by early April.[73]

The Serb strategy of ethnic separation and international negotiations for BiH

Following the European Community's instruction that all remaining SFRY republics declare their intention to become independent by 23 December 1991, BiH and Macedonia had both opted for independence.[74] Serbia and Montenegro instead claimed the right to be the legal successor of the SFRY and maintain their status as republics; but the UN refused to recognise the continuity of the SFRY and compelled them to jointly request recognition, just as all SFRY successor states had. And so, together, Serbia and Montenegro formed the Federal Republic of Yugoslavia (FRY), the Constitution of which was adopted on 27 April 1992.

The Prosecution argued that Milošević had established the FRY with the expectation that the RSK and RS would someday join the Federation, and indeed, Article 2 of the FRY Constitution left a door open to "other member republics."[75] Moreover, from February 1992 onward, the constitutional frameworks of the RSK and the RS were aligned with that of the FRY for eventual unification.[76] Still, Defence witnesses denied the Prosecution's proposition that the aim to join 'Serb-designated territories' in BiH with Serbia had driven the Serb war effort there. Čedomir Popov, for instance, rejected the notion of Serbian hegemony by pointing out that the RS had remained a part of BiH after 1995.[77]

The international community made the lifting of sanctions subject to the FRY's recognition of all the newly independent former Yugoslav republics, and in particular of Croatia and BiH. This did not happen and the Prosecution asserted that the refusal of Yugoslav leaders to do so was due to their plans for a future state that would include parts of each of these countries.[78] FRY leaders discussed the recognition of these republics at the 18 August 1992 session of the Council for Harmonisation, where Milošević suggested that any recognition of Croatian independence ought to be conditional, applying only to parts of the country not under UNROFOR protection.[79] In a heated discussion of whether or not to recognise the state of BiH, Milošević again applied conditions.[80] But Prime Minister Milan Panić not only saw full recognition as a necessity, he insisted that it should be accompanied by a declaration that the FRY had no territorial aspirations in Bosnia. Arguing that the Bosnia problem would be resolved by the outcome of war waged among the three nations there, Milošević and his loyalists were willing to recognise the state but not its government.[81]

The Prosecution viewed Serb engagement in peace negotiations as having been motivated by the desire to maximise territorial gains and legitimise new borders with the blessing of the international community. The Defence presented the involvement of Serbia and the FRY in peace talks as proof of a genuine effort to stop the ethnic violence, though, and Defence witnesses claimed that Milošević and Serbia had been dedicated to peace and had demonstrated this by accepting all five peace proposals for BiH.[82] In truth, consenting to these proposals had not required any considerable concessions from Milošević; each plan, brokered by the international community, was based on a strategy of territorial separation that at least partially aligned with the objectives laid out by Serbs.

The Cutileiro Peace Plan and ethnic separation

The very first peace proposal for BiH – the Cutileiro Peace Plan, named after Portuguese Foreign Minister Jose Cutileiro – was an EU-sponsored plan developed with the hope that it could prevent the outbreak of war. It was based on a February 1992 working paper titled, "Statement of Principles for a New Constitutional Arrangement for BH," which put forward an independent Bosnia and Herzegovina consisting of three constituent units based upon ethnicity, but without territorial contiguity for any of the three ethnic groups and without an option to secede.[83] The Statement stipulated that BiH would maintain its existing borders and that sovereignty would be realised first through the republic and then through the constituent units, leaving BiH internally divided into three ethnic territories. The Defence position was that the equal but divided Bosnia envisaged in the Cutileiro Plan could have secured the peace; and in fact, Serbs had insisted on an ethnic division of BiH and Milošević had been prepared to recognise an independent Bosnia only on that basis.[84]

Karadžić favoured the cantonisation of BiH, also on an ethnic basis. At the peace conference in Lisbon that led to the Cutileiro Plan, he expressed that the Yugoslav crisis could be resolved quickly if a political agreement was reached for BiH that gave full sovereignty to all three constituent peoples in a confederation.[85] Still, Bosnian Serbs and Bosnian Croats both accepted the Cutileiro Plan, while Bosnian Muslim leadership opposed the division of BiH along ethnic lines. They preferred a unitary and multinational model and saw the Cutileiro Plan as endorsing fractures within BiH that would weaken the state, making it easier for Serbia and Croatia to carve it up at some later stage. Negotiations continued until August 1992 despite repeated failures to reach an agreement and amid an atmosphere of escalating violence.

After August, negotiations were overtaken by other events, although the Serbs maintained that their acceptance of the Cutileiro Plan exhibited their dedication to a peaceful resolution of the BiH crisis. But the peacemaking rhetoric of Serbs and their apparent cooperation during negotiations did not tell the full story. At an RS Assembly session on 18 July 1994, Karadžić said that the maps offered by Cutileiro had been completely unacceptable but were useful as the basis for future negotiations because they legitimised Bosnian Serb demands that BiH be divided on an ethnic basis and that they be awarded 45–50 per cent of Bosnian territory.[86]

Belgrade's view of the shortcomings and benefits of the Cutileiro Plan was revealed in an official note written by the Federal Ministry of Foreign Affairs, dated 9 August 1994, which indicated that all three parties in BiH had

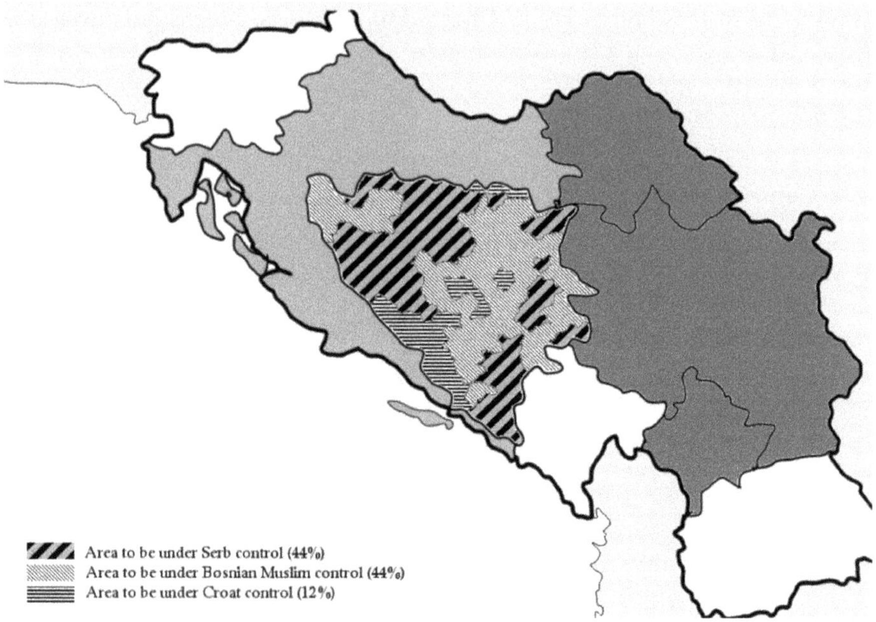

Map 5.3 The Cutileiro Peace Proposal (source: Data from the Geographic Information Systems Unit of the ICTY).

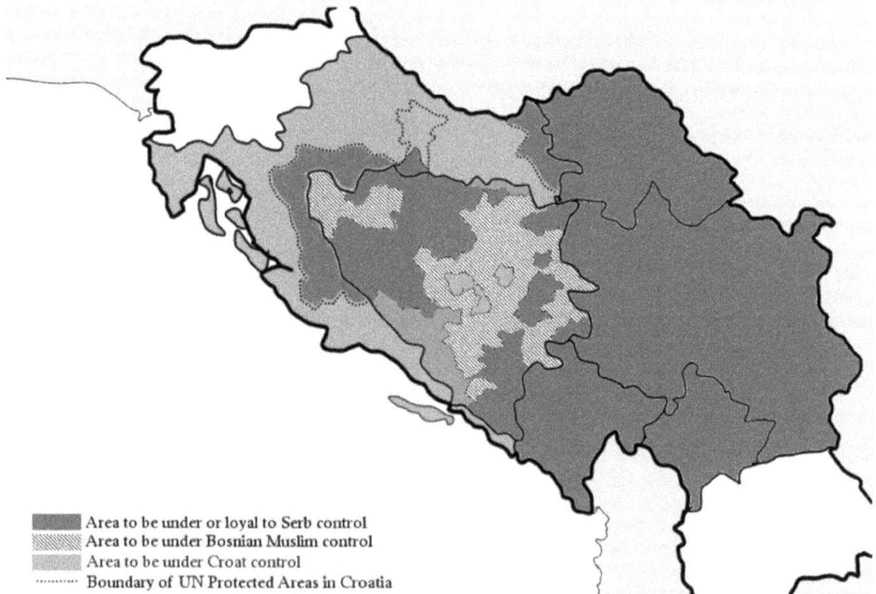

Map 5.4 De facto Serb control under the Vance Plan (for Croatia) and the Cutileiro Plan (for Bosnia) (source: Data from the Geographic Information Systems Unit of the ICTY).

initially accepted the plan but that Bosnian Muslims had later rejected it, which was said to have been their fatal mistake, not only because it led to war but because all later peace plans – with the exception of the Vance–Owen Plan – proved to be more favourable for the Serbs than for the Muslims. In conclusion, the note read that the "value of the Cutileiro Plan rested with [the fact] that the International Community . . . showed its readiness to legalise and verify" Serb-claimed territories in BiH. "Unfortunately," it continued, "even after the two-year war in this former Yugoslav republic, these borders have not been formally recognised."[87] For Serbs, the Cutileiro Plan was just a first stepping stone. Even in combination with the Vance Plan it did not secure optimal territorial contiguity, as corridors in the north and east of BiH would have remained predominantly Muslim.

The London Conference, August 1992

In July 1992, as negotiations on the Cutileiro Plan continued, foreign news media aired the first disturbing images of non-Serb detainees in Serb-run detention camps in northern Bosnia and the world finally saw the nature of the violence that was aimed at civilians in the conflict zone.[88] The international community called for an emergency conference in London, scheduled to take place in the last week of August. Political leaders from the Republics of Serbia and Montenegro and from the Federation discussed the Conference at the 18 August session of the State Council for Harmonisation. Federal Prime Minister Panić introduced reports about ethnic cleansing in BiH, and his boldness in addressing the topic unsettled other participants at the meeting. When Milošević interrupted, trying to stop him, Panić only became more emboldened. He said the UN had informed him that ethnic cleansing of Muslims had begun near Jajce and had asked him to put an end to it.[89] In blunt language, Panić called for FRY and Serbian leaders to stop the war, end the ethnic cleansing, and cut financing for the conflict in BiH. He said he was unpersuaded by the argument articulated by Bosnian Serbs that they were merely defending themselves.[90] Panić then confronted meeting attendees over Serb aggression in the name of "Greater Serbia," which he described as the idea that Serbs in Bosnia would "get rid of the others and join Serbia one day."[91]

With no unanimous position reached in the meeting, the Serbian delegation led by Milošević and the federal delegation led by Dobrica Ćosić and Milan Panić set off for the London Conference, where Milošević and Panić clashed publicly. In another session of the Council for Harmonisation held upon their return to Belgrade, Milošević expressed his displeasure over the outcome of the Conference, which had produced a final document he found unacceptable because part of the Conference conclusions called on the FRY to stop intervening outside its borders.[92] Indeed, the final London Conference text bound all participants to fulfil their obligations to: cease cross-border interventions; restrain the Bosnian Serbs from taking territory by force and expelling local populations; restore the civil and constitutional rights of people in Kosovo and Vojvodina and in Sanđak; influence the Bosnian Serbs to close their detention camps; comply with international humanitarian law and in particular the Geneva Conventions; and permit the return of refugees to their homes.[93] The wording of the text suggested that representatives of Serbia and Montenegro, and of the FRY, had agreed with the characterisation that the FRY was involved in interventions beyond its borders, in internationally-recognised Croatia and BiH. Milošević was furious about this, saying in the Council session that the final version of the document had not been discussed, and that if it had, the FRY delegation would have denied such implications.[94] Nonetheless, the London Conference introduced new rules for the conflict and established a new negotiating platform known as the International Conference on the Former Yugoslavia (ICFY), headed by US diplomat Cyrus Vance and his UK colleague David Owen.[95]

The Vance–Owen Peace Plan (VOPP) and ethnic separation

Negotiations led by Vance and Owen were held between the summers of 1992 and 1993. Talks opened with the presentation of five possible models for the Bosnian state; and a loose federation of ethnic units, which would not be geographically contiguous, prevailed.[96] But problems arose when the map had to be drawn, and it became clear that agreement on the shape of ethnic units would not be easily reached.

The Bosnian Serbs initially proposed a contiguous territory comprising 75 per cent of BiH for themselves, including everywhere Serbs were a majority and where they owned a majority of the land. Serbs also claimed areas where – according to their own calculations – they would have had a majority were it not for genocide committed during the Second World War.[97] In the end, the Vance–Owen Peace Plan (VOPP) map was a compromise that accounted for the territorial desires of all three parties. It divided BiH into ten provinces, the boundaries of which were drawn according to ethnic, geographic, historical, and other relevant factors, including economic viability. These provinces were not necessarily ethnically contiguous and, in some instances, their borders cut through municipal boundaries; and in an attempt to avoid ethnic labels, the provinces were assigned only numbers and place names.[98] Still, each ethnic group would have a majority in three of the ten provinces, and Sarajevo – where Muslims were the majority – would be assigned an "open" status, to be administered equally by the three constituent peoples.[99]

The Bosnian Croat delegation greeted the plan with enthusiasm, accepting the constitutional principles, the ceasefire agreement, and the map.[100] This wasn't surprising in light of the fact that the three proposed Croat-majority provinces were large territories that bordered on Croatia and extended into Central Bosnia.[101] The Bosnian government delegation opposed the map but accepted the constitutional and military principles of the proposal. The

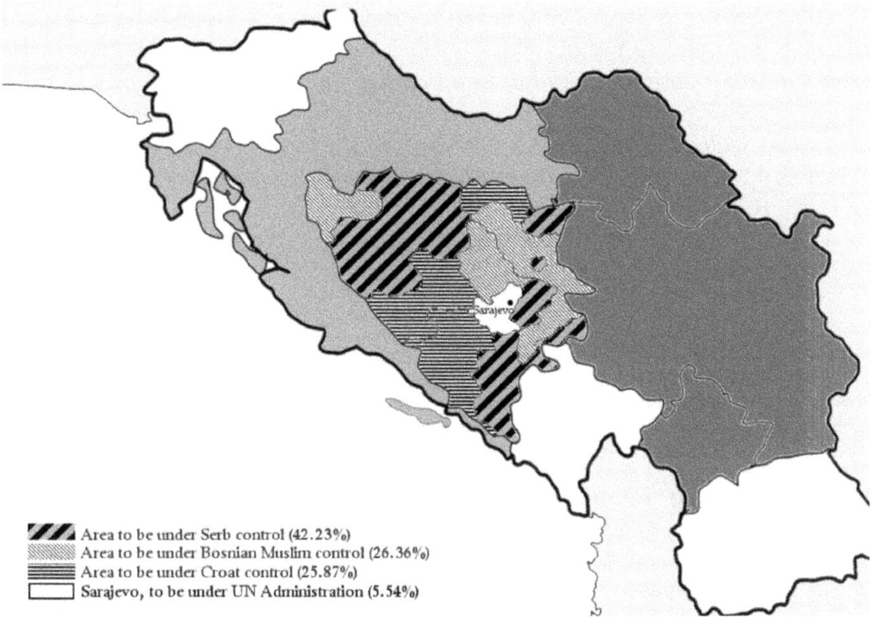

Map 5.5 Vance–Owen Peace Plan (source: Data from the Geographic Information Systems Unit of the ICTY).

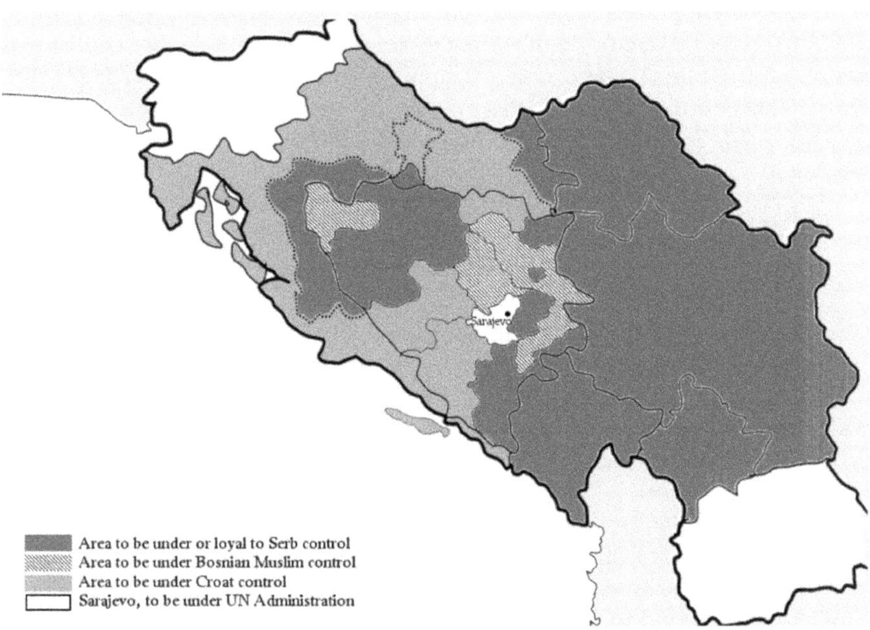

Map 5.6 De facto Serb control under the Vance Plan (for Croatia) and the Vance–Owen Plan (for Bosnia) (source: Data from the Geographic Information Systems Unit of the ICTY).

Bosnian Serbs expressed several reservations about the proposal, but accepted the map as a starting point, with the one major objection that it lacked the corridors they desired in order to guarantee the contiguity of Serb territories.[102] To that end, they insisted that the Posavina corridor in Northern Bosnia be widened; they demanded territory on the left bank of the Neretva River in Herzegovina; and they claimed the Muslim-majority municipalities of Foča, Rogatica, Višegrad, and Bratunac along with Skelani and Goražde – all for geostrategic reasons.[103] The negotiations failed to produce a settlement, and in fact seemed to incite greater violence.

Milošević and the VOPP negotiations

Two of the most interesting joint meetings of Bosnian Serb, Croatian Serb, and Serbian leaders took place at the sessions of the State Council for Harmonisation held on 9 and 21 January 1993, where an "all Serbian" position for the next round of VOPP negotiations in Geneva was discussed. These were the first meetings to which representatives from the RSK and the RS were invited, and they included leaders such as Karadžić, Momčilo Krajišnik, and General Ratko Mladić from the RS, and Assembly President Mile Paspalj and Prime Minister Zdravko Zečević from the RSK.[104] The Bosnian Serb strategy was focused on insisting on recognition of the RS and then integrating Serbia, Montenegro, the RSK, and the RS.[105]

Milošević supported RS leaders but stressed how important it was that the public accept de facto ethnic separation and the notion of "constituent peoples."[106] Dobrica Ćosić noted that the formation of a state or federation was a long-term objective that could be realised step-by-step.[107] Yet, Milošević felt Serbs had achieved unity and said the issue was simply how to legalise it:

> objectively and according to our relations, such as political, military, economy, cultural and educational, we have that unity. The question is how to get the recognition of the unity now, actually how to legalise that unity. How to turn the situation, which de facto exists and could not be de facto endangered, into being de facto and *de jure*?[108]

Milošević underlined that, without war, the goal of ethnic separation never would have been realised.[109]

Ethnic separation in BiH was discussed again in the next session of the Council, on 21 January 1992, when it was explicitly approved by political and military leaders from the FRY, the Republics of Serbia and Montenegro, and the RS and RSK. Serbian Foreign Minister Jovanović gave a long speech supporting the division of BiH, but he warned of the perception that "ethnic cleansings are palm-offs" and recommended using "the peacetime process of the exchange of inhabitants," which he claimed would occur if conditions in Bosnia became so unpleasant that non-Serbs chose to "rush off to their original provinces." After that, he said, "everything else is a matter of technique, including the break-up of Bosnia into three parts."[110] Jovanović predicted that ethnic homogenisation in BiH could be achieved in a couple of years.[111]

Because not all Serb territorial claims could be justified by the ethnic principle alone, Bosnian Serb leaders Momčilo Krajišnik and Nikola Koljević agreed that they should use economic arguments when negotiating peace proposal maps to avoid relinquishing any territory taken for geostrategic reasons.[112] But VJ Chief of Staff General Života Panić shared his concern that some of that territory – in Eastern Bosnia – was at risk of being lost militarily, and that stepping in to save it could risk the pretence that the FRY was not involved in the war in BiH. According to General Panić, Serbs there were disgracefully unprepared to fight and were "running away, leaving everything."[113] While he felt that "[VJ] manpower should not be allowed to go into foreign territory," he was determined to hold the strategic gains made by Serb forces and argued that "volunteers should be found, people who will rescue that part of the territory.... We must not lose control."[114]

Failure of the VOPP

With the leaders of the three ethnic groups in BiH unable to reach an agreement, Cyrus Vance and David Owen turned to Milošević for help in convincing the Bosnian Serbs to accept their Plan.[115] And Milošević was willing; the map they proposed essentially honoured ethnic separation and, though it did not establish territorial contiguity, he considered it a good start. He had grown uncomfortable with the international isolation that had resulted from UN sanctions on the FRY and calculated that, if he persuaded the Bosnian Serbs to accept the VOPP, the sanctions may be lifted. As a consequence of the pressure exerted by Milošević and by the international community, Karadžić signed the two remaining documents of the Vance–Owen peace agreement package – the Provincial Map and the Agreement on Interim Arrangements – on 2 May 1993. However, he stipulated that his signature would be invalidated if the RS Assembly did not accept the plan at its next session, later that week.[116]

At the RS Assembly session held on 5 and 6 May 1993, Bosnian Serb leadership debated the VOPP in the presence of federal and republican dignitaries as well as Greek Prime Minister Kosta Mitsotakis. Karadžić called the plan catastrophic, claiming it denied Bosnian Serbs their right to self-determination. Still, he concluded that the Assembly had to accept the VOPP or risk an attack by NATO forces.[117] As other Bosnian Serbs spoke in strong opposition to the plan, Milošević attempted to save the VOPP, speaking twice to urge its acceptance. He acknowledged that Serbs had only partly achieved their goal, which he said would yet be reached, but he said that it should not come at further cost to the people of Serbia, who had been faced with UN sanctions for almost a year.[118] Milošević did not convince

RS Assembly members, who decided to let the Bosnian Serb population vote directly on the VOPP in a referendum held from 15 to 16 May 1993 – when they voted overwhelmingly against its acceptance.[119]

Until that point, international officials tasked with addressing the conflict had prioritised a negotiated peace settlement over justice for victims, fearing that talks could be disrupted or may fall apart if Serb leaders were charged. But the idea of a UN court that would take on cases of mass atrocities had been floating around since August 1992.[120] If the RS Assembly had voted to adopt the VOPP, a UN war crimes court may never have come into being; but with the VOPP definitively failing and the war intensifying, the UN established the International Tribunal for the Former Yugoslavia (ICTY) on 25 May 1993 in Resolution 827, with a mandate to investigate and prosecute individuals accused of crimes committed in the conflicts that occurred in the break-up of the SFRY.

The Owen–Stoltenberg Peace Agreement, 1993

With all its attention put toward the peacemaking effort, and huge expectations vested in the VOPP negotiations, the international community and the UN had resisted pressure to engage in peace *enforcement*. Yet, as a result of the UN weapons embargo imposed in 1992, the official Army of BiH remained weak compared to the Serb and Croat forces, and became dependent on costly and clandestine weapons imports from countries such as Iran. That reality moved the Clinton Administration to push for a "lift-and-strike" initiative in 1993, by which the weapons embargo for the Bosnian Muslims was to be lifted and air strikes launched from outside the territory, to protect the Bosnian Muslim population from atrocities. The United States saw this as a way to attack Serb military positions from the air without engaging NATO troops on the ground; a task that would be left to the Bosnian Muslims, who would finally be adequately armed to do so. On 29 June 1993, a draft lift-and-strike Resolution was put before the UN Security Council that, if adopted, would have exempted BiH from the arms embargo so that it could exercise its "inherent right to self-defence." No country actually opposed the Resolution, but it was defeated by a majority of abstentions, and the UN weapons embargo remained in force until the end of the war in 1995.[121]

According to President Bill Clinton, the United States had trouble convincing European allies to adjust or end the weapons embargo, which made the Bosnian Muslims an easy target for well-equipped Serb forces. Clinton said European leaders used humanitarian grounds as public justification for the embargo, reasoning that more arms would mean more bloodshed, but privately objected to it on the basis that an independent BiH would be "unnatural" as the only Muslim-majority state in Europe. French President François Mitterrand apparently expressed quite bluntly that BiH did not belong in Europe, and some British officials spoke of a need to restore a

"Christian Europe." Clinton felt that they favoured the embargo precisely because it disadvantaged BiH.[122]

After the failure of the VOPP, Cyrus Vance was succeeded by Norwegian diplomat Thornvald Stoltenberg. Stoltenberg worked with David Owen in the next round of negotiations, in Geneva, which resulted by late August 1993 in the Owen–Stoltenberg Peace Proposal. It envisaged a division of Bosnia into a Serb part with 53 per cent of the territory, a Muslim part with 30 per cent, and a Croat part with 17 per cent. Predictably, the Bosnian Muslims rejected the plan and the RS Assembly accepted it unconditionally.[123] The Bosnian Croats also endorsed the Plan but demanded more territory. They had proclaimed the Croatian Republic of Herceg-Bosna on 28 August 1993, with its capital in Grude, in southwestern Bosnia.[124] The entity's new Assembly protested the territories given to Croats in the plan, which were the poorest in natural resources, were inhabited by less than 50 per cent of the Croats living in BiH, and lacked a single large city, advanced communications, and industrial, scientific, cultural, and religious facilities.[125]

The Washington Agreement, 1994

Two additional attempts to broker an agreement failed and, by the end of 1993, it was clear that completely new negotiating tactics were called for.[126] A turning point came in early 1994 with the active involvement of the

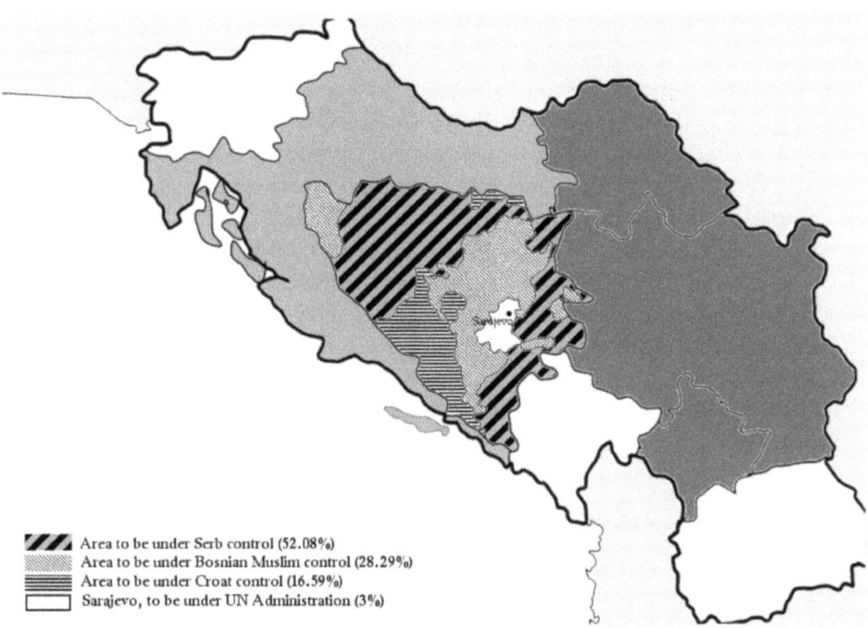

Map 5.7 Owen-Stoltenberg Peace Plan (source: Data from the Geographic Information Systems Unit of the ICTY).

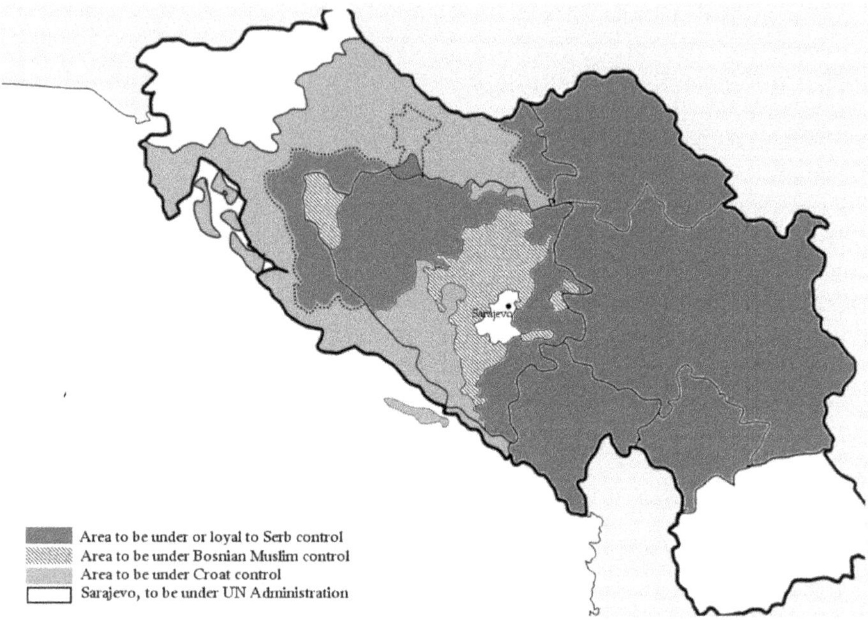

Map 5.8 De facto Serb control under the Vance Plan (for Croatia) and the Owen–Stoltenberg Plan (for Bosnia) (source: Data from the Geographic Information Systems Unit of the ICTY).

United States, which resulted in a pact between the Bosnian Muslims and Bosnian Croats known as the Washington Agreement. Signed on 1 March, it outlined a framework for a federation of majority Bosnian Muslim and Bosnian Croat areas in BiH and also contained a preliminary agreement for a confederation between the proposed federation and Croatia.[127] The Agreement made the creation of a Muslim-Croat Federation a milestone for future peace talks and it ended the war between Bosnian Croats and Bosnian Muslims for increased territory, which had been triggered by the VOPP maps and the conflict resolution model based on ethnic division of territories. This was an important moment in Croatian politics that gave an opportunity to President Tuđman to distance himself unequivocally from previous plans to partition BiH.

The Contact Group Plan, 1994

In April 1994, this fresh approach to negotiations spurred the formation of the Contact Group, consisting of representatives from the Russian Federation and the United States, with appointees from the ICFY, the UN, and the European Union – which was represented by France, Germany, and the UK.[128] In July, the Contact Group presented a proposed map of BiH to representatives from

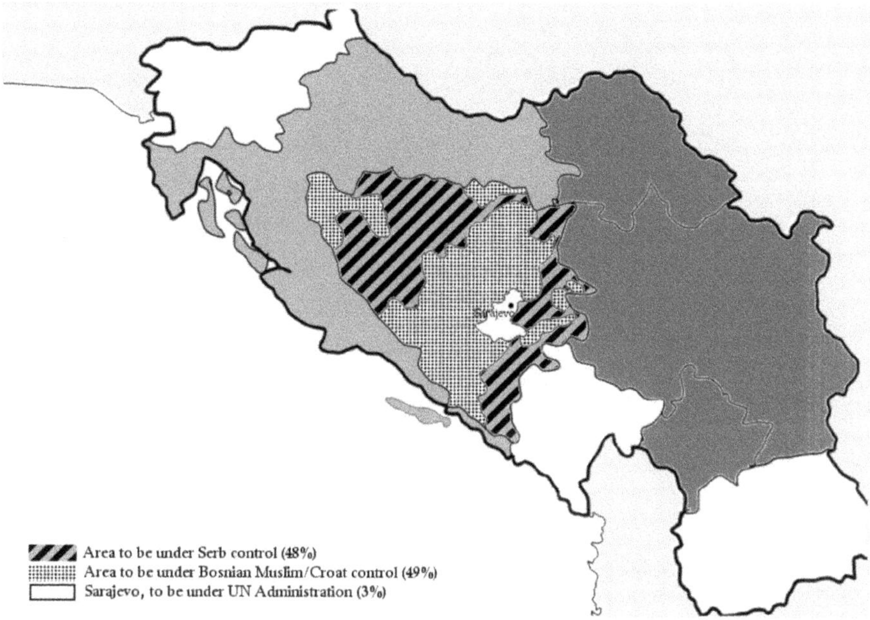

Map 5.9 Contact Group Peace Plan (source: Data from the Geographic Information Systems Unit of the ICTY).

the Bosnian Muslim-Croat Federation and to the Bosnian Serbs. Territorial distribution was nearly even, with 51 per cent going to the Federation and 49 per cent to a Bosnian Serb entity.[129] After significant pressure from the UN Security Council and the EU Council of Ministers, as well as from governments and NGOs worldwide, the Bosnian Muslim-Croat Federation finally accepted the map at the end of July. But, even with Belgrade lobbying on behalf of the Contact Group Plan, Bosnian Serb leadership did not accept it.[130]

At a Supreme Defence Council meeting in August, Milošević expressed frustration with the defiance of RS leaders who had rejected the Contact Group map. He explicitly cited a "unanimous policy" among Serbs in the FRY, BiH, and Croatia – revealing that Serb leaders had indeed shared a common plan, as alleged by the Prosecution. He credited that policy with having saved the FRY from war while still allowing Belgrade to aid in the creation of the RS and RSK, which led, he said, to the "ultimate goal … [of a] Republika Srpska, stretching over a half of the territory of the former Bosnia and Herzegovina!"[131] As Milošević saw it, the real victory of the war in BiH was that the international community was legitimising significant Serb territorial conquests, which he called "the maximum that many have never even dreamed of."[132]

Showing more pragmatism than politicians from the RS, Milošević appreciated how crucial it was that the Contact Group Plan be accepted; and he

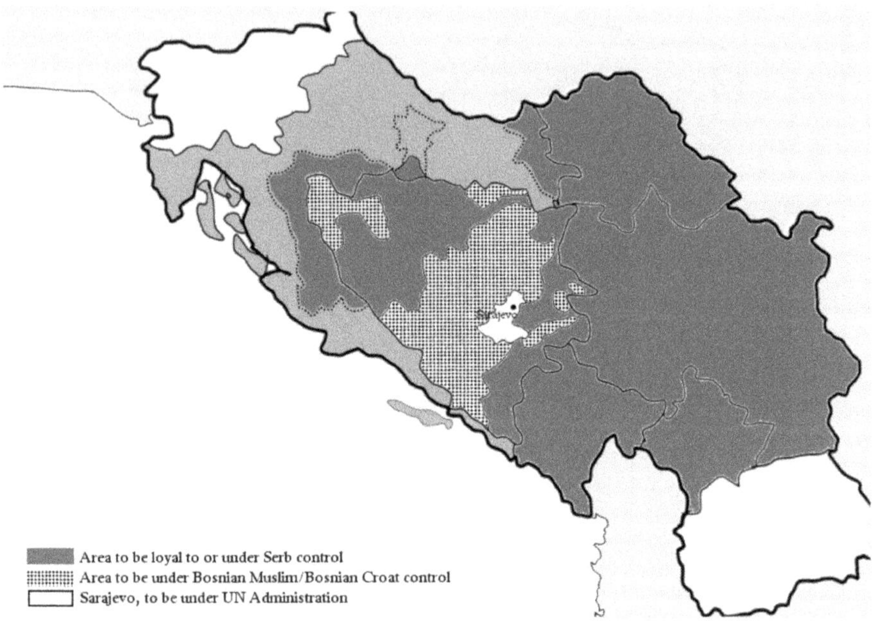

Map 5.10 De facto Serb control under the Vance Plan (for Croatia) and the Contact Group Plan (for Bosnia) (source: Data from the Geographic Information Systems Unit of the ICTY).

felt it was impossible to expect that the Serbs would be granted more than half of BiH territory.[133] He rebuffed the complaints of RS leaders that they could not accept the map because their territory was not compact enough. Milošević reminded them that:

> when you put together Serbia and Montenegro, then the whole eastern part is more than compact, because there is a territorial corridor … with territorial sovereignty permitting the passage of military convoys and everything else needed for a very compact western part.[134]

He warned that there were dangers in conquering too much territory, because the population-to-territory ratio could make it difficult to "cover it with settlers." Besides, he said, having taken half of Bosnian territory was an achievement to be proud of; adding, "Republika Srpska is twice the size of Montenegro, one-and-a-half the size of Slovenia, and it is being disputed as not big *enough*?!"[135] Milošević was not only satisfied with the amount of territory seized by Serbs, but he anticipated that it would be united with the FRY, noting that this would increase the size of Yugoslavia by one-fourth and the population by one-tenth. He said there was "an offer to create a military alliance with Russia" that would make the VJ the "single strongest army in the Balkans."[136]

Serbian and FRY leaders publicly promoted the Contact Group Plan and, under international pressure, ostensibly sanctioned Bosnian Serb leadership for rejecting it, by imposing a blockade on the RS. Analysts often use this as proof that Milošević did not control Bosnian Serb leaders and that his relationship with Karadžić and Mladić was dysfunctional and vitriolic.[137] It's true that there were periods of disagreement; but even in the most strained of times, aid from Belgrade kept reaching the Bosnian Serbs. The sanctions announced in August 1994 were never really imposed, as Milošević himself confirmed at a closed meeting held one year later when, responding to the suggestion by Bishop Irinej that the blockade be lifted, Milošević told him that the blockade was merely a formality and that "aid flows daily."[138] This was an important revelation in court, for leaders in Belgrade had insisted that they had ended their cooperation with the RS.

The evolving relationship between Milošević and Karadžić was marked by what some interpreted as a 'good cop/bad cop' dynamic, but it was more complex than that. And although Karadžić's stubbornness might have given the impression of a deeper rift, Milošević was always able to exercise ultimate control on the most important issues. The Prosecution articulated this in a court filing, saying that "Milošević and the Bosnian Serb leadership may have had their differences, but the evidence suggests that his influence over them – when he wanted to use it – continued through to 1995" and was rooted in his "total and absolute support of the RS economy and its war."[139] Karadžić himself had talked about his disagreements with Milošević in front of the RS Assembly in May 1994. He said that the most serious disputes had accompanied the Vance–Owen negotiations, but admitted that "without Serbia ... [we] would not have been able to make war."[140] Still, even if the relationship between Milošević and Karadžić had begun to deteriorate over time, the relationship between Milošević and Mladić had remained strong.[141]

The Srebrenica genocide: a precursor for Dayton Peace negotiations[142]

The Contact Group Plan represented a significant gain for Bosnian Serbs regarding territorial contiguity; but they still had reason to drag out negotiations while they created a situation on the ground that concretely assured them several crucial strategic areas that had to be seized by force, including Muslim-majority enclaves in Eastern Bosnia. By mid-1993, the vaguely-defined term "ethnic cleansing" had entered the lexicon of official texts along with descriptions of other crimes such as "forcible expulsions" and "mass killings."[143] It was an important development when UNSC Resolution 819, issued on 16 April 1993, included the term "genocide" for the first time in condemning the actions of Serb paramilitary units in Eastern Bosnia and required Serbia and Montenegro – as the FRY – to take all measures within its power to prevent it.[144] Resolution 819 also proclaimed Srebrenica a UN-protected Safe Area and tasked UNPROFOR with regulating the humanitarian situation in the enclave. Some countries, including the United States, supported Resolution 819 only on the condition that the original term "Safe Haven" was replaced by "Safe Area," because a Safe Haven presupposed full military protection for which 15,000 ground troops would be needed while a Safe Area was simply assumed to insure a "certain degree of security," the level of which was never explained in detail, but should have been.[145]

UN debates on the status of Srebrenica led to a Security Council fact-finding mission under the leadership of Ambassador Diego Arria of Venezuela, at the end of April 1993. Ambassador Arria testified as a Prosecution witness and recounted that he and his UN colleagues had witnessed what resembled an "open air prison." Arria described Srebrenica as a place where "slow motion genocide" had been taking place and said the suffering of the people in the area took the Mission by surprise; they were shocked by what they witnessed on the ground and realised that the situation had never been accurately presented to the UNSC.[146] The Mission recommended that the UN proclaim five other places in BiH as UN Safe Areas as well, all of which were under threat of being taken over by Serb forces. Upon their return to New York, UN Resolution 824 of 7 May 1993 added Goražde, Žepa, Tuzla, Sarajevo, and Bihać to the list of UN Safe Areas in Bosnia, with the intent to protect civilians and obstruct Serb strategic designs.[147] Bihać, Srebrenica, Goražde, and Sarajevo were of particular strategic importance to Serbs in achieving territorial contiguity.

In the months and years that followed, it became obvious that the proclamation of Srebrenica as a Safe Area did not protect civilians there from the attack of Serb forces. And in the summer of 1995 – despite seeking refuge at the UN compound six kilometres northwest of Srebrenica, in Potočari – women and children were separated from the men and older boys by Serb armed forces, in the presence of Dutch UN peacekeepers.[148] Neither the UN's diplomatic response nor the presence of peacekeepers on the ground prevented the only official genocide in Europe since 1945, when the execution of some 8,000 Bosnian Muslim men followed the Serb takeover of the enclave.[149]

Evidence presented at the ICTY pertaining to the takeover of Srebrenica was summarised in the 16 June 2004 Half-Time Judgement, delivered at the end of the Prosecution part of the case. It described the sequence of events leading to the fall of the enclave as having started with Radovan Karadžić's "Directive for Upcoming Operations," addressed to the Command of the 1st Krajina Corps and including specific details regarding the engagement of the Drina Corps, which operated in Eastern Bosnia. The Directive called for "well-thought-out combat operations [that] create an unbearable situation of total insecurity with no hope of further survival or life for the inhabitants of Srebrenica and Žepa."[150] Prosecution witness General Rupert Smith, who was the Commander of UNPROFOR at the time of the takeover of Srebrenica, testified that the Directive gave instructions to "squeeze and compress, both physically and in terms of a way of life, the existence of those enclaves."[151] Further, the Directive stated that if UNPROFOR left the Safe Areas, "the Drina Corps command shall plan an operation … with the task of breaking up and destroying the Muslim forces in these enclaves and definitively liberating the Drina valley region,"[152] which General Smith understood to mean that, if the UN withdrew, the enclaves would be "done away with."[153]

On 6 July 1995, Serb forces launched an attack on Srebrenica that lasted five days. Bosnian Muslim forces present in the area, many of whom had surrendered their weapons to peacekeepers, did not have the military capacity to resist.[154] On 11 July, Srebrenica fell. As he toured the town afterward, VRS Commander Ratko Mladić called it "Serbian Srebrenica" and said Serbs had finally taken "revenge on the Turks."[155]

After Srebrenica

There was confusion within the international community about how to react to the fall of Srebrenica. French President Jacques Chirac offered the most radical solution, suggesting that Srebrenica be regained by force and returned to the Muslims. The question was who would take the lead in doing so. British Foreign Secretary Malcolm Rifkind had repeated on several occasions that UN forces in BiH were not there to take up arms. And the Americans, who backed the French initiative in principle, were not willing to assist with material support.[156] Many of Chirac's colleagues, as well as the media, interpreted his initiative as political grandstanding that was never meant to go beyond rhetoric.[157]

In Srebrenica, the deportation of Bosnian Muslims began immediately after Serb forces entered the town on 11 July. The next day, the UN Security Council passed Resolution 1004, demanding that Serbs suspend their offensive and allow humanitarian assistance to reach civilians in the region.[158] But the Resolution did not inspire any response on the ground and the presence of UN peacekeeping forces was inadequate to prevent mass atrocities; and within weeks, satellite images disclosed traces of fresh burial sites and mass graves in the vicinity of the enclave.[159] On 10 August, UN Resolution 1010 cited alleged breaches of international humanitarian law and many reports of missing persons from the Safe Areas. It demanded that the Bosnian Serbs permit the UNHCR and the ICRC to enter both Srebrenica and Žepa to register detainees, and that Serb forces guarantee these detainees' safety. But Serb forces had already been engaged for weeks in mass executions of Bosnian Muslim men and boys, and in covering up these crimes.[160]

By August 1995, the United States had taken the lead in negotiations and, for the first time, an aggressive negotiation style was matched by military threat: if Serb artillery forces did not withdraw, NATO would strike. This eventually led to Operation Deliberate Force, in which NATO bombed Bosnian Serb positions, pressuring the Serbs to either accept US conditions for a political settlement of the crisis or risk military defeat.[161] The bombardment lasted two-and-a-half weeks, which was long enough to prove to Serb forces that the international community was serious and long enough to convince Milošević that he must compel the Bosnian Serbs to agree to negotiations – which he did.[162]

In court, both Prosecution and Defence witnesses who held high-level positions in the FRY government during the fall of Srebrenica made distinctions between the moment they claimed to have first heard about the fall of the enclave and the moment they claimed to have learned about the atrocities committed during and after its takeover. In this way, they rationalised their own inaction to prevent the killings, and that of Belgrade.[163] Defence witness Vladislav Jovanović said he learned of the fall of the enclave on 13 July and testified that he met with Milošević immediately afterward to discuss it. According to Jovanović, Milošević appeared very surprised and angry to hear the news, especially because he had reportedly tried to dissuade General Mladić from completing the takeover.[164] Indeed, David Harland – who served as a Political Advisor to the Commander of UNPROFOR and was Head of Civil Affairs for the UN in BiH from 1993 to 1998 – claimed that Milošević had met with Mladić in Belgrade just four days before Srebrenica fell.[165] However, General Rupert Smith testified that Milošević had also received a coded cable on the day of the takeover, which informed him that "the BSA [VRS] is likely to separate the military-age men from the rest of the population."[166]

According to General Smith, Milošević met with Mladić just four days *after* the enclave fell, on 15 July.[167] Yet, the killings in and around Srebrenica went on for weeks, and Belgrade took no action to stop them. On the contrary, as events in Srebrenica increasingly occupied international diplomatic, military, and political discussions, Serb forces advanced to seize nearby Žepa. The UNSC discussed the situation in Žepa, including a reference to a Contact Group statement. This somewhat routine discussion could easily be interpreted as showing that the UNSC *nominally* took the position of the Muslims seriously, but nothing more. Such an interpretation would come to be significant for decisions made by the top political and military leadership in Belgrade.[168] They were led to assume – accurately – that nobody was going to make any fuss about Žepa. Nobody did at the time. Žepa fell on 25 July; ethnic cleansing of the area followed unimpeded.[169]

The Republika Srpska and war-related losses

Maps depicting the ethnic composition of BiH before and after the war were compelling visual evidence of the gravity of crimes committed in territories that later became part of the RS. A number of municipalities with an absolute or relative Muslim majority on the 1991 map (on the left) were seized in order to achieve Serb strategic goals, and many that had been predominantly Muslim before the war – but had a Serb majority on the 1998 map – featured in the Bosnia indictment against Milošević as the sites of mass atrocities.

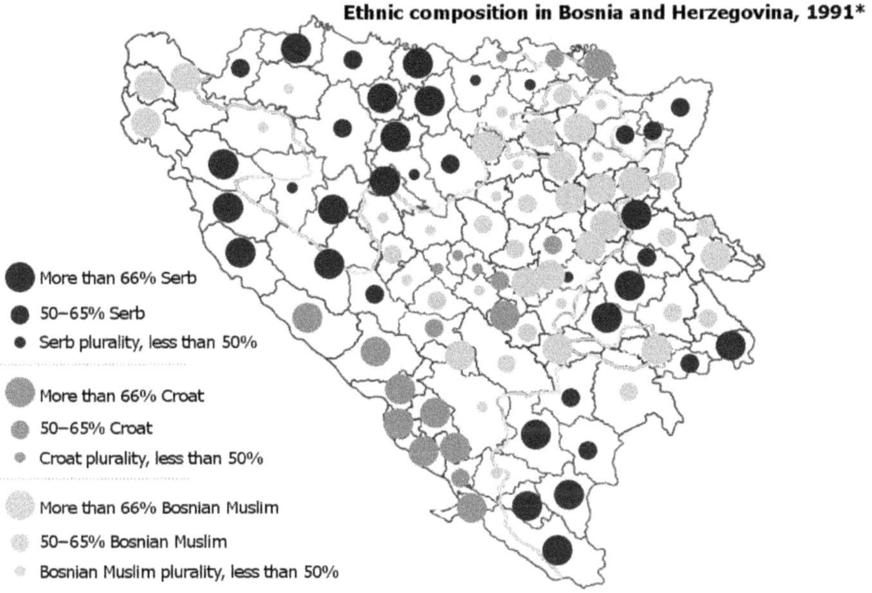

Map 5.11 Ethnic distribution in BiH before the war (1991) (source: ICTY OTP's Demographic Unit).

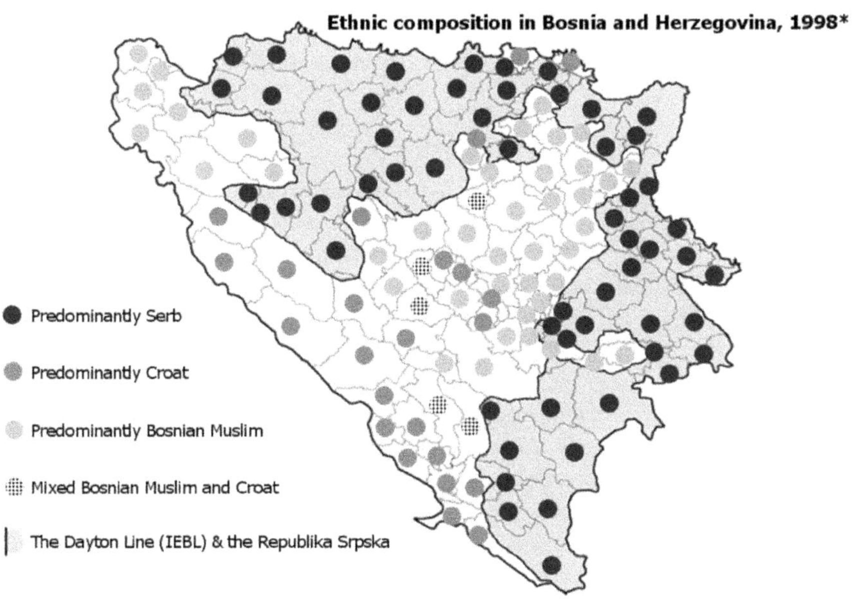

Map 5.12 Ethnic distribution in BiH after the war (1998) (source: ICTY OTP's Demographic Unit).

This changing ethnic distribution in BiH as a consequence of the war has been among the most damning proof of the planned nature of the crimes committed by Serb forces. In Srebrenica, for example, of 29,198 inhabitants in 1991, 73 per cent were Muslim; but in 1997, the total population was only 7,442 and just seven people were Muslim.[170] Demographic evidence presented at the trial showed that similarly drastic population shifts occurred throughout the part of BiH that became the Republika Srpska. In 1991, 344,803 Muslims lived in that territory, but by 1997–1998, only some 2 per cent of the pre-war total remained.[171] Preliminary results of Bosnia's 2013 census, the first official census since 1991, indicate that the population of Muslims has increased considerably in Eastern Bosnia since the immediate post-war period, to over 190,000. And in Srebrenica, of 15,242 inhabitants, over 8,000 are now Muslims.[172] Still, after nearly two decades of NGO- and government-sponsored refugee return efforts, returnees continue to face intimidation and even violence, especially in the case of 'minority returns' – in which people who now represent minorities come home to their communities of origin.[173]

Estimates of numbers of deaths due to the war in BiH range from about 25,000 to 329,000. For the Milošević trial, the OTP's Demographic Unit arrived at an estimate of 102,622 war-related deaths, of which 47,360 (46 per cent) were military and 55,261 (54 per cent) were civilian victims. This figure, measuring "war-related" deaths, includes not only those killed and missing, but those who died due to harsh living and working conditions during the war. Still, a minimum number of those killed by direct war actions is 67,530; of this number, 40,948 were military and 26,582 were civilian, and 45,980 were Muslims, 12,642 were Serbs, 5,629 were Croats, and 3,279 were "others."[174]

Obscured evidence about Srebrenica crimes

The fall of Srebrenica was preceded by preparations that warned of events to come and should have alarmed international observers. A large number of empty buses moved from Serbia to Eastern Bosnia, for example, for later use in transporting civilians to killing sites in Bosnian Serb-controlled territory, sometimes as far as 150 kilometres away from Srebrenica. The intelligence capabilities of some countries have left lingering questions about whether they, or the UN, received information beforehand that the takeover was likely; and a lack of evidence for the period before or during the weeks of mass atrocities has led to speculation about why details of political and military activity were suppressed.

The UN has no intelligence capacity of its own and depends on the services of its member states, especially the United States and Canada, and to a lesser extent the UK.[175] Various sources have confirmed the existence of US intelligence on the Srebrenica genocide, including recordings of intercepted telephone conversations between FRY and RS military leaders from 17 June 1995.[176] And, the Dutch Institute for War Documentation (NIOD), investigating the role of Dutch UN peacekeepers in the fall of Srebrenica, noted that a meeting took place between Carl Bildt – who succeeded Lord David Owen as the EU representative in negotiations – and former US Vice President Al Gore, along with two others, on or about 3 August 1995 at the White House. In this meeting, intercepted communications between Milošević and General Mladić relating to the "fall of the Safe Area" were specifically referred to and read from by Gore.[177]

At the time, the United States officially denied the existence of intercepted communications related to Srebrenica through a statement made by then CIA Director John Deutch.[178] But records of an SDC session held in August 1995, which were unavailable to the United States when Deutch issued his denial, made it clear that Milošević and Mladić had spoken "on the occasion of the attack on Žepa and Srebrenica," as Milošević referred to one of their conversations himself.[179] One plausible reason for the official disavowal by the United States of intelligence that indicated the intent of Serb forces to commit crimes, or which revealed that crimes were in process, may be the fact that knowledge of such intelligence exposes states to possible allegations of complicity in genocide, since it is the duty of any and every of state to prevent that crime.[180]

The "swap of territories" strategy

For many observers, the fall of the Safe Areas in Eastern Bosnia was not unexpected; and from at least June 1995, the recognition that they could not be defended had been expressed publicly. Calling Srebrenica's future "gloomy," US diplomat Sandy Vershbow had said that international negotiators were seriously considering a swap of territories – i.e. Eastern Bosnian enclaves would be given to Bosnian Serbs in exchange for larger territories elsewhere to be given to Bosnian Muslims, in order to make the map "more coherent."[181] Milošević had actually talked as early as August 1994 about an exchange of territories, at a meeting of the SDC. He had displayed detailed knowledge of the ethnic composition of BiH, citing Ozren, Doboj, and "perhaps Derventa and some other parts" as necessary Serb gains, which he felt "could easily be acquired in negotiations between the two sides in exchange for some vital features that the Muslims need … [such as] Vogošća, Ilijaš and Hadžići."[182] At another SDC session one month later, Milošević commented on the importance of Sarajevo and several other strategic areas to the "swap of territories" approach he believed the United States would endorse. In order to "correct the maps," he explained, the Americans would "insist on reciprocity for the eastern enclaves and on widening of the corridor." He said the notion of Republika Srpska military leaders that they could not give up any "land that a Serbian soldier acquired with his rifle" was "unacceptable to the international community."[183]

Speaking in August 1995 to the RS Assembly, Radovan Karadžić also hinted at a territorial exchange. He boasted that the RS had forcibly incorporated many areas where Serbs were not previously the majority and indicated that these territories may be expendable in negotiations. But he warned that areas where Serbs had always been a majority, which he called "our traditional territories," had to be retained.[184] He continued:

> Don't let this get around, but remember how many of us there were in Bratunac, how many in Srebrenica, how many in Višegrad, how many in Rogatica, how many in Vlasenica, in Zvornik, etc. Due to strategic importance they had to become ours, and practically no one is questioning it anymore.[185]

And indeed, in the aftermath of the summer of 1995 – during which Srebrenica and Žepa fell in BiH and Knin Krajina fell in Croatia – the international community appeared keen to accept military conquests as the basis for a final peace settlement.

Among the most telling statements reflecting how the fall of Bosnian enclaves was viewed by international negotiators came from then US Secretary of State Warren Christopher, who said that their takeover had "created a circumstance that in some ways, tragically enough, makes the shape of the peace simpler than it would have been in the past."[186] Christopher also talked in similar terms about the recapture of the RSK in August 1995 by Croatian Armed Forces in Operation Storm and the subsequent exodus of Croatian Serbs from the area. He said that these developments were "simplifying matters," implying that ethnic homogeneity was necessary in the contested territories in order to resolve the conflict and achieve peace.[187]

In an SDC session held in the wake of Operation Storm, Serbian and FRY leaders were extremely judgemental of how weak and inadequate they felt the defence of Knin had been. RSK Minister of Defence Milan Martić had ordered an evacuation of the civilian population one day before Croatian forces started Operation Storm; and the timing of the order implied that the abandonment of the RSK and the evacuation of the Serb population were prearranged.[188] Milošević sharply criticised the conduct of RSK leaders, especially Martić, for having compelled civilians to leave the Krajina and for the fact that the SVK had not engaged with Croatian forces at the front line. He claimed that Belgrade would have been prevented from coming to the rescue of Croatian Serbs, even if the VJ "had done a stupid thing on that day and decided to help them," alleging that SVK columns "blocked all the roads while fleeing together with the population." Milošević did not shy away from inferring that SVK and RSK leadership had utterly capitulated, asking why the FRY would "defend those territories, which they left running away as fast as they could?!"[189] Still, when Milošević did nothing to reverse the Serbs' military defeat in the RSK, his inaction further fuelled rumours that he had in fact agreed to a swap of territories.

The Dayton Peace Agreement

The final round of peace negotiations for Bosnia took place between 1 and 21 November 1995, in Dayton, Ohio. The principle negotiators were Alija Izetbegović, President of BiH; Franjo Tuđman, President of Croatia; and Milošević, President of the Republic of Serbia, on behalf of the Bosnian Serbs. According to US General Wesley Clark, Milošević's knowledge of BiH terrain and his influence over RS leaders were apparent during negotiations. In carving out the map of Sarajevo, for instance, Milošević decided which parts of Sarajevo he was willing to return to the Federation of BiH, which parts should be given to the RS, and where a sovereign road should be allowed between Sarajevo and the last and only remaining Bosnian Muslim enclave of Goražde in Eastern Bosnia, without consulting anyone from the RS.[190] And when the time came, Milošević signed the Dayton Agreement as a guarantee, promising to produce the signatures of Bosnian Serbs later, which indeed he did.[191]

The negotiations resulted in a final map that divided BiH into two entities: the Bosnian Muslim-Croat Federation was awarded 51 per cent of the territory and the RS was granted 49 per cent. In other words, the Dayton Peace Agreement accepted the situation on the ground as a *fait accompli*, cementing Serb military gains as the basis for an internal partition of BiH and validating, for some Serbs, the legitimacy of the war's objectives. But another side effect

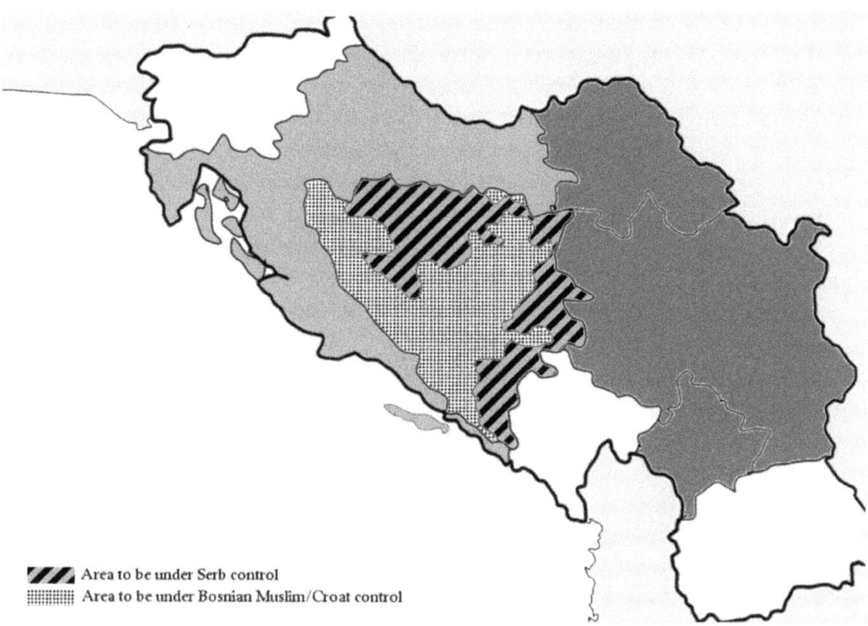

Map 5.13 The Dayton Agreement (source: Data from the Geographic Information Systems Unit of the ICTY).

of Dayton was the rather positive spotlight it shone on Milošević as the principle negotiator for all Serbs.

In court, General Clark testified that the Bosnian Serbs had allowed Milošević to represent them in Dayton because he held such considerable de facto power over them; and that this power meant Milošević had not been blind to the actions and operations of the RS. Clark recalled a meeting he attended with Milošević, together with US envoy Richard Holbrooke and others, on 17 August 1995. When Holbrooke asked Milošević whether he should deal with Milošević or directly with the Bosnian Serbs, Milošević said the terms of an agreement should be given to him so that Serbians could vote on it in a referendum, asserting that the Bosnian Serbs would not disobey the will of the Serbian people.[192] By then it was known that General Mladić's forces had committed crimes in Srebrenica.[193] During the conversation – Clark claimed – Milošević admitted knowing about Mladić's plan in advance.[194] His admission stunned the Americans.[195]

The transformative value of the evidence on Milošević's de facto and *de jure* power during the conflict in BiH

SDC records as evidence of individual and state responsibility

Notes from Supreme Defence Council sessions (SDC) were first made available to the OTP by Belgrade authorities in August 2003, but only for inspection by Prosecution researchers. After they were assessed to be relevant, an official request for all SDC records was made, and when the documents were handed over in December 2003, the Prosecution plan was to tender a large portion of these records into evidence through General Momčilo Perišić – who was interviewed as a potential Prosecution witness in late 2003 and early 2004. In the end, General Perišić was not called to testify and the SDC records were therefore tendered as evidence as part of a report that analysed their content.

Minutes were provided for almost all SDC sessions, but stenographic notes were not provided for 21 of those sessions.[196] It appeared that in 17 of those 21 meetings, for reasons that remain unclear, no official stenographic recordings had been made at all. Zoran Lilić, the presiding member of the SDC from 1993 to 1997, testified that this was usually at the initiative of Milošević, who felt some topics were too sensitive to be heard by an "outsider" (referring to the personnel tasked with recording the meetings on audio tape and making stenographic notes).[197] Notably, most of the missing records were from 1995 – the year when atrocities were committed in Srebrenica and the Serbs worked to consolidate territorial gains in BiH. Eleven of the 18 sessions held in 1995 were apparently not recorded by a stenographer.

SDC documents and protective measures

Negotiations between the Prosecution's trial team and Belgrade over terms for the handover of SDC records delayed their procurement by the OTP. Belgrade was willing to relinquish the notes of Council sessions only if Serbian officials were allowed to redact parts that they estimated were a risk to "vital state interests" because of their potential use in the genocide lawsuit filed by BiH against Serbia at the International Court of Justice (ICJ). The OTP's trial team rejected Serbia's request for protective measures, arguing that the transparency of the legal process could not, and should not, be compromised, especially not in order to protect Serbian national interests in another lawsuit before another UN court. In December 2002, the trial team decided to pursue the Rule 54 *bis* procedure – by which the Court can issue an order compelling states to produce documents – and submitted its request on 6 May 2003, clarifying the position of the OTP that ICTY proceedings against Milošević should in no way be compromised by "collateral interests in the ICJ case."[198]

A court hearing was scheduled for 3 June and the OTP's team was confident of success; but on 24 May, contrary to the written recommendation of Prosecutor Nice – who was in charge of the trial – ICTY Chief Prosecutor Carla del Ponte wrote to Serbian Minister of Foreign Affairs Goran Svilanović and conceded to the protection of selected parts of SDC documents.[199] The conditional acquisition of SDC materials brought attention to an unresolved question at the ICTY, namely: What is the value of the evidence in mass atrocities trials if it remains hidden from the public? Obviously, material sought by the OTP was important to the Tribunal's goal of delivering final verdicts, and one could reason that as long as judges had access to it, there should be no objection to that evidence being protected from public view. Yet, arguably, evidence from trials that deal with political violence and mass atrocities should especially be accessible to the public, regardless of whether final judgements are reached.

What emerged from the process of acquiring the SDC records was that dual, and conflicting, approaches – on the one hand legal and on the other political – were shaping ICTY prosecutions. Proponents of the legal approach advocated transparency in court proceedings and a focus on public access to the evidence, insisting that states must cooperate with ICTY rules and that every effort must be made to avoid applying protective measures to evidence. Prosecutor Nice fell into this camp and saw no legal basis for del Ponte's letter to Svilanović. He considered any direct deals with Belgrade not only unnecessary but potentially counterproductive, because they could have created unintended precedents that would have affected the acquisition of documents in the future.[200] But del Ponte pursued the political approach, with the direct support of a number of diplomatic, political, and public relations aides within the OTP who had been directly involved in the creation of the OTP's cooperation policy. They argued that some documents would never have been handed over to the ICTY if not for negotiations conducted behind closed doors.[201]

The fact that Serbia had conditioned their submission of requested documents may have remained buried inside the OTP, except that public interest was triggered by the February 2007 ICJ Judgement in *BiH* v. *Serbia and Montenegro*. The ICJ judges determined that genocide had indeed been committed in BiH but that Serbia was not responsible for its commission; yet they made this decision without access to the complete SDC records and still held Serbia responsible for failing to *prevent* genocide under the Genocide Convention.[202] The next month, an article in the *New York Times* prompted heated public debate over the protective measures that had been applied to SDC records.[203] Carla del Ponte confirmed to the author of the article that she had written to Svilanović in May 2003 and said that, in the end, she had agreed to the protections because the documents were so important to the conviction of Milošević.[204]

Although it is possible that the deal with Belgrade was helpful in bringing requested documents into the courtroom, del Ponte's consent to protections had been premature. The matter was to be litigated and her choice to deal with Belgrade when legal possibilities had not yet been exhausted led to the impression among many observers that the ICTY lacked respect for transparency and the administration of justice, as well as for the right of victims and the public to know what had happened and how. Further, questions that surrounded the deal benefitted Serbia the most, for they led to heightened criticism of the ICTY and meant that parts of the SDC records were kept from use as evidence in the ICJ lawsuit.

Lifting the protection of SDC records and the legacy of the Perišić judgement

In 2006, Momir Bulatović published his book *Unspoken Defence*, in which he recounted the time he had spent with Milošević as he prepared for testimony as a Defence witness. The book referred to various documents Milošević had planned to tender during Bulatović's testimony; and an analysis of the book completed by the OTP in October 2006 showed that Bulatović had quoted from protected portions of a number of SDC transcripts.[205] Still, the OTP made no efforts to challenge the original decision on protection or to sanction Bulatović – who could have been investigated for contempt – and Serbian authorities were silent, taking no steps to try him in domestic courts for divulging state secrets. The question arose as to how it was possible that neither the lawyers who presented the Bosnian genocide case before the ICJ, nor the ICTY Prosecution team, had used the publication of these parts to initiate legal proceedings that would lift the protections.[206] Yet it was almost five more years before the majority of protections were reversed, during the trial of former VJ Chief of Staff General Momčilo Perišić. On 24 March 2011, as closing arguments were made in the Perišić case, the news broke that the Trial Chamber had decided to lift the seal from many SDC documents.[207] Though not every protected record was made public, the decision represented a huge leap forward toward transparency and focused public attention on them.[208] But their weight as evidence came under public scrutiny again after the Appeals Chamber acquitted Perišić in February 2013. Had the significance of SDC documents been overstated? What did an acquittal say about the content of the records, their importance, and the reasons for their protection? And why would FRY authorities bother to insist on redactions if the protected parts of SDC records were not damaging to Serbia?

What formerly protected parts of SDC records revealed

The protected parts of SDC records presented at the Milošević trial covered a variety of topics, and exposed opinions and decisions related to the planning and execution of strategies that concerned territories in BiH and Croatia. Portions that related to the status of VJ officers serving in the Croatian Serb and Bosnian Serb armies – the VRS and the SVK – accounted for the largest number of redactions. SDC members had invested considerable effort into hiding the true nature of military engagement by VJ officers in these armies, and SDC records made clear that they had been concerned about being implicated as a warring party in the conflicts in neighbouring states, which were by then recognised as independent.[209]

In 1992, anticipating the independence of BiH, the PSFRY had ordered the JNA to return all Bosnian military conscripts serving in Serbia, Macedonia, and Montenegro to their original locations in BiH.[210] Then in April, before the FRY was constituted at the end of that month, the PSFRY issued a Decision on JNA Withdrawal from BiH that called for 15 per cent of troops in Bosnia – all from Serbia and Montenegro – to be pulled out. Those who remained were originally from BiH, and by leaving behind JNA military infrastructure to the Bosnian Serbs, the PSFRY laid the foundation for formation of the VRS.[211]

General Ferenc Vegh, a retired General and former Commander of the Hungarian Defence Forces, testified on military issues for the Prosecution. He asserted that "as long as the military organisations stationed on the territory of BiH were subordinated to the JNA, they operated on the theory and practice of 'one army.' "[212] With the withdrawal of the JNA and the creation of the VRS, Vegh concluded, the two officially independently functioning armed forces "co-ordinated and harmonised activities and support" and operated in "exceptionally close co-operation."[213] A Protected Witness for the Prosecution testified that ties between the two armies were so close that when the JNA formally withdrew from BiH, JNA officers there simply became officers of the VRS.[214] General Morillon, Commander of UNPROFOR during the war in BiH, also testified that the JNA had been "repainted" into the VRS in May 1992. According to Morrillon, all the ammunition, fuel, logistics, and weapons used by the VRS came from the JNA.[215] He was convinced that Belgrade had exercised authority over the VRS for the duration of the war in BiH, through General Mladić.[216] He led the executive command body of the VRS, the General Staff, and yet was paid by the VJ throughout the period relevant to the Bosnia indictment.[217]

The interoperability of forces from the FRY, Serbia, Montenegro, the RS, and the RSK was discussed regularly at SDC meetings; and Milošević himself suggested in December 1992 that RS and RSK leaders should be invited to confer on the defence of those two entities and the support they could get from the FRY.[218] In discussions of the VRS that unfolded at subsequent meetings, Bulatović and Milošević took the position that officers serving in the VRS should be given the choice to become officers of the VJ. They had originally been JNA officers and had stayed on in BiH to establish the VRS, and according to Bulatović, had remained because they were obliged to be there while Serb political and military leaders pursued a common state policy.[219] But there was concern among Council members, including Milošević, that if arrangements for keeping VJ officers in the VRS were ever to become public they would hurt the interests of the FRY by confirming its military engagement in BiH.[220]

Yet, Milošević desired to continue supporting the efforts of Serb armies abroad, for the FRY had "carried a great burden in order to help them form." While he worried that the presence of VJ officers outside FRY borders could result in sanctions from the international community, he felt that withdrawing these officers from the VRS would be "counterproductive," could "weaken their combat readiness," and may even "prove fatal for some units."[221] It was his opinion that financial assistance to the Serbs in BiH could continue, but material support had to end, and he argued that the FRY "should send them some general-purpose aid, and it should be up to them how to spend it." According to Milošević, assistance totalling 19 trillion dinars had already flowed into the RS and RSK, which he said amounted to "50 percent of the [FRY] budget, i.e. 2 million dinars per citizen of this country."[222]

Throughout 1993, the SDC grappled with how to regulate the status of VJ officers serving in the VRS and SVK, which numbered in the thousands. In October, with the question on the agenda yet again, General Perišić offered a possible answer, explaining that the General Staff had "devised a temporary formation in the Yugoslav Army." He admitted that this was "not entirely in conformity with the law," but said "we cannot see a better solution."[223] In the discussion that followed, a spectrum of concerns was raised about the exact wording and formulation of a new Decision on the regulation of these officers. It was obvious that top FRY political and military leaders were very much aware of the legal and diplomatic ramifications they could face if their involvement with the Serb armies was discovered, with Bulatović going so far at one point as to warn that the FRY could be under sanctions for ten years if their management of VRS and SVK officers was ever made public.[224]

At the following session, a draft Order regulating the status of VJ officers serving in the VRS and the SVK was prepared for signing, and General Perišić explained its implementation. Two 'Training Centres' would be established within the General Staff of the VJ – the 40th would administer officers serving in the VRS, and the 41st would administer officers in the SVK. This way, Perišić said, they would have the same rights "as if they were in the Yugoslav Army here ... except that they are physically absent, they're on the front." He claimed that the Law on Service in the Yugoslav Army offered no alternative solution.[225]

The proposal of General Perišić to establish the 40th and 41st Training Centres was adopted, and they eventually became the 30th and 40th Personnel Centres. Zoran Lilić, FRY President at the time and *primus inter pares* among the three SDC members, actually signed the Decision that created them, in November 1993.[226] He testified that JNA soldiers who were not citizens of either Montenegro or Serbia were brought under the 30th Personnel Centre to resolve their status.[227]

Financial, military, and political assistance from the FRY to the RS and RSK was vitally important to maintaining the capacity of Serb military formations to wage war and seize territory; and this assistance continued long after the end of the conflicts in Bosnia and Croatia in 1995. In fact, minutes of the 56th SDC session, held on 5 September 1996, revealed that the 30th Personnel Centre remained an important part of RS military infrastructure at that time – almost a year after the signing of the Dayton Peace Agreement. In that session, the Council decided that all VJ officers who had served in the 30th Personnel Centre and whose term had expired would need to remain in BiH until elections were held later that month, after which they could return to their original units or deploy to other posts.[228]

The SDC and the Six Strategic Objectives

The Six Strategic Objectives adopted by the RS Assembly in May 1992 were never explicitly cited in any meeting of the Supreme Defence Council; however, the Sarajevo area, the Drina valley, and the Posavina corridor – all named in the Objectives – were discussed. And although Milošević never openly referred to the Six Strategic Objectives, he did infer them, even citing the strategic importance of the Posavina corridor in connecting the "eastern and western parts of Republika Srpska" and linking the RS "to the east with Serbia" in his February 2002 Opening Statement at the ICTY. He suggested then that regular dialog among international negotiators about the corridor meant that military operations there had been justified.[229]

Records from SDC meetings after the fall of Srebrenica and Žepa presented some of the Council's most vigorous exchanges and most blatant criticism of the VRS. At the session held on 29 July 1995, General Perišić called the events that had taken place in both enclaves a "response to the provocations" of local people and blamed "the unprincipled conduct of the international community," which he said was capitalising on Serb mistakes to create a "pretext to proceed with preparations for massive air strikes."[230] Milošević expressed similar concerns about NATO bombing in the next session, on 14 August, if Bosnian Serbs did not agree to negotiate on the basis of the situation on the ground. He warned that the VRS must stop trying to seize more territory by force and implied that failed attempts by Mladić to do so had been foolish, recounting a conversation he had with the General in which Mladić had admitted suffering heavy losses and negative results in attempts to conquer more territory.[231]

References to the fall of Srebrenica and Žepa in these SDC meetings were never accompanied by condemnations or calls for an investigation, despite the fact that the execution and transport of men and boys from Srebrenica was still ongoing at the time. In the August meeting, Milošević revealed that he had been in communication with Mladić before and after the fall of Srebrenica, but also "on the occasion of the attack." He recalled warning Mladić that even though the military price of the attack had been "inexpensive ... the political price could be a million times higher," and he told the SDC that there had been an unfortunate "lack of synchronization" between the military and the political.[232] And so, while Milošević was critical of Mladić for making choices with "negative results," it was the high political price – not the atrocities – that troubled Milošević, who was beginning to see the repercussion of these events play out and worried about their potential impact on negotiations.

Though parts of SDC records had been protected from the public, the Trial Chamber saw them in their entirety when deciding the 2004 Half-Time Judgement, in which the judges determined whether there was enough evidence to continue with the charge of genocide against Milošević in the Defence part of the case. Their Judgement was that genocide charges should be upheld in the municipalities of Brčko, Prijedor, Sanski Most, Srebrenica, Bijeljina, Ključ, and Bosanski Novi; and they concluded that there was sufficient evidence showing Milošević had been a participant in a Joint Criminal Enterprise – together with Bosnian Serb leadership – with the intention to destroy, in part, the Bosnian Muslims as a group.[233]

This Judgement essentially sealed the fate of Milošević, even if the trial had come to a conclusion. He never would have had time to introduce evidence on the BiH part of the case, and the Half-Time Judgement would probably have been the basis for the Final Judgement. As it is now, the Half-Time Judgement is the closest thing to a judgement in the Milošević trial, and is a valuable legal document that summarises the law, legal theories, and evidence of the case.

The SDC and evidence on VJ combat units in BiH

Political and military leaders of the FRY and Serbia and Montenegro insisted throughout the 1990s that they were not a party to the wars in Croatia or BiH.[234] In his Opening Statement, Milošević asked the Court why it wanted to "make Serbia and Serbs responsible for the war in Croatia and BiH," claiming that he knew nothing about the charges alleged in the indictment and had only been aware that "there was fighting going on [in BiH]," which he said the FRY had made an effort to stop.[235] However, SDC records in combination with the testimonies of a number of Prosecution witnesses provided valuable evidence that the VJ had played both a direct and indirect role in combat operations in Croatia and BiH.

Among the most compelling accounts of Yugoslav military activities in BiH came from a Protected Witness for the Prosecution who was a VJ combatant in the 72nd Brigade. The unit was trained in the Serbian town of Pančevo, and the trainees supervised members of a special police unit from Knin – a clear example of inter-army cooperation.[236] The Witness testified that sometime during the night in January 1993, approximately 300 men from his unit crossed the border into Bosnia; but before they did, they changed their uniforms, replacing the VJ insignia with symbols of the VRS given to them by their superior officers. Once across the border, they met the VJ's 63rd Parachute Brigade from Niš and joined them in an attack on the village of Skelane in Eastern Bosnia, across the Drina River from Serbia. The soldiers drove people from their homes by launching hand-held rockets, then set fire to haystacks and shot at fleeing villagers. Eventually, they threw grenades into houses to make sure that no one was hiding inside.[237]

The deployment of VJ units in Bosnia was discussed at an SDC session held in February 1994 when Momir Bulatović, the President of Montenegro, demanded an explanation for the deaths of several young Montenegrins in combat in BiH, leading to extensive debate about the presence of VJ units there without the Council's authorisation.[238] This topic had been broached at a session in December 1992 as well, when an Army representative had said there were no plans to engage VJ combat units on BiH territory but that a decision would have to be taken by the SDC if they were to be deployed.[239] In the February session, Bulatović protested that VJ units – in this case a parachute brigade from Belgrade – had been mobilised in BiH without an SDC order. General Perišić admitted the brigade was in BiH but insisted the soldiers had all deployed voluntarily. He said "without volunteerism or without proclaiming a state of war," VJ units could not be engaged without SDC approval.[240]

Perišić insisted that the deployment of these troops must be kept secret, but Bulatović and FRY Prime Minister Radoje Kontić, a fellow Montenegrin, said there was no point, claiming it was well known in Montenegro that several young men from the town of Nikšić had been killed in combat in BiH. As the discussion continued, Bulatović was adamant that the SDC had to take a position on the issue. He had been confronted by Serbian politician Vojislav Šešelj about the deaths of these soldiers and told the Council, "When Šešelj knows, everyone knows."[241]

Cross-border engagement by the FRY as a warring party in BiH would have qualified the war as an international armed conflict, but FRY authorities preferred to be able to claim that it was a civil war and therefore an internal armed conflict, subject to different standards. And so, from both historical and legal points of view, participants at SDC meetings were right to be concerned about the consequences of revelations that VJ formations were present in Croatia and BiH. The VJ could have legally engaged outside of the FRY only with the consent of the federal government, in the service of the UN or a competent international organisation, or on the basis of a bilateral or multilateral agreement on military cooperation with the states in question. Yet, the 30th and 40th Personnel Centres had been set up to administer forces in the RS and RSK even though neither enjoyed state sovereignty and therefore could not establish such cooperation agreements, and the FRY was not officially at war with any of its neighbouring states.[242]

Further, FRY laws stipulated that all members of the VJ had to be FRY citizens, which applied to forces administered by the 30th and 40th Personnel Centres just as it did to the rest of the Army.[243] Addressing the political ramifications of conducting combat operations across the border of another independent state, General Ferenc Vegh wrote in his Expert Report that it constituted a violation of territorial sovereignty. He testified that, in his opinion, every action of an armed force could be considered the action of a state; and that armed forces, which are under political control, only cross borders as the result of political decisions.[244]

The SDC and the promotions of VJ officers serving in the Serb armies

The testimonies of Zoran Lilić, Borisav Jović, and Branko Kostić – who had all served as members of the PSFRY or FRY – were helpful in explaining many of the policies implemented by Serbian political and military leaders for post-Yugoslav 'Serb-designated territories,' but they did not fully account for how officers of the JNA, and later the VJ, became the keystones of military structures in the RS and the RSK. SDC records filled in the gaps by providing evidence on the relationship between the VJ and the VRS and SVK. It was clear from SDC notes, for instance, that engagement in the conflicts in Croatia and Bosnia was an asset toward the promotion of VJ officers. On numerous occasions, contributions on the battlefields in Vukovar, the Dubrovnik area, Knin Krajina, Eastern Bosnia, and other sites of notorious atrocities were referenced when an officer was recommended for advancement.[245] And SDC records showed that the VJ had not only sent much-needed personnel to the VRS and SVK throughout the war, but that the SDC had regularly promoted VJ officers serving in the VRS and SVK during the same period.

In fact, it is little wonder that Belgrade authorities chose to protect the portions of these records that detailed the promotions and retirements of VJ officers serving in the VRS and SVK, for the redacted parts revealed that the SDC had even verified promotions proposed by RS and RSK authorities.[246] Still, minutes from a session in June 1995 make it clear that Milošević's word was the ultimate authority for the promotion of officers to senior ranks in the VRS and SVK, and that Karadžić accepted the decisions of Milošević and the SDC. This was an important example of how the SDC exercised power as a de facto superior body to the Main Staff of the VRS.[247]

FRY and Serb military institutions inter-operated in non-combat and civilian functions, too. Milan 'Mrgud' Milanović – who was first appointed Assistant Minister of Defence in the SAO of Slavonia, Baranja, and Western Syrmia in November 1991 and was reappointed for the last time in October 1995 – testified that he received his pay from the VJ for that entire period of time, as did other functionaries of the Ministry of Defence, both civilian and military. Milanović told the court that it was "well known that officers of the Army of the Republic of Serbian Krajina were active-duty officers of the Army of Yugoslavia and … received their salaries from the Army of Yugoslavia." He said close links between the Ministry of Defence and the Army had led to the decision to bring the Ministry under the umbrella of the VJ.[248]

The SDC and financial support for the wars in Croatia and BiH

Financial support by the FRY was essential to RSK and RS war efforts and Prosecution witness General Rupert Smith underlined the controlling power of a paymaster, saying "the man who pays the cheque is usually the person who is in command."[249] SDC records show that, following the formation of the RSK and RS, their armies were primarily financed from the FRY budget; and one of the first comprehensive accounts of the extent of this aid was presented by General Panić in a February 1993 session. Panić reported that there were 2,500 commanding officers from the VJ serving in the VRS, and 700 in the SVK, and said he received requests for arms every day. "We send what we can," he told the Council, but he reported problems with the purchase of artillery and tank ammunition, which he said was run "through different channels."[250] Panić pleaded that money be found to finance the production of ammunition to meet the needs of both the VJ and the VRS.[251]

Although the FRY was not officially at war, the greatest part of its budget went to the VJ, and much of the VJ's stock to the RSK and RS. Federal Prime Minister Kontić, who was in charge of the federal budget and its distribution, was alarmed by the financial strain being created by expenses of the VJ and requests from the Serb Republics. He called it "an extremely complex problem" but said there was no way to consolidate the budget when it had to "bear such costs."[252] The financial burden for the FRY became almost unbearable over time and led the government to print more money, resulting in hyperinflation. In June 1993, the SDC discussed how to pay over 2,000 officers and soldiers whose salaries had been stopped as a consequence of budget shortfalls – which were due, among other things, to UN sanctions and the lack of import and customs revenues. Kontić called the situation "more than catastrophic" and suggested that FRY leaders assess how to continue issuing dinars and "still avoid collapse."[253]

Four months later, in October, the printing of money to finance the VJ was again debated and Kontić expressed strong opposition to continuing the practice. But Milošević advocated for continued financial backing of the Army by any means, saying "the Army is not interested where the federal budget will secure the funds ... the essential thing is that the Army gets the money."[254] On several occasions in court, most notably during his cross-examination of the Prosecution expert on finance, Morten Torkildsen, Milošević denied that the FRY had ever financed the military infrastructure or war effort by printing money – officially known as the "primary emission of money." He claimed he "was always against it."[255] But former FRY President Zoran Lilić testified that the primary emission of money had been an important source of financing after the introduction of UN sanctions in 1992, and said President Milošević had wielded influence regarding "decisions of that kind."[256]

Reforms were introduced in 1994 to control hyperinflation, but the financial demands of the RSK and RS remained a serious threat to the stability of the FRY. In March 1994, General Perišić expressed his concerns about financing the Serb armies, saying that the RS had requested 522 million dinars for everything from equipment, to construction of facilities and housing, to strategic war reserves for the VRS. A total of 829 million dinars were requested by the RS and RSK together, and Perišić stressed that the SDC needed to decide just how much the FRY could actually afford to pay.[257] Still, military aid appears to have continued to flow.[258]

The SDC and the fall of the SAOs

Despite attempts by Serb leaders to conceal their wartime collaboration, SDC records uncovered the effort that had been made from Belgrade to control military developments in the RSK and the RS. In May 1995, the loss of the SAO of Western Slavonia, in Croatia, prompted General Perišić to develop a series of proposed actions to be taken in the event of an attack by Croatian forces on the SAO of Krajina and its capital Knin. Perišić felt that RSK leaders should seek approval from authorities in the FRY before making important political and military decisions, and he brought up the possibility of VJ engagement in Croatia in the event of aggression against the RSK, especially in Eastern Slavonia. In the event of an escalation, Perišić said that refugees from the RSK and volunteers from the FRY could be equipped and formed into military units and sent to fight in the SVK. All of Perišić's proposals were adopted by the SDC.[259]

Several months after the fall of Western Slavonia, Croatian forces launched an attack on the central part of the RSK and on Knin. The operation, known as Storm, began six days after a 29 July session of the SDC at which Perišić had reported that Croatian forces planned to carve up RSK territory along several key axes. He had concluded that if the Croatian Army was successful, the SVK would be obliterated and the RSK dismantled.[260] And as Perišić predicted, Operation Storm led to a swift military defeat of the SVK.[261]

Yet, despite the fall of the RSK, the SAO of Slavonia, Baranja, and Western Syrmia (SAO SBWS) remained in Serb hands and the attention of SDC members turned to raising the capability of the VJ's 11th Corps, which operated there.[262] Strategies to strengthen the Serb military presence in Croatia in the aftermath of Operation Storm did not materialise, though. On the contrary, at the 29 August 1995 session of the SDC, the 40th Personnel Centre was abolished.[263] Eventually, the SVK was abandoned and the FRY continued to finance and support only the VJ's 11th Corps.[264] In October, General Perišić reported on the military situation in both the RS and SAO SBWS and re-emphasised the danger of a Croatian-Bosnian Muslim military alliance, warning that an offensive could be launched in Western Bosnia.[265] But by January 1996, the war in BiH was over and the SAO SBWS was peacefully reintegrated into the Croatian state.

What the evidence revealed about discord between Milošević and RS leaders

Away from the courtrooms of The Hague, some trial observers, historians, and legal scholars have suggested that the Prosecution's evidence on the influence Milošević held over Karadžić and Mladić was relevant only for the period up to early 1993 and then from August to December 1995. In their view, no evidence was presented on Milošević's involvement in and criminal responsibility for crimes committed from early 1993 to late July 1995, crucial to proving the charge of genocide in Srebrenica.[266] But, while it's true that serious disagreements may have tempered the relationship between Milošević and Karadžić – first in August 1994, and then again a year later in the aftermath of the Srebrenica massacre and during preparation for peace talks in Dayton – General Mladić remained on good terms and in regular communication with Milošević for the duration of the war.

Moreover, despite any disagreements with RS leaders, SDC records showed that the VJ General Staff favoured providing assistance to the VRS in order to prevent its defeat and maintain the territorial integrity of the Republika Srpska.[267] Discussions about the blockade that had purportedly been imposed by the FRY on the RS in August 1994 were among the redactions made by authorities in Belgrade. The 24th SDC session, on 9 August, occurred around the time the blockade was introduced, after the refusal of RS leadership to accept the Contact Group Peace Plan. Minutes from that session revealed that the blockade never did really sever aid to the RS; in fact, both the VRS and SVK were said to be serving "the interests of the Serbian people."[268]

In September 1994, the question of whether to abolish the 30th Personnel Centre was discussed by the SDC. Momir Bulatović felt the Centre had become a liability to "the realisation of political objectives," and therefore should be closed.[269] Yet aid streamed into the RS unabated, and in April 1995, Ratko Mladić reported to the RS Assembly that the VJ was providing the VRS with weapons and equipment amounting to 50 per cent of its needs.[270] In his statement to the Investigative Judge of the District Court of Belgrade after his arrest in March 2001, Milošević himself addressed these expenditures, admitting that everything "from a needle to an anchor" had been provided to the VRS.[271]

Milošević also openly expressed a willingness to bring Karadžić forcefully in line if needed, revealing even to Western diplomats the extent of his de facto power and just how far he would go to get his way. On one occasion, in a June 1995 meeting with UK diplomat Ivor Roberts regarding the UN hostage crisis – when Serb forces captured and held some 400 UN troops in order to pressure the international community not to engage in air strikes against Bosnian Serb positions – Milošević agreed to help negotiate the release of the hostages, saying he would send Jovica Stanišić, then Head of the DB, to threaten the Bosnian Serbs. When Roberts inquired as to what threats Milošević would use, he told him: "Stanišić will tell Karadžić that I will have him killed if he doesn't release the hostages. He knows I can do it."[272]

While this heavy-handedness certainly may have played a role in discord that developed between Belgrade and RS leadership, internal disagreement among RS leaders was also a factor. At the SDC session held on 23 August 1995, Mladić was asked about the international community's refusal to deal with Karadžić in negotiations. He said RS leadership was deeply divided and blamed Serb "enemies" for attempting to create a schism among Bosnian Serbs, between "Karadžić's men and Mladić's men."[273] He proposed a meeting of FRY and RS leaders to reach an agreement on how to present their shared interests in upcoming peace talks.[274]

A meeting was held two days later, in Dobanovci, and all participants were sworn to secrecy upon the arrival of Mladić. Milošević praised VRS officers and, obviously satisfied with the territorial gains that had been made and ready to seal them off, he said that if Muslims refused the peace, it would be made clear to them that they would be left with "the sword of Damocles hanging over them in the form of General Mladić."[275] A second meeting was held in Dobanovci on 29 August to discuss the composition of the Serb delegation at forthcoming negotiations in Dayton. Under the mediation of Orthodox Patriarch Pavle, an agreement was reached according to which Milošević would represent all Serbs at Dayton, side-lining Karadžić from the talks.[276] Eventually, Milošević's leadership was accepted by both Karadžić and Mladić; but they had little choice, since by the time talks began, each had been indicted by the ICTY and would have been apprehended for transfer to The Hague if they had travelled.

Weeks after the Dayton Peace Agreement was signed in Paris, at a session of the RS Assembly held in December 1995, Momčilo Krajišnik put forth a new strategic goal to divide Serbs from Muslims and Croats, saying that no one had the right to make them to stay together.[277] But with the talks concluded, Milošević felt that Serbs in Bosnia had achieved success and he hailed the victorious creation of a Serb "state." Speaking at an SDC session on 6 December, Milošević stressed that there never had been a Serb majority from Zvornik to Foča, but that the Serbs "took all of it," and that despite being a minority in Sarajevo, too, the Serbs had gotten the southeastern part and Pale, which "covers as much territory as the entire Sarajevo does." He explained that "when a state is being created ... one cannot insist on particular spots, such as: 'This quarter is Serbian, so we should annex it to this side.' "[278]

Milošević remained critical of RS leaders who were not content with the amount of territory they were awarded by the international community, insisting that the creation and preservation of the Republika Srpska was a triumph. He called the conflict a "defensive war," but said that if more territory had been taken, the Serbs would have been fighting a war of conquest because "more than half of the territory does not belong to us." He moralised that "by taking away something that belongs to someone else, you are digging graves for your future grandchildren and preparing a new war."[279] Yet, he also spoke triumphantly about the RS having been established "where no Serbian country had ever existed before" and called this "a historic achievement."[280] And Milošević's sense of triumph was understandable; by the end of 1995, the RS was not only ethnically homogenous, but covered almost half of BiH territory, despite Serbs constituting only 33 per cent of the population. Plus, he had another reason to feel he had prevailed, as it seemed at first that he would not be indicted by the ICTY for crimes committed by Serb forces in BiH.

Notes

1 Amended Indictment, 22 November 2002. Herinafter, the Bosnia Indictment.
2 See: Testimony of Branko Kostić (25 January 2006), 47617–47618 and (8 February 2006), 48189–48190; Testimony of Borisav Jović (19 November 2003), 29293–29294; Testimony of Milan Kučan (21 May 2003), 20956.
3 Testimony of Stjepan Mesić (1 October 2002), 10538–10544. The PSFRY session took place on 12, 14 and 15 March 1991. Also see: Testimony of Branko Kostić (7 February 2006), 48181–48188; and Borisav Jović, *Last Days of the SFRY*, Exhibit P596.2a, 255–271. For Milošević's speech, see Exhibit P328.29.
4 Borisav Jović, *Last Days of the SFRY*, Exhibit P596.2a, 271–278. On page 278, Jović explains why Serbia returned to the Presidency, saying that: "Defending the Serb nation's right to self-determination is realistically impossible without the JNA, because the Serb nation is not armed." He also cited the risk that the Presidency could have been taken over "by separatists and those intent on destroyingYugoslavia" had they not returned.
5 Testimony of Stjepan Mesić (1 October 2002), 10560.
6 Ibid.
7 Ibid., 10559–10563.
8 Testimony of Stjepan Mesić (2 October 2002), 10657.
9 Testimony of Stjepan Kljuić (15 July 2003), 24393 and 24459–24460.
10 Testimony of Hrvoje Šarinić (21 January 2004), 31263–31268.
11 Ibid., 31267.
12 Dušan Bilandžić, "Najveća Razilaženja," *Nacional*, 25 October 1996.
13 Testimony of Ratko Marković (20 January 2005), 35382.

14 Ibid., 35385.
15 Smilja Avramov, *Postherojski rat Zapada protiv Jugoslavije* (Belgrade: Akademija za diplomatiju i bezbednost, 1997), 140–141. An English translation of these pages of the book was tendered into evidence as: "The Post-Heroic War of the West against Yugoslavia," Exhibit P817a. Also see: Testimony of Smilja Avramov (8 September 2004), 32510.
16 Testimony of Smilja Avramov (8 September 2004), 32510.
17 Testimony of Ante Marković (23 October 2003), 28026.
18 Ibid., 28026–28027.
19 Ibid., 28027.
20 Testimony of Hrvoje Šarinić (21 January 2004), 31267.
21 Testimony of Stjepan Mesić (2 October 2002), 10657. The Trial Trancript reads that Tuđman described the shape as an "oblong role." It should read "oblong roll." The author was able to decipher the intended meaning by accessing the original quote by Tuđman, when he used the Croatian word *kifla*. Also see a summary of the ICTY testimony of Josip Manolić, a former Croatian Minister and one time ally of Tuđman, who quoted Tuđman's use of the word *kifla* when appearing in 2006 as a witness in the trial of six Herceg Bosnia leaders: "Tuđmanova naklapnja i želje," *Sense*, 3 July 2006.
22 Testimony of Milan Babić (20 November 2002), 13111–13113 and 13575–13576.
23 Testimony of Vojislav Šešelj (5 September 2005), 43655–43656.
24 Testimony of Ante Marković (15 January 2004), 30916–30918.
25 Testimony of Ante Marković (23 October 2003), 28026.
26 Testimony of Hrvoje Šarinić (22 January 2004), 31334–31335.
27 Ibid., 31324–31335 and (21 January 2004), 31266–31267.
28 Testimony of Hrvoje Šarinić (21 January 2004), 31263–31264.
29 Ibid., 31267–31268.
30 "Transcript of the meeting between Franjo Tuđman and others and members of the Presidency of BiH," 8 January 1992, Exhibit P641.3a, 13–14 and 32.
31 Dragoljub Todorović, interview (9 June 2005). From the Geneva meeting between Dobrica Ćosić and Franjo Tuđman, also see: "Joint Declaration of 30 September 1992," in *The International Conference on the Former Yugoslavia: Official Papers*, 458.
32 Testimony of Hrvoje Šarinić (22 January 2004), 31268.
33 Ibid.
34 Intercept of Conversation between Slobodan Milošević and Radovan Karadžić, 12 June 1991, Exhibit P613.8a.
35 Intercept of Conversation between Slobodan Milošević and Radovan Karadžić, 8 July 1991, Exhibit P613.21a; 29 July 1991, Exhibit P613.24a; 31 July 1991, Exhibit P613.25a; 6 August 1991, Exhibit P613.26a; 9 August 1991, Exhibit P613.30a; and 13 September 1991, Exhibit P613.63a.
36 Ibid., 6 August 1991, Exhibit P613.26a.
37 Ibid., 14 November 1991, Exhibit P613.117a.
38 Ibid., 17 December 1991, Exhibit P613.140a.
39 Ibid.; and Intercept of Conversation between Radovan Karadžić and Branko Kostić, 17 December 1991, Exhibit P613.141a.
40 Intercept of Conversation between Radovan Karadžić and Jovica Stanišić, 21 December 1991, Exhibit P613.144a.
41 The full title of the Decision was:

> Decision on promulgation of autonomous regions as unquestionable parts of the federal state of Yugoslavia and as constituent parts of the federal unit of Bosnia and Herzegovina and on separation of settlements of one municipality and their integration into another municipality.

See: Judgement, *Prosecutor* v. *Krajišnik*, No. IT-00–39-T, 27 September 2006, 28, para. 57. Also see: "Statute of the Autonomous Region of Krajina...," 16 September 1991, Exhibit P730a; and "Map of Serbian Autonomous Districts (SAOs)," Exhibit P343.1a.

42 In September 1991, three large areas in BiH – Eastern and Old Herzegovina, Bosnian Krajina, and Romanija – were proclaimed Serb Autonomous Regions (SAOs), followed by Semberija-Majevica, Northern Bosnia, and Birač in November. See: "Decision on Pronouncing and Conducting the Plebiscite of the Serb People in Bosnia and Herzegovina," 24 October 1991, Exhibit P740a.

43 Intercept of Conversation between Slobodan Milošević and Radovan Karadžić, 19 September 1991, Exhibit P613.67a.

44 "Decision on Pronouncing and Conducting the Plebiscite of the Serb People in Bosnia and Herzegovina," 4.

45 "Decision ... to Sanction the Serbian Autonomous Districts Proclaimed in Bosnia and Herzegovina," No. 37–02/91, 21 November 1991, Exhibit P741a.

46 "EC Declaration Concerning Condition for Recognition of New States," 16 December 1991, Exhibit P826.5; "Yugoslavia for the Third Time," Epoha No. 12, 7 January 1992, Exhibit P808a.

47 Testimony of Branko Kostić (14 February 2006), 48430.

48 Intercept of Conversation between Radovan Karadžić and Slobodan Milošević, 30 December 1991, Exhibit P613.151a.

49 Testimony of Branko Kostić (14 February 2006), 48431.

50 Ibid.

51 Ibid., 48431–48432.

52 "Instructions issued by the SDS for the Organization and Activity of the Organs of the Serbian people in Bosnia and Herzegovina in Extraordinary Circumstances," 19 December 1991, Exhibit P434.3a.

53 Deronjić implemented the Instructions in the Bratunac municipality, reporting back to Karadžić about the outcome at a meeting in Pale. Deronjić was indicted by the Tribunal and pleaded guilty to charges related to his involvement in the commission of crimes in the Srebrenica area in 1995. He was sentenced to ten years and died in a Swedish prison in May 2007.

54 Testimony of Miroslav Deronjić (23 November 2003), 29632.

55 Intercept of Conversation between Slobodan Milošević and Radovan Karadžić, 15 January 1992, Exhibit P613.162a.

56 Intercept of Conversation between Radovan Karadžić and Budimir Košutić, 7 February 1992, Exhibit P613.171a.

57 For example, see: "Proclamation issued by the main board of the Serbian Democratic Party of BiH, inviting all Serbs to abstain from voting in the referendum," 1 February 1992, Exhibit P731a.

58 Trial Transcript, Defence Opening Statement (14 February 2002), 258.

59 Testimony of Branko Kostić (14 February 2006), 48433.

60 Ibid., 48469–48470.

61 United Nations Security Council, Resolution 237, S/RES/237, 22 May 1992.

62 Testimony of Miroslav Deronjić (26 November 2003), 29633. Also see: Miroslav Deronjić, Witness Statement, 25 November 2003, Exhibit P600a, para. 63.

63 See: "Decision on Strategic Objectives of the Serbian People in Bosnia and Herzegovina," 12 May 1992, Exhibit P451.12a.

64 For example, see: Testimony of Mihailo Marković (17 November 2004), 33557; Testimony of Branko Kostić (14 February 2006), 48436. Marković and Kostić handled questions from the Prosecution about the corridors differently, with Marković admitting their necessity for territorial contiguity and Kostić inferring that brutality in the corridors was simply the by-product of a "bloody civil war."

65 "Map of Serb controlled areas ... as of 30 December 1992," Exhibit P809.

66 The last strategic objective, calling for access to the sea, was abandoned early in the war. No serious attempts to advance toward Dubrovnik were made once the Vance Peace Plan became effective in 1992.
67 Testimony of Zoran Lilić (18 June 2003), 22745–22746.
68 Regular attendees included Đorđe Blagojević, Federal Minister of the Interior; Pavle Bulatović, former Federal Minister of the Interior and Federal Minister of Defence as of December 1992; Nikola Šainović, first as Deputy Prime Minister of Serbia and then as Prime Minister of Serbia as of February 1993; Milo Đukanović, the Prime Minister of Montenegro; and Svetozar Stojanović, Special Advisor to the President of FR Yugoslavia. Occasionally others would join, including General Života Panić, Chief of the General Staff of the VJ and Vladislav Jovanović, Federal Minister of Foreign Affairs. Some of the most interesting discussions took place during sessions at which the entire political and military leadership of the RS and RSK were also present.
69 Testimony of Vladislav Jovanović (22 February 2005), 36384.
70 "Stenographic transcript of the 3rd session of the Supreme Defence Council (SDC)," 23 July 1992, Exhibit P667.3.1a, 2–4.
71 For notes from the session in B/C/S, see: "Stenographic notes from the Council for the Co-ordination of positions of State Policy," 11 August 1992, Exhibit P469.41, 136.
72 For notes from the session in B/C/S, see: "Stenographic notes from the Council for the Co-ordination of positions of State Policy," 18 August 1992, Exhibit P469.42, 71.
73 Testimony of Čedomir Popov (16 December 2004), 35514. See Article 2 of the RS Constitution in: "Serbian Republic of Bosnia-Herzegovina," in Blaustein and Blaustein, *Constitutions of Dependencies and Special Sovereignties*; available as Exhibit 319.1a.
74 "EC Declaration Concerning Condition for Recognition of New States."
75 Testimony of Ratko Marković (24 January 2005), 35549. Also see: "Federal Republic of Yugoslavia," in Blaustein and Blaustein, *Constitutions of Dependencies and Special Sovereignties*, Article 2.
76 Testimony of Ratko Marković (24 January 2005), 35504–35505.
77 Testimony of Čedomir Popov (16 December 2004), 34622–34623.
78 "Stenographic notes from the Council for the Co-ordination of positions of State Policy," 18 August 1992, Exhibit P469.42, 51–54.
79 Ibid., 55.
80 Ibid., 55–57.
81 Ibid., 53–54.
82 For example, see: Testimony of Vladislav Jovanović (22 February 2005), 36463. Jovanović was the Serbian and FRY Minister of Foreign Affairs before representing the Federation as a diplomatic representative at the UN.
83 "Statement on Principles for New Constitutional Arrangement for Bosnia and Herzegovina," 22 February 1992 (Lisbon). The Statement is available in: Snežana Trifunovska, ed., *Yugoslavia Through Documents: From its Creation to its Dissolution* (Dordrecht: Martinus Nijhoff, 1994), 171 and 517–519.
84 For example, see: Testimony of Branko Kostić (7 February 2006), 48110–48111; Testimony of Vladislav Jovanović (14 February 2005), 36133–36135.
85 "Dr. Karadžić before Beginning of Meeting in Lisbon," *Glas*, 22 February 1992, 2.
86 Robert Donia, *The Assembly of Republika Srpska: 1992–1995*, Expert Report, 29 July 2003, Exhibit P537.2a, 64. Also see: "Transcript of minutes of RS Assembly Meeting, 42nd session," 18 and 19 July 1994, Exhibit P538.21.1a, 4–5.
87 Testimony of Čedomir Popov (16 December 2004), 34621–34622. Also see: Federal Ministry of Foreign Affairs, "Brief Information on the so-called Cutileiro's Plan for the former BiH," 9 August 1994, Exhibit P810a.

88 Maggy O'Kane, "Muslims' Nightmare under the Long Yugoslav Sun," *Guardian*, 29 July 1992; Roy Gutman, "Ethnic Cleansing: Yugoslavs Try to Deport 1,800 Muslims to Hungary," *Newsday*, 3 July 1992; Roy Gutman, *A Witness to Genocide* (New York: Macmillan, 1993).
89 "Stenographic notes from the Council for the Co-ordination of positions of State Policy," 18 August 1992, Exhibit P469.42, 18.
90 Ibid.
91 Ibid., 19.
92 See notes from the session in B/C/S: "Stenographic notes from the Council for the Co-ordination of positions of State Policy," 3 September 1992, Exhibit P469.43, 11–24.
93 Testimony of Kosta Mihailović (17 December 2004), 34778. Also see: Exhibit P813, Snežana Trifunovski, *Yugoslavia Through Documents*, 694–718.
94 "Stenographic notes from the Council for the Co-ordination of positions of State Policy," 3 September 1992, Exhibit P469.43, 13.
95 David Owen, *Balkan Odyssey* (Oxford: Indigo, 1995), 24–31. Owen's book was entered into evidence as Exhibit C18. Vance was appointed on behalf of the UN and Owen on behalf of the EU. Lord Owen testified as Chamber's witness on 3 and 4 November 2003.
96 The options were:

1 a centralized state;
2 a centralized federal state with significant functions carried out by 4–10 regions;
3 a loose federal state of three ethnic units, not geographically contiguous;
4 a loose confederation of three ethnically determined republics with significant independence, possibly even in the security field;
5 a Muslim state, created through partition, with Serbian territory becoming part of Yugoslavia and Croat territory becoming part of Croatia.

See: Owen, *Balkan Odyssey*, 65.
97 United Nations Security Council, *Report of the Secretary-General on the International Conference on the Former Yugoslavia*, No. S/25015, 24 December 1992.
98 Testimony of Lord Owen (3 and 4 November 2003), 28402-28403, 28516. See also: Owen, *Balkan Odyssey*, 97.
99 "Opening Address of Lord Owen at the first plenary session" in United National Security Council, *Report of the Secretary-General on the Activities of the International Conference on the Former Yugoslavia*, No. S/25050, 6 January 1993.
100 Owen, *Balkan Odyssey*, 98.
101 Laura Silber and Allan Little, *Yugoslavia: Death of a Nation* (London: Penguin, 1995), 226.
102 Lenard J. Cohen, *Broken Bonds: Yugoslavia's Disintegration And Balkan Politics in Transition* (Boulder: Westview Press, 1995), 256. Owen, *Balkan Odyssey*, 97–98, 104–105.
103 Report on a meeting with the Bosnian Serbs and Croats, 4 January 1993 and meeting with the Bosnian Serb delegation, 15 January 1993. Owen, *Balkan Odyssey*, 61–62, 69, 141.
104 See notes from the session in B/C/S: "Stenographic notes from the Council for the Co-ordination of positions of State Policy," 9 January 1993, Exhibit P469.40.
105 Ibid., 6–9.
106 Ibid., 34–38.
107 Ibid., 68–70.
108 Ibid., 69.
109 Ibid., 70.

110 See notes from the session in B/C/S: "Stenographic notes from the Council for the Co-ordination of positions of State Policy," 21 January 1993, Exhibit P469.39, 20.
111 Ibid.
112 "Stenographic notes from the Council for the Co-ordination of positions of State Policy," 21 January 1993, Exhibit P469.39, 22–23.
113 Ibid., 34.
114 Ibid.
115 Testimony of Lord Owen (3 November 2003), 28379-28380. "Report of ICFY Co-Chairmen's Visit to Belgrade and Zagreb," 6 January 1993. Also see: David Owen, telegram to Douglas Hurd, 7 January 1993, in Owen, *Balkan Odyssey*, 102–103.
116 United Nations Security Council, *Report of the Secretary-General on the Activities of the International Conference on the Former Yugoslavia: Peace Talks, Athens, 1–2 May 1993*, No. S/25709, 3 May 1993. Also see: Owen, *Balkan Odyssey*, 158.
117 "Transcript of minutes … [of] the 30th Session of the Republika Srpska National Assembly," 5 and 6 May 1993, Exhibit P538.9.1a.
118 Ibid., 94–97. Also see: Testimony of Robert Donia (11 November 2003), 28747–28749; and (12 September 2003), 26495–26496.
119 Owen, *Balkan Odyssey*, 164.
120 Owen, Balkan Odyssey, 103. Michael P. Scharf, *Balkan Justice: The Story Behind the First International War Crimes Trial Since Nuremberg* (Durham, NC: University of North Carolina Academic Press, 1997), 44, 51–90. Scharf quotes Cherif Bassiouni, who said that a political settlement was the priority at the time and that justice was not perceived to be "an inducement to that end." Also see: Chris Stephen, *Judgement Day: The Trial of Slobodan Milošević* (New York: Atlantic Books, 2004), 89–92.
121 See: Kenneth Manusama, *The United Nations Security Council in the Post-Cold War Era: Applying the Principle of Legality* (Leiden: Koninklijke Brill, 2006), 258–259. Also see: NIOD, *Srebrenica: A "Safe" Area* (Amsterdam: Boom Uitgeverij, 2002), 127.
122 Taylor Branch, *The Clinton Tapes: Wrestling History with the President* (New York: Simon & Schuster, 2009), 9–10. Clinton said that Germany and its leader Helmut Kohl held a different view and were in favour of adjusting the UN arms embargo, but that it failed in part because Germany did not hold a seat in the UN Security Council.
123 "Transcript of minutes of the RS Assembly Meeting 34th session," 27 August–1 October 1993, Exhibit P538.13.1a.
124 "Basic Decision on Establishing and Proclaiming HR BiH issued," *Narodni List*, 28 August 1993; "Decision on Constituting the House of Representatives of the HR H-B," *Narodni List*, 28 August 1993.
125 "Fax to ICFY from President of the Chamber of Economic Affairs of the Croatian Community of Herzeg-Bosna," 30 August 1993, 15.
126 After the Owen–Stoltenberg Plan, the so-called "Invincible Package" was introduced in September 1993, and the European Union Action Plan (EUAP) in November 1993. On 5 November, the EUAP was presented in a paper entitled "Joint Action on the Former Yugoslavia," which outlined 28 issues on which future discussions should focus, capturing all major points as developed from the EC's first involvement in 1991 through the shaping of the Invincible Package in the summer of 1993. See: Owen, *Balkan Odyssey*, 204, 208, 232–234, 237–241.
127 Owen, *Balkan Odyssey*, 178, 232, 263, 288–9, 384–386. See: *Washington Agreement*, Peace Agreements Digital Collection: Bosnia and Herzegovina, United States Institute of Peace, www.usip.org/sites/default/files/file/resources/collections/peace_agreements/washagree_03011994.pdf (accessed 18 January 2016).

128 United Nations, *Letter from the Secretary-General addressed to the President of the Security Council*, No. S/26066, 8 July 1994.
129 Owen, *Balkan Odyssey*, 272, 300–308.
130 Ibid. Also see: United Nations, *Letter from the Secretary-General addressed to the President of the Security Council*, No. S/1994/1074, 19 September 1994.
131 "Stenographic transcript of the 25th session of the Supreme Defence Council," 30 August 1994, *Prosecutor* v. *Perišić*, Exhibit P00778.E, 37.
132 Ibid., 39.
133 Ibid., 37.
134 Ibid., 46.
135 Ibid., 53.
136 Ibid., 41.
137 For example, see Bob de Graaff, "The Difference between Legal Proof and Historical Evidence: The Trial of Slobodan Milošević and the Case of Srebrenica," *European Review* 14, no. 4 (2006): 505.
138 "Notes from a meeting held in Dobanovci (Serbia) between Slobodan Milošević and the Bosnian Serb leadership," 29 August 1995, Exhibit P469.20a, Meeting Record, 11.
139 Prosecution Response to Amici Curiae Motion for Judgement of Acquittal Pursuant to Rule 98 *bis* (Public Version), 3 May 2005, para. 309.
140 "Transcript of RS Assembly Meeting 40th session," 10 and 11 May 1994, Exhibit P538.19.1, 51 (in B/C/S). Also see: Donia, *The Assembly of Republika Srpska: 1992–1995*, 62.
141 See: Testimony of Witness Hrvoje Šarinić (21 January, 2004), 31279–31280. Borislav Mikelić, a Croatian Serb politician and a close associate of Milošević, told Šarinić that Mladić was "two hundred percent" loyal to Milošević. Also see: Hrvoje Šarinić, Witness Statement, 6 December 2003, Exhibit P641.2a, para. 42–44; and "Minutes of the 42nd session of the Supreme Defence Council," 23 August 1995, *Prosecutor v. Perišić*, Exhibit P00713.E.
142 Parts of this chapter have been published previously. See: Geoffrey Nice and Nena Tromp, "Bosnia and Herzegovina," in *The United Nations Security Council in the Age of Human Rights*, eds Jared Genser and Bruno Stagno Ugarte (Cambridge: Cambridge University Press, 2014).
143 See the following United Nations Security Council Resolutions: 771, 13 August 1992; 779, 6 October 1992; 780, 6 October 1992; and 808, 22 February 1993.
144 United Nations Security Council, Resolution 819, No. S/RES/819, 16 April 1993.
145 NIOD, *Srebrenica: A "Safe" Area*, 774–775.
146 Testimony of Diego Arria (10 February 2004), 31724. Mission members – all UN Security Council Ambassadors – foresaw a massacre, and even genocide. See: United Nations, *Report of the Security Council Mission Established Pursuant to Resolution 819 (1993)*, No. S/25700, 30 April 1993. Also see: Exhibits P645.16-P645.22 – a collection of media reports on the activities and comments of the Mission, some in English and some in B/C/S.
147 United Nations Security Council, Resolution 824, No. S/RES/824, 6 May 1993.
148 See: Mark Danner, "Bosnia: The Great Betrayal," *New York Review of Books*, 26 March 1998. For a more detailed reconstruction of the role of the UN and Dutch peacekeepers, see: NIOD, *Srebrenica: A "Safe" Area*, Parts II and III.
149 See: Decision on Motion for Judgement of Acquittal (16 June 2004), Schedules A through F (hereinafter the Half-Time Judgement), para. 202–219. Also see: Judgement, *Prosecution* v. *Popović et al.*, No. IT-02-88 (10 June 2010). In the *Popović et al.* case, six people were tried for genocide in Srebrenica. In the Judgement, the number of executions following the fall of Srebrenica was estimated to

have been as high as 7,826, although the Trial Chamber noted that only 5,336 victims of execution had been positively identified. All six Accused were found guilty in first-instance and appeals proceedings.

150 "Directive for Further Operations Op. No. 7," 8 March 1995, Exhibit P553.2a, 10; Half-Time Judgement, para. 204; Testimony of General Rupert Smith (9 October 2003), 27303.

151 Testimony of General Rupert Smith (9 October 2003), 27304.

152 "Directive for Further Operations Op. No. 7," 11; Half-Time Judgement, para. 204.

153 Testimony of General Rupert Smith (9 October 2003), 27304.

154 General Rupert Smith, Witness Statement, 14 August 1996, Exhibit P552, para. 76.

155 "Transcript of Video clip of Mladić and Krstić walking through Srebrenica (V000–0642 & V000–1605)," Exhibit P514.7, 9. Also see: Testimony of Dražen Erdemović (25 August 2003), 25148–25150.

156 NIOD, *Srebrenica: A "Safe" Area*, 2423.

157 In his memoirs, former British Prime Minister John Major qualified the French initiative as a "hair raising plan." See: John Major, *The Autobiography* (London: Harper & Collins, 1999), 545.

158 United Nations Security Council, Resolution 1004, No. S/RES/1004, 12 July 1995.

159 See: Andreas Zumach, "US Intelligence Knew Serbs were Planning an Assault on Srebrenica," *Basic Reports*, no. 47 (16 October 1995); Cees Wiebes, "Intelligence and the War in Bosnia 1992–1995: The Role of Intelligence and Security Services," in *Srebrenica: A "Safe" Area*; and Charles Lane and Thom Shanker, "In Bosnia: What the CIA Didn't Tell Us," *New York Review of Books*, 9 May 1996.

160 For example, see: Judgement, *Prosecution* v. *Popović et al.*

161 For an analysis of Deliberate Force ten years after the Operation, see: Ryan C. Hendrickson, "Crossing the Rubicon," *NATO Review*, no. 3 (Autumn 2005). It is available as an excerpt online at: www.nato.int/docu/review/2005/issue3/off-print_autumn_eng.pdf (accessed 10 July 2010).

162 NIOD, *Srebrenica: A "Safe" Area*, Appendix XIII.

163 Testimony of Vladislav Jovanović (16 February 2005), 36354; Testimony of Zoran Lilić (17 June 2003), 22616–22617.

164 Testimony of Vladislav Jovanović (16 February 2005), 36349–36350.

165 Testimony of David Harland (18 September 2003), 26981.

166 Testimony of General Rupert Smith (9 October 2003), 27316; "Code Cable Z-1139 'UNFP Policy, and Information for the Security Council'," 11 July 1995, Exhibit P553.15.

167 Testimony of General Rupert Smith (9 October 2003), 27329.

168 According to ICTY demographer Ewa Tabeau, 116 people from Žepa were killed in atrocities that followed its fall. See: Velma Šarić, "Demographics of Bosnian War Set Out," IWPR, *Tribunal Update*, no. 739, 4 May 2012, https://iwpr.net/global-voices/demographics-bosnian-war-set-out (accessed 4 April 2015). Also see the ICTY Judgement in the Tolimir case, in which three killings in Žepa were qualified as genocide.

169 For more discussion see: Geoffrey Nice and Nena Tromp, "Bosnia and Herzegovina."

170 Ewa Tabeau, Jakub Bijak, Arve Hetland, and Marci Zoltkowski, *Ethnic Composition, Internally Displaced Persons and Refugees from 47 Municipalities of Bosnia and Herzegovina, 1991 to 1997–98*, Expert Report, 4 April 2003, Exhibit P548.2, 76.

171 Half-Time Judgement, para. 232.

172 Samir Karić, "Od 200.000 Bošnjaka, u Foči ostale 3.000," *Oslobođenje*, 10 November 2013. Available at: www.oslobodjenje.ba/vijesti/bih/od-20000-bosnjaka-u-foci-ostale-3000 (accessed 23 September 2014).
173 Astri Suhrke and Mats Berdal, eds, *The Peace In Between: Post-War Violence and Peacebuilding* (New York: Routledge, 2012), 80–83.
174 The latest ICTY number of victims of the war in Bosnia and Herzegovina – which does not break down the military versus civilian deaths – is 104,732 persons, of which 68,101 were Muslims, 8,858 Croats, 22,779 Serbs and 4,995 others. See: Ewa Tabeau and Jan Zwierzchowski, "A Review of Estimation Methods for Victims of the Bosnian War and the Khmer Rouge Regime," in *Counting Civilian Casualties: Introduction to Recording and Estimating Nonmilitary Deaths in Conflict*, eds Taylor B. Seybolt, Jay D. Aronson, and Baruch Fischhoff (New York: Oxford University Press, 2013).
175 Wiebes, "Intelligence and the War in Bosnia 1992–1995," 226.
176 See: Zumach, "US Intelligence Knew Serbs were Planning an Assault on Srebrenica." Zumach writes that US intelligence services intercepted communications starting 17 June 1995 and listened daily to conversations between Perišić and Mladić, who were planning the attack on Srebrenica. Zumach is quoted in Wiebes, "Intelligence and the War in Bosnia 1992–1995," 221.
177 Wiebes, "Intelligence and the War in Bosnia 1992–1995," 193 and 221.
178 Deutch wrote a reply to Charles Lane and Thom Shanker for their article, "In Bosnia: What the CIA Didn't Tell Us." He wrote: "rumors of intercepted communications between Generals Perisic and Mladić last summer ... remain exactly that – rumors the US Government cannot substantiate." See: John Deutsch, "The CIA and Bosnia: An Exchange," *New York Review of Books*, 6 June 1996.
179 "Stenographic transcript of the 41st session of the Supreme Defence Council," 14 August 1995, *Prosecutor* v. *Perišić*, Exhibit P00797.E, 24.
180 United Nations General Assembly, Convention on the Prevention and Punishment of the Crime of Genocide, 9 December 1948.
181 Silber and Little, *Yugoslavia: Death of A Nation*, 352.
182 "Stenographic transcript of the 25th session of the Supreme Defence Council," 30 August 1994, *Prosecutor* v. *Perišić*, Exhibit P00778.E, 38.
183 "Stenographic transcript of the 39th session of the Supreme Defence Council," 29 July 1995, Exhibit P667.30.1, 25.
184 "Transcript of the 53rd session of the RS Assembly," 28 August 1995, Exhibit P538.24.1a, 70.
185 Ibid.
186 Lee Michael Katz, "Peace Hope for Bosnia: Use of Force," *USA Today*, 19 September 1995.
187 Human Rights Watch, *Croatia: A Decade of Disappointment – Continuing Obstacles to the Reintegration of Serb Returnees* (September 2006); Warren Christopher, in *Death of Yugoslavia*, "Pax Americana," Part VI, produced by Brian Lapping Associates, BBC, 1995.
188 For the text of the Evacuation Order, see: "Orders by Milan Martić dealing with planned evacuation of the population," 4 August 1995, *Prosecutor* v. *Gotovina et al.*, No. IT-06–90, Exhibit D00137.E.
189 "Stenographic transcript of the 41st session of the Supreme Defence Council," 14 August 1995, *Prosecutor* v. *Perišić*, Exhibit P00797.E, 26–27.
190 Testimony of General Wesley Clark (15 and 16 December 2003), 30379–30380.
191 Ibid., 30380.
192 Ibid., 30371.
193 Ibid., 30373.
194 Ibid., 30489.

195 Ibid., 30495.
196 For the sessions dated 23 April 1996, 21 May 1996, and 18 February 1997 (the 52nd, 53rd, and 61st session respectively), the OTP did not request records and nothing at all was provided.
197 Testimony of Zoran Lilić (17 June 2003), 22580–22581. The Chief of the Military Cabinet was also the secretary of the SDC, and was responsible for sending invitations, determining the agenda, collecting and distributing working material for meetings, and keeping records of the sessions. There were two Chiefs of the Military Cabinet between 1992 and 2000: Colonel Slavko Krivošija, from June 1992 to December 1995; and Colonel Slavoljub Šušić, from January 1996 to March 1999.
198 Prosecution Response to the 6 May 2003 Submission by Serbia and Montenegro Regarding Outstanding Requests for Assistance, 20 May 2003, para. 13.
199 Marlise Simons, "Serbia's Darkest Pages Hidden from Genocide Court," *New York Times*, 8 April 2007.
200 Geoffrey Nice, "Del Ponte's Deal," *London Review of Books*, 13 December 2010.
201 The politicisation of the OTP under del Ponte's mandate has been praised by some and criticised by others. For example, see: Simons, "Serbia's Darkest Pages Hidden from Genocide Court"; Geoffrey Nice, "Hidden from Public View," *New York Times*, 16 April 2007; and Lisa Clifford, "Del Ponte Denies Belgrade Deal Claim," IWPR, *Tribunal Update*, no. 498, 27 April 2007. Serge Brammertz, who followed del Ponte as Chief Prosecutor of the ICTY, also expressed support for this approach, telling the *Guardian* that, "Linking EU enlargement to the arrest of the fugitives has been a really successful tool in the past, and has been instrumental in the arrests of the fugitives of the last years." See: Julian Borger, "The Hunt for the Former Yugoslavia's War Criminal: Mission Accomplished," *Guardian*, 3 August 2011.
202 See: International Court of Justice, Judgement, "Case Concerning Application of the Convention on the Prevention and Punishment of the Crime of Genocide," *Bosnia and Herzegovina vs. Serbia and Montenegro*, 26 February 2007. Available at: www.icj-cij.org/docket/files/91/13685.pdf (accessed 23 September 2014).
203 See: Simons, "Serbia's Darkest Pages Hidden from Genocide Court." The topic had also been raised in a 2005 article, but it was largely ignored until the ICJ verdict. See: Hugh Griffiths and Ana Uzelac, "Justice at What Price?" IWPR *Tribunal Update*, no. 407, 18 November 2005.
204 Del Ponte reportedly agreed "that 'reasonable' portions of the records be kept under seal." See: Simons, "Serbia's Darkest Pages Hidden from Genocide Court."
205 Momir Bulatović, *Neizgovorena odbrana: ICTY vs. Slobodan Milošević* (Belgrade: Zograf, 2006).
206 Edina Bećirević, "New Light Shed on Belgrade Role in Bosnian War," IWPR, *Tribunal Update*, no. 526, 27 November 2007.
207 For example, see: "ICTY Lifts Seal from Supreme Defence Council Document in Momčilo Perišić Case," *Sense Tribunal*, 25 March 2011.
208 Decision on Prosecution Request for Change in Status of Certain Exhibits Admitted under Seal, *Prosecutor* v. *Perišić*, No. IT-04–81-T, 23 June 2011. Parts of the collection have been made available online by the Sense News Agency at: www.sense-agency.com/home/icty.59.html (accessed 2 March 2013). Protections were lifted from transcripts of selected sessions relevant to the Perišić case, namely the 5th, 6th, 9th, 12th, 14th–22nd, 25th, 27th, 28th, 30th, 31st, 35th, 37th, 38th, 41st, 44th, 56th, and 58th. Protections were also lifted from the minutes of the following sessions: 9th, 12th, 14th–16th, 18th, 21st–25th, 27th, 31st–33rd, 35th, 37th, 39th, 41st, 44th, 45th, 56th, and 58th.

209 ICTY rulings and the Bandinter Arbitration Commission have determined the date of recognition for Croatian independence as 8 October 1991, and not 15 January 1992, as the Defence claimed. The independence of BiH was determined by the ICTY to have been recognised as of 7 April 1992.
210 Branko Kostić, *Not To Be Forgotten*, Excerpt, Exhibit D333.72e, 179–180.
211 Ibid.
212 General Ferenc Vegh, Expert Report, 23 December 2003, Exhibit P644, 57.
213 Ibid.
214 Testimony of Witness B-127 (16 July 2003), 24597 and 24623.
215 Testimony of General Philippe Morillon (12 February 2004), 31963 and 32000.
216 Ibid., 32003–32004.
217 General Ratko Mladić was officially retired on 28 February 2002 and received a Serbian state pension until 24 March 2005, when it was suspended due to pressures from the Tribunal. See: "Mladiću penzija još nije odmrznuta," B92, 2 June 2011, www.b92.net/biz/vesti/srbija.php?yyyy=2011&mm=06&dd=02&nav_id=516252 (accessed 6 October 2014).
218 "Stenographic transcript of the 6th session of the Supreme Defence Council," 9 December 1992, *Prosecutor* v. *Perišić*, Exhibit P00788.E, 19.
219 "Stenographic transcript of the 9th session of the Supreme Defence Council," 2 June 1993, *Prosecutor* v. *Perišić*, Exhibit P00789.E, 19.
220 Ibid., 25.
221 Ibid., 30
222 Ibid., 31.
223 "Stenographic transcript of the 14th session of the Supreme Defence Council," 11 October 1993, *Prosecutor* v. *Perišić*, Exhibit P00709.E, 32.
224 Ibid., 33–36.
225 "Stenographic transcript of the 15th session of the Supreme Defence Council," 10 November 1993, *Prosecutor* v. *Perišić*, Exhibit P00780.E, 19.
226 Testimony of Zoran Lilić (17 June 2003), 22591.
227 Ibid., 22591–22592.
228 "Minutes from the 56th session of the Supreme Defence Council," 5 September 1996, *Prosecutor* v. *Perišić*, Exhibit P00768.E, 4.
229 Trial Transcript, Defence Opening Statement (17 February 2002), 257.
230 "Minutes from the 39th session of the Supreme Defence Council," 29 July 1995, *Prosecutor* v. *Perišić*, Exhibit P00763.E, 2.
231 "Stenographic transcript of the 41st session of the Supreme Defence Council," 14 August 1995, *Prosecutor* v. *Perišić*, Exhibit P00797.E, 24.
232 Ibid. The presentation of this evidence represented the first time Milošević's own words betrayed that he had indeed communicated with RS leadership during the attack, despite repeated denials of this fact.
233 Half-Time Judgement, para. 289. Also see: para. 309.
234 For example, see: Radovan Radinović's contribution at the 6th SDC session: "Stenographic transcript of the 6th session of the Supreme Defence Council," 9 December 1992, *Prosecutor* v. *Perišić*, Exhibit P00788.E, 16.
235 Trial Transcript, Defence Opening Statement (14 February 2002), 256–257.
236 Testimony of Witness C-175 (2 September 2003), 25919 and 26032–26033. Also see: Reynaud J.M. Theunens, *The SFRY Armed Forces and the Conflict in Croatia & JNA Activity in BiH and JNA (VJ) Support to Bosnian-Serb Forces*, Expert Report, 16 December 2003, Exhibit P643.1.
237 Ibid., 25917–25930.
238 See: "Stenographic transcript of the 18th session of the Supreme Defence Council," 7 February 1994, *Prosecutor* v. *Perišić*, Exhibit P00782.E, 55–61.
239 "Stenographic transcript of the 6th session of the Supreme Defence Council," 9 December 1992, *Prosecutor* v. *Perišić*, Exhibit P00788.E, 17.

240 "Stenographic transcript of the 18th session of the Supreme Defence Council," 7 February 1994, *Prosecutor* v. *Perišić*, Exhibit P00782.E, 56–57.
241 Ibid., 58.
242 Lawyers Committee for Human Rights, "Analysis of the Issue of the Legality or Illegality of the Creation of the 30th and 40th Personnel Centres of the VJ," 3.
243 Ibid.
244 Vegh, Expert Report, 22.
245 For instance, see: "Stenographic transcript of the 37th session of the Supreme Defence Council," 13 June 1995, *Prosecutor* v. *Perišić*, Exhibit P00786.E, 32–33; and "Stenographic transcript of the 13th session of the Supreme Defence Council," 7 September 1993, Exhibit P667.13.1a, 9.
246 Ibid.
247 See: "Stenographic transcript of the 37th session of the Supreme Defence Council," 13 June 1995, *Prosecutor* v. *Perišić*, Exhibit P00786.E.
248 Testimony of Milan Milanović (8 October 2003), 27245.
249 Testimony of General Rupert Smith (9 October 2003), 27368.
250 "Stenographic Notes of the 7th Session of the FRY Supreme Defence Council," 10 February 1993, *Prosecutor* v. *Perišić*, Exhibit P00771.E, 27–28.
251 Ibid.
252 Ibid., 29.
253 "Stenographic transcript of the 9th session of the Supreme Defence Council," 2 June 1993, *Prosecutor* v. *Perišić*, Exhibit P00789.E, 9.
254 "Stenographic transcript of the 14th session of the Supreme Defence Council," 11 October 1993, *Prosecutor* v. *Perišić*, Exhibit P00709.E, 28.
255 Trial Transcript (11 April 2003), 19069.
256 Testimony of Zoran Lilić (17 June 2003), 22622.
257 "Stenographic transcript of the 19th session of the Supreme Defence Council," 16 March 1994, *Prosecutor* v. *Perišić*, Exhibit P00783.E, 6.
258 "Stenographic transcript of the 22nd session of the Supreme Defence Council," 11 July 1994, *Prosecutor* v. *Perišić*, Exhibit P00784.E, 2.
259 "Minutes from the 36th Supreme Defence Council Session," 12 May 1995, *Prosecutor* v. *Perišić*, Exhibit P00749.E.
260 "Minutes from the 39th session of the Supreme Defence Council," 29 July 1995, *Prosecutor* v. *Perišić*, Exhibit P00763.E, 2–3.
261 "Stenographic transcript of the 41st session of the Supreme Defence Council," 14 August 1995, *Prosecutor* v. *Perišić*, Exhibit P00797.E, 26–27.
262 Ibid., 20.
263 "Minutes from the 43rd session of the Supreme Defence Council," 29 August 1995, *Prosecutor* v. *Perišić*, Exhibit P00708.E, 1–2.
264 "Minutes from the 44th session of the Supreme Defence Council," 6 September 1995, *Prosecutor* v. *Perišić*, Exhibit P00765.E, 1.
265 Minutes of the 46th session of the Supreme Defence Council, 11 October 1995, 5.
266 For example, see: de Graaff, "The Difference between Legal Proof and Historical Evidence," 505.
267 See: "Stenographic transcript of the 25th session of the Supreme Defence Council," 30 August 1994, *Prosecutor* v. *Perišić*, Exhibit P00778.E.
268 "Minutes from the 24th session of the Supreme Defence Council," 9 August 1994, *Prosecutor* v. *Perišić*, Exhibit P00755.E, 2.
269 Ibid., 95.
270 "Transcript of the 50th session of the RS Assembly," 15 and 16 April 1995, Exhibit P538.22.1a, 18.
271 "Statement by Milošević in relation to financial matters," Exhibit 427.3a, 2.

272 Ivor Roberts, *Conversations with Milošević* (Oxford: Oxford University Press, 2013), 48.
273 "Minutes of the 42nd session of the Supreme Defence Council," 23 August 1995, *Prosecutor* v. *Perišić*, Exhibit P00713.E, 2.
274 Ibid.
275 "Notes from a meeting held in Dobanovci (Serbia) between Slobodan Milošević and the Bosnian Serb leadership," 29 August 1995, Exhibit P469.20a, Meeting Record, 5.
276 Ibid., 16–19.
277 See: Donia, *The Assembly of Republika Srpska*, 69. Also see: Testimony of Robert Donia (12 September 2003), 26519.
278 "Stenographic transcript of the 47th session of the Supreme Defence Council," 6 December 1995, Exhibit P667.47.1a, 10.
279 Ibid., 9.
280 Ibid., 6.

6 The plan for Kosovo

Keeping Kosovo in Serbia by changing the ethnic composition

In the aftermath of Dayton, as Milošević celebrated the double victory of the creation of Republika Srpska and its acceptance by the international community, he may have had a real chance to pursue a second phase of his career without culpability for political violence and mass atrocities. But, he failed to pass the test of Kosovo, the political potency of which had remained charged among the Serb nationalists on whose votes and support he relied. Any compromise from Milošević on the issue of Kosovo bore the risk of being seen as weakness among his nationalist supporters, and could have affected his ability to retain power.

This chapter addresses the fifth of Milošević's goals – the domination of Kosovo – a project that began early in his tenure and, though it may have taken a backseat to conflicts in neighbouring states, continued throughout the 1990s. Efforts to achieve this goal became increasingly ineffective in the face of rising opposition from the majority ethnic Albanian population, leading to a full-scale war in 1999 and the commission of grave crimes against civilians. The Kosovo indictment alleged that, from 1 January 1999 to 20 June 1999, Milošević was a participant in a Joint Criminal Enterprise, the purpose of which was to expel a significant number of Kosovo Albanians from Kosovo in order to ensure Serb control of the province. FRY forces allegedly operated "at the direction, with the encouragement, or with the support" of Milošević during this time; and their efforts to create an "atmosphere of fear and oppression" were said to have resulted in the displacement of some 800,000 civilians. These forces were also accused of having systematically destroyed homes, farms, and cultural and religious institutions, and of murdering Kosovo Albanian civilians and raping Kosovo Albanian women. As President of the FRY during the period in question, Milošević exercised command authority over the Yugoslav Army and the Federal MUP.[1]

From 1990 to 1999, the major goal of Serbian policy in Kosovo was to keep the province under Serbian rule – by maintaining the status quo, creating an apartheid system, and then enforcing this policy through violence. The Prosecution saw the conflict in Kosovo and the mass atrocities committed by Serb forces there in 1998 and 1999 as a part of Milošević's strategy to hold on to Kosovo, arguing that Serbia had been determined to prevent Kosovo

Albanians from regaining any form of autonomy and had used their resistance as an excuse to respond with disproportionate force. The Defence claimed that the Kosovo Liberation Army (KLA) had unleashed the violence, in 1997, and that Serbia and the FRY had responded to acts of terrorism as any state would.

In the trial record, the Kosovo conflict can be seen through the lens of various events, against the contrast of two opposing views. Controversy surrounds a number of issues, such as the Račak massacre and its role in triggering subsequent events – including the Rambouillet negotiations, the failure to negotiate a peace, and the NATO military intervention. As was true for the Croatia and BiH indictments, it was important to reconstruct Milošević's de facto and *de jure* powers during the years pertinent to the Kosovo indictment; though, during the Kosovo conflict, he tried to obscure decision-making processes related to the use of force so that he could not be directly linked to crimes. And although he was President of the FRY at the time of the war in Kosovo and bore responsibility for deployment of the armed forces, it was again his de facto power that was more important to understanding his actions and his state of mind.

In establishing the role Milošević played in the Kosovo conflict, the Prosecution followed the trail of an ad hoc body known as the Joint Command for Kosovo and Metohija (or just the Joint Command). After submitting requests to Belgrade for documents related to the Joint Command for many years, some of them finally arrived during the Defence part of the case and were used in the cross-examination of Defence witnesses. Milošević called a number of VJ and MUP officers who had been engaged in combat in Kosovo in 1998 and 1999, and who referred in their testimony to contemporaneous documents relating to combat there. These documents were of significant evidentiary value, as they exposed the military objectives of Serb forces in Kosovo and their use of violence against civilians. The fact that obtaining these documents had been such a challenge also exposed Serbia's post-war effort to keep evidence of its wartime policies from the ICTY and the public.

Serbia's policy of apartheid in Kosovo

After 1990, Serbia governed Kosovo through an expensive model of administration that relied on a large police force, creating a system of repression and oppression that amounted to a police state.[2] Blatant abuses of the individual and collective human rights of Kosovo Albanians by Serbian lawmakers, political institutions, and police were recorded by various national and international NGOs, which routinely sent reports of these abuses to Milošević and other Serbian and FRY politicians, officials, and government agencies.[3] Once in The Hague, his receipt of these reports meant that Milošević could not claim ignorance to what had occurred in Kosovo. In legal terms, he was shown to be 'on notice.'

Human rights reports on discrimination against Kosovo Albanians, some of which were tendered into evidence, were corroborated and complemented by the testimonies of several Prosecution witnesses.[4] In July 1990 the Serbian Parliament passed the "Law on Labour Relations in Special Circumstances," which allowed for dismissals based on arbitrary criteria and at the same time legalised the recruitment of Serbs only – and not ethnic Albanians – for posts in Kosovo.[5] The Law further obliged workers of Albanian origin to sign a document attesting that they accepted the political and other measures taken by Serbian authorities in Kosovo.

Subsequently, a number of laws had been adopted that set the ground for an apartheid society, and Prosecution witnesses described the process through which ethnic Albanians had been dismissed from their jobs in favour of Serbs and Montenegrins. Speaking often from their own experience, witnesses testified about the unemployment that affected Kosovo Albanians when large numbers of employees in public enterprises and institutions – such as hospitals, media organisations, and schools – were let go.[6] There were also mass dismissals of Kosovo Albanians from positions in industry. And in some cases, employees of Kosovo Albanian origin were told to sign a declaration of loyalty to state authorities or face dismissal.[7] Albanian-language media was targeted, too, when the broadcasts of Albanian Radio and Television were restricted and influential newspapers were closed.[8] This led to the establishment of parallel systems of public services – an official system for Kosovo Serbs and another unofficial system for Kosovo Albanians.

One of the most disturbing consequences of Serbian apartheid politics in Kosovo was the exclusion of ethnic Albanian children from the school system. A new school curriculum was introduced in 1990 and 1991 by the Serbian authorities and Kosovo Albanian teachers who refused to implement it were dismissed.[9] And Prosecution witness Sabit Kadriu – a teacher himself – testified that by the start of the school year in September 1991, Kosovo Albanian teachers were prevented from entering school premises at all.[10] As a consequence, approximately 400,000 children did not attend school for almost two years, during which a parallel education system was formed, with classes held in private homes.[11]

The University of Priština was affected as well: the University Assembly and several faculty councils were dissolved, and provisional organs staffed predominantly by Serbs were established instead.

Failed negotiations to normalise life in Kosovo, 1996–1998

Serbia's strategy in Kosovo faced little serious opposition from Kosovo Albanian political leadership for many years due to the non-violent resistance espoused by Ibrahim Rugova, the President of Kosovo from 1992 to 2000. Although the Kosovo Albanian majority never accepted Serbian rule, Rugova was determined to avoid violence. His party, the Democratic League of Kosovo (LDK), which won unofficial elections in May 1992, did not take action against the deteriorating social and economic position of ethnic Albanians. For the sake of peace the LDK accepted the parallel system that emerged, creating de facto Kosovo Albanian government structures, schools, and health services, paid for by a voluntary solidarity tax largely collected from diaspora.[12]

This diaspora rapidly expanded in the early 1990s as younger generations of Kosovo Albanians, unable to get an education or job at home, began leaving the province in large numbers and settling abroad.[13] The UN reported that 300,000 Kosovo Albanians had left Kosovo by the end of 1992 and, citing allegations ranging from torture and mistreatment in detention to restrictions on freedom of information, expressed concerns about the safety of remaining ethnic Albanians.[14] Yet Serbia was reluctant to engage in dialogue with Kosovo Albanians for fear that this would inevitably lead to political compromises and probably to a change – or reversal – in the province's status.

Bilateral talks were eventually scheduled in 1996 and included representatives of several Serbian political parties. Milošević's SPS did not attend, but participation by the New Democracy Party (*Nova demokratija*, or ND), a coalition partner of the SPS, implied support from Milošević. The talks were mediated by the Bertelsmann Science Foundation and a diplomatic organ from the Vatican led by Monsignor Paglia of the Community of San Egidio; and they went reasonably well, until Milošević decided to withdraw his support.[15]

Veton Surroi, a Kosovo Albanian publisher-turned-politician and owner of the influential daily *Koha Ditore*, was also involved in the talks. He testified that Kosovo Albanian delegates had been motivated to negotiate by an understanding that, unless they worked with Serbs to improve living conditions, Kosovo was on a path to a war.[16] Serbian negotiators had also expressed that the status quo could not be maintained and that a wave of violence was imminent without some sort of change.[17] The negotiations resulted in a document titled "Joint Recommendations on the Kosovo Conflict," which was meant to serve as the basis for future talks about the status of the province.[18] But the most concrete outcome of the talks was the so-called San Egidio Education Agreement, according to which the school system was to be normalised and Albanian teachers and students were to return to classrooms.

The Serbian delegation submitted the "Joint Recommendations" to Milošević, and eventually he and Rugova both signed the Education Agreement in September 1996.[19] However, no tangible steps were taken to implement the Agreement and Kosovo Albanian students took to the street in late 1997, in protests that were violently quelled by Serbian police with tear gas and truncheons. On 23 March 1998, a follow-up document laid out implementation measures for the Agreement and the Institute of Albanology reopened on 31 March, but hardly any other faculty or institution followed suit. International mediators began to openly question the goodwill of Serbia;

and despite several more, albeit half-hearted, attempts to address the implementation of the Education Agreement, it lost any relevance by 1998 as violence rapidly spread across Kosovo.[20]

A failed strategy to change Kosovo's ethnic composition through reforms

In her Expert Report for the Prosecution, historian Audrey Budding explained how the Kosovo Albanian majority had become such an obstacle to Serbian control of the province. She wrote that the communist Partisans made serious efforts during the Second World War to win the support of Kosovo Albanians and had ensured after the war that Kosovo became an autonomous province that Serb interwar colonists could not return to.[21] And indeed, the emigration of Serbs from Kosovo and the immigration of Albanians to Kosovo during the war did change the ethnic composition in the province to the advantage of Kosovo Albanians. Then, from the 1950s, there was a steady rise in their numbers.[22] By 1961, Kosovo Albanians constituted 67 per cent of the population and ten years later, more than 70 per cent. Kosovo Albanian political and intellectual elites flourished, and after 1966, they took over leadership of the province.[23]

These demographics were interpreted by Serbia's nationalist elites as the result of an intentional anti-Serb effort meant to create an ethnically homogenous, i.e. Albanian, Kosovo; and this interpretation became a powerful motif in Milošević's propaganda.[24] The Defence alleged that consistently high Kosovo Albanian birth rates combined with what it described as a systematic expulsion of the Serb population from the province beginning in the nineteenth century, amounted to a political strategy of ethnic cleansing. Defence expert Slavenko Terzić asserted that it was "almost impossible to find an instance of such ethnic cleansing by the Serbs; instead, it is the Serbs, unfortunately, who were the victims."[25] According to Terzić, "the final phase" of the ethnic cleansing of Serbs in Kosovo was "carried out under communist rule by the [Albanian] political leadership" of the province. He said these leaders could have promoted "the multi-cultural and multi-ethnic nature of Kosovo and Metohija," but instead were responsible for what he called the "great drama of the Serbian people in Old Serbia."[26]

The changing ethnic balance in Kosovo demanded attention and new political and administrative solutions. In 1968, acknowledging the unchangeable reality of the Kosovo Albanian majority, Dobrica Ćosić had been the first to suggest splitting Kosovo into Serbian and Kosovo Albanian parts.[27] He again raised this option in September 1990, arguing for a division based not on ethnic criteria but on more pragmatic parameters, so that Serbia would retain ore mines and Serbian holy places such as Gračanica and Gazimestan. Ćosić's plan envisaged eastern and central Kosovo for ethnic Albanians, and the northern and western parts for Serbs, with the Ibar River as a border. But his proposal was ignored, overshadowed by Milošević's triumph in revoking

Kosovo's autonomy. Still, Ćosić continued to make the argument for partition in similar terms in his book *The Writer's Notes*, published in 1992, in which he stated that it would lead to a lasting solution to the Serb-Albanian question in Kosovo.[28]

This idea was picked up by Aleksandar Despić, then President of the SANU, who told SANU members in a 1997 address that the partition of Kosovo solved a problem that had become too heavy a burden for Belgrade.[29] Dušan Bataković, a diplomat and expert on the history of Kosovo, took the idea further, advocating in early 1998 for the cantonisation of Kosovo – the same model Serbs had espoused for the partitioning of BiH. Bataković argued that this would preserve the multiethnic composition of Kosovo while enforcing distinct rights for cantons with a Serb majority.[30]

But Milošević never considered the partition of Kosovo an option; nor did he accept demographic realities in the province. Indeed, his politics from 1990 onward were concentrated on establishing Serb dominance through the imposition of laws and decrees that he hoped would alter the demographic balance there. First, he created a fund to finance the return of Serbs and Montenegrins to Kosovo.[31] This was complemented in 1991 by the "Decree on the Conditions, Ways and Means for Distributing Agricultural Land" to citizens wanting to live and work in Kosovo, which made loans available to Serbs to encourage them to move there.[32] In 1992, the "Programme for the Development of Kosovo" was adopted, providing further financial assistance to Serbs, to build houses, establish businesses, and create cultural establishments, schools, and infrastructure.[33]

Human rights observers, along with Kosovo Albanian politicians and human rights activists, protested these attempts by Serbian authorities to gain greater influence in Kosovo through government-sponsored settlement programmes. Still, they continued; though with little success.[34] And a resettlement programme for refugees from the RS and RSK also failed. According to Milošević, the number of refugees from these entities that resettled in Kosovo amounted to a mere 0.7 per cent of the total number that entered the FRY before the Dayton Agreement.[35] Therefore, he argued, one could not accuse him or Serbian authorities of having implemented a policy to change the demographic structure of the province. But it wasn't for lack of trying, and Kosovo Serb political leaders had been sharply critical of Belgrade's failure to fulfil its promise to resettle 100,000 Serbs to Kosovo.[36]

Kosovo after 1995

As tensions in Kosovo were slowly reaching their boiling point, other conflicts in the former Yugoslavia had ignited. Milošević had kept Kosovo out of the talks in Dayton, but instead of securing the status quo, this in fact shifted the dynamics. For, by ignoring Kosovo at Dayton, the space was created for an alternative approach to the conflict by a new generation of Kosovo Albanians. The international community's failure to address the Kosovo crisis at this opportunity undermined Ibrahim Rugova's political authority. His peaceful front had failed to bring results and his party had engaged in a misguided public campaign which claimed the Kosovo issue would be resolved through negotiations in Dayton, giving the impression that the province was days away from independence; but of course it wasn't.[37]

According to Veton Surroi, Rugova's policy of peace was so passive that it had devalued peaceful politics over time and paved the way to violence.[38] Younger Kosovo Albanians, dissatisfied with the slow progress of non-violence and dialogue, took up arms, organising themselves into the Kosovo Liberation Army (KLA). The first violent incidents ascribed to the KLA took place in 1995, escalating in frequency and scope by 1997 – when the political situation in Kosovo finally caught the attention of the international community. By the spring of 1998, clashes between Serbian police forces and the KLA became more frequent and violent, and various monitoring organisations reported on a fully-fledged armed conflict as early as March.

The turning point for the intensity of the conflict was a massacre at the family compound of Adem Jashari, a local KLA commander in the Drenica area who had become notorious for attacks on Serbian security forces. In an attempt to capture Jashari, Serbian police attacked the entire Jashari family compound in early March 1998, killing not only Adem, but nearly every member of his family, including women and children. Shocking pictures of the victims were disseminated via the Internet by Kosovo Albanian activists, launching Jashari as a martyr and the Serbian authorities as villains.[39]

The defence narrative on the proliferation of violence in Kosovo

In November 1992, the Serbian Assembly had issued a Declaration on the Rights of National Minorities, in which Albanian separatists were blamed for the human rights situation in Kosovo. The Declaration described the history of the province as one of "ethnic cleansing of Serbs and Montenegrins" meant to facilitate the creation of a "Greater Albania." Milošević echoed this at the trial, asserting that 150,000 Serbs – one-quarter of the total Kosovo Serb population – had been expelled from Kosovo between 1878 and 1912. He also emphasised the suffering of Kosovo Serbs during the Second World War, claiming that 10,000 Serbs had been killed and hundreds of thousands expelled from Kosovo between April 1941 and August 1942.[40] He accused Albanian nationalists of everything from chauvinism to terrorism and said they were a continued threat to Serbs.[41]

Prosecution witnesses rejected the idea that Greater Albania ideology drove Kosovo Albanian policy.[42] Mahmut Bakalli, a communist functionary from Kosovo who appeared as the trial's first witness, testified that any prospect of a Greater Albania was the creation of Serbian political propaganda and aimed at casting the Albanians in a sinister light.[43] When cross-examined by Milošević about the existence of a Greater Albania during the Second

World War, Bakalli said it had been a fascist and Nazi creation, not representative at all of Albanians, the majority of whom joined anti-fascist movements in Albania, Macedonia, and Kosovo.[44] He said political efforts to create an independent Kosovo or a Republic of Kosovo within the FRY were never part of any scheme to eventually realise a Greater Albania. Even though 90 per cent of the population was ethnically Albanian, he explained "the Republic of Albania is an Albanian state, Kosova is a state of Kosovars."[45]

Ibrahim Rugova also testified, citing his party's (the LDK) primary objective in the early 1990s as democracy for all of Kosovo's citizens, with a secondary goal to create a Kosovar republic in the SFRY.[46] In October 1991, the LDK had issued a document titled "Statement with Three Options," in which three possibilities for the status of Kosovo were laid out in the event of changes to internal SFRY borders resulting from the independence of some Yugoslav republics. The first option was a Republic of Kosovo within Yugoslavia, the second was independence for Kosovo, and the third was a common state for all Albanians living in the SFRY – similar to the goal espoused by Serbia for Serbs across the former Federation. Rugova testified that the LDK preferred an independent Kosovo.[47]

In court, Milošević presented Rugova with a Memorandum allegedly written in the 1990s by Kosovo Albanian intellectuals, in which they demanded the re-drawing of borders in order to create an independent state that would unite all ethnic Albanian territories. He asked Rugova to comment on the map attached to the Memorandum.[48] Rugova replied that there were many such maps in circulation, but that his party had sought independence above all else since the dissolution of Yugoslavia. Nonetheless, Milošević maintained that Rugova and the Kosovo Albanian leadership supported a Greater Albania, and that they sought to incorporate not only Albania and Kosovo but also parts of Macedonia.[49] Shukri Buja, a former KLA commander who testified for the Prosecution, confirmed that the KLA – not the LDK – had indeed intended at one time to liberate occupied Albanian territories that included areas in Macedonia, Serbia, and Montenegro, but said the negative response of international policy makers compelled the KLA General Staff to reconsider their political objectives; and the decision was made to concentrate only on Kosovo.[50]

Internationalisation of the Kosovo conflict

Throughout the 1990s, Milošević kept Kosovo out of international mediation and diplomacy by insisting that tensions there were an internal matter to be dealt with by Serbian and FRY authorities.[51] The first time the Kosovo conflict was addressed in an international setting was at a September 1997 meeting of the Contact Group – the informal group of representatives from influential countries created to supervise policy in Southeastern Europe. Although the Contact Group had been mandated to monitor implementation of the Dayton Peace Agreement, the alarming security situation that was developing within Serbia led to the inclusion of Kosovo on their agenda, and they issued a joint statement calling on authorities to begin dialogue and create conditions for the return of refugees. They also voiced support for implementation of the San Egidio Education Agreement. And, while the Contact Group did not support independence for Kosovo, they called for enhanced status for the province.[52] Beginning in January 1998, the Contact Group met every month to evaluate the quickly evolving situation in Kosovo, especially focusing on reports of escalating violence and human rights abuses.[53]

The Jashari family massacre in March 1998 intensified diplomatic activity. The Contact Group condemned Belgrade authorities' use of violence, called for independent forensic experts to investigate, and asked the FRY to prosecute and punish those responsible. A majority of Contact Group representatives had dealt directly with Milošević in the past, and they appealed to him personally to take rapid and effective steps to stop the violence and find a political solution through dialogue. Moreover, they imposed a deadline of ten days for the withdrawal of Serbian special police units from Kosovo and threatened new international sanctions for the FRY if it wasn't met.[54]

Contact Group meetings were marked by the strong dissenting voice of Russian Minister of Foreign Affairs Yevgeny Primakov, who echoed the rhetoric of Milošević that Kosovo be treated as an internal Yugoslav affair. Primakov, who later appeared as a Defence witness, recorded in his memoir that the United States, United Kingdom, and other European countries had proposed in the March 1998 meeting that economic sanctions be imposed on the FRY, to his dismay. Primakov believed they wanted to discipline Milošević, or even depose him; and he proposed an arms embargo instead, with limited sanctions.[55] On 31 March, the UN banned arms sales to Serbia, imposed economic sanctions, and – in UNSC Resolution 1160 – established a committee to monitor the situation in Kosovo.

At the April 1998 Contact Group meeting, the Group stated firmly that it opposed the independence of Kosovo and called for the start of dialogue. And for the first time, they referred to excessive use of force by the VJ, which was said to mark a significant change in the extent and nature of the conflict.[56] In a 'carrot and stick' approach, the Contact Group soon promised Belgrade full integration into the international community if it met the Group's demands – a particularly tempting proposal for Serbia because so-called outer wall sanctions meant that the FRY could not become a member of international organisations such as the UN or the IMF.[57] The Contact Group stipulated that if the FRY did not comply with the conditions it had laid out in March, funds held internationally by the FRY and Serbian governments would be frozen; in other words, if Belgrade exhibited noncompliance and blocked dialogue with the Kosovo Albanians, the FRY would be subject to a series of economic sanctions. The Russian Federation distanced itself from these measures and proposed, instead, to condemn Kosovo Albanian terrorism and commit to preserving the territorial integrity of all countries in the region.[58]

A strongly worded Statement on Kosovo issued by the foreign ministers of the Contact Group in London on 12 June 1998 was indicative of yet another level of alarm in the international community. For the first time, the Group demanded access to Kosovo, alleging that indiscriminate armed interventions were "causing many civilian casualties and forcing tens of thousands of inhabitants to flee their homes." Belgrade's use of force was described as "massive and disproportionate" and was said to have led to "widespread destruction and the deliberate displacement of large numbers of people."[59] Serbia turned to Russia for advice and support and President Boris Yeltsin met with Milošević on 16 June 1998.[60] Yeltsin pressed Milošević to accept the internationalisation of the Kosovo conflict and to allow OSCE monitors into the province. Primakov characterised the meeting as a triumph of Russian diplomacy that had averted a military intervention against Belgrade.[61] But for Serbia, the meeting was a disappointment because Russia did not support Serbia's military approach to the Kosovo crisis. Milošević knew then that even if the FRY were ultimately to win the conflict by force, it would still face total international isolation.

The July meeting of the Contact Group used the Yeltsin-Milošević meeting and its outcomes to press for an increase in the OSCE Monitoring Mission presence in Kosovo. The Group warned those outside the FRY to stop supplying financial support, arms, or training to the warring sides, in compliance with UNSC Resolution 1160.[62] Under the threat of military intervention for defying UNSCR 1160, and then facing ceasefire demands in Resolution 1199, Milošević engaged in a series of meetings with American diplomat Richard Holbrooke, reaching a final agreement on 13 October 1998 that was unofficially known as the Milošević-Holbrooke Agreement.

The Agreement consisted of 11 points and included a very strict implementation timetable. Addressing the Serbian public, Milošević announced that an accord had been reached to resolve the problems in Kosovo by peaceful political means, saying the threat of military intervention against the FRY had been eliminated.[63] The Agreement envisaged an international presence in Kosovo and concentrated on two major issues – a political solution based on Contact Group principles defined on 2 October 1998, and establishment of rules and procedures for elections in Kosovo to be held by November 2009.[64] The OSCE was asked to engage as part of a peaceful settlement of the Kosovo conflict, and an agreement on the newly formed Kosovo Verification Monitors (KVM) was signed on 15 October.[65]

The KVM had a mandate to verify compliance by all parties in Kosovo with UNSC Resolution 1199, as well as to report progress or noncompliance to the OSCE Permanent Council, the UNSC, and other organisations. Various Prosecution witnesses involved with the KVM testified that Serbia did not cooperate. For instance, Milošević made a habit of ignoring queries of a technical nature, such as requests for information regarding the strength and equipment of the armed forces in Kosovo.[66] Further, according to witnesses, the KVM never had unlimited access to MUP and VJ sites and even had difficulty getting information on training schedules for VJ exercises or advance notice of troop movements, despite official agreements.[67] The KVM reported these continuous breaches, and yet combat involving MUP and VJ forces simply continued.[68] Meanwhile, Belgrade complained that implementation of the Milošević-Holbrooke Agreement required a reduction of its military units, and that the KLA was relying on this reduction to seize more territory.

From the Račak massacre to negotiations in Rambouillet

By the end of 1998, the threat of a humanitarian catastrophe in Kosovo became a reality. Independent reports from all sides estimated that by November of that year, there were about 300,000 internally displaced persons in Kosovo facing a severe winter and no prospect of a quick return to their homes.[69] A UNHCR survey showed that between the end of 1998 and 23 March 1999, some 349,000 Kosovo Albanians were displaced altogether, with 200,000 displaced internally.[70]

But it was the Račak massacre, which took place on 15 January 1999, that led the international community to change its rules of engagement and demand a political solution from the parties to the armed conflict. The massacre, which resulted from the same Serbian police techniques used at the Jashari compound, was triggered by information that three KLA terrorists suspected of killing two Serbian policemen were hiding in Račak. Serbian police forces surrounded the village in the middle of the night and killed approximately 45 unarmed people.[71]

The Contact Group condemned the Račak massacre at its 22 January 1999 meeting in London, stating that no amount of provocation could justify what had taken place. It called on the FRY to stop all offensive actions in Kosovo and facilitate the safe return of refugees from the Račak area. Further, the Group requested full cooperation with the ICTY from the FRY, in order to ensure that those responsible for the massacre were brought to justice.[72] At a meeting one week later, the Contact Group insisted that the parties to the conflict accept principles of a peaceful settlement set out by the Group, which offered substantial autonomy to Kosovo. Negotiations to refine the proposal were scheduled for 6 February at Rambouillet Castle, near Paris.[73]

The failure of the Rambouillet negotiations

The Prosecution argued that the Rambouillet talks – which took place through mid-March – were an example of Serbia's unwillingness to come to a political compromise on the status of Kosovo. Serbia ostensibly, and for the first time, appeared agreeable to negotiations under international mediation on the issue. But a number of witnesses testified that Serbia never took the negotiations seriously.

The 15-person Kosovo Albanian delegation at Rambouillet consisted of representatives from Rugova's LDK and from the KLA, along with independent delegates such as Veton Surroi. Professor Fehmi Agani – who was murdered by Serbian security forces in May 1999 – headed the delegation.[74] And Hashim Thaci, head of the political directorate within the KLA General Staff, led the representatives of the KLA.[75] The Serbian delegation comprised republican and federal officials, including Milan Milutinović, then President of Serbia; Ratko Marković, Deputy Prime Minister of Serbia; and Nikola Šainović, Deputy Prime Minister of the FRY; as well as other officials with close ties to Milošević.[76]

The Rambouillet Peace Proposal, presented as the last resort for finding a political solution to the Kosovo problem, was based on the Dayton Peace Agreement formula and consisted of both a political component and a military component. The political component did not give full independence to Kosovo, but offered substantial autonomy with a very clear framework for how political and judicial systems would operate and human rights would be respected. The military component was meant to secure implementation of the Proposal.[77]

One of the strongest indications of Serbia's disinclination to cooperate was that the armed conflict in Kosovo intensified as the peace negotiations were underway. Knut Vollebaek, a Norwegian diplomat participating in the OSCE's Kosovo Mission, testified that there was an increased presence of the VJ in Kosovo by March, in violation of the Milošević–Holbrooke Agreement, and that the local population had lost confidence in the KVM. It became clear to Vollebaek that a military presence tasked with keeping the fighting factions apart was necessary; and this is what the OSCE advocated at Rambouillet. In fact, Vollebaek personally tried to convince Milošević, who was not at the talks, to accept an international military presence.[78]

The absence of Milošević at the negotiating table was another sign that the Serbs did not take the negotiations seriously, and many foreign negotiators who testified for the Prosecution spoke of how important Milošević's presence had been in Dayton. In Rambouillet, there were two rounds of negotiations – from 6 to 23 February and from 23 February to 15 March – and FRY and Serbian delegates appeared to be unauthorised to make decisions on their own, contacting Milošević every day. Despite his physical absence, Milošević clearly held the ultimate power.[79] Serbian delegates openly stated that they only had the authority to discuss the political component of the agreement, not the military component, and they made it clear that once political negotiations were completed, Milošević would give them instructions for the next step.[80]

Prosecution witnesses who were present at Rambouillet throughout the negotiations agreed that a change of attitude within the Serb delegation occurred after 23 February. According to Wolfgang Petritsch, an Austrian diplomat in charge of the negotiations on behalf of the EU, the Serbian delegation consisted of well-versed experts with whom international negotiators had been dealing since mid-1998 and who, up to 23 February, were negotiating in good faith.[81] Indeed, in a meeting with the Contact Group on

20 February, there were strong signals that Serbia and the FRY could live with the political agreement that had been crafted.[82] The sense was that the Serbs were ready to sign, as indicated in a letter sent on 23 February by Serbian delegation member Professor Ratko Marković, addressed to the three principle negotiators, Christopher Hill (US), Wolfgang Petritsch (EU), and Boris Mayorski (Russia). Marković said that the FRY was willing to discuss the scope and character of an international presence in Kosovo in order to implement the agreement that would be accepted in Rambouillet.[83] But things were about to change.

On 8 March 1999, Petritsch accompanied German Foreign Minister Joschka Fischer to a meeting with politicians in Belgrade. In private talks – Fischer with Milošević and Petritsch with Milutinović – they realised the Serbs had done an about-face and were not only intent on rejecting the military component of the draft agreement but also the political component. Petritch concluded that "something happened, so to speak, after the 23rd of February when this letter was written to us. There was a total change of attitude." He believed it was Milošević who had, "between the 23rd of February and the 15th of March, decided not to continue the path of negotiation."[84]

Still, Kosovo Albanian negotiators who appeared in court testified that they never felt the Serbian delegation had been moving towards an agreement, even prior to 23 February. Ibrahim Rugova, for example, said he got the impression from the outset that the Serbs were not serious.[85] And, the Kosovo Albanians had indeed appeared more cooperative and more prepared to reconcile internal differences for the sake of peace. There was unanimous agreement among members of their delegation that Rugova, Thaci, and Surroi should sign the agreement, each as representatives of different groups and points of view within the Kosovo Albanian population.[86]

Madeleine Albright, the then US Secretary of State, explained to the Kosovo Albanian delegation that if neither they nor the Serbs signed an agreement, the negotiations would be perceived as a total failure; but if only the Serbs refused to sign, the international community would call for military intervention aimed at stopping violence against civilians. Despite the fact that the draft proposal did not allow for independence, the Kosovo delegation signed in the end, with the condition that a clause be added permitting a referendum on the status of Kosovo in three years' time.[87] But this alone gave the Serbs grounds to criticise the draft, for once a referendum was held, the independence of Kosovo was surely to become a reality. The Serbs interpreted the clause as an internationally sanctioned step towards Kosovo's independence.

Milošević complained that the bar at Rambouillet was set higher than Serbia could accept, and perceived it as an ultimatum for unconditional surrender. Responding to Milošević in court, Petritsch denied any bias against Serbia. He said the fact that the Russian Federation had agreed to parameters set by the Contact Group, and had been fully involved in preparations for Rambouillet was "ample proof that there was no scam, no dictate, no ultimatum." In his opinion, negotiations had been challenging and lengthy but "quite positive, and unfortunately, after the 23rd of February collapsed, to the dismay and disappointment of many, including some in the Yugoslav delegation."[88] Petritsch stressed how important it had been to Russia that the negotiation process result in a peaceful solution, in order to prevent a NATO intervention.[89] He recalled that the Russian member of the negotiating team had even suggested to Milošević at one point that, if it would be helpful, the whole agreement could be re-examined and the negotiating started all over again. Although this went well beyond the mandate of this negotiator, it showed how keen the Russians were to reach an agreement.[90]

With no political solution reached by 23 February, though, and the international community growing impatient with ongoing violence by FRY and Serbian forces against the civilian population, the prospect of a military intervention grew by the day. And Milošević was increasingly noncompliant. In a message sent on 22 March by Robin Cook and Hubert Védrine, the Foreign Ministers of Great Britain and France, they urged him to accept a political resolution and avert military intervention.[91] In his reply, Milošević set out the same arguments he reiterated during the trial, accusing the international community of supporting Kosovo Albanian separatism and asserting that the talks in Rambouillet were not negotiations at all.[92] He said negotiators should be ashamed of their threats of NATO intervention, which would pit the Alliance against "a small European nation, just because it protects its territory from separatism ... [and] terrorism" and also expressed open contempt for Kosovo Albanians for the first time, claiming Serbia was simply defending "its historical dignity against scoundrels who know nothing about history or dignity."[93]

Milošević further asserted in the letter that the draft agreement had been published in the Albanian language newspaper owned by Surroi before the talks even started, saying that this proved the Rambouillet negotiations were predetermined. "Of course, we have nothing against preparing a draft document before the start of the talks," he said, "But we are strongly against not having talks at all, and being asked to sign something."[94] Milošević also indicated that he had accepted the prospect of a military intervention, asking, "Is it really possible for a normal person to think that somebody who is being threatened will not show the intention to defend himself?"[95]

On 23 March 1999, the same day the letter was published, the KVM withdrew from Kosovo completely. It had become impossible for monitors to fulfil their mandate due to the presence of increasing numbers of FRY and Serbian combat forces and the escalation of violence.[96] Numbers of deployed police and VJ forces exceeded what was permitted by earlier agreements and they were engaged in combat operations.[97] According to US General Wesley Clark, Commander of NATO forces at the time, there had been a systematic build-up of units in Kosovo in January and February 1999, and it was rumoured that Serbia was planning a "final solution" to the problem of Kosovo.[98] By March, garrisons were increasingly inaccessible to the KVM, who were even stopped at gunpoint by armed guards.[99] And by around 20 March 1999, it seemed that FRY and Serbian forces were fully prepared for combat.[100]

The defence narrative on Račak, the Rambouillet negotiations, and NATO intervention

The Prosecution argued that the Račak massacre was not an isolated incident and was foreseeable in light of the immoderate military campaign that had started in mid-1998 and had continued despite the KVM presence. But the Defence said the incident had been fabricated – a claim Milošević made in both of his Opening Statements. He framed the massacre as a creation of the international community meant to justify an already pre-planned military intervention, and said that forensic experts from many countries had been invited to investigate the crime site and had all found that those killed had been members of the KLA, because it was clear that each of them had shot and fired a weapon at the police. According to Milošević, the KLA commander in the region had even admitted in a speech after the war that it was his fighters who had died bravely in Račak.[101]

Pointing a finger at the United States specifically, Milošević characterised the Americans as having used Kosovo to pursue an aggressive post-Cold War agenda by siding with local nationalists. He said the American administration had double standards regarding terrorism and asserted that they had planned the NATO intervention in advance but, until media reports of a massacre in Račak, could not justify it.[102] Milošević alleged that Kosovo Albanians had formed the KLA (which he called a terrorist organisation) with the assistance of the international community, under the leadership of the United States and with the guidance of the CIA, with the objective to cleanse Kosovo of Serbs and other non-Albanians. He said the United States was using terrorism to realise its strategic goals and accused the Clinton Administration of defining terror based on its own self-interests. He claimed that:

> When the victims are Americans or the people they protect, then the killers are terrorists who deserve the worst possible sentences.... When, on the other hand, the Serbs are victims, as was the case in Kosovo, then, in the worst of cases, those killers were only referred to as the armed Albanians.[103]

According to Milošević, Kosovo Albanians had been strengthened and supported in their struggle not only by the United States, but simultaneously by Islamic extremists. He cited the powerful Kosovo Albanian lobby on Capitol Hill, the Albanian drug mafia, and sponsorship by Osama Bin Laden, and saw no contradiction in the United States and Bin Laden supporting the same cause.[104] Milošević claimed that deployment of the KVM, the framing of the Račak massacre, and the Rambouillet talks were all parts of a plan to humiliate Serbia and the FRY.[105] But this Defence narrative was in stark contrast to KVM reporting, from which it appeared that, despite being informed of disproportionate and indiscriminate use of violence by FRY and Serbian forces, Milošević had taken no action to stop it.[106]

NATO intervention and attempts by Serbia to change the ethnic composition of Kosovo through the commission of crimes

Once NATO bombing began in the end of March 1999 and the mass exodus of Kosovo Albanians became daily news, questions arose as to how the international community had not taken adequate measures to protect civilians from what many saw as predictable consequences of the intervention. Considering the amount of intelligence compiled and presented – by the KVM and others – indicating that the Serbian military build-up in early 1999 was a preparation for war, it remains puzzling that the commission of mass atrocities against Kosovo Albanians was not anticipated. Indeed, various intelligence sources had found evidence of a plan, allegedly devised by FRY and Serbian leaders and known as Operation Horseshoe, to cleanse Kosovo Albanians from Kosovo.

In court, Milošević denied the existence of Operation Horseshoe, saying it, too, was a fabrication of the international community – notably, of Germany – aimed at mobilising public opinion against Serbia in order to legitimise the actions of NATO.[107] But Prosecution witness Ratomir Tanić, a former Serbian intelligence agent and negotiator, testified that the plan had existed. He said that Horseshoe was not an official operational name; and while he was not able to say when the term was first colloquially, he connected it with a pre-existing JNA plan that had been prepared in the case of an aggression against Yugoslavia from Southeastern Europe. The plan was designed to protect against the Albanian population of Kosovo taking the side of a foreign aggressor by placing the JNA in seven defensive positions that formed a semi-circle, from which they would neutralise Albanian strongholds. According to Tanić, the plan was pulled from the archives and reactivated in the 1990s.[108]

Tanić testified that there was resistance to the plan in circles close to Milošević, and claimed that General Perišić and Jovica Stanišić were both dismissed over their opposition.[109] According to Tanić, these high-ranking officials felt the lack of an external aggressor made use of Army and police special units legally questionable. He said those who opposed the plan preferred a political solution in combination with only selective use of force.[110] Milošević challenged Tanić's testimony, particularly his allegations that Milošević had prepared for ethnic cleansing by establishing a commission to coordinate these efforts. Yet, Tanić told the Court that the State Commission for Kosovo had been founded to implement Milošević's "private will outside the legal institutions" and cited a letter written by General Perišić to Milošević on 23 July

1998 as proof.[111] Perišić had expressed concern about illegal use of the VJ and said that the command of VJ units had been left to unauthorised persons. He also criticised the practice of avoiding the official hierarchy and chain of command, which the Prosecution saw as evidence of Milošević's criminality.[112]

In his letter, Perišić assessed the security situation bluntly. He said "the situation in Kosovo and Metohija could have been overcome if a STATE OF EMERGENCY had been declared in time," upon his recommendation in April 1998 (emphasis in original). He called the deployment of Yugoslav Army units in Kosovo illegal and said "the repercussions for the state are well-known."[113] Perišić insisted that the mobilisation of armed forces required the satisfaction of constitutionally-stipulated precursors and pleaded that military facilities and units not be used outside the legal and constitutional framework.[114] He also opposed attempts by members of the MUP to have some VJ units subordinated to them, and condemned the fact that leading party functionaries and close associates of Milošević distributed tasks, including to the Commander of the Priština Corps, which Perišić said had led to "illegal, unsystematic, and inadequate use of VJ units."[115]

General Božidar Delić, who testified as a Defence witness, claimed there was no need for a state of emergency to be declared in Kosovo, as suggested by Perišić, because VJ units had been deployed there to fight terrorism according to Articles 470 and 473 of the Rules of Service of the VJ. These Articles allowed for peacetime units to be used in the "struggle against renegades, sabotage, terrorists, and other hostile or enemy armed groups."[116] The Defence suggested through Delić that the Rules of Service of the VJ trumped constitutional and other legal provisions for the use of the armed forces. But the Prosecution argued that state institutions and political elites of the FRY chose not to declare a state of war in Kosovo because *de jure* command structures would then place responsibility on Milošević as Supreme Commander and on his subordinates in the chain of command. According to the Prosecution, the choice by Milošević and his collaborators to obscure this *de jure* line of command indicated their awareness that what they were doing was criminal.

When resettlement and land reform decrees of the late 1980s and early 1990s did not shift the ethnic composition of Kosovo in favour of Serbs, some parties had pressed for mass expulsions of Kosovo Albanians. Among the first references to this strategy came in the Political Programme of the Serbian Radical Party (*Srpska Radikalna Stranka*, or SRS), made public in February 1991, which reflected the ideology of SRS leader Vojislav Šešelj and his reinterpretation of Greater Serbia ideology. Šešelj articulated a long list of goals to be achieved in Kosovo, including suppression of the "uprising" by Kosovo Albanians as well as the expulsion of 360,000 citizens.[117]

In a speech on 27 February 1999, when Šešelj was a Deputy Prime Minister of Serbia, he said that "if NATO bombs us, we Serbs will suffer casualties, but no Albanians will be left in Kosovo."[118] In court, Šešelj insisted that the speech had actually been meant to *deter* a potential aggression, by warning of the dangers of US imperialism. He said the Americans always caused many civilian casualties, and claimed he had been expressing his concern that US bombing would, yet again, bring devastating results.[119] But Šešelj had done more than express concern, saying, "Surely the Americans do not believe that if they attack us, we will allow [for] armed bands and disloyal citizens ... who can hardly wait to stab us in the back. We will not..."[120]

The transformative value of the evidence on Milošević's de facto and *de jure* responsibility for crimes in Kosovo

SDC records and Kosovo

SDC records were evidence of the development and implementation of the plan for Kosovo. Despite the potentially explosive situation that existed in the province throughout all of the 1990s, the SDC had of course been overwhelmingly focused on the wars in Croatia and BiH in the early part of the decade. From time to time, though, the issue would arise; for Kosovo was seen as a chronic security risk during the Milošević era and FRY authorities made sure VJ forces there were sufficiently supplied.[121] Indeed, SDC members expressed concerns about the chance that an armed rebellion could be encouraged in Kosovo by "foreign elements" – i.e. Serbian and Montenegrin extremists or Albanian Muslim extremists – years before they turned their full attention to the province.[122] And when Perišić assured the SDC in April 1995 that every Kosovo town had a military presence, Milošević said security in the province would be preserved by such a demonstration of force, because "fear keeps the house safe."[123]

By the summer of 1998, Kosovo had become the SDC's main agenda item. At the session held in June 1998, Perišić reported that 31 cases of armed conflict had occurred near the border in less than three months, and that about half of these instances involved the attempted infiltration of Kosovo by "terrorists" – resulting in casualties including five VJ soldiers.[124] He said that successful negotiations with Kosovo Albanian leaders would reduce the tension and terrorism (and loss of life); otherwise, he predicted that hostilities would rise, especially in the north and west of Kosovo. Perišić pushed for a political solution.[125] But Milošević did not rule out an Army mobilisation, saying the VJ should be prepared to counter any form of foreign intervention that might threaten the sovereignty and territorial integrity of the FRY.[126]

At the October 1998 SDC meeting, in the wake of UNSC Resolution 1199 – which called for a ceasefire – Perišić underlined the fact that failure by the FRY to fulfil the requirements set out in the Resolution would lead to the use of force by NATO and other UN countries. He also summarised all potential military scenarios, and said that the international community believed military activity would boost KLA forces and possibly lead to an all-out armed rebellion. Warning that the VJ had enough supplies for only a short-term operation, Perišić recommended that everything possible be done to avoid inviting air strikes.[127]

Milan Milutinović agreed with Perišić and was optimistic that tensions might calm in Kosovo as the FRY had already met most of the requirements of UNSCR 1199. Milo Đukanović – participating for the first time as the President of Montenegro and thus a voting member – also supported Perišić and stressed the necessity that all conditions of the Resolution be fulfilled immediately, without question. He urged Milošević to make a public statement welcoming representatives of international legal institutions, including the ICTY, to investigate allegations of crimes against civilians in Kosovo. Đukanović reminded the Council that the country was not in the mood for a fight, despite the rhetoric of some politicians, and that the wars in Croatia and Bosnia had already led to a "dramatic process of sobering-up."[128] Momir Bulatović said, further, that financial concerns could not be ignored. He urged the SDC to understand "that there is no money in government safes, that the social problems are way out of proportion, and that we are not allowed to resort to deficit financing."[129] Still, Milošević contended that the FRY had met *all* demands of UNSCR 1199. He claimed that it was those imposed on the Albanians which remained unfulfilled and that Albania persisted in trying to supply military equipment and ammunition to parties in the FRY. He also asserted that US diplomat and Kosovo negotiator Christopher Hill had said that "the problematic side was not the Serbian side but the Albanian side."[130]

Milošević instigated the dismissal of Perišić as Chief of Staff of the VJ at the next meeting of the SDC, on 24 November, on the basis that he had held the position of Chief of Staff for "an unusually long period of time."[131] Đukanović raised his voice in opposition, calling Perišić a "proven authority," but to no avail.[132] At the session held in December, new Chief of Staff General Dragoljub Ojdanić reported on the political and military situation in Kosovo. He said that insufficient engagement by the MUP on border security-related tasks was problematic because the VJ was operating in a hostile environment in the province, where he claimed 90 per cent of the population was aligned with the KLA.[133] Personnel issues were then discussed, and Đukanović was again critical, this time of the proposed promotion of General Nebojša Pavković as Commander of the Priština Corps. Pavković was a controversial figure and Đukanović felt the Priština Corps had acted outside its legal bounds; but Milošević praised Pavković as "exceptionally capable" and denied illegal behaviour by the Corps.[134] Đukanović did not attend the last recorded meeting of the SDC, held on 23 March 1999, on the eve of the Federal Assembly's declaration of war and the start of NATO bombing.

The Joint Command for Kosovo and Metohija

Since Belgrade authorities claimed the SDC did not meet after the NATO intervention began, the Prosecution had to establish which political body or individual was in command of FRY armed forces in Kosovo after 23 March. Documents of the Joint Command for Kosovo and Metohija revealed that it had represented an unofficial, de facto line of decision-making, command, and deployment of these forces in 1998 and 1999. This was part of the same pattern of concealment used during the Croatian and the Bosnian conflicts, wherein *de jure* political and military responsibly was obscured.

Yet, Milošević's *de jure* position for the period relevant to the Kosovo indictment was different than the positions he held during the time of the Croatian and Bosnian conflicts. From June 1997 to October 2000, he was President of the FRY and was therefore the automatic presiding member of the SDC; and so lawyers at the ICTY – and probably judges – expected that the crimes committed in Kosovo by Yugoslav forces would thus be more easily linked to Milošević on the basis of his *de jure* powers, making prosecution and conviction relatively straightforward. But proving the case against him was more challenging in practice, not least because the *de jure* command body, the SDC, purportedly never convened after 23 March 1999. Indeed, Serbian authorities have never offered a satisfactory explanation as to which political body took on the role of Supreme Commander during the war in Kosovo, and in communications with the OTP, implied that the VJ in fact had no civilian commander-in-chief during the military intervention there.[135]

It is notable that the SDC met eight times during Dobrica Ćosić's one-year tenure as FRY President and 56 times during Zoran Lilić's four-year Presidency, but was said to have met only nine times in the three years that Milošević held the position. The Prosecution challenged the official position of the FRY that the SDC did not convene once the state of war was declared, arguing that it was difficult to accept that state leadership would cease holding meetings of whatever body was in supreme command of the armed forces from the day a war was proclaimed. Then again, this made evidence of the Joint Command – the apparent de facto commanding body – even more significant in exposing the involvement of Serbian and Yugoslav forces in the commission of mass atrocities in Kosovo. But powerful VJ and MUP lobbies actively tried to prevent the release of Joint Command documents, foiling early expectations that the Kosovo indictment would be easier to prove than the two other indictments.

The Joint Command remained something of a mystery to the Prosecution for some time; but evidence of the Supreme Command Staff – the wartime formation of the General Staff of the VJ – was discovered by OTP investigators by the spring of 2001. The Supreme Command Staff was subordinate to the Supreme Command, the highest civilian leadership body for military forces.[136] Zoran Lilić testified that the Supreme Command consisted of all three members of the Supreme Defence Council (the Presidents of the FRY, the Republic of Serbia, and the Republic of Montenegro), the Presidents of both Chambers of the Federal Assembly (the Chamber of Republics and the Chamber of Citizens), the Federal Prime Minister, the Minister of Defence, the Minister of Foreign Affairs, and the Minister of Internal Affairs. According to Lilić, two documents adopted by the SDC served as the basis for the formation of the Supreme Command.[137]

General Nebojša Pavković, who commanded the Priština Corps at the time of the Kosovo military campaign and was later promoted to Commander of the 3rd Army, revealed more about how the Supreme Command functioned when he gave an extensive interview to Serbian broadcaster RTS in October 2000.[138] After the Kosovo campaign, Pavković had been promoted to Chief of Staff of the VJ; a position he still held when he spoke with RTS and said that it was the President of the FRY who acted as Supreme Commander and gave authority to the Chief of Staff.[139] Pavković described the Supreme Command as an advisory body, designed only to give counsel and lacking authority to issue executive orders – a task that was left to the President according to the principle of seniority. Pavković explained that all members of the Supreme Command were "commanders on a certain level" but said that during the Kosovo conflict, "the Supreme Commander – and the President – was Slobodan Milošević."[140]

The Prosecution needed to determine who commanded FRY forces during the state of war from 24 March to 10 June 1999 and through which bodies, and this required deconstructing the connections between *de jure* and de facto command structures and Milošević. Yet, investigators had little evidence about the Supreme Command. In their search for more, they discovered that a parallel line of command had been exerted through the extraconstitutional and ad hoc body known as the Joint Command. The Prosecution's position, expressed in an Expert Report by Philip Coo, was that the Supreme Command had been atop the chain of command but the Joint Command had been responsible for the coordination of activities of the VJ, the MUP, and other armed Serb organisations in Kosovo in 1998 and 1999.[141]

Evidence on the Joint Command indicated that it was formed in the summer of 1998, many months before the March 1999 NATO intervention or the proclamation of a state of war.[142] The Prosecution asserted that this command had two threads – one moving through the command structure and the second through networks Milošević had cultivated with individuals from VJ and MUP leaders.[143] General Pavković, who was part of the Joint Command, confirmed that cooperation between police and army units in Kosovo had been coordinated through political actors.[144]

In April 2002, the Prosecution submitted a request to Belgrade for documents related to the Joint Command, but Serbian authorities did not produce them, and suggested they may have been destroyed in NATO bombing.[145] Still, their reply by itself contained some valuable information, including that the Joint Command for Kosovo and Metohija had been formed by the President of the FRY via an oral order in June 1998.[146] Further correspondence regarding the Prosecution's request did not produce new results and Belgrade insisted that no documents of the Joint Command could be located for the period between 1 November 1998 and 19 June 1999. But this official position was contradicted by a chance discovery when Serbian authorities provided the Prosecution with 85 documents in response to a completely different request for assistance, in June 2003. One of these documents, the inclusion of which was presumably an oversight, was dated 15 April 1999 and was titled "Military Secret Order (Strictly Confidential 455–148)"; and it was clearly issued by the Joint Command for Kosovo and Metohija.[147] The document carried the stamp of the Military History Institute's Military Archive in Belgrade – information that led to a second request by the Prosecution for Joint Command documents.

The battle for documents from the state archives in Belgrade

Eventually, a modest collection of 15 Joint Command documents was handed over to the Prosecution on 15 November 2005, almost three years after the first request was sent. By then, the Prosecution part of the case was long over and all Defence witnesses for Kosovo had all testified – meaning that the majority of the documents could not be put into evidence through a witness before the March 2006 end date of the trial. The documents were not of a command hierarchy that led to Serbian or FRY political leaders and were mostly operative orders regarding combat matters from 22 March to 16 April 1999; yet, the existence of the documents at all exposed the insincerity of Belgrade authorities' initial claims that they had been lost in the NATO bombardment.

Evidence the Prosecution did acquire on the Joint Command indicated that the purpose of the body was to plan military operations in Kosovo against the ethnic Albanian population, through a system of local headquarters.[148] Testimony and documentation revealed that the Joint Command had been established, ad hoc, on the authority of Slobodan Milošević. It functioned under the supervision of high-level officials from his party, the SPS.[149] Operational activity was directed through loyal individuals within selected MUP and VJ units, allowing Milošević to avoid using *de jure* command structures and making it more difficult to prove his responsibility as the leader of the FRY and Commander-in-Chief of its armed forces during the Kosovo conflict.

Though Belgrade authorities had claimed the Joint Command was founded by an oral order of the President, the first written evidence of it was found in records of an SDC session held on 9 June 1998, when a plan to suppress terrorism in Kosovo was drawn up. General Perišić emphasised at the time that whether the engagement of military forces was necessary was a decision for the SDC and other federal organs.[150] One day later, on 10 June, at the 16th Session of the SPS Main Board, Milošević appointed a three-member working group to coordinate political developments in Kosovo.[151]

There was little consensus on how to deal with the Kosovo crisis. General Perišić's reference to the authority of the SDC and other federal institutions reflected his view that constitutional and legal prescriptions for use of the armed forces had to be respected; a position he reinforced in his 23 July 1998 letter to Milošević – in which he complained about the unconstitutional use of VJ units in Kosovo and drew attention to risky and unjustified shifts from *de jure* to de facto decision-making processes for use of VJ forces.[152] In October, just several months later, Perišić was dismissed as VJ Chief of Staff.

The Prosecution contended that the Joint Command had been designed to divert attention from and obscure evidence of the *de jure* responsibility Milošević held for crimes committed in Kosovo from January to June 1999. A number of Defence witnesses contradicted this view and downplayed the role of the Joint Command. Police General Obrad Stevanović, who testified that he participated in about ten Joint Command meetings, denied for instance that the Joint Command had directed actions of the MUP in Kosovo.[153] And General Božidar Delić admitted that a group of federal- and republic-level politicians had been present in Priština at the relevant time, to observe the situation and engage in talks with the Albanians, but he denied that the Joint Command had given any orders to units and insisted that he would never have carried out a military order given by a politician.[154]

In cross-examination, the Prosecution asked General Delić to comment on a Joint Command order dated 6 July 1998, signed by Delić himself, which had been sent to subordinate brigades and further down to their subordinate units.[155] And to reinforce the point, the Prosecution also produced an order issued by the 125th Motorised Brigade in which reference was made to another order of the Joint Command that banned VJ units from executing any action "without the approval of the Joint Command for Kosovo and Metohija."[156] Yet, Delić continued to deny the authoritative function of the Joint Command, referring to it as "just a notion." He said he had complied with orders because they came from his commanding officer in the Priština Corps, maintaining that the Joint Command was "just a coordination body."[157] Denial by Defence witnesses of the extent of power of the Joint Command, despite concrete and persuasive evidence, actually reinforced the significance of that evidence.

And, in light of the evidence, Milošević's choice of Defence witnesses remains puzzling. He called participants in the military campaigns in Kosovo in 1998 and 1999 to the stand, thereby exposing them to cross-examination based not only on Prosecution evidence but also on the contents of documents they brought to the courtroom. At times, these witnesses enabled the court to hear evidence that had been requested by the Prosecution from Serbia but was not received or presented; and a majority of them confirmed, and occasionally strengthened, the Prosecution's case against Milošević. For example, as one of Milošević's legal advisors, Dobroslav Ognjanović, later explained, the Defence had called Vojislav Šešelj only in order to have him say a few sentences. This was a considerable risk because they knew Šešelj could not be controlled and, in the end, Šešelj's testimony went on for several weeks, exposing him also to a lengthy cross-examination.[158]

The production of documents contemporaneous to the Kosovo indictment period

A number of documents brought into the trial by Defence witnesses exposed the extent to which Serbian authorities had exercised control over FRY cooperation with the ICTY. As noted earlier, post-Milošević political elites had cultivated a two-track approach to assisting the ICTY. On one hand, they implemented the proclaimed policy of cooperation by handing over high-level indictees, such as Milošević, General Pavković, Jovica Stanišić, and Franko Simatović. On the other hand, Belgrade authorities tried to control the flow of evidence to the ICTY, needed to prove charges laid out in indictments – both as far as how and when documentary evidence was provided and whether it was possible to access witnesses. This manifested in the struggle the OTP had in obtaining (or not obtaining) requested documents from federal and republic archives, as with SDC and Joint Command records.

Revelations that Serbian authorities had held back key documents from the OTP came to light in the courtroom when Milošević started to call Defence witnesses for the Kosovo indictment and some of them produced material in court that the Prosecution had been unable to tender as evidence, either because it had been requested but not received or had been received after the Prosecution part of the case. Several requests had been submitted for the daily reports, combat logbooks, and war diaries of VJ commanders and units operating in the Priština Corps, for instance. The Prosecution believed that brigades and units subordinated to the Corps were involved in sweep-up operations for the Kosovo conflict. But by the time the Defence case began in September 2004, many of the requested documents were yet to be produced by Belgrade, and the majority of the documents that were provided were either exculpatory or irrelevant because they were outside of the requested period.[159]

Serbia rejected the OTP's implication that the government was hiding or withholding evidence, noting that Serbia had been cooperative despite a heavy toll. A representative of the Serbian government reminded the Court that Serbian authorities had arrested and surrendered Milošević, and that late Prime Minister Zoran Đinđić had taken responsibility for these actions and had subsequently been assassinated. Indeed, the investigation into Đinđić's murder revealed that a longer list of officials had been targeted, including ministers responsible for cooperation with the ICTY. Serbia's legal representative dismissed the Prosecution's "armchair perspective" as unrealistic in terms of the tangible challenges faced by the government.[160]

The VJ commission for cooperation with the ICTY

While the battle between the Prosecution and Serbian authorities over the production of documents was waged in the courtroom from December 2002 until the very end of the trial in March 2006, the dynamics shifted upon commencement of the Defence part of the case. During Rule 54 *bis* litigation in 2003, by which the Prosecution had sought a Court order compelling Serbia to produce certain documents, the Trial Chamber had ruled against the production of war diaries as overbroad – a decision the Prosecution found surprising, and never accepted. But the Chamber's position was that cooperation between the OTP and Serbia was not something for which the Defendant and his Defence team could be held responsible. And indeed, these requests for assistance were sent to the state *ex parte*, or without notification to Milošević and his legal advisors; thus, the Defence could not know what was requested or provided by the state to the Prosecution.[161]

The Prosecution nevertheless argued that any possibility that different standards were applied by Serbia – one to the Defence and another to the Prosecution – should be explored.[162] This issue was never resolved, however, and the Prosecution simply tried to acquire as many documents as it could as they were brought in, identified, or relied on in some way by Defence witnesses. In 2005, some of these documents included war diaries and log books, as well as *post facto* statements of VJ officers involved in Kosovo military campaigns that were produced for Defence purposes by the VJ Commission for Cooperation with the ICTY, a semi-state body that existed from April 2002 to April 2003.

The Prosecution team was pleased by the appearance of any genuine contemporaneous documents from the indictment period, but was concerned about *post facto* statements, reports, and maps, which might have offered new and unexpected interpretations of the Kosovo evidence and could have cast reasonable doubt on the crimes charged. The Prosecution addressed each document introduced by Defence witnesses, raising questions as to the method of production and the reliability of any documents produced by the Commission, the purpose and function of which it viewed sceptically. Aware of the existence of the Commission since its establishment in 2002, the Prosecution had argued in a written submission to the court in May 2003 that it had actively assisted ICTY indictees in preparing their defences.[163] The submission quoted a media report that asserted that a team of VJ officers had been engaged in selecting documents from the military archives in a search for evidence that would favour persons indicted by the Tribunal.[164] The report specifically expressed concerns that the Commission had aided Milošević, noting that the background knowledge which informed some of the questions he posed in court would have required he have access to "sensitive information from the time when he was already in jail."[165]

The testimony of retired General Božidar Delić was based on hundreds of pages of reports, statements, and maps that had been produced under the guidance and support of the Commission, and this material – along with Delić's testimony – exposed the role of the Commission in preparing evidence intended to assist the Defence and not meant to fulfil the truth-seeking mandate of the ICTY more generally. Delić said that he had prepared for his courtroom appearance by making use of a list of events he received from the Commission, which he was asked to address in graphic and textual form.[166] In order to help him do that, the Commission had provided him access to all the original documentation he needed, including some that had been requested by the Prosecution but had not been provided by Belgrade. During his testimony, Delić showed the court copies of operational logs and the war diary of his brigade, which had been provided to him by the Commission.[167] Among these, the Prosecution identified some of the very materials it had sought for over three years and it requested permission to examine full versions of the documents, leading the judges to compel Delić to hand over his war diary, despite his protestations.[168]

Following Delić's first day in court, the OTP trial team sent an urgent request to then Serbian Minister of Defence Pravoslav Davinić, requesting documents relating to the establishment, functioning, and dissolution of the VJ Commission for Cooperation with the ICTY. Despite the high urgency of the request, sent on 6 July 2005, it was not until two months later that 24 documents were handed over. The documents described the Commission as an advisory and organising body tasked with analysing and studying the work of the ICTY, in order to make proposals as to the type and extent of cooperation of the Yugoslav Army and the Defence Ministry with the Tribunal.[169] This included, for instance, a stipulation "not to carry out requests which could endanger state security without the consent and the decision of the Supreme Defence Council."[170]

The founding of the Commission had been prompted by the trial of Milošević and the fact that it would deal with crimes allegedly committed by JNA and VJ officers.[171] But some of these same officers were part of the Commission's Expert Team, such as General Milan Gvero, who, at the time the Commission was formed, had already been charged by the ICTY and was subsequently tried and sentenced for crimes committed in Srebrenica in 1995.[172] In fact, according to Delić, most of the Commission's 40 members were active duty VJ officers with the rank of Colonel and Lieutenant Colonel, along with five or six retired JNA officers.[173]

The Commission was abolished in April 2003 by the decision of Boris Tadić, almost immediately after he became the Serbian Minister of Defence, yet it collected over 10,400 documents during its short-lived existence. It also compiled new material, including combat maps and statements taken from VJ officers who were direct participants in combat incidents.[174] The Defence had clearly been given access that had been denied to the Prosecution; but when the Prosecution pressed General Delić to explain discrepancies between the official and actual intent of the VJ to cooperate with the ICTY, he spoke of difficulties in locating documents due to the bombing of VJ installations and the lack of an electronic register system, which he said could make the search for some documents take months if not years.[175] But it did not pass unnoticed in the courtroom that Delić seemed to have been more successful in expediently locating documents relating to crimes allegedly committed by the KLA. He explained that he had been collecting this documentation because he was the only VJ officer who had been asked to testify as an expert at the ICTY in a case against KLA members, including former Kosovo Prime Minister Ramush Haradinaj.

Delić had indeed been asked by the Prosecution team on the *Haradinaj et al.* case to write an expert military report – a fact originally kept from the Milošević Prosecution team – and the VJ Commission had facilitated access to any documents the General deemed relevant.[176] This was viewed by the Prosecution for the Milošević case as a display of selectiveness or bias in the search for and production of documents, an allegation which eventually made it impossible for Delić to appear in the Haradinaj trial. Further, by appearing as a witness on behalf of Milošević, Delić exposed himself to the scrutiny of cross-examination, in which the Prosecution addressed evidence that Delić had been seen by a witness destroying an undefended house with a tank in 1999.[177] Still, in the Serbian media General Delić's testimony was initially evaluated as positive for Milošević, with some media calling it a serious blow to the Prosecution's case.[178] And Delić himself seemed to be very satisfied with his appearance in court, bragging in an interview that he had single-handedly refuted the testimony of 26 Prosecution witnesses.[179]

In truth, the Haradinaj Prosecution team should never have accepted General Delić as an expert witness because of his position as a commanding officer during the time period relevant to the indictment. Given his participation as an active VJ officer during the Kosovo conflict, and one who was accused by other witnesses of committing crimes, he could be called to the stand only as a fact witness. Not only was he unable to be objective about the subject of his expert testimony, but his PhD dissertation indicated that he was biased against and hostile toward Kosovo Albanians; and this also emerged in cross-examination. The General's PhD thesis, entitled "Preparation and Engagement of Defence Forces in the Prevention and Crushing of Armed Insurgency in Kosovo and Metohija," was written sometime between 1996 and 1997 and was presented in court by the Prosecutor. In a paragraph discussing the demographic structure of Kosovo, Delić used the derogatory term *Šiptars* to refer to Kosovo Albanians and called Kosovo "the mother country of the Serbian people, the ethnic space of Serbs." He asserted that Kosovo Albanians had worked systematically to drive out Serbs while simultaneously expanding their own numbers through a high birth rate.[180] In court, Delić confirmed that his views had not changed, calling it "an incontestable fact" that this demographic redistribution in Kosovo had been deliberate.[181]

The Prosecution asked General Delić to elaborate on who the enemies were whose insurgency had to be prevented and crushed – referring to the dissertation title – and he could not provide a straightforward answer, admitting that it could not be the KLA since they appeared on the scene after he wrote his thesis. He was also questioned about a claim made in the thesis, that Serbs and Montenegrins in Kosovo had "been issued light infantry weapons." Their safety, he wrote, was thus "ensured, as they can offer resistance and defend their homes and families."[182] When asked to clarify if that meant that the Serb and Montenegrin population was already armed in 1997, General Delić confirmed that they were indeed armed by then, as civilian defence units.[183]

The boomerang effect of defence evidence: VJ war diaries and daily combat reports

Although the VJ Commission was abolished in 2003, materials collected from the archives as well as those prepared under its supervision remained in VJ custody; and those relating to the Kosovo indictment period were used by Defence witnesses as late as 2006. The Prosecution urged the court to disregard *post facto* documents created by the Commission, in favour of materials contemporaneous to the events in question, and this approach eventually bore fruit when several Defence witnesses produced parts of original war diaries and operational logs of their units when pressed about the nature of their *post facto* statements.[184] The court successfully compelled these witnesses, and in some cases the Serbian authorities, to provide the complete war diaries of particular brigades and units.[185]

Once the full war diaries of General Delić's 549th Motorised Brigade, as well as those of other brigades and units commanded by General Miloš Đošan, Colonel Vlatko Vuković, and Major Janoš Šel, were made available, they together provided the basis for some of the most compelling evidence heard at the trial. These war diaries showed that VJ combat units had planned and started combat actions in Kosovo, in cooperation with MUP forces, immediately after NATO air strikes began on 24 March 1999. The NATO bombardment started just before 20:00, and a state of war was proclaimed by Federal authorities at 23:00.[186]

The Prosecution argued that, in anticipation of the NATO attacks, a plan had been devised to implement a sweep-up operation by both VJ and MUP units, and NATO attacks were then used as a cover to expel as many ethnic Albanians as possible from Kosovo in order to change its ethnic composition and enable political rule by the Serb minority. The war diary of the unit commanded by Colonel Vuković noted that Combat Group 2 carried out a mission according to a confidential order dated 23 March 1999 – a day before the bombing began – and a Prosecution source claimed that Vuković had told his men on 24 March that the Albanians must be driven from Kosovo so that there would "not be even an Albanian ear" left in the province.[187] But the Defence position, which was supported by every VJ officer called to testify, was that the NATO air campaign, not FRY troops, caused the humanitarian catastrophe in Kosovo. In fact, Defence witnesses asserted that

NATO had fabricated the notion of Serb crimes to cover for its own aggression. Colonel Vuković asserted during his cross-examination, for instance, that these accusations "enabled NATO to target everything in Kosovo and Metohija indiscriminately."[188]

The semantics of the evidence: cleaning up, sweeping up, mopping up, or ethnic cleansing?

During the conflict in Kosovo, the BBC and CNN had aired images of fleeing civilians that reporters characterised as resulting from "ethnic cleansing" but which Defence witnesses such as former FRY Military Prosecutor Radomir Gojović routinely attributed to NATO aggression. When these broadcasts were played in court, Gojović insisted that there was "no evidence of ethnic cleansing" in Kosovo.[189] And in his Opening Statement at the start of the Defence case, Milošević had asserted that any history of ethnic cleansing in Kosovo had been systematically conducted by the Kosovo Albanian majority against Serbs and Montenegrins.[190] Former Serbian Minister of Foreign Affairs Vladislav Jovanović reiterated this view when asked by Milošević about the origin of the term, claiming its use had risen in the 1980s amid fears among Serbs that they would be cleansed from Kosovo.[191]

Still, the term 'ethnic cleansing' was used throughout the Prosecution part of the case by witnesses referring to the crimes committed by Serb forces in Croatia, BiH, and Kosovo. And Defence assertions on this issue did not reflect historical facts about the origins of the term or evidence from war diaries, in which VJ officers regularly used the word *čišćenje* – which was translated in a number of ways by different ICTY translation and interpretation services, as "cleaning," "cleansing," "sweeping up," or "mopping up." The Defence rejected the allegation that the term referred to a cleansing of the Kosovo Albanian civilian population, and said it had only been used to imply a military "mopping up" of territory after anti-terrorist actions that involved enemy combatants. But, in contemporaneous documents brought to the attention of the court by Defence witnesses, various interpretations of the term emerged.

The Prosecution tracked the use of the term *čišćenje* in the war diary entries of Colonel Vuković's unit and General Delić's and General Đošen's brigades. The diary of Vuković unit offered some of the most explicit evidence of forced expulsions of the civilian population from Kosovo villages, with the term *čišćenje* accompanying descriptions of operations that could hardly be passed off as mopping-up activities on the battlefield. For instance, in a series of entries from the end of March 1999, villages named in the Kosovo indictment as sites of atrocities and deportations were consistently listed as sites of operations that followed a similar pattern: FRY forces would "intervene" in an area, "seal off" towns and villages, and thousands of civilians would move en masse towards the border. The entry for 28 March 1999 noted that "during the day about two thousand people passed by in the direction of the Ćafa Prušit border crossing."[192]

Day after day, the entries were almost identical. On 29 March 1999, forces were said to be "ready for intervention along the Orahovac–Oštrozub axis" and some thousand people reportedly "passed by in the direction of the Ćafa Prušit border crossing."[193] On 30 March, 2,000 people from four more villages were said to have moved toward Ćafa Prušit; and on 31 March, 1,000 more from two others.[194]

When Colonel Vuković testified as a Defence witness, the Prosecution challenged him in cross-examination with evidence of crimes committed in Bela Crkva on 25 March 1999, including the execution of a large number of villagers on a river bank.[195] Vuković claimed that his combat unit had passed through Bela Crkva between 5:00 and 5:30 but had not engaged in fighting because they did not encounter any terrorists there; yet the war diary entry of his brigade from that day used the word *čišćenje* in relation to Bela Crkva, and the Prosecution asked him to explain what had needed mopping up if no terrorists had been present there. In fact, of five KLA strongholds in the area, four of them – Drenovac, Dragobob, Nišor, and Mališevo – were not attacked at all.

Vuković told the Court that the term "čišćenje" referred to "cleaning or cleansing, exclusively as part of an operation against the terrorists, just as you use the word 'cleaning' in everyday life where you're separating ... something good from something bad."[196] Vuković offered the same definition given the day before by Air Force General Đošan, who had explained it as the process of separating the good from the bad, or "separating the terrorists from the rest of the population."[197] When the Prosecution had presented General Miloš Đošen with entries from the war diary of his unit in which the word *čišćenje* was used, he had remarked that the word was "a clumsy choice, but it was used very often." He said it had a "very broad meaning," but referred in this context to "fighting against terrorists, Šiptar terrorists."[198] Asked by the judges to elaborate, General Đošan told them that *čišćenje* was the process of "removing them, taking them captive, and even killing terrorists in a war. That is to say, destroying terrorists."[199]

When Colonel Vuković responded the same way about use of the term on the following day, Prosecutor Nice intervened, suggesting that he had either spoken with General Đošan or "with someone else who has explained to you how you're going to get around the problem of this use of the word 'čišćenje.'"[200] As the term *čišćenje* became increasingly troublesome for the Defence, Milošević raised the issue with multiple witnesses. General Geza Farkaš echoed others, responding that the Army's rules defined the term to include "the clearing of a minefield" or, "in the sense of terrorists [as] mopping up."[201] However, evidence from war diaries and operational logs spoke for itself.

Sanitising the terrain or hiding the crimes?

Another contemporaneous source that provided valuable evidence was the wartime notebook of Serbian Police General Obrad Stevanović. The notebook was not a war diary per se, but it contained entries about Stevanović's appointments as well as lists of tasks. When Stevanović appeared as a Defence witness, the Prosecution used the opportunity to explore the notebook's contents in cross-examination, bringing forth powerful evidence about plans to remove the traces of crimes committed by Serbian forces in Kosovo.

Milošević understood the evidentiary significance of the notebook, too, and in his questioning of Stevanović, pre-emptively addressed the word *asanacija*, or sanitation, which appeared in several entries; for he knew the Prosecution would contend that it alluded to the removal of corpses. He asked the General to explain what the "mop-up or sanitisation of the terrain" referred to and Stevanović replied that this was a "well-known military concept." He conceded that "other terms might be used in other languages" but said it denoted

> the burying of corpses after battle in the legally prescribed manner as well as livestock that were killed, and generally cleaning up the area ... to protect the people to ensure their safety and security and normal functioning of life in general.[202]

They went on discussing the meaning of the term *asanacija* in the context of the Geneva Convention of 1906 and the second Hague Convention of 1907, each of which referred to the obligation of all parties to find, identify, and bury the dead after battle. Milošević asked outright if *asanacija* could refer to "the cases that were mentioned, the transportation of bodies from Kosovo to the territory of central Serbia, for example," and Stevanović resolutely rejected this possibility. "Events of that kind ... have nothing to do with the concept of clearing up the battlefield and sanitisation of the terrain as I explained it a moment ago," he said. Pressed by Milošević as to who would have had a motive to rebury bodies in that way, General Stevanović reckoned that the likely culprit was someone who wished to ascribe alleged crimes to Serbia, not "somebody who wanted to cover them up."[203]

One page of Stevanović's notebook consisted of shorthand from a meeting, including the notes "President," "No corpse – No crime," "They will use evidence of crimes to justify aggression," "Simultaneous cleaning up of territories," and "Clearing up the terrain is the most important."[204] Stevanović was asked about the word "President" and whether it was a reference to a meeting at the President's office, and if the President was the Accused, Milošević. He answered affirmatively.[205] This evidence, which revealed that planning for the cover-up of crimes had taken place in Milošević's office, was powerful evidence of his criminal state of mind.

Awareness of criminality and attempts to hide evidence

The Prosecution contended that killings and mass expulsions of Kosovo Albanians were among the chief objectives of Serbian policy in Kosovo and that the activities of FRY and Serbian forces in Kosovo were therefore criminal. The coordinated use of buses – often with two policemen per bus to accompany those being transported out of Kosovo to Macedonia or Albania – was proof, the Prosecution argued, of strategic planning and implementation before the launch of air strikes. The Defence maintained that the flight of Kosovo Albanians was due to the NATO bombardments and failed to explain why transport vehicles were full of Kosovo Albanian refugees while Serbs remained in Kosovo or fled to Serbia, even as Serbia was also being bombed.

The evidence suggested that Serbian forces had controlled the flow of Kosovo Albanian refugees by surrounding villages and leaving only one corridor through which civilians could exit to border crossings, either into Albania or Macedonia, or occasionally to Montenegro.[206] And reports that Kosovo Albanians were forced to hand over their passports and other identity documents at border crossings was a particularly damning indication that their expulsions had been organised and that FRY and Serbian authorities sought to prevent refugee return. Many witnesses testified that identity documents were confiscated from Kosovo Albanians specifically and, that the majority of these confiscations took place along the Kosovo–Albania border or en route to the border, and that the practice was not limited to one checkpoint but occurred across different municipalities.[207]

Starting in May 1999, the remains of some Kosovo Albanians killed in Kosovo were removed for reburial in Serbia. This was further evidence that Serbian officials were aware of the criminal actions of VJ and MUP forces; for, if the dead in Kosovo were indeed KLA combatants, and were thus legitimate targets in the conflict, it made no sense that Serbian authorities would go to the trouble of moving hundreds of bodies across the border. In his book, Momir Bulatović wrote that this decision was linked to several miscalculations on the part of Milošević. According to Bulatović, when the intervention started, Milošević had reckoned that NATO bombing would not last longer than a week because of public pressure in NATO countries. But, not only did NATO bomb Serbia for over two months, but Serbian ally Russia aligned itself with the international community. When Milošević was informed by Russian special envoy Victor Chernomyrdin that Russia would not support Serbia, he finally understood that his policy had failed and that Serbia would lose Kosovo.[208] Milošević and his close associates, understanding consequences of the loss of the Kosovo territory, started to plan how to relocate the bodies of Kosovo Albanians killed in the conflict.[209]

The Prosecution's case was that, under the cover of NATO bombings, FRY and Serbian armed forces engaged in an ethnic cleansing operation with a goal to alter the ethnic composition of Kosovo in favour of Serbs through a carefully prepared and executed campaign consisting of mass deportations, destruction of property, and killings of Kosovo Albanian civilians. A report prepared by Prosecution Expert Witness Patrick Ball found that over 10,000 Kosovo Albanians were killed in just March through June of 1999 and that clear patterns of killings and refugee flow were evident during that time. Ball, a statistician, noted the unlikelihood that these patterns "would result simply from ad hoc decision-making" on the part of civilians.[210] But the Defence blamed the exodus of civilians on NATO bombardments that it claimed were on populated areas with no military targets. And though the Defence did acknowledge that a major military campaign was conducted by the FRY starting immediately after the NATO air strikes began, it insisted that operations were aimed only at KLA terrorist forces and claimed these forces were using the bombings as strategic support to gain territory.

It is worth mentioning that in the ICTY trial of *Milutinović et al.* – known as the case of the 'Kosovo Six' – the Judgement recognised that people left their homes for a variety of reasons during the conflict in Kosovo, noting that some were instructed by the KLA to leave, that some left to avoid the fighting between the KLA and FRY and Serbian forces, and some left to avoid NATO bombing close to where they lived.[211] However, it emphasised that Kosovo Albanian witnesses at the trial "gave a broadly consistent account of the fear that reigned in towns and villages across Kosovo, not because of the NATO bombing, but rather because of the actions of the VJ and MUP, and associated forces, that accompanied it."[212] In other words, no witness in the trial who had crossed a border due to the conflict (i.e. those who were externally displaced) said that the NATO bombing had caused their departure from Kosovo. The Judgement also underlined the fact that the NATO bombing in Serbia, most notably in Belgrade, did not lead to an exodus of Belgrade citizens in numbers anywhere near those who left Kosovo. The Trial Chamber did not find, therefore, that NATO bombing was the cause of the mass displacement of Kosovo Albanians from Kosovo. The judges also excluded the ongoing armed conflict between KLA forces and FRY and Serbian units as the cause, because the fighting between these factions that had been taking place since mid-1998 had led to the displacement of many civilians, but most had remained in Kosovo as internally displaced people.[213]

The *Milutinović et al.* Judgement also qualified the reburial of over 700 civilians killed in Kosovo and transferred to secondary burial sites in Serbia as a crime for which the FRY and certain government officials were responsible, naming Milošević, Serbian Minister of Internal Affairs Vlajko Stojiljković, and Chief of the MUP Vlastimir Đorđević, among others. The Judgement noted that "the fact that the persons involved felt this concealment to be necessary in the first place" indicated that "they knew that the great majority of the corpses moved were victims of crime, as opposed to5combatants or people who perished during legitimate combat activities."[214] In his notebook, General Stevanović had written the word "Izbica," and this was significant for the Prosecution because the remains of Kosovo Albanian civilians who were killed at Izbica had been discovered in 2001 in a secondary grave in Serbia, in Batajnica.[215] The Prosecution contended – as the Milutinović Judgement had – that the relocation of killed civilians demonstrated a recognition that their killings had been criminal.

The impact of the evidence: the Scorpions Video

The cross-examination of Obrad Stevanović, who had helped the Prosecution establish the evidentiary value of the Kula Camp Video, was crucial to the presentation of another damning piece of video evidence that showed the killing of Bosnian Muslims from Srebrenica by members of the Scorpions – a Serbian paramilitary group first formed in 1991 in Eastern Croatia. The Scorpions were also engaged in Kosovo in 1999 and Prosecution witnesses had referred to the unit's crimes there; yet, the Prosecution was unsure that the judges would allow the Scorpions Video to be introduced in the Defence part of the trial, and asked General Stevanović for his assistance. He readily agreed, unaware of the Pandora's box he was helping to open.

The extraordinary video showed the executions of six Bosnian Muslim boys and men that took place some three weeks after the fall of Srebrenica in the small village of Godinjske Bare, several kilometres from Sarajevo and about 150 kilometres from Srebrenica. The footage confirmed accusations made by Prosecution witnesses and proved that the Scorpions had operated, and criminally, for a number of years and across a wide territory. Combined with the testimony of these witnesses, the video also verified connections between the Serbian MUP and members of the Scorpions who fought in the wars in Croatia, BiH, and Kosovo. And in light of what the Scorpions had done in Croatia in 1991 and BiH in 1995, the exposure of the Scorpions Video raised important questions about why Belgrade had called on them again in 1999 to fight in Kosovo.

The Scorpions Video was shown in the courtroom during the Prosecution's May 2005 cross-examination of General Stevanović. As a rule, Prosecution evidence of direct probative value should have been tendered into evidence during the Prosecution's part of the case, which had concluded in February 2004; and in order for the video to have been officially admitted into evidence, the Prosecution would have had to request that its case be reopened. Instead, the OTP decided that their primary goal was simply to get parts of the video shown in court. And this proved wise, because the effect of the video was felt immediately – inside and outside the courtroom.

The video began with close-up shots of members of the Scorpions, as they were blessed by a local Orthodox priest before departing to fight in BiH. The Prosecution was aware of their identities and asked Stevanović if he knew any of them. He vehemently denied that he did.[216] Stevanović also rejected the idea that any unit subordinated to the Serbian MUP's Public Security Sector – for which he had worked – had operated in the RS or had been involved in killing people from Srebrenica.[217] When the Prosecution presented Stevanović with evidence that the Serbian MUP sent 350 members of the Special Purpose Police Units (PJP) to the Trnovo front in June 1995, Stevanović claimed that it had to be mistake.[218] This was where the Scorpions had filmed the crimes they committed; but even after being presented with a series of documents that further illuminated connections between the Serbian MUP and the Scorpions, Stevanović insisted that he had no knowledge of the unit.[219] Unable to find a credible explanation for the content of the reports he found himself reading, Stevanović went so far as to claim that whoever wrote them may have been delusional.[220]

This lengthy preparation by the Prosecution provided the groundwork to justify showing the part of the Scorpions Video that included the executions of six civilians. And indeed, that groundwork was important when, after the first of these distressing images were played, Defence counsel Stephen Kay objected to the video and qualified it as sensationalism. He argued that the witness could not respond to the content in a useful way and that the Prosecution was merely trying to publicise undisclosed material, saying "It's not cross-examination."[221] And so, to clarify, Prosecutor Nice turned to Stevanović and explained that he was "suggesting this film shows Scorpions executing prisoners from Srebrenica."[222]

Stevanović responded with shock, calling the video "one of the most monstrous images I have ever seen on a screen." He said the Prosecutor knew "full well" that the killings it portrayed had "nothing to do with me or the units I commanded."[223] Yet, when compelled by Judge Robinson to reply to the Prosecutor's suggestion that the victims were prisoners from Srebrenica, Stevanović said that he did not intend to cast doubt on what the Prosecutor's claims, but that he did not know anyone appearing in the video.[224] The Prosecutor then asked Stevanović if he had ever met Slobodan 'Boca' Medić, the leader of the Scorpions, and Stevanović said that he had actually met him several times in 1995, when he visited the small town of Erdut in the Baranja part of the Croatian SAO of SBWS with Milan Milanović, alias Mrgud.[225] Erdut was the base and training camp run by Željko 'Arkan' Ražnatović, and was supervised and financed by Radovan Stojičić, the head of the Serbian MUP Public Security Directorate. Judge Bonomy invited Stevanović to comment on his previous testimony, in which he had refuted any possibility that the Scorpions were affiliated with the Public Security Sector, and still, Stevanović firmly persisted in his denial of the possibility.[226] But it would become clearer and clearer that this affiliation was a fact.

In the days that followed the presentation of the video, the Prosecution pursued several leads on links between the crimes shown in Trnovo in BiH, in July 1995, with crimes committed in Podujevo in Kosovo, in March 1999, by members of the same unit. In Podujevo, women and children from several families had been ordered to line up against a wall, and were shot; 14 were killed and five children were seriously wounded.[227] The Prosecution obtained documents that had appeared as evidence in a 1999 domestic criminal trial of two Scorpions members for these murders. In fact, it was the Serbian MUP that had prepared both documents for the earlier trial, upon request of the domestic court.

The first document, a report, stated that the two accused men were indeed members of the Scorpions and that the unit was formed of 128 volunteers, with Slobodan Medić, alias Boca, as its commander and Srđan Manojlović, alias Srle, as his Deputy. The unit had apparently been transferred to the reserve formation of the MUP SAJ with the approval of Police Colonel-General Vlastimir Đorđević, who was the head of the Public Security Directorate of the Serbian MUP at the time and who was indicted in 1999 by the ICTY for crimes committed in Kosovo in 1998 and 1999. The report noted that the Scorpions were put under the leadership of Zoran Simović, commander of the Belgrade SAJ, on 27 March 1999 – one day before the killings in Podujevo took place. In court, Stevanović insisted that he knew nothing about this and said that the law did not allow for a complete unit to be drafted into the reserve forces.[228]

The second document repeated the history of the Scorpions unit, underlining the fact that it had been engaged by the SAJ in the past for certain tasks in Eastern Slavonia.[229] The reservists were said to have been activated on 25 March 1999 and given uniforms of the PJP. The unit was sent back to Serbia on 8 April 1999 and was then re-engaged on 25 April 1999, when 108 members of the unit were sent to Kosovo Polje, only to be discharged again as soon as 9 May 1999.[230] Witnesses indicated that the unit was sent back to Serbia for the second time because they had once again committed crimes during operations.[231]

Stevanović had little choice but to accept the facts as written by his colleagues from the MUP. He insisted that the reserve police could only recruit individuals, and not units, but said that if such a unit was indeed drafted into the reserve composition of the SAJ against the existing law, it would require the authorisation of a government minister.[232] What was not presented to Stevanović during the last part of the cross-examination, but was already in evidence, was an entry in his own notebook from 22 April 1999, which said that men from Šid were coming in PJP uniforms.[233] This was an important entry because various Serbian human rights organisations had previously identified Šid, a small town in Vojvodina, in the north of Serbia, as the place where Scorpions members had moved in 1995 after the reintegration of the SAO of SBWS into the Republic of Croatia.[234]

Milan 'Mrgud' Milanović, who was the Minister of Defence in the SAO of SBWS until the end of 1995 and who knew the Scorpions well, testified as a Prosecution witness in October 2003, one year before the OTP obtained the Scorpions Video. Although he was not examined on the Scorpions crimes committed in BiH, Milanović explained some of the links between the police and military structures of Serbia, the RSK, and the RS and named a number of individuals who had played roles in every stage of the armed conflicts from 1991 to 1999. He described how, after the fall of Vukovar, he was asked by the director of an oil company to organise security for the company's oil fields, which were on the line between RSK and Croatian forces. Milanović went to the nearby village of Banovci and talked to the local Territorial Defence commander, Slobodan Medić, who was just 21 years old at the time. And Milanović also testified to meeting Živko Trajković in 1992.[235] Trajković was the MUP official who was in charge of the Scorpions in March 1999 when they committed their first crimes in Kosovo. When Milanović visited the oil fields in Đeletovci, he would take Trajković with him, and that was how Medić and Trajković had met.[236]

Apparently, Medić named the unit the Scorpions (*Škorpioni*) in 1994. The unit originally consisted of 100 to 150 men who were frequently mobilised by the SVK and engaged in combat as a part of its Slavonia-Baranja Corps.[237] Milanović organised the Scorpions to fight in the 1994–1995 Operation Spider in the Bihać pocket, an area in Western Bosnia of great strategic importance for the Serbs. He testified that the Scorpions were subordinated in the Bihać region to the SVK, but to the RS MUP in Trnovo – where they also fought in 1994 – and to the Serbian MUP in Kosovo in 1999.[238] According to Milanović, it was Radovan 'Badža' Stojičić, the Head of the Serbian MUP's Public Security Sector, who approached him in 1994 with concerns about problems in the RS and asked that a battalion from Eastern Slavonia be formed to help out. Milanović approached Medić and the Scorpion unit was engaged.[239] Obrad Stevanović's testimony that he had met Medić through Milanović in 1995 confirmed the role of Milanović as the link between the Serbian MUP and the Scorpions.[240]

Milanović was again instrumental in the deployment of the Scorpions during the Kosovo war in 1999, when Medić offered the services of his unit on the condition they be subordinate to the Serbian MUP and not to the VJ. Milanović claimed that Momir Gavrilović, alias Gavra, a Serbian MUP official active in the SAO of SBWS who was dead at the time of Milanović's testimony, had warned him that MUP leaders planned to pin the killings of Albanians in Kosovo on volunteer groups. Several days later, Milanović received a call from Vlastimir Đorđević informing him of the killings in Podujevo.[241] According to Milanović, Đorđević called Medić only three weeks later to redeploy the Scorpions.[242]

Milošević's examination-in-chief of General Stevanović took place before the Scorpions Video was shown, but Milošević had asked if any paramilitary formations had been under the control of any state authority. Stevanović denied that possibility, and said that the presence or activity of paramilitary groups would have been against the law and never would have been sanctioned the police or army.[243] However, this was an unsustainable assertion given evidence that connected every major paramilitary group – including the White Eagles, the Serbian Volunteer Guard (Arkan's men), the Serbian Radical party units, and the Scorpions – with the Serbian MUP.

It is not surprising that witnesses such as Stevanović, a state official, denied contact and cooperation with paramilitaries. The whole concept of "unruly" paramilitaries was constructed in order to deflect responsibility from armed forces and official chains of command. Ton Zwaan, who testified for the Prosecution as an expert on genocide, explained the "monopoly of violence" that is exercised by states. This monopoly is normally centralised, but if is not functioning or if certain groups are deliberately excluded from it, some groups may claim their own monopoly and use unlawful violence for their own ends. Similarly, in the commission of mass atrocities or genocide, a state may encourage and allow violence as a means to support its political goals; but in some genocidal processes, central authorities may no longer maintain the monopoly of violence but instead give permission, directly or indirectly, to groups of perpetrators to commit mass atrocities.[244] According to Zwaan, the actual murder and killing that takes place, which he calls the "ultimate phase" of a genocidal process,

> may be done by state agents, often special units of police and/or military personnel ... exempted from the rule of law, and usually also from normal military discipline, but also by special auxiliary or paramilitary groups indirectly linked to the central state authority.[245]

Zwaan describes a "flywheel effect" that occurs as a consequence of impunity – meaning that once a genocidal process is under way, the commission of crimes can gather speed like a flywheel, running more smoothly as time passes and as perpetrators become more experienced and efficient.[246]

Collateral trials for crimes committed by the Scorpions in BiH and Kosovo

The presentation of the Scorpions Video in court elicited unprecedented reactions in Serbia, where the state's participation in the wars of the 1990s had been kept from the public as much as possible. The excerpts played at the trial were followed by a broadcast of the entire videotape on Serbian television the same evening, unleashing a public debate on the role of Serbia in the conflicts in Croatia, BiH, and Kosovo.[247] However, instead of resulting in a catharsis – triggering a shift in attitudes and a public accounting for Serbia's political and criminal responsibility for mass atrocities committed against non-Serbs – the initial shock and any guilt it activated was soon diluted by counter-narratives produced by nationalist elites and state bureaucracies, which portrayed Serbs as having been the primary victim nation in the Balkans for centuries.[248]

Nonetheless, Serbian authorities were left with little choice but to respond to the crimes exposed in the video, in which the perpetrators could be easily identified as Serbian citizens. Within 24 hours of its broadcast on Serbian television, several Scorpions members were arrested and, in October 2005, five of them were indicted. Slobodan Medić, Pera Petrašević, Aleksandar Vukov, Branislav Medić, and Aleksandar Medić were charged with the killings of six men from Srebrenica in a crime that was described as having been committed under the direction of an unidentified VRS commander. In the trial, no connection to the Serbian MUP was addressed.[249]

The trial attracted considerable media attention and raised high expectations, not only regarding the pursuit of justice but also concerning the reaction of Serbian authorities and the Serbian public to mass atrocities committed by Serbian armed forces in BiH. However, the narrow scope of the indictment insured that any criminal responsibility was applied only to the perpetrators themselves; it demanded no accountability from higher-level authorities and made no mention of genocide in Srebrenica. The *Medić et al.* Judgement, pronounced on 10 April 2007, reflected these limitations and was a letdown for families of the victims, even though four of the five accused were found guilty of war crimes. Slobodan Medić and Branislav Medić were each given 20 years in prison; Petrašević, the only one who confessed to the crime, was sentenced to 13 years; Aleksandar Medić was sentenced to five years; and Vukov was acquitted.[250] Slobodan Medić died in a car crash in December 2013 while on leave from prison.

Informed observers, such as local NGOs, criticised the Judgement and said that justice had not been done because, while the criminal responsibility of the perpetrators was exposed, their ties to state officials and organisations were obscured. This allowed elites to carry on using the rhetoric of victimisation as a buffer against state responsibility, framing the West as blindly determined to collectively punish Serbs. For example, now Prime Minister of Serbia Aleksandar Vucic , who was then the Secretary General of Šešelj's SRS, stated in 2005 that a "media campaign against the Serb people and state" was intended to lead to the "unobstructed arrest of Ratko Mladic and the formal abolition of Republika Srpska."[251]

Scorpions members were not charged in the domestic courts with genocide, but with war crimes.[252] This was also true for MUP officials at the ICTY, where Jovica Stanišić and Franko Simatović were charged for crimes against humanity in Srebrenica, and not genocide. Their ICTY indictment did, however, refer to the Scorpions as having been a special unit of the Serbian MUP's State Security while fighting in BiH, and of the Serbian MUP's Public Security while fighting in Kosovo.[253] During the joint trial of Stanišić and Simatović, former Scorpions member Goran Stoparić testified as a Prosecution witness that the unit had been transferred to Trnovo on the orders of Belgrade and had been paid by the Serbian DB.[254] In April 2013, Stanišić and Simatović were acquitted of all crimes in a first instance Judgement, meaning that the Scorpions killings are not a part of the ICTY record in any conviction that ties Belgrade to mass atrocities in BiH.

Crimes committed by Scorpions members in Kosovo were also included in the ICTY indictment of General Vlastimir Đorđević. The Đorđević Prosecution team introduced extensive evidence during the trial regarding the unit and their status, so that a detailed reconstruction of a crime in which the Scorpions are said to have served with the SAJ in Podujevo at the end of March 1999 is encapsulated in the Đorđević Judgement.[255] Controversies regarding the status of the unit were addressed in the Judgement; and the judges determined that it had functioned as a separate unit in Kosovo, wearing the same uniforms as the SAJ, but with a Scorpions insignia on the arm.[256] The court found that Đorđević, who appeared in the Kula Camp Video, had played a key role in the incorporation of the Scorpions into the MUP, ordering their deployment to Kosovo in March of 1999 as well as their redeployment in April 1999, despite his knowledge that members of the unit had committed crimes in Podujevo on 28 March.[257] The fact that the unit was redeployed is a powerful illustration of the climate of impunity that existed among Serbian authorities for perpetrators of war crimes.

Notes

1 Second Amended Indictment, 16 October 2001. Hereinafter, the Kosovo Indictment.
2 Testimony of Frederick Abrahams (3 June 2002), 6100. The Prosecution also dealt extensively with the notion of a 'police state' in the cross-examination of Police General Obrad Stevanović. See: Testimony of General Obrad Stevanović (31 May 2005), 40154. Also see: Helsinki Committee for Human Rights, "Report on the Escalation of Repression in Serbia," Exhibit P446.9.
3 Testimony of Frederick Abrahams (3 June 2002), 6102.
4 See: Tadeusz Mazowiecki, *Situation of Human Rights in the Territory of the Former Yugoslavia,* United Nations, Nos. A/47/666 and S/24809, 17 November 1992, Exhibit P771a.
5 See: "Law on Labour Relations Under Special Circumstances," 26 July 1990, Exhibit P526.14a.
6 Ibid., paras 100, 105–106, and 113.
7 Testimony of Adnan Merovci (23 May 2002), 5442–5444; Testimony of Ibrahim Rugova (3 May 2002), 4194–4195.
8 Testimony of Veton Surroi (18 April 2002), 3370–3372 and 3439–3440.
9 Mazowiecki, *Situation of Human Rights in the Territory of the Former Yugoslavia,* para. 105.
10 Testimony of Sabit Kadriu (6 March 2002), 1618–1619.
11 Ibid., 1619–1620; Testimony of Ibrahim Rugova (3 May 2002), 4198–4199. Also see: Baton Haxhiu, Rule 92 *bis* Witness Statement, 22 May 2002, Exhibit P169; and Testimony of Rahim Latifi (22 April 2002), 3637–3640.
12 Testimony of Ibrahim Rugova (3 May 2002), 3999–4000.
13 Mazowiecki, *Situation of Human Rights in the Territory of the Former Yugoslavia,* para. 100 and 104.
14 Ibid., para. 99–113.
15 Ratomir Tanić, Witness Statement, 19 July 2000, Exhibit P151, 1 and 9.
16 Testimony of Veton Surroi (18 April 2002), 3382–3383 and 3450–3451.
17 Ibid., 3384.
18 See: "Joint Recommendations on the Kosovo Conflict, Halki meeting 1997, Bertelsmann Science Foundation," Exhibit P102.
19 Testimony of Veton Surroi (18 April 2002), 3385.
20 Ibid., 3386, 3389, and 3441–3445.
21 Audrey H. Budding, *Serbian Nationalism in the Twentieth Century: Historical Background and Context*, Expert Report, 11 April 2003, Exhibit P508, 10.
22 See: Dušan Breznik, "The Population of Kosovo," *Yugoslav Survey* 30, no. 4 (1989).

23 Ibid., 29.
24 Ruža Petrović, "Composition of Yugoslavia's Population 1991," *Yugoslav Survey* 33, no. 1 (1992). Also see: Slavenko Terzić, *Kosovo and Metohija in the 20th Century*, Expert Report, Exhibit D259a, 48–66.
25 Terzić, *Kosovo and Metohija in the 20th Century*, 47.
26 Ibid., 50.
27 For example, see: Dobrica Ćosić, *Kosovo*, (Belgrade, Novosti: 2004), 72, 74. Excerpt, Exhibit P802a, 8. Ćosić's position on a partition of Kosovo as a permanent solution for the Kosovo problem was discussed during the testimony of Slavenko Terzić. See: Testimony of Slavenko Terzić (9 December 2004), 34400–34419.
28 In B/C/S, see: Dobrica Ćosić, *Piščevi zapisi: 1992–1993* (Belgrade: Filip Višnjić, 2004), 21 and 231. Ćosić writes on page 21 that he presented the idea of a partition of Kosovo to Milošević in January 1992, but he rejected it. On page 231, he reports also having presented the idea to Cyrus Vance and David Owen in January 1993.
29 Testimony of Mihailo Marković (17 November 2004), 33479. Marković acknowledged the existence of such plans among Serbian elites, naming Ćosić and Aleksandar Despić as proponents of partition.
30 Dušan T. Bataković, "The Serbs in Kosovo-Metohija: War, International Protectorate and National Catastrophe," Project Rastko – Kosovo and Metohija, www.rastko.rs/kosovo/istorija/batakovic/batakovic_serbs_of_kosovo.html (accessed 30 October 2014).
31 Official Gazette of the Socialist Republic of Serbia, No. 35/90, item 555.
32 Official Gazette of the Republic of Serbia, No. 43/91, item 553.
33 Official Gazette of the Republic of Serbia, No. 54/92, item 1360.
34 Mazowiecki, *Situation of Human Rights in the Territory of the Former Yugoslavia*, para. 104.
35 Trial Transcript, Defence Opening Statement (15 February 2002), 302.
36 See the interview with Momčilo Trajković in *NIN*, 15 July 1994, 14–16.
37 Testimony of Veton Surroi (18 April 2002), 3373.
38 Ibid.
39 Prosecution Witness Adnan Merovci exclaimed during cross-examination that Jashari should have received a Nobel Prize for his contributions to freedom and democracy. Testimony of Adnan Merovci (24 May 2002), 5516.
40 Trial Transcript, Defence Opening Statement (31 August 2004), 32222–32223.
41 Ibid., 32223.
42 For example, see the exchange between Milošević and Merovci on this issue: Testimony of Adnan Merovci (24 May 2002), 5484–5488.
43 Testimony of Mahmut Bakalli (19 Februay 2002), 633–663.
44 Ibid., 634.
45 Ibid., 605–606.
46 Testimony of Ibrahim Rugova (3 May 2002), 4192.
47 Ibid., 4195–4196.
48 Testimony of Ibrahim Rugova (6 May 2002), 4337–4339.
49 Ibid., 4339–4340.
50 Testimony of Shukri Buja (5 June 2002), 6353.
51 For example, see: "Stenographic notes from the Council for the Co-ordination of positions of State Policy," 11 August 1992, Exhibit P469.41, 95 (in B/C/S). Milošević insisted that Kosovo be treated as an internal political issue.
52 "Statement on Kosovo of the Contact Group Foreign Ministers," 24 September 1997, Exhibit P791.1.
53 For example, see statements on Kosovo from the Contact Group: on 8 January 1998, Exhibit P791.2; on 25 February 1998, Exhibit P791.3; on 9 March 1998, P791.4; and on 25 March 1998, Exhibit P791.5.

54 See: "Statement on Kosovo of the Contact Group Foreign Ministers," 29 April 1998, Exhibit P791.6, para. 9.
55 Yevgeny Primakov, *Years in Big Politics*, Excerpt of pages 338–358, Exhibit P794.2a, 5–6.
56 See: "Statement on Kosovo of the Contact Group Foreign Ministers," 29 April 1998, para. 4.
57 "Statement on Kosovo of the Contact Group Foreign Ministers," 8 July 1998, Exhibit 791.8, para. 10. Also see: Enver Hasani, "The 'Outer Wall' of Sanctions and the Kosovo Issue," *Perceptions* III, no. 3 (September–November 1998). Available at: http://sam.gov.tr/wp-content/uploads/2012/01/ENVER-HASANI.pdf (accessed 11 January 2013).
58 Primakov, *Years in Big Politics*, Excerpt, 8–9.
59 "Statement on Kosovo of the Contact Group Foreign Ministers," 12 June 1998, Exhibit P791.7, para. 3.
60 The joint statement was submitted to the United Nations by then Russian Ambassador to the UN Sergey Lavrov. See: United Nations Security Council, Letter from the Permanent Representative of the Russian Federation, No. S/1998/526, 17 June 1998, Annex.
61 Primakov, *Years in Big Politics*, Excerpt, 11.
62 "Statement on Kosovo of the Contact Group Foreign Ministers," 7 July 1998, para. 4 and 6.
63 See: Marc Weller, *The Crisis in Kosovo 1989–1999* (Cambridge: Documents & Analysis Publishing, 1999), 279. The page was entered into evidence as Exhibit P94/1.
64 Ibid.
65 Testimony of Knut Vollebaek (8 July 2002), 7641–7642.
66 For example, see: William Walker, Rule 92 *bis* Witness Statement, Exhibit P228, 39–40; Testimony of William Walker (11 June 2002), 6780–6781; Testimony of Major General Karol John Drewienkiewicz (11 April 2002), 2842–2843.
67 Testimony of Major General Karol John Drewienkiewicz (11 April 2004), 2853–2854; Testimony of Colonel Richard Ciaglinski (16 April 2002), 3169–3171.
68 Testimony of Major General Karol John Drewienkiewicz (11 April 2004), 2853–2855; Testimony of Colonel Richard Ciaglinski (16 April 2002), 3147–3148. Also see: John Crosland, Rule 92 *bis* Witness Statement, 9 July 2002, Exhibit P253A.
69 United Nations Security Council, *Report of the Secretary-General prepared pursuant to Resolutions 1160 (1998), 1199 (1998) and 1203 (1998) of the Security Council*, No. S/1998/1068, 12 November 1998, 14–15. Also see: Testimony of Alice Mahon (1 March 2006), 1315–1318.
70 Neil Wright, Rule 92 *bis* Witness Statement, 5 February 2002, Exhibit P234.
71 See: Kosovo Indictment, para. 66 and Schedule A.
72 "Contact Group – Chairman's Conclusions," 22 January 1999, Exhibit P791.9.
73 "Statement by the Contact Group issued in London," 29 January 1999, Exhibit P791.10.
74 Testimony of Veton Surroi (18 April 2002), 3405–3408, 3412–3413, and 3457–3461. Agani was known as the architect of the parallel system of Kosovo Albanian institutions that arose in response to Serbia's discriminatory policies. While Rugova was the face of the LDK, Agani held great influence behind the scenes, shaping much party policy. For more on Agani and his murder, see: Gabriel Partos, "Fehmi Agani," *Guardian*, 27 May 1999.
75 Testimony of Shukri Buja (5 June 2002), 6350–6351.
76 There were 12 members in the delegation, representing both FRY and Serbian institutions.

77 Testimony of Wolfgang Petritch (2 July 2002), 7221–7224.
78 Testimony of Knut Vollebaek (8 July 2002), 7655–7658.
79 Testimony of Wolfgang Petritch (2 July 2002), 7219–7221.
80 Ibid., 7252–7254.
81 Ibid., 7227–7231.
82 Ibid., 7227–7228.
83 Ibid., 7229–7230.
84 Ibid., 7235.
85 Testimony of Ibrahim Rugova (3 May 2002), 4217–4218.
86 Testimony of Wolfgang Petritch (2 July 2002), 7289–7290.
87 *The Fall of Milošević*, directed by Dai Richards, produced by Brian Lapping Associates, BBC, 2001.
88 Testimony of Wolfgang Petritch (2 July 2002), 7271.
89 Ibid., 7243–7244.
90 Ibid.
91 Testimony of James Bisset (24 February 2006), 48845–48846.
92 Milošević replied to Ministers Cook and Védrine in a *Politika* article. For an English translation, see: "You Don't Have the Right to Threaten Other Countries and their Citizens, or Arrange Their Lives," 23 March 1999, Exhibit D336. Also see: Testimony of James Bisset (24 February 2006), 48863–48864.
93 Ibid. *Note*: In the original, Milošević did not use the word *pacovi*, which would be translated as 'rats,' but *hulje*, which was translated by the courtroom interpreters as 'scoundrels.' When the Exhibit was presented in court and the word 'rats' was read aloud, Milošević insisted on correcting the transcript, stressing that he had written *hulje*. See: Trial Transcript (24 February 2006), 48847.
94 Ibid.
95 Ibid.
96 Testimony of Colonel Richard Ciaglinski (17 April 2002), 3256–3257.
97 Testimony of General Klaus Naumann (13 June 2002), 6998–7001.
98 Testimony of General Wesley Clark (15 December 2003), 30404–30407.
99 Testimony of Colonel Richard Ciaglinski (16 April 2002), 3151–3154. Also see: Testimony of Major General Karol John Drewienkiewicz (12 April 2002), 2945.
100 Testimony of Colonel Richard Ciaglinski (17 April 2002), 3258.
101 Trial Transcript, Defence Opening Statement (15 February 2002), 397–405.
102 Trial Transcript, Defence Opening Statement (31 August 2004), 32241–32243.
103 Trial Transcript, Defence Opening Statement (15 February 2002), 404–405.
104 Trial Transcript, Defence Opening Statement (31 August 2004), 32252–32253 and 32240–32242.
105 Ibid., 32209, 32242–32243, and 32251.
106 For example, see: Testimony of Colonel Richard Ciaglinski (16 April 2002), 3151–3154; and Testimony of Major General Karol John Drewienkiewicz (12 April 2002), 2945.
107 Trial Transcript, Defence Opening Statement (14 February 2002), 244–245.
108 Testimony of Ratomir Tanić (15 May 2002), 4949–4952 and 4996–4997.
109 Ibid., 4936 and 4995–4996.
110 Ibid., 4996–4997.
111 Testimony of Ratomir Tanić (21 May 2002), 5198–5199.
112 General Perišić's letter was published in a book titled *Vatre i Potop* ("Fire and Flood"). An English translation was tendered into evidence. See: "Letter dated 23 July 1998, to Slobodan Milošević from Momčilo Perišić published in the book Fire and Flood," Exhibit, P150a.
113 Ibid.
114 Ibid.
115 Ibid.

116 Testimony of General Božidar Delić (20 September 2005), 44397. Also see: Phillip Coo, "Part I: Organisation and Command & Control Measures (January–June 1999)," *Forces of the FRY & Serbia in Kosovo*, Expert Report, Part I, Exhibit P318.1.

117 "Policy Declaration of the Serbian Radical Party," 23 February 1991, Exhibit P458.2a.

118 "Transcript of Šešelj's Speech," Exhibit P821.1. Also see: *The Fall of Milošević*, BBC, 2001; and Testimony of Vojislav Šešelj (15 September 2005), 44167.

119 Testimony of Vojislav Šešelj (23 August 2005), 43025–43026.

120 Testimony of Vojislav Šešelj (15 September 2005), 44167–44169.

121 For example, see: "Stenographic transcript of the 23rd session of the Supreme Defence Council," 21 July 1994, *Prosecutor* v. *Perišić*, Exhibit P00785.E, 9. General Kovačević read a list of "long-term forces ready for operation," noting that there were "1,580 men with 40 tanks, 36 personnel carriers, 121 artillery weapons, 36 anti-aircraft weapons – equivalent to two battalions" in the Kosovo area.

122 "Stenographic transcript of the 25th session of the Supreme Defence Council," 30 August 1994, *Prosecutor* v. *Perišić*, Exhibit P00778.E, 13.

123 "Stenographic transcript of the 35th session of the Supreme Defence Council," 13 April 1995, *Prosecutor* v. *Perišić*, Exhibit P00795.E, 29.

124 "Stenographic transcript of the 5th session of the SDC (chaired by Slobodan Milošević)," 9 June 1998, Exhibit P667.70.1a, 6.

125 Ibid., 8.

126 Ibid., 10.

127 "Stenographic transcript of the 6th session of the SDC (chaired by Slobodan Milošević)," 4 October 1998, Exhibit P667.71.1a, 7–8.

128 Ibid., 16.

129 Ibid., 18.

130 Ibid., 22–24.

131 "Meeting notes from the 7th session of the Supreme Defence Council," 24 November 1998, Exhibit P469.29a, 3.

132 Ibid., 4.

133 "Stenographic transcript of the 8th session of the SDC (chaired by Slobodan Milošević)," 25 December 1998, Exhibit P667.73.1a, 7.

134 Ibid., 24.

135 Testimony of General Geza Farkaš (10 November 2005), 46435.

136 Coo, *Forces of the FRY & Serbia in Kosovo*, Part I, Section D, para. 1–6.

137 Testimony of Zoran Lilić (17 June 2003), 22569. The documents were titled: "Strategy of Armed Battle" and "Military Doctrine of the FRY."

138 General Nebojša Pavković was indicted, tried, and convicted of crimes committed by Serb armed forces in Kosovo in 1998 and 1999 in *Milutinović et al.* See: Judgement, *Prosecutor* v. *Milutinović et al.*, No. IT-05–87-T, 26 February 2009.

139 "Belgrade RTS Television First Program, 1900 GMT," 20 October 2000, Exhibit P319.90, 3.

140 Ibid.

141 Testimony of Philip Coo (10 September 2002), 10004–10005.

142 "Decision on the Proclamation of a State of War…," 24 March 1999, Exhibit P319.11a.

143 Coo, "Part II: Kosovo Operations Narrative," *Forces of the FRY & Serbia in Kosovo*.

144 "VJ Website regarding Pavković on MUP Announcement," 14 June 2001, Exhibit P319.53.

145 Trial Transcript, Rule 54 *bis* Motion Hearing (10 March 2003), 17538. Also see: Prosecution Response to the 6 May 2003 Submission by Serbia and Montenegro Regarding Outstanding Requests for Assistance, 20 May 2003, 8, note 27.

146 Ibid.
147 Prosecution Submission of Joint Command Order of 15 April 1999, 27 February 2004, Annex A.
148 Testimony of Shukri Aliu (5 July 2002), 7597.
149 Testimony of Zoran Lilić (18 June 2003), 22656–22658.
150 "Stenographic transcript of the 5th session of the SDC (chaired by Slobodan Milošević)," 9 June 1998, Exhibit P667.70.1a, 9.
151 Testimony of Zoran Lilić (18 June 2003), 22687. Also see: "Minutes of the 16th Session of the Main Committee of the Socialist Party of Serbia," 10 June 1998, Exhibit D142a.
152 "Letter dated 23 July 1998, to Slobodan Milošević from Momčilo Perišić published in the book Fire and Flood," Exhibit P150a.
153 Testimony of Obrad Stevanović (2 June 2005), 40410–40421.
154 Testimony of General Božidar Delić (11 July 2005), 42125–42127.
155 Ibid., 42137.
156 Ibid.
157 Ibid., 42138.
158 See Ognjanović's statement in: *Milošević on Trial*, directed by Michael Christofferson, Team Productions, 2007.
159 Trial Transcript, Rule 54 *bis* Motion Hearing (3 June 2003), 21661.
160 Ibid., 21666–21667.
161 See the comments of Stephan Kay, assigned legal counsel for the Defence:

> Disclosure issues between the Prosecution and the government of Serbia have nothing to do with this Accused and Mr. Nice continually makes his complaint as though it's against the Accused.... This is not a matter under his control and therefore to make continually points against the Accused on this matter is indeed unfair.

Trial Transcript (26 October 2005), 45746.
162 Trial Transcript (26 October 2005), 45750.
163 Prosecution Response to the 6 May 2003 Submission by Serbia and Montenegro Regarding Outstanding Requests for Assistance, 20 May 2003, para. 15.
164 Ibid.
165 Ibid. The original article referenced by the Prosecution was: "Army Commission for Cooperation with the ICTY Abolished," *Defence & Security*, no. 75 (April 2003).
166 Testimony of General Božidar Delić (11 July 2005), 42087–42088.
167 Testimony of General Božidar Delić (10 July 2005), 42100–42101; and (18 July 2005), 42408.
168 Ibid. (18 July 2005), 42406–42408; and (19 July 2005), 42481–42483.
169 See the Decision in B/C/S: "Decision of the Ministry of Defence on forming an expert commission ... for analysis of the praxis of the ICTY," No. 486–1, 26 March 2001, Exhibit P921.1.
170 Letter from Lieutenant General Zlatoje Terzić to Minister Slobodan Krapović, 16 July 2001, 3.
171 Yugoslav Army General Staff, "Analysis of the hitherto trial before the Hague Tribunal, problems and proposals of measures," 20 February 2002, Exhibit P921.8a, 1.
172 Testimony of General Božidar Delić (28 September 2005), 44762–44764.
173 Testimony of General Božidar Delić (10 July 2005), 42108. Also see: "Army Commission for Cooperation with the ICTY Abolished," *Defence & Security*. The following names were referred to as members of the Commission: Slavoje Terzić, General Geza Farkaš, General Radomir Gojović, Nikola Grujina, Aca Tomić, Slobodan Rajčević, Miloje Pršić, Gvozden Petrović, Radovan Labus, and Dragiša Rašković.

174 For example, see evidence brought into the courtroom by General Božidar Delić in Defence Exhibits D300.430-D300.436.
175 Testimony of General Božidar Delić (11 July 2005), 42077.
176 Ibid. (20 July 2005), 42675–42676; and (21 June 2005), 41232.
177 Ibid. (12 July 2005), 42248–42254.
178 For example, in B/C/S, see: "Dokazao sam da Ešdaun laže," Internet Novine Srpske, www.srpskadijaspora.info/vest.asp?id=6383 (accessed 30 October 2014). In English, this headline reads, "I have proof that Ashdown is a liar."
179 Delić said, *inter alia,*

> I have taken 26 "scalps" ... I have refuted the testimonies of 26 Prosecution witnesses – among whom were colonels and generals from Western countries ... I have proved on the spot that they were forgers, amateurs, and complete ignoramuses. That troubled the prosecutors and the judges. Whenever they [presented] evidence, I said it was a forgery and I succeeded to prove my claims.

(This article appears in Serbian and was translated by the author.) See: P. Stojković, "Zemlju nema ko da brani," *Arena 92*, 26 February 2008, http://revija92.rs/code/navigate.php?Id=599&editionId=15&articleId=70 (accessed 4 April 2015).
180 Testimony of General Božidar Delić (11 July 2005), 42119.
181 Ibid.
182 Ibid., 42120.
183 Ibid.
184 Members of the VJ involved in the Kosovo campaign and called as witnesses for the Defence included: General Božidar Delić, General Miloš Đošan, General Milan Kotur, Colonel Vlatko Vuković, Major Janoš Šel, Husein Sarvanović, Krsman Jelić, and Zlatko Odak.
185 For example, see: Trial Transcript and Testimony of Colonel Vlatko Vuković (27 October 2005), 45836–45839, 45871–45872, 45876–45877, and 45929–45930. Also see: Testimony of Major Janoš Šel (30 November 2005), 46831–46842. Major Šel, after several initial confusing and evasive answers, eventually admitted to having kept daily operative reports in two notebooks and directed the Court to the official location where they were kept. Subsequently, the Court issued an oral order to the Serbian authorities on the following day to provide a copy of the notebooks.
186 "War Diary of the 2nd Motorised Battalion," Excerpt, Exhibit D322.3e, 2.
187 Trial Transcript (12 December 2005), 47294.
188 Testimony of Colonel Vlatko Vuković (27 October 2005), 45928–45929.
189 Testimony of General Radomir Gojović (22 March 2005), 37615–37616.
190 Trial Transcript, Defence Opening Statement (31 August 2004), 32222–32223.
191 Testimony of Vladislav Jovanović (15 February 2005), 36171–36172.
192 "Map reflecting entries in Vuković's diary," Exhibit P930.1. Also see: "War Diary of the 2nd Motorised Battalion," 6–7. Towns named in both the diaries and in the indictment include Bela Crkva, Celine, Nogavac, Velika Kruša, Retimlje, Randubrava, and Rogovo, among others.
193 "War Diary of the 2nd Motorised Battalion," 6–7.
194 Ibid., 6.
195 Testimony of Colonel Vlatko Vuković (1 November 2005), 46075–46076.
196 Testimony of Colonel Vlatko Vuković (1 November 2005), 46119.
197 Testimony of General Miloš Đošan (31 October 2005), 45950.
198 Testimony of General Miloš Đošan (31 October 2005), 45966.
199 Ibid., 45966.
200 Testimony of Colonel Vlatko Vuković (1 November 2005), 46152.
201 Testimony of General Geza Farkaš (9 November 2005), 46349.

202 Testimony of General Obrad Stevanović (26 May 2005), 39908–39909.
203 Ibid. (2 June 2005), 40378–40382.
204 Ibid. (2 June 2005), 40378–40382.
205 Ibid., 40382–40383.
206 See: Heike Krieger, ed., *The Kosovo Conflict and International Law: An Analytical Documentation 1974–1999* (Cambridge: Cambridge University Press, 2001), 60.
207 Nike Peraj, Rule 92 *bis* Witness Statement, 15 February 2002, Exhibit P143Aa, 9 (in B/C/S); Sabit Kadriu, Witness Statement, 10 December 2000, Exhibit P50a, 20 (Kadriu wrote: "I only had ... my identification papers by now. The Serb took it.... The identification papers of all my companions were also confiscated"); Rahim Latifi, Rule 92 *bis* Witness Statement, 28 April 1999, Exhibit P107A, 3; and Martin Pnishi, Redacted Rule 92 *bis* Witness Statement, 4 April 2000, Exhibit P299A, 4 (Pnishi wrote: "civilians were forced to drop their ID cards on the ground").
208 Momir Bulatović, *Pravila ćutanja* (Belgrade: Narodna knjiga, 2004), 333.
209 Testimony of Aleksandar Vasiljević, (12 February 2003), T 15760; (13 February 2003) T 15970–15972 15998–16005; Testimony of Obrad Stevanović, (2 June 2005), T 40381–40383.
210 Patrick Ball, Wendy Betts, Fritz Scheuren, Jana Dudukovich, and Jana Asher, *Killings and Refugee Flow in Kosovo, March–June 1999*, Expert Report, 3 January 2002, Exhibit P67, 3–4.
211 Judgement Summary, *Prosecutor* v. *Milutinović et al.*, 3.
212 Ibid.
213 Ibid.
214 Ibid.
215 A "secondary grave" is the grave of a victim who was originally buried elsewhere before they were exhumed and reburied.
216 Testimony of General Obrad Stevanović (1 June 2005), 40283–40286.
217 Ibid., 40287.
218 Ibid., 40251.
219 Ibid., 40254–40256.
220 Ibid., 40255.
221 Trial Transcript (1 June 2005), 40278.
222 Ibid., 40279.
223 Testimony of General Obrad Stevanović (1 June 2005), 40279.
224 Ibid.
225 Ibid., 40269–40270.
226 Ibid., 40290.
227 Judgement, *Prosecutor* v. *Đorđević*, No. IT-05–87/1-T, 23 February 2011, 483–500.
228 Testimony of General Obrad Stevanović (1 June 2005), 40541–40543.
229 Ibid., 40543–40544.
230 "Report on engagement of reserve formations ... signed by Commander Živko Trajković," Exhibit P870.7a.
231 Testimony of General Geza Farkaš (10 November 2005), 46449–46450.
232 Ibid., 40435–40437.
233 "General Obrad Stevanović's personal diary," Exhibit D299. 440a, 84. Also see; Testimony of General Obrad Stevanović (7 June 2005), 40610.
234 For more on the history of the Scorpions, see (in B/C/S): *Škorpioni od zločina do pravde* (Belgrade, Humanitarian Law Centre, 2012). Available at: www.hlc-rdc.org/wp-content/uploads/2012/06/Skorpioni.pdf (accessed 11 January 2013).
235 Testimony of Milan Milanović (8 October 2003), 27241 and 27254.
236 Milan Milanović, Witness Statement, 28 June 2003, Exhibit P550, 31.
237 Ibid., 32.

238 Testimony of Milan Milanović (14 October 2003), 27431.
239 Milan 'Mrgud' Milanović, Witness Statement, 32.
240 Testimony of General Obrad Stevanović (1 June 2005), 40281.
241 Milan 'Mrgud' Milanović, Witness Statement, 33.
242 Ibid., 34.
243 Testimony of General Obrad Stevanović (26 May 2005), 39958–39961.
244 Ton Zwaan, *On the Aetiology and Genesis of Genocides and other Mass Crimes Targeting Specific Groups*, Expert Report, November 2003, Exhibit P639, para. 14 and 29. Also see: Testimony of Anthony Zwaan (20 January 2004), 31168–31169.
245 Ibid., para. 30.
246 Ibid., para. 37–39.
247 See: "Almost all Belgrade Print Media Deaf Mute," 2 June 2005, Helsinki Committee of Human Rights in Serbia, www.helsinki.org.rs/tjsrebrenica_t04.html (accessed 30 October 2014).
248 See: "The Scorpions Case: Denial of Genocide," in *Self-Isolation: Reality and the Goal*, the Annual Report of the Helsinki Committee for Human Rights in Serbia (2007), 451–454.
249 Belgrade District Court War Crimes Chamber, Indictment (Amended), *Medić et al.*, No. KTRZ 3/05, 9 October 2006. Available at: www.tuzilastvorz.org.rs/html_trz/OPTUZNICE/O_2006_10_09_ENG.pdf (accessed 15 January 2013).
250 See: Vesna Peric Zimonjic, "Serb 'Scorpions' Guilty of Srebrenica Massacre," *Independent*, 11 April 2007. In January 2014, Slobodan Medić died in a car crash while on leave from prison. See: Sasa Milosevic, "Fatal Privilege for Serbian War Criminal," *The World Post*, 29 January 2014, www.huffingtonpost.com/sasa-milosevic/fatal-privilege-for-serbi_b_4644136.html (accessed 4 April 2015).
251 "Vućić: 'This is an anti-Serb campaign,'" 6 June 2005, *Kurir*, as quoted in: "The Scorpions Case: Denial of Genocide," 457.
252 Ibid., 266–268.
253 Prosecution Notice of Filing of Third Amended Indictment, *Prosecutor* v. *Stanišić & Simatović*, No. IT-03–69-PT, 10 July 2008, para. 61.
254 "Former 'Scorpion' Soldier Testifies about Links with Serbian Secret Police," *Sense Tribunal*, 14 December 2010. Also see: "Shifting the Blame on a Family Clan in the 'Scorpions'," *Sense Tribunal*, 15 December 2010.
255 Judgement, *Prosecutor* v. *Đorđević*, para. 1928.
256 Ibid., para. 206.
257 Ibid., para. 1930.

7 The unmaking of the leader

From the early days of the conflict in the former Yugoslavia, Milošević was demonised by his political opponents and the world media. After the conflict in Croatia took a violent turn and subsequently expanded into BiH, *Time* magazine published a June 1992 front-page article titled "Slobodan Milošević: Butcher of the Balkans." In a sharp analysis, the author attempted to capture the essence of Milošević as a man and as a politician, describing his political tenure – at the time lasting only a couple of years – with more refinement than the title suggested.[1] The unflattering nickname stuck, though, and not least because Milošević exposed himself as ruthlessly determined to retain power and achieve his strategic goals in the years that followed. Almost three decades after his march to power, historical evaluations of Milošević's leadership have evoked the suggestion of seventeenth-century mathematician Blaise Pascal that the story of world history would have been different if Cleopatra's nose, which attracted Mark Antony and thereby led to the fall of the Second Triumvirate, had been shorter. Applied to Milošević, the question is: "Would the recent history of the SFRY and its people have turned out differently if Milošević had not visited Kosovo in April 1987?"

It was in 1987 that Milošević discovered his charismatic appeal to the public somewhat accidentally, during his first two visits to Kosovo; and he embraced his newfound influence with the eager vigour of a politician who yearns for power and has found a way to be noticed in a dense political landscape. His metamorphosis from communist functionary to the cult leader of all Serbs occurred in several seconds – just the time it took for him to say those now famous words, "No one is allowed to beat you." Serbian nationalists, who understood that their emerging movement needed to be validated in order for it to transform successfully into a political force, sought a Serbian communist official who could push their agenda in federal and republican institutions. And so, in 1987, when his pragmatism converged with their ideology in that sound bite in Kosovo, Serbian nationalists found their man in Slobodan Milošević. And, while it appears that Milošević spoke those particular words spontaneously (although in a less heroic context than his propagandists might have suggested), events that led up to that utterance and its treatment afterward were reflections of the well-oiled media machine that supported his early rise to power.

As much as Ivan Stambolić concluded in retrospect, somewhat reluctantly, that taking his protégé under his wing had been his biggest political mistake, an analysis of Milošević's political career reveals that his power grew through support on several fronts and not only because Stambolić had been his early champion. But it was one thing to conquer power in Serbia and another to hold on to it; and Milošević's ability to retain power is partly explained by the dominant political culture in the Yugoslav state, stretching back to 1918. In 73 years, Yugoslavia never experienced democracy and relied heavily on authoritarian leadership. The death of strong leader Josip Broz Tito in 1980 created an opening for another authoritarian leader to emerge; and it was in this space that Milošević materialised as a politician. He was empowered by the Communist Party, but encouraged and supported by Serbian nationalist elites, who used the political confusion created by Tito's death as an opportunity to resurrect old grievances about the position of Serbia within the SFRY. They espoused nationalism as the basis for re-defining the constitutional status of Serbia, but in fact used the ideology to facilitate social and political change, legitimise their power and secure Serb domination.

Although there is merit to the argument that the history of the former Yugoslavia might indeed have turned out differently had Milošević not risen to power, Serbian nationalists would have found someone else to direct the expansionist programme that had been their objective for over a century. Yet, while Milošević came to power on the wings of an already potent nationalist movement, it is important to underline that he was not simply a puppet of that project. Indeed, once he rose to power, he became its most powerful executor. His agenda to unite "All Serbs in a Single State" was his path to criminality; but at any stage of the aggression and violence, he could arguably have stopped or severely impeded the Serb war effort by cutting military aid. Instead, he increasingly embraced criminal behaviour in order to address both cross-border territorial aspirations and domestic political challenges.

The path to self-destruction

Like many other politicians with extensive and autocratic powers, Milošević fell into the trap of self-isolation, relying on a shrinking circle of advisors over the course of his tenure. Eventually, he operated in an environment that resembled a royal court, with individuals competing to ingratiate themselves to Milošević as if to a monarch. He grew accustomed to the flattery, even seduced by it, and accepted the uncritical and untruthful representations of political reality that fawning loyalists offered him.[2]

Milošević's former associates testified that he became obsessively concerned about his status and power as time passed, showing intolerance towards fellow party members and perceiving their public success as rivalry. Borisav Jović wrote about the methodical way Milošević dealt with potential competitors or those who expressed opposing views, marginalising or eliminating them before they gained too much political influence. According to

Jović, Milošević had no scruples about carrying out political purges when he felt threatened.[3] Indeed, open political clashes had become a hallmark of Milošević's political style by 1995; and he used state-controlled media to publicly denounce individuals while simultaneously applying political pressure to isolate or simply dismiss them. Jović himself received this treatment in 1996, upon the publication of his first book, when he was dismissed initially from the position of SPS Vice-President before Milošević also asked him to resign as a member of the Serbian Parliament. Jović did as he was asked, for he knew from experience that Milošević would get his way.[4]

Zoran Lilić gave a similar account of the changing atmosphere in the SPS, underlining Milošević's increasing intolerance of opposition within his own party. Lilić said that SPS members who criticised policies advanced by Milošević, his wife, and his inner circle very quickly either left the party of their own free will or were forcibly expelled.[5] And when a showdown occurred immediately after the signing of the Dayton Peace Agreement among Milošević's closest associates – some of whom were critical of the power-sharing arrangement Milošević had with his wife – Milošević was unconcerned, believing he could afford the standoff given his newly acquired patronage by the West.[6] Yet, Milošević had failed to address the challenges of Serbian society that could have helped him win back the popular domestic support he once enjoyed. Serbian citizens, weary of the domestic problems that accumulated over years of negligence and corruption – and augmented by the regional and international isolation of the FRY – expected improvements to their daily lives. But Milošević's regime was not ready, capable, or willing to tackle these problems.[7]

Milošević had survived mass protests against his regime by Serbian political opposition in 1991, 1992, and 1993. Still, any anti-war discourse failed to seriously challenge his bellicose politics, and Milošević responded by insisting that Serbia was not at war and that his policies had successfully prevented the escalation of neighbouring conflicts into Serbian territory. And further, while his open support to Serbs outside of Serbia was condemned by some people inside Serbia, it was expected by many others, including a number of opposition leaders – who criticised Milošević whenever he exerted public pressure against RSK or RS leadership. In fact, opposition leaders such as Vojislav Šešelj, were actually more militant and extreme than Milošević. Thus, most of the persistently democratic, non-nationalist, and anti-war opposition to Milošević came from civil society and not from within political parties.

The wars in Croatia and BiH became a salient issue for Serbian voters after Dayton – when they seem to have finally grown weary of the poverty that resulted from UN sanctions and military expenditures, as well as the criminalisation of Serbian society that had occurred during Milošević's rule. Local elections held in the autumn of 1996 were a test of domestic support for Milošević, but a coalition of opposition parties – the Democratic Movement of Serbia (*Demokratski pokret Srbije*, or DEPOS) – won in several major cities including Belgrade. When Milošević and his political allies tried to alter the election results, they provoked the largest and most persistent street protests Serbia had ever seen. The protests lasted into 1997 and, eventually, Milošević had to accept the election results, bending under combined domestic and international pressure.[8] He remained in power, though, and after Serbia's presidential elections in December 1997, was appointed by the Federal Assembly as President of the FRY; with Milan Milutinović stepping into Milošević's old role as President of Serbia.

In 1998, he turned to Kosovo again, apparently believing that Serbia could resolve the simmering conflict there by trying to remake the demography of the province and then govern it from Belgrade. This was not only a grave political miscalculation but also exposed the irrational and impractical side of his political strategy. How could such a goal be achieved? Did he really think he could get away with another war on another non-Serb population? His choice to use force against civilians in Kosovo, reflecting the criminality he had displayed during the conflicts in Croatia and BiH, reversed any mercy he had been offered after Dayton. And what had seemed in 1990 to be a political triumph for Serbia, and for Milošević personally, led nine years later to the capitulation of Serbian Kosovo policy and to the political downfall of Milošević. Already in 1998 Milošević was already aware of the grave consequences of his approach to the Kosovo crisis in 1998. Momir Bulatović recorded a conversation with Milošević explaining why he appointed Bulatović's Deputy Nikola Šainović to run the team tasked to deal with Kosovo. Milošević explained to Bulatović that he did not appoint him as he wanted to spare him from being indicted by The Hague Tribunal, something Milošević expected to happen to all those who were in the chain of political, military, and police command for Kosovo and Metohija.[9]

Following defeat in Kosovo at the hands of NATO and the KLA, Milošević faced opposition at home and isolation abroad, and he clung precariously to power. The last stage of his rule was characterised by rash decision-making and paranoia. In 2000, still in office and still convinced that he held superior political authority among Serbs, he called for elections to be held one year early. It remains unclear why he decided to take such a gamble. In July of that year, the FRY Assembly adopted amendments to the Constitution according to which the President of the FRY would no longer be appointed, but would be elected by Serb citizens in a direct vote; thus, if he had not called for early elections, he would have held on to power at least until the end of 2001.[10] Nevertheless, early elections were held, and Milošević – ill-advised, over-confident, and disconnected from reality – lost.

Tanks under the command of trusted General Božidar Delić waited on the outskirts of Belgrade for orders to move towards the city centre, but Milošević chose not to engage them to defend his regime.[11] Instead, he simply walked away, accepting his electoral defeat and surrendering his power against the advice of his wife, who urged him to make use of the force.[12] In the aftermath of the loss, he did not offer his resignation as President of the SPS, which Jović noted would have been "totally natural," but called for a party congress.[13] He was re-elected as SPS President, but the party no longer held any significant power and Milošević did not even seek a seat in the Assembly. Milošević seemed almost reconciled to what was to come.

From a populist leader to a common criminal

The contradictions that shaped Milošević and marked his behaviour have been regularly noted by those who have had direct dealings with him. Warren Zimmerman, former US Ambassador to the SFRY, saw two people in Milošević: an authoritarian leader, ready to use force in the creation of a Greater Serbia, who spoke Serbian and despised Westerners; and a polite, pleasant, and cooperative diplomat who spoke English and reminisced about his banking days in New York. According to Zimmerman, this second Milošević was in charge of correcting the damage that the first Milošević had caused. Reflecting on Zimmerman's observations of Milošević as two-faced, Slobodan Antonić evokes a Jekyll-and-Hyde analogy; but, in the case of Milošević, it was not a potion that transformed him from gentleman into beast, but power.[14] And, indeed, "power for the sake of power" has been underlined as the most important modus operandi of his leadership by a wide spectrum of scholars, diplomats, fellow politicians, ICTY prosecutors, and journalists.

The Milošević regime had commissioned crimes against non-Serbs in Croatia, BiH, and Kosovo using official military and police infrastructures as well as seemingly ad hoc paramilitary groups that operated with impunity. The "flywheel" effect of this impunity apparently ran smoothly as long as the regime was willing to protect those who engaged in such crimes. And individuals from armed formations that operated during the wars – many of whom appeared with Milošević in the Kula Camp Video – had continued to commit crimes on behalf of Milošević in peacetime, against his political opponents. A number of politically-motivated murders carried out in Serbia during his leadership exposed him as a common felon; and predictably, any impunity enjoyed by Milošević and his supporters while he was in power did not endure regime change in 2000.

By 2003, the criminality of the former regime was laid bare in several court cases that demonstrated the importance of facing the past not only to ensure an accurate historical record but also to support domestic stability and security. It was after the assassination of Prime Minister Zoran Đinđić in March of that year that the full extent of political violence and intimidation tactics used by Milošević loyalists was uncovered. The investigation into Đinđić's murder led to several notorious JSO members, who revealed information during questioning that helped resolve several other political assassinations that had occurred in the course of Milošević's reign – including that of Ivan Stambolić. In the Stambolić Judgement, delivered in 2005, the judges concluded that Milošević had indeed ordered the killing of his political rival and one-time mentor.[15]

From leading the project of Serb nationalism to ordering the killing of his political opponents, Milošević seemed to believe he would never be held accountable for his actions. And so, years after his ouster from power, skeletons from the Milošević era keep haunting Serbia. In January 2014, for instance, based on information given to the police by Milorad "Legija" Luković, two former State Security (DB) officials were brought into custody as suspects in the 1999 murder of journalist Slavko Ćuruvija.[16] Legija offered his account of Ćuruvija's murder – true or false – while he was already in prison for the roles he played in the murders of Đinđić and Stambolić and in the attempted murder of opposition politician Vuk Drašković. Legija named Radomir Marković, former Head of the Serbian DB, as a third suspect in Ćuruvija's assassination. Marković was already serving a 40-year sentence for his part in the 1999 conspiracy to murder Drašković.

Milošević's courtroom performance

Milošević was arrested on 31 March 2001 by Serbian police, and on 28 June, he was transferred to The Hague. It was St Vitus' Day, when Serbs commemorate the lost Battle of Kosovo Polje; and also the day, only 12 years earlier, on which he had given his historical sabre-rattling speech at Gazimetan and had announced new battles ahead for Serbs that could not be won "without the resolve, bravery, and sacrifice of the people."[17] On 12 February 2002, Milošević sat in a courtroom in The Hague, representing himself against charges that included genocide.

As President of Serbia and later of the FRY, Milošević had accumulated extensive *de jure* and de facto powers that the Prosecution argued had made it possible for him to control political and military institutions in Serbia, Montenegro, the SFRY and the FRY, as well as those established by Serb leadership in Croatia and BiH. In all three indictments against him, the Prosecution addressed Milošević's unique position as an omnipotent leader of all Serbs. This stemmed from his *de jure* power as President, and was reinforced and extended by the de facto power that resulted from the acceptance by Serbs outside Serbia of Milošević as their leader, too.

This de facto power was further strengthened by the willingness of politicians from other Yugoslav republics – even those who actively opposed Serbian politics under his rule – to deal with Milošević as if he was indeed the leader of all Serbs, inducing representatives of the international community to do the same. The Defence underlined Milošević's extensive powers, too, but stressed that they were legitimate and based on his qualities as a leader who, unlike other communist politicians at the time, was prepared to take risks to deliver what was expected from him. The Defence also argued that he had been the protector of Serbs everywhere and in particular those living in Kosovo, Croatia, and BiH – places, the Defence claimed, Serbs' national existence had been threatened by Kosovo Albanians, Croats, and Bosnian Muslims.

The trial proceedings revealed Milošević as a man who refused to see the consequences of his political actions, defending in court the very views that had led him to engage in multiple conflicts. Still, he was ready to put up a good fight against the international community and its Tribunal. Daily broadcasts of the trial made him a symbol of resistance not only in Serbia but among newly-won supporters worldwide, who cheered him for what they saw as his struggle against the new world order and globalism.[18]

Appraisals of Milošević's courtroom performance have ranged from "bad" to "brilliant," with authors from Serbia tending to see it in a particularly positive light.[19] Borisav Jović praised Milošević for a brilliant defence strategy and felt he had successfully defended both Serbia and the Serbian people.[20] This favourable assessment is shared by Serbian scholar Slobodan Antonić, who argues that Milošević had to defend himself not before the ICTY but in the court of history.[21] According to Antonić, Milošević skilfully examined Defence witnesses and uncovered the deceit of Prosecution witnesses.[22] He dedicates an entire chapter in his recent book to evaluating the testimonies of Prosecution witnesses as untruthful.[23] For Antonić, Milošević exposed the trial as a farce.[24]

The attitude Milošević took on in the courtroom undoubtedly contributed to positive assessments by his sympathisers. He was not intimidated, and in fact manifested a sense of superiority, displaying a contempt for the court, the Prosecution, and the international community. In one of his first courtroom appearances, he taunted the Prosecutor, saying he had the "intellectual level of a seven-year-old child – or rather, let me correct myself – a retarded seven-year-old."[25] Indeed, his most extreme language was not directed against Croats, Bosnian Muslims, or Kosovo Albanians but against the international community. He accused Europe of a "lack of honour and cannibalism" for what he perceived as media attacks on his children and attempts by NATO to kill him and his family, and he reminded the court that "according to international law, and according to US law, the murder of a foreign head of state is a crime."[26]

Milošević's loyalty to his wife Mira Marković remained unwavering. He could find no fault in her, and he became doting and emotional in court when he talked about her and their family. In fact, he paid tribute to her in his February 2002 Opening Statement, praising her achievements before the judges and the world and deriding the media focus on his family in general. He called the publication of her books in over 30 languages a "testimony of the superhuman efforts ... of an intellectual against war, against national conflicts, against violence and primitivism." And he said she had been the victim of "the most savage media campaign, with the most grievous lies and fabrications being bandied about" and claimed that both his children had been forced into isolation by similar "slander."[27]

The affection and loyalty Milošević expressed for his immediate family showed his capacity to be a loving, proud, and protective husband and father, but starkly contrasted with the aloof and arrogant demeanour he exhibited in court towards the judges, lawyers, the international community, and even victims. In courtroom grandstanding, Milošević liked to emphasise that it was not he alone on trial, but the entire Serb nation – framing Serbs as victims and further dismissing the impacts of his wartime policies. Indeed, Milošević hardly ever demonstrated that he understood the extent of suffering he had inflicted on ordinary people through the violence of war. He seemed detached from the realities depicted by the evidence and by witness testimonies, and showed no concern that the strategies he employed had left Croatia, BiH, and Kosovo in shambles. The way he occasionally challenged the truthfulness of victims' accounts revealed his lack of empathy for their suffering; and as time passed, he toned down this aggressive approach, possibly because his treatment of victims had not gone unnoticed.[28] In fact, Prosecutor Nice later recalled being astonished at Milošević's treatment of a woman who testified to having witnessed the killing of her own children, saying he "showed no feelings whatsoever for her." Nice concluded that "Milošević had a heart of stone."[29]

Throughout the trial, Milošević played the role of a wronged leader who was forced to defend his political legacy against defamation. He distanced himself from his influence over the military; and unlike many other political leaders in the region, was never spotted wearing a military uniform and never seemed at ease among soldiers. His preference was for a dark suit, white shirt, and tie – the uniform of a political bureaucrat – and Milošević obviously enjoyed being treated as an equal to powerful international dignitaries, as he had been during the Dayton negotiations in 1995.[30]

Timothy McFadden, head of the UN Detention Unit, observed Milošević daily once he was transferred to The Hague. He described Milošević as disdainful of lower-level witnesses as well as court and Prosecution officials but said he relished the opportunity to deal with high-level witnesses.[31] In a courtroom exchange with former RSK President Milan Babić – who Milošević had always viewed as a political subordinate – Milošević could not hide his pleasure in mocking Babić. Babić had testified for the Prosecution that politicians had used code words to refer to arms, including the terms "planks," "wooden bars," "flour," "sugar," and "batteries." During his cross-examination, Milošević revisited this claim, asking Babić what terms were used for actual blankets, flour, oil, sugar, medicines, and all the other things that were sent as aid. "If 'flour' was used as a term for ammunition," Milošević asked, "what term was used to denote flour proper?" Babić answered: "Well, flour was called flour."[32] Milošević clearly felt a sense of triumph.

Yet, while Milošević did take a certain predictable satisfaction from outmanoeuvring witnesses over whom he once held political authority, facing the international diplomats and politicians who testified against him should have represented the ultimate humiliation. General Wesley Clark, Lord David Owen, Lord Paddy Ashdown, and many others with whom he had met frequently when he was President no longer saw him as a political partner. They represented the world of powerful men, and he, a defeated politician who had gambled his power away. Nonetheless, or perhaps because of this, Milošević "took on the task of a lawyer with enthusiasm." However, according to Prosecutor Nice, Milošević "was an appalling defence attorney" who "should have used the weapon we all knew he possessed – his charm." Nice reflected that, if Milošević had done so, he "might have been surprised with the effect."[33]

Milošević's inexperience as a lawyer was apparent in various ways, including in his tendency to invent and evade to get out of uncomfortable and unfavourable situations. And when he was caught, he would simply continue as if nothing had happened or as though he had not tried to obscure the truth. This denial or distortion of reality – which may have been effective when he was an omnipotent leader – did not work to Milošević's advantage in the courtroom, where every accusation he made had to be supported and every word he spoke could be challenged by counter-evidence. When his cross-examination strategy was shown to be flawed on several occasions, Milošević curiously pressed ahead without acknowledging his error, as if he did not grasp the legal consequences of such mistakes.

One such instance came in early 2003 during Milošević's cross-examination of Prosecution witness General Aleksandar Vasiljević, the former Head of JNA Counterintelligence, whom he questioned about the involvement of Momir 'Gavra' Gavrilović, a Serbian DB official, in the war in Croatia.[34] In his testimony, Vasiljević mentioned that Gavrilović had been assassinated in Belgrade in August 2001 and that the assassins remained at large. Milošević claimed he didn't know about the assassination, leading Vasiljević to exclaim with disbelief that the whole country knew about it.[35] What made Milošević's denial even more absurd was the fact that, only four months earlier, Gavrilović's assassination had been a subject of his cross-examination of Prosecution witness Jovan Dulović, a wartime reporter for the Serbian independent weekly *Vreme*. Dulović had testified about rumours that Gavrilović was assassinated after he visited FRY President Vojislav Koštunica and provided him with information about ties between State Security and the Mafia.[36]

Another notable example of Milošević's clumsy handling of difficult evidence concerned his approach to the Kula Camp Video. In the 1997 video, Red Berets leader Franko Simatović was recorded addressing Milošević, the guest of honour, and saying explicitly that his unit had been formed on 4 May 1991 at the time of the break-up of the former Yugoslavia. Milošević was also seen and heard on the video remarking that he had read the reports of a senior Red Berets officer. The video was dramatic, irrefutable evidence of Milošević's knowledge of the establishment of a paramilitary unit engaged in unlawful activities from 1991. But, for the purposes of a criminal trial, his reaction to the video in court was almost more telling. He continued to insist that the unit was established only after the war, in 1996, and the ludicrousness of this assertion revealed more about his guilt than an experienced courtroom lawyer representing him would ever have allowed.

These courtroom episodes were reflective of Milošević's character generally. Witnesses painted a picture of a politician who had been pleasant and well informed at meetings, yet manipulative and dishonest when it suited him. Former head of the Kosovo Verification Mission William Walker recalled just one example of Milošević's capacity to ignore plain truths. Walker had received a letter from the FRY Foreign Ministry with instructions about what the KVM could and could not do, and where. As Walker put it, this was "totally out of line with the agreement," and so he mentioned the letter to Milošević, who denied knowing of it and, even after Walker showed him a copy, said, "I haven't seen the letter. It doesn't exist."[37]

In his cross-examination of Walker, Milošević's inexperience in the courtroom was particularly on display. At one point, he showed Walker photographs of some of the victims who died during the Račak massacre in January 1999. Milošević contended that the photographs, which the Prosecution had already tendered as evidence, had been staged. He asked Walker to identify evidence of blood in the pictures he was shown, and Walker pointed to very visible blood stains. Milošević then asked Walker again and repeatedly whether the photographs he had shown him – which were not taken by Walker – had been "rigged," finally prompting an intervention by Judge May, who told Milošević, "if you make allegations of that sort, you must support them with evidence."[38]

Later, during his cross-examination of US General Wesley Clark, Milošević seemed to come dangerously close at times to introducing potentially inculpatory lines of questioning. Clark had testified about his experience in negotiations with Milošević, which took place not long after the fall of Srebrenica, and had recalled challenging Milošević's authority to control the Bosnian Serbs in upcoming peace talks, asking him: "Mr. President, you say you have so much influence over the Bosnian Serbs, but how is it then, if you have such influence, that you allowed General Mladić to kill all those people in Srebrenica?" According to Clark, Milošević said that he "warned Mladić not to do it, but he didn't listen to me."[39] Challenging this important evidence – which indicated Milošević's prior knowledge of what took place in Srebrenica – Milošević denied that he and Clark had ever discussed Srebrenica at all, and then he also denied that he had ever been in the position to give orders to General Mladić. This was not something General Clark had suggested, but Milošević knew very well that evidence of this authority could hurt him. Judge May interrupted, telling Milošević that, if he wanted, he could give evidence on this issue in due course, but that he had to limit his cross-examination to only matters the witness could address. Still, as if he could not help himself, Milošević turned to General Clark and told him, "General Mladić did not order any execution of people in Srebrenica. I believe that this was done by a group of mercenaries."[40]

Amateur mistakes such as these allowed the judges to make determinations about Milošević's personality and motives that would not have been possible if he were represented by professional counsel. And his lack of legal experience not only manifested in what were sometimes bewildering and bizarre courtroom exchanges, but also in inefficiencies that hindered the pace of the trial, which was due to be concluded by the end of April 2006. This was a dire prospect for Milošević, who had introduced little evidence on the BiH indictment, meaning that the genocide charges against him would have been judged based on evidence presented by the Prosecution. That evidence had been examined by the judges for the Half-Time Judgement, and they had concluded that genocide charges were indeed warranted for several sites in north and east Bosnia.[41]

The prisoner

In the last month of the trial, Milošević was a man struggling with his health and with an enormous workload. He had spent the previous five years of his life in his small prison cell in Scheveningen, in The Hague, which had also served as his office. Not surprisingly, his daily life – structured by a rigid daily prison routine – was scrupulously recorded by detention authorities. On court days, he rose and called his wife before he left for court at 8:00, where he would remain from 9:00 to approximately 14:00. Back in the detention unit, he would have a meal and one hour of exercise before spending most afternoons in meetings with legal advisors, preparing for his next court appearance. In the evenings, Milošević liked to read thrillers by bestselling authors such as John Grisham.[42]

When he was not in court, Milošević slept longer, exercised more, and sometimes even visited an art class before starting his work. He listened to Frank Sinatra, or watched DVDs he received from visitors who smuggled them in. Although Milošević had use of a computer, he was not allowed to access the Internet or use email, and so he communicated with the outside world only by telephone. All of his phone calls and visits, except those with recognised legal advisors, were monitored.[43]

Milošević's health was a great concern of UN Detention Unit managers. He had arrived with diagnoses of hypertension and a heart condition, which required medication. Presenting his own case had forced Milošević to work long hours to meet procedural deadlines and prepare for the courtroom, and his blood pressure rose so dangerously as a result that the court reduced the trial schedule to a three-day week. Curiously, he was still allowed to smoke despite his condition; something the Prosecution addressed in its filings.[44]

Concerns about periodic depression had occasionally been voiced by Milošević's close associates during his tenure, when he would disappear from Belgrade for days at a time, and some worried about this while he was in detention. But Detention Unit head Timothy McFadden felt that Milošević had only a "limited inclination toward depression."[45] And, although Milošević refused to see a psychiatrist individually, he did attend group sessions with other prisoners, in which signs of depression or any other significant clinical problem were not observed in him. Instead, McFadden ascribed

Milošević's moodiness and unhappiness to the limited contact he had with his family.[46]

Even with considerable distance between them, the relationship between Milošević and his wife remained very close. McFadden – who had access to reports of all of Milošević's telephone conversations – commented on their "extraordinary relationship" and wondered how Milošević was able to manipulate a whole nation but could not manage his wife. She was very much engaged in overseeing his legal and political contacts and when she pressed Milošević to do something he did not want to do, Milošević rarely pushed back; though he was apt to ignore her instruction. When he failed to follow her advice, she would scold him and remind him that many bad outcomes could have been avoided if he had listened to her in the past. McFadden described her as "very volatile." Yet, for Milošević, his wife remained his most trusted and appreciated source of "information, comfort, motivation, and strategy" and he relied on her guidance until the end.[47]

When the situation for Milošević's family became difficult in 2003 after the assassination of Zoran Đinđić, anxiety about their well-being put additional strain on his health. Facing legal battles in Serbia, Mira Marković moved to Russia in order to avoid a trial, and this self-imposed exile made it impossible for her to travel. And so, her visits to The Hague stopped. Her presence in Milošević's life was perceived as so important that when his health subsequently deteriorated, McFadden suggested to his superiors that one antidote may be to bring Marković from Russia with some sort of deal for her immunity from arrest. But this would never have been possible, given the criminal investigation against her in Serbia.

Marković had helped Milošević maintain his links with the SPS, and support of the party was especially important for Milošević at this time. When the family's financial situation worsened in the spring of 2003 and he could not pay his Belgrade household staff or afford airline tickets for his rotating legal associates, the SPS mobilised to generate funds. And with his wife in exile, Milošević took over communications with the various national and international groups that were providing him with legal and other assistance.[48]

The daily surveillance of Milošević's behaviour revealed, and sometimes confirmed, sides of his personality that are important to understanding his previous political conduct. Complaining at one point that his legal associates from Serbia made him feel he was "surrounded by fools," he candidly remarked that the problem was of his own making, for he had surrounded himself with fools throughout his career for fear of being challenged by those more competent and intelligent.[49] Indeed, his ten-year political reign was marked by regular fallings out with anyone who expressed criticism of Milošević, his family members, or his political tactics or strategies, leaving room only for those who would not contradict him.[50]

Contrary to the disdain Milošević was said to have felt for legal staff – and which he displayed in the courtroom towards the *amici curiae* – McFadden reported that Milošević was actually "fond" of the *amici*, and it was true that his legal associates did coordinate with them to discuss defence strategy and the questioning of witnesses.[51] But by hiding the fact that he was making use of the services of a substantial legal team, Milošević maintained the appearance of a disproportionate judicial proceeding in which he was just one man against the rest of the world. His rejection of imposed Defence counsel can in fact be analysed though this lens; for not only would this have denied Milošević very important air time on national and international television, it would also have undermined the David and Goliath dynamic that had brought him sympathy from a number of powerful international lawyers, writers, activists, and politicians. A committee, known as Freedom for Slobodan Milošević, had formed and was active in analysing evidence and promoting the Defence narrative. And Milošević had also developed an interesting following of prominent intellectuals including Noam Chomsky, Peter Handke, and Diana Johnstone, all of whom were on his list of potential Defence witnesses.

McFadden's reports from the Detention Unit reveal the amicable side of Milošević's character as well, which had been noted by Stambolić and Jović – who had known him in his early days in politics – but also by international mediators who had worked with Milošević over a decade of various peace negotiations. In detention, Milošević was described as cooperative and popular among the other detainees, who liked and respected him and even concerned themselves with his health and diet.[52] But the Prosecution maintained throughout the trial that the charming façade Milošević wore hid his more sinister nature, and a US Embassy employee, reporting on the work Milošević did while in detention, underlined this, noting his masterful ability to work "behind the scenes, through third parties, and leave few fingerprints."[53]

Despite his capacity for manipulation and duplicity, former associates of Milošević described him as a poor strategist. In fact, his lack of strategic thinking was criticised by his allies and used by his opponents. Borisav Jović observed that Milošević's strategic failures were due sometimes to bad strategy and sometimes to his misjudgement of a situation; but said that he was usually able, by resorting to pragmatism or scheming, to find his way out of hopeless situations. Over time, Jović felt this had given Milošević a false confidence that he was invulnerable.[54] This belief Milošević had in himself, which at times surpassed the bounds of reality, led him to feel that he was winning in the courtroom, and this fired him up so that he was combative and willing to work despite his unstable health. His sense that he was out ahead in the trial may also partly explain his choice of Defence witnesses. Or maybe, by the time his Defence case started in September 2004, he was simply putting on a show, aware that it really did not matter anymore what he did in court. With his wife in Russia, his health deteriorating, and the financial strains of his defence mounting, he may have given up hope of any favourable outcome.

In the months before his death, Milošević's persistent requests to receive medical treatment in Russia seemed his only means to fulfil his desire to be reunited with his wife again. Evidence was mounting against him, sometimes through the testimonies of his own witnesses, and it was set to mount further when Momir Bulatović took the stand. The Prosecution considered Bulatović an ideal witness for cross-examination; for he had first-hand knowledge of many important events discussed at the trial and had also been a regular participant at many of the important meetings that were featured in evidence. Until the very end, it was unclear whether Milošević would risk calling Bulatović and give the Prosecution the opportunity to cross-examine him on key evidence for all three of the indictments Milošević was charged in. It would have been a major exercise, and one which would have provided much of the structure for the Prosecution's closing arguments, as Bulatović's testimony was expected to have covered all ten years of Milošević's political tenure.

Milošević spent the entire week preceding his death with Bulatović, preparing for testimony – an exercise known by lawyers as 'proofing.'[55] On the Friday evening of 10 March 2006, Bulatović left the prison after working the whole day with Milošević.[56] The next morning, Milošević was found dead in his cell and the prison record noted that the last person who had seen him alive was his faithful comrade Momir Bulatović. In his 2007 book *ICTY vs Slobodan Milošević: Unspoken Defence*, Bulatović referenced a report made available by Professor Miloš Stojiljković from the University Hospital in Odense, Denmark, which noted that traces of Rifampicin[57] – a medicine that was not officially prescribed to him – had been found in Milošević's blood in January 2006. The question of who provided Milošević with the drug remains, and whether he knew he was consuming it. Stojiljković's report indicated that Rifampicin could have interacted with other medications that were prescribed to Milošević to control his hypertension, and could have been the reason those medications were ineffective.[58]

Upon Milošević's death, some fellow detainees signed a joint letter, in memoriam. Among the signatories were Croatian General Ante Gotovina, and several Bosnian Croat commanders.[59] Milošević's funeral was held in the courtyard of his family house in Požarevac. It was a private ceremony without the military or state honours usually reserved for a former head of state. In place of the national anthem, his friends and loyal supporters said their goodbyes with the Russian song "Moscow Nights." Notably absent were his family.[60] Mira and their son Marko – indicted in 2003 and still fugitives to this day – faced criminal charges if they returned to Serbia. But in the Požarevac main square, 20,000 people from across Serbia and beyond paid their last respects to a political leader they still saw as a hero.[61]

Notes

1 James L. Graff, "Butcher of the Balkans," *Time*, 8 June 1992.
2 Ibid., 158.
3 Jović, *Knjiga o Miloševiću*, 17.
4 Borisav Jović, Witness Statement, para. 6.
5 Testimony of Zoran Lilić (17 June 2003), 22557.
6 Jović, *Knjiga o Miloševiću*, 160–165.
7 Ibid., 160–165.
8 The Prosecution did not deal in detail with this period of Milošević's political tenure. The majority of evidence on this time was introduced through Jović's *Knjiga o Miloševiću* (see 163–173, especially). For more on events in 1996 and 1997 in B/C/S, also see: *Lex, pištaljke i laži: Hronologija gradjanskog i studentskog protesta 17.11. 96–04.02.97* (Belgrade, Helsinki Committee for Human Rights, 1997).
9 Bulatović, *Pravila ćutanja*, 291.
10 Jović, *Knjiga o Miloševiću*, 182–185.
11 Delić was allegedly stopped by General Nebojša Pavković, Chief of Staff of the VJ and his superior; though Delić later denied that he had been awaiting an order to move. For his comments, see: Stojković, "Zemlju nema ko da brani."
12 See (in English): Maroje Mihovilović, "The Perfect Criminal Couple," *Nacional*, no. 539, 13 March 2006, www.nacional.hr/en/clanak/23828/the-perfect-criminal-couple (accessed 31 October 2014).
13 Jović, *Knjiga o Miloševiću*, 182–185.
14 Warren Zimmerman, *Origins of a Catastrophe: Yugoslavia and its Destroyers* (New York: Times Books, 1996), 26; Slobodan Antonić, *Slobodan Milošević: još nije gotovo* ("Slobodan Milošević: It's Not Over Yet") (Belgrade: Vukotić medija, 2014), 7–8.
15 The Judgement in the trial for the Stambolić assassination is available in Cyrillic at: www.reportingproject.net/peopleofinterest/profil.php?profil=21 (accessed 18 January 2016).
16 "Radisavljević: Legija je otkrio ubice Ćuruvije; Vučić: Niko neće biti izuzet," *Blic*, 14 January 2014.
17 "Speech, Gazimestan," 28 June 1989, Exhibit D251.1e.
18 Jared Isreal, "A Conversation with Ambassador Borislav Milošević, Slobodan's Brother," The Emporer's New Clothes, 2 June 2002, http://emperors-clothes.com/news/borislav (accessed 4 April 2015).
19 Between 2009 and early 2015, two books published in the Serbian language have dealt with the trial record, Milošević's courtroom performance, and events in the aftermath of his death. See: Antonić, *Slobodan Milošević*; and Borisav Jović, *Od Gazimestana do Haga Vreme Slobodana Miloševića: vreme Slobodana Miloševića* (Belgrade: Metaphysica, 2009). In Jović, especially see the chapters titled: "Odbrana pred Haškim tribunalom" [Defence before the Hague Tribunal], "Tragičan ishod i reagiranje javnosti" [A Tragic Outcome and the Reaction of the Public]; and "Svedočenje pred haškim tribnalom" [Testimony before the Hague Tribunal] (these titles have been translated from Serbian by the author).
20 Jović, *Od Gazimestana do Haga*, 200.
21 Antonić, Slobodan Milošević, 448.
22 Ibid., 430–442, 448–455.
23 Ibid., 430–442.
24 Ibid., 448.
25 Trial Transcript, Status Conference (30 October 2001), 147.
26 Trial Transcript, Defence Opening Statement (18 February 2002), 469–471.
27 Ibid.
28 For example, Milošević chose not to cross-examine some witnesses, such as Shyhrete Berisha, a young mother who lost her children in a mass execution in Suva

Reka. The cross-examination was instead conducted by an *amicus curiae* on behalf of the Defence. See: Testimony of Shyrhete Berisha (10 July 2002), 7906.

29 See the interview with Geoffrey Nice in *Jutarnji List*, 8 December 2007.

30 For a look at the atmosphere during the Dayton negotiations in November 1995, see: *Death of Yugoslavia*, "Pax Americana," Part VI, produced by Brian Lapping Associates, BBC, 1995.

31 See: US Department for War Crimes Issues (S/WCI), "ICTY: AN INSIDE LOOK INTO MILOSEVIC'S HEALTH AND SUPPORT NETWORK," Diplomatic Cable, 12 November 2003. Although McFadden denied disclosing any information to the United States by which they produced this classified cable, the ICTY investigated McFadden for possible contempt of court and found that he had breached ICTY rules by leaking information about Milošević to US officials. However, they found no grounds to charge him because they did not believe his intention was "willful interference with court proceedings." For more, see: "No charges against Hague leak warden," B92, 19 July 2011, www.b92.net/eng/news/crimes.php?yyyy=2011&mm=07&dd=19&nav_id=75520 (accessed 4 April 2015).

32 Testimony of Milan Babić (22 November 2002), 13292–13293; and (3 December 2002), 13758–13759.

33 Ivana Miloradović, "There Was Pressure on Our Work," *NIN*, 15 May 2008.

34 Testimony of Major General Aleksandar Vasiljević (14 February 2003), 16093–16094.

35 Ibid.

36 Testimony of Jovan Dulović (17 October 2002), 11763–11765. Also see: US Department of State Bureau of Democracy, Human Rights, and Labor, "Country Reports on Human Rights Practices – 2001: Yugoslavia, Federal Republic of," 4 March 2002, www.state.gov/g/drl/rls/hrrpt/2001/eur/8369.htm (accessed 30 October 2014).

37 Testimony of William Walker (11 June 2002), 6786–6787.

38 Ibid. (12 June 2002), 6862–6864.

39 Testimony of Wesley Clark (15 and 16 December 2003), 30372–30373.

40 Ibid., 30490.

41 Decision on Motion for Judgement of Acquittal, 16 June 2004 (the Half-Time Judgement).

42 See: "ICTY: AN INSIDE LOOK INTO MILOŠEVIĆ'S HEALTH AND SUPPORT NETWORK."

43 Ibid.

44 Ibid.

45 Ibid.

46 Ibid.

47 Ibid.

48 Ibid.

49 Ibid. It is not clear whether Milošević said this directly to McFadden or if McFadden repeated what someone else told him (hearsay).

50 Ibid.

51 Ibid.

52 Ibid.

53 Ibid.

54 Jović, *Knjiga o Miloševiću*, 16–18.

55 Bulatović published the full text of the proofing in: Bulatović, *ICTY vs Slobodan Milošević: Neizgovorena odbrana* (Niš: Zograf, 2008).

56 Ibid., Chapters XVII and XVIII.

57 Rifampicin is a bactericidal antibiotic commonly included in the drug cocktail used to treat tuberculosis and meningitis.

58 See: Bulatović, *Neizgovorena odbrana*, 314–315.

59 "Na osmrtnici za Miloševića potpisan i Ante Gotovina" and "Gotovina: Izrazio sam sućut Miloševićima jer sam katolik," *Jutarnji list*, 14 March 2006. Note that three other Croatian detainees, Dario Kordić, Vinko Martinović, and Miroslav Bralo – who were in a different part of the detention unit and had no contact with Milošević – did not sign. Kordić stated through his lawyer that he had not done so out of respect for the victims.
60 "Kako su sahranjeni Tito, Tuđman i Milošević," *Danas*, 3 October 2014.
61 Ibid.

Conclusion

Slobodan Milošević did not die an innocent man. When his life ended he was a defendant against whom the case at the ICTY had not been concluded, against whom guilt had not yet been 'hammered home' as, in time, it may have been had he survived.

Surprisingly the ICTY has seemed keen to forget this trial altogether. Perhaps ICTY senior management were only interested in verdicts, and 'guilty!' verdicts at that; to them this unfinished trial might have seemed to be a failure that brought no verdict and thus no valuable conclusion of any kind. If that was what they thought they would have been wrong. However, being remote from the courtroom they could hardly be blamed for missing what the trial actually delivered.

For those in court day in, day out – where each day *had* to be filled with evidence even if in jumbled order – the experience was something between trying to decode detail in the frieze of a Greek temple that told the story of a war and grabbing the 'Breaking News' or 'ticker' or 'crawler' of news at the bottom of TV screens that presses information from many sources on the viewer but that is gone to be replaced by something else as soon as it is read; the 'ticker' of this trial lasted over 2,000 hours.

On every court day evidence of importance would appear but then be gone so fast it might be missed for its *lasting* value because all focus had to be on what it revealed immediately about Milošević as a criminal. Everything else of scholarly interest – such as the role of the Serbian state or the multi-layered Balkan history that explained what happened or the reasons humans behave in way they do in conflicts – *had* to be set aside, at least for the time being.

And so, with no substantial ICTY 'outreach' dedicated to the trial – during the trial or more particularly after Milošević's death when constructive outreach could have generated interest in the trial record – the huge trial archive might have languished until rediscovered one day long in the future by researchers with years to devote to analysing it. Allowing that to happen would be to waste a present opportunity. The time to decode the 'frieze' and to make a first attempt to grab detail from the 'ticker' is now. The daily 'show' of the trial – beamed direct to Serbia and around the Balkans for casual consumption – presented processions of significant individuals – some of them witnesses, others spoken of by witnesses – progressions of ideas that drove the wars – sometimes hidden sometimes revealed – together with sequences of maps and a kaleidoscope of other imagery. Experts of many kinds painted pictures from various standpoints – sometimes cautiously, sometimes with over-commitment to a cause that destroyed their integrity but lifted the hem of garments of deception. And the lawyers did what they could to fit all this material to a concept of the individual criminal culpability of a single human, who had acted and reacted in a complex world that was only in part his own construction.

And yet from this material – reviewed at leisure not as it races from short-term memory of the 'daily show' – conclusions emerge, not just about Milošević the criminal (if he was) but about bigger issues. The purpose of this book has been to give some life to these conclusions.

Serbian state ideology

Since the nineteenth century, a distinct Serbian state ideology – also known loosely as 'Greater Serbia' – has been manifest in aspirations by Serbs for creation of a state that would include all Serbs scattered across the Western Balkans in Croatia, Kosovo and BiH. The creation of a single Serbian state in its ethnic borders was designed to include ethnically mixed areas which had been claimed by the Serbs on a historical or geopolitical basis; making such claims had led in the past to ethnic cleansing and mass atrocities. The interests of other ethnicities in the mixed areas had been of no consequence in the past; they were of no consequence in the 1990s; it is unlikely they will ever be of real consequence in the future if they stand in the way of the Serbian state project when next pursued at gunpoint.

The trial record allowed the Prosecution – and now allows scholars – not only to trace the violence associated with attempts to create a larger Serbian state since the nineteenth century but to expose clear links between historical Greater Serbia thinking and Milošević's policy of territorial expansion. Although he and his associates avoided any explicit mention of Greater Serbia, their policy of "All Serbs in a Single State" in the 1990s and Greater Serbia plans were very similar. Milošević had been selected (initially by Serbs in Kosovo) to lead this project of which he was not the creator. He was not even the person who revived the project in the 1980s; and he barely dared speak its name. The long process of that revival had initially been driven by others who were not inclined to climb into the driver's seat of the vehicle – call it a train – they had fired up and re-started. Milošević was in a sense simply the driver of the train, although a very willing driver once he had his hands on the controls. The train's progress was blocked by defeats: in Croatia with Operations 'Flash' and 'Storm,' in Bosnia when the Dayton Peace Agreement allowed for the existence of Republika Srpska but blocked its immediate annexation by Serbia; in Kosovo when NATO took sides and bombed Serbia into its loss of Kosovo that achieved its surprising independence. But the train was not derailed. Train driver Milošević was pushed off the footplate as the train slowed down. The train did not stop. It has not stopped. It is rolling still.

Or, to quit the analogy, the Serb state project is not dead and might never die; it assumes ever new forms – reduced or enlarged – depending on internal and external political circumstances. The tragedy for the other unconsidered ethnicities is that Serbia's ideology can only ever be realised through new territorial borders drawn by violence, probably mass violence.

International community

From this first conclusion others follow, especially about international actors – collectively the international community – that demonstrated recurring characteristics when all three conflicts are reviewed together. The most alarming conclusion, on one reckoning, may be that even if the international community understood the danger of the Serbian state project this did not stop the project being afforded some support coming as the inevitable consequence of determined international resistance to creation of a Muslim state in the heart of Europe. Better, it might be thought, to tolerate an unfortunate but Christian project that has brought wars and may bring more bloodshed than to see strong near contiguous Muslim entities in Europe – Milošević's 'Green Transversal' – from Bosnia through Kosovo, Albania, and Macedonia towards Turkey. The route to deciding whether this is alarmist conjecture or alarming conclusion comes via other milestone conclusions, each evidence-based and often free of any doubt.

The most notable and concrete of a cluster of these milestone conclusions is that whatever the international community's underlying motivations may have been, its invariable response to a Balkan problem was ethnic separation. Backing for the policy of ethnic division in BiH was in fact remarkably easy to come by among representatives of the international community. Witnesses testified that the rumoured partition agreed to as early as the 1991 Karađorđevo meeting had actually enjoyed European support, because Europe was not prepared to allow the formation of a unitary BiH, with a Muslim majority.[1] This – it must be recalled – preceded any significant ethnic violence. Further highly persuasive evidence of European support for this proposed ethnic division can be found in what those who may have supported it in 1991 did in subsequent years. In the period from February 1992 to December 1995, international negotiators brokered five peace plans, all of which were based, to varying degrees, on the principle of ethnic separation. The first, the Cutileiro Peace Plan – proposed two months before war broke out in BiH – evoked the arrangement Tuđman and Milošević had reportedly discussed at Karađorđevo one year earlier. Ethnic separation of BiH was also the basis of the Vance–Owen Peace Plan of 1993, which proposed the creation of ten cantons. During negotiations for the Vance–Owen Plan, violence escalated as Serbs and Croats fought for more territory, anticipating that conquered territories would be awarded to them at the negotiating table. As it happened, negotiations failed by mid-1993, as they did for two subsequent peace proposals: the Owen–Stoltenberg Peace Plan of 1993 and the Contact Group Peace Plan of 1994, each of which was premised on ethnic separation.

Although Serbs were pleased with the ethnic separation principle reflected in these plans, none afforded them enough of the territorial corridors they felt they needed in order later to unify a Serb state; so, they fought for more. They succeeded in dividing Bosnia with the approval of the international community not just by insisting that territorial gains on the ground – obtained though they had been by genocide – be reflected in the final, fifth peace 'settlement' at Dayton, but through the skilful use of anti-Muslim rhetoric that warned of the 'Green Transversal.' As a result, Republika Srpska, validated as an entity at Dayton, may well achieve separation from the rest of Bosnia at some stage and perhaps join Serbia proper.

Milošević, the all-Serbs wily negotiator at Dayton, rarely spoke publicly in derogatory terms about any ethnic group. He preferred to refer instead to global threats of fascist or Islamist domination and his words reflected the private thoughts of some Western politicians, who – according to Bill Clinton's account – expressly opposed the establishment of a Muslim majority state in the heart of Europe.[2]

Conclusions about the ethnic separation as a solution for Bosnia's political composition leads to an inferential conclusion about the international community's overall strategic motivation. This latter conclusion, that the international community was resistant to creation of a Muslim state in the heart of Europe, can find support, some would say, in the internal territorial divisions of post-war Bosnia and Kosovo, that make them weak and not fully functional as states. Serbia, on the other hand, has been encouraged to enter Europe faster than either Bosnia or Kosovo. It is an irony to observe that the ICTY's work cannot be criticised for being an example of one-sided 'victor's justice' because it tried individuals from all sides of the conflict, but that it could, instead, be noted as achieving 'perpetrator's justice' because the state of the worst perpetrators has benefitted by war crimes, first at Dayton and ever since.

The leader

Milošević spent his four years in court behind a mask, literally laughing only once when he and his witness Šešelj cracked a laboriously prepared joke at Geoffrey Nice's expense – and on that occasion everyone in court laughed except Šešelj, for whom even a rehearsed joke about an enemy had to be taken seriously.[3]

Out of court Milošević was, it was said, polite to guards and other such staff and he was polite to the only junior member of the Prosecution team who spoke to him when handing over documents in court. There was no other direct contact with him and his mask was for Serbs at home: this, his mask said, was a man who would yield nothing.

Information from the prison showed him to have been popular with – and even fatherly in a way to – others facing ICTY trials, whatever their ethnicity.

The Prosecution and the judges took different views of Milošević's behaviour in court. The judges thought him satisfactorily polite most of the time but it was they who had granted him – unasked – the privilege of being seated when he addressed them or questioned witnesses. It was hard to see why a defendant representing himself and facing grave charges would be free of the standard obligation to stand when addressing a court, a posture in which the near contempt of the seated slouch is much harder to show. But since there was no consensus among those in court on his general demeanour there is clearly not much to learn from it. He was, by way of reminder, dismissive or contemptuous of 'lowly' witnesses however much they had suffered and something of a respecter of authority. But these characteristics may be found in many others and do not help us understand his character, his political conduct or his potential for criminality.

Yet there was much to discover from the evidence beyond the subjective views of those in court.

First, a significant negative: there was no evidence – none – of his behaving badly before his promotion in 1987 by the Kosovo Serbs to be their leader and the leader of all Serbs.

He was trained in law and spoke good English; he had lived in America; he worked as a banker and was a Communist Party apparatchik. Uxorious to a fault, he was clearly fond and even proud of his two children, unusual though some thought them to be. He was clever, clearly, and possessed of a good memory. His courtroom corrections of errors in interpretation that were unfavourable to him while questionning witnesses showed an ability to perform more than one task simultaenously and to do so with a straight face. He rarely if ever 'let on' when an error in interepration was favourable to him. In court, as in political life, he showed cunning.

To come to prominence serving the plans of others is not an unusual path for successful politicians. The trigger Milošević needed to turn him into an isolated and immensely powerful leader – for such he clearly became – is probably itself a matter of little significance. The fact is that he was converted into, or became, such a leader. And he did this despite a general lack of enthusiasm for public speaking and a resolution never to be seen in uniform or to meet troops anywhere near a battlefield. Within a year or so of being first promoted to represent the Kosovo Serbs he made the 1989 speech to about a million Serbs at Gazimestan in the heart of Kosovo that promised ethnic battles ahead, exciting an expectant crowd, as aspiring leaders sometimes must, to gain adulation.

Milošević was not a man easy to pigeonhole. No white suit and no military uniform and no flamboyance. Some urbanity – he liked whisky with politicians and diplomats and seemed to have no note taker most of the time he was with them.

Was Milošević a man of contradictions so complex as to defeat forensic or historical analysis? Not at all – and it was, in combination, evidence and the trial process itself that says as much. Any properly recorded criminal trial illuminates, magnifies, and clarifies what is its proper concern. The record of the Milošević trial process, with Milošević acting as his own counsel, does precisely that. Such was the effect of the trial process that, on occasions in court, one single presentation by Milošević provided dispositive proof about particular crimes. To understand this extraordinary effect of Milošević's conduct in court it is essential also to remember earlier norms: US President Harry Truman faced no trial and was never interviewed about Hiroshima and Nagasaki. UK Prime Minister Winston Churchill was not tried for or interviewed about the carpet bombing of Dresden. US Presidents Eisenhower, Kennedy, Johnson, Nixon, and Ford faced no interrogation or trial over Vietnam. That was not how the world then worked. At best those men would write memoirs and historians would try to disentangle some truth from personal propaganda. Perhaps only with the Chilcott inquiry into the British government's war in Iraq or with trials such as Milošević's may political leaders start to face what world citizens want their leaders to face. Notable historic exceptions were the trials of leaders at the post-Second World War Nuremberg and Tokyo Tribunals.

And yet, while many or most historical or present-day trials conducted by professional lawyers will leave some uncertainty – whatever the verdicts about their clients – Milošević took the dangerous step of representing himself and thus leaving certainty behind. Had he been represented by a professional lawyer but given no evidence himself, *some* conclusions, even some formal convictions, would have emerged. But by his presenting arguments to the judges, his questioning of Prosecution witnesses and his calling of his own Defence witnesses he left the Prosecution better placed than they could ever have hoped to analyse who Milošević was, what he did and why.

From evidence and the trial process what can be concluded – what would have been proved – about the required criminal state of mind – the *mens rea* – of this man charged for war crimes committed over a ten-year period? Preface consideration of that by some questions: Was he driven by a criminal mind every minute of every day? Probably – almost certainly – not. Whenever the possibility of living lawfully and being a respected member of international society existed, was he likely to enjoy that? Definitely. Would he, at the same time, enjoy a sense of power and superiority in secretly running an armed conflict in another state by instructing General Ratko Mladić or the Red Berets? Certainly. These 'certainties' – if they are – must fit and be consistent with other certainties that may become the true legacy of this trial.

One example of this legacy of certainties can be inferred from Milošević's reaction in court to the Kula Camp Video that recorded a 1997 celebration of the formation in 1991 of the Red Berets. The video remains one of the best pieces of evidence in the case; it led to several conclusions. When confronted by the video in court Milošević had no personal record but his own to defend and no one else to blame. The video showed him walking uncomfortably among uniformed armed men and listening to speeches that detailed crimes Red Berets members had committed without dissent. His presence at the ceremony gave him no leeway. He knew that this was evidence of early criminality in 1991 that he could not evade, explain, or escape. So he met it with an absurd and manifestly false proposition – that the Red Berets commander was boasting and lying about the date of their creation. The words addressed by the men in uniform to Milošević, as recorded on the video, are sufficient to understand how nonsensical his challenge to the evidence was. What Milošević said in court about the video was technically not 'evidence' as he was not giving evidence on oath. It was a lie nonetheless. And it was the lie that hammered home the truth. From this video, and from Milošević's reaction to it in court, it is possible to conclude that by May 1991 the state of Serbia – that paid for the Red Berets and that was kept aware of what they did – and Milošević were acting criminally and knew beyond doubt that they were acting criminally. They had embarked on a criminal plan to use paramilitary forces on territories now independent – Croatia and Bosnia – to achieve ethnic separation in Serbia's hegemonic interest, and to do so by mass violence. Had Milošević had something intelligent to say in reaction to the video, or even had he said nothing – or if represented had his counsel said nothing – there might have been less certainty. His engagement in the legal process that he did not 'recognise' gave the game away. He was, and would surely have been proved, guilty for this activity; he was a guilty man working within a guilty state.

This evidence was particularly important to the Prosecution team that, as part of its duty to prove 'widespread and systematic' crimes of many kinds, was determined to establish things that could be seen as unequivocally criminal by non-lawyers quite as much as by lawyers and judges. Sending paramilitaries off to kill citizens of other independent states was a crime. The non-lawyer citizen could readily understand that. Milošević understood it. His state associates understood it. The state 'understood' it. It was a crime to which there was no defence.

Controlling the post-conflict narrative

A problem for users of the Milošević trial record is that states and international organisations simply cannot be relied on to tell international courts the whole truth or not to corrupt international courts' processes by forcing them to indict or not to indict someone, by keeping evidence from the courts or by forcing evidence onto the courts. States in particular are likely – bound perhaps – to do these things in their own interests and there is not a lot of point in being upset about it. That is what states do and always have done. What is important for academic, journalistic, and other users of an international court's record is to be able to rely on its integrity despite the vulnerabilities of such courts to this form of corruption. This may require a detailed understanding of why a particular a state would be willing to interfere with processes that it will publicly protest are independent.

It might always be expected that a state that has been in conflict owes a duty to itself – as opposed to any responsibility it may owe to the international community – to ensure that an adequate but 'favourable' record is left of its own history in a conflict. And, in reality, states may always choose to obscure their role in the commission of mass atrocities.

Serbia's interactions with the ICTY, once properly understood, provide an excellent case study of such state behaviour. They can also give the user of the Milošević trial record confidence in the integrity of that record or at least of the parts shown not to have been in any way corrupted by state or other organisational pressure.

Serbia's state elites have invested great effort since the fall of the Milošević regime in 2000, in keeping evidence away from courts that, according to their calculations, might implicate Serbia itself as a party in the commission of genocide in BiH at the ICJ. The condition set by Belgrade that portions of important evidence (in particular the Supreme Defence Council records) be protected from public scrutiny came without any legal or state security justification. The protection of the evidence that could have revealed direct involvement of Serbia in the war in Bosnia showed Serbia's understanding of its culpability.

Reflecting on the history of Serbia's cooperation with the ICTY, the mere fact that the Belgrade authorities selected parts of important evidence for protection raised high expectations in the public that the protected parts would show the extent of Milošević's criminal responsibility at the ICTY but also state responsibility that might have been established at the ICJ. History shows that states are rarely willing to admit the crime of genocide for at least three reasons, all of which are explanatory of Serbia's conduct at the ICTY.

First a state accused and found liable for breaches of the Genocide Convention at the ICJ will most likely be ordered to pay enormous reparations to the damaged party. This would deter any government – whether the conflict regime or a post-conflict successor regime – from a genocide confession.

Second, a court's recording that genocide has been committed becomes a permanent historical record, which will forever stain that state. By creating some counter-narrative essential to defeat a genocide allegation, the state's elites contribute to equalisation of criminal and historical responsibility, or even cast the victims as principle villains.

Third, refusal to admit crimes committed by a former regime frees the successor regime to pursue the 'unfinished' geopolitical objectives that their predecessors failed to achieve despite the commission of mass atrocities.

It can be argued that Serbia's effort in controlling the flow of evidence that might implicate Serbia or its high-level officials in the commission of genocide in BiH at the ICJ and the ICTY have been successful. The 'legal history' of war crimes in BiH – to date – exonerates Serbia of the crime of genocide.

Simultaneously with its relative successes at the ICTY and ICJ, Serbia has been engaged in process of recasting the histories of Bosnia and Kosovo – smaller states lacking awareness of the need to be in control of writing their own histories. If not challenged by alternative views, Serbia's control of post-conflict narrative might leave Serbia with a cleaner history than it deserves, allowing post-conflict elites to pursue the ideology of unification of all Serbs, however named.

Moreover, two decades after Milošević left the station (back to the train analogy) to embark on his journey towards a state for all Serbs, the train still rolls on. Milošević was pushed from the running board and sent to The Hague, but the train did not stop, and has not stopped. A number of Serbia's current political elites see the Serbian state project as unfinished business, and hope yet to change the western borders of the state, to encompass the Republika Srpska. In fact, in 2013, Prime Minister Ivica Dačić publicly stated that insuring preservation of the RS was more important for Serbia than keeping Kosovo within Serbia.[4]

The right to know

The fact that some Serb leaders continue to promote an ideology akin to the one with which Milošević rode to power makes public access to trial records even more important. Citizens in general – and victim groups in particular – have the right to know what happened during the wars spurred by that ideology in the 1990s. Attempts by elites to control the legal process and the historical narrative by keeping important documents away from courts should be less effective now that national and international courts can compel states to cooperate. The protection or withholding from the public of evidence should be possible only on the most solid legal grounds, for obscuring the truth from those who are entitled to know it – the public, and especially victims – can undermine the integrity of any trial, finished or unfinished.

There is a tendency in the Balkans to look for rubber stamps and depend, perhaps too much, on what is 'authorised.' A judgement by the Tribunal may have led to a more general acceptance of certain conclusions about Milošević and the Serbian state project, even by some Serbs; and without a judgement, conclusions presented elsewhere – such as in books like this – may be ignored or viewed with scepticism. But that would be a mistake. The record of the trial provides material from which individuals can, if able to research properly, draw their own conclusions and be untroubled by the lack of a rubber stamp. In states – notably Bosnia and Kosovo – where history is being manipulatively rewritten by Serbia and by Serbs, the value of this documentation cannot be overstated. Indeed, over time, the citizen's ability to understand this and other trial records may democratise the holding of leaders to account. Judges and lawyers do not necessarily have the last word.

Notes

1 Testimony of Ante Marković (23 October 2003), 28027.
2 Branch, *The Clinton Tapes*, 9–10.
3 Testimony of Vojislav Šešelj (7 September 2005), T 11962.
4 "Dačić: Opstanak Republike Srpske mnogo važniji državni interes nego opstanak Kosova u okviru Srbije," *Blic*, 26 April 2013.

Selected bibliography

Books and reports

Antonić, Slobodan. *Slobodan Milošević: još nije gotovo*. Belgrade: Vukotić medija, 2015.

Arendt, Hannah. *Eichmann in Jerusalem: A Report on the Banality of Evil*. New York: Penguin, 1963.

Armatta, Judith. *Twilight of Impunity: The War Crimes Trial of Slobodan Milošević*. Durham, NC: Duke University Press, 2010.

Avramov, Smilja. *Postherojski rat Zapada protiv Jugoslavije*. Belgrade: Akademija za diplomatiju i bezbednost, 1997.

Bass, Gary Jonathan. *Stay the Hand of Vengeance: The Politics of War Crimes Tribunals*. Princeton: Princeton University Press, 2000.

Beloff, Nora. *Tito's Flawed Legacy: Yugoslavia and the West Since 1939*. London: Westview, 1985.

Bennett, Christopher. *Yugoslavia's Bloody Collapse: Causes, Course and Consequences*. London: Hurst, 1995.

Bilandžić, Dušan. *Historija SFRJ: glavni procesi, 1918–1985*. Zagreb: Školska knjiga, 1985.

Bilsky, Leora. *Transformative Justice: Israeli Identity on Trial*. Ann Arbor: University of Michigan Press, 2004.

Biserko, Sonja. *Yugoslavia's Implosion: The Fatal Attraction of Serbian Nationalism*. Oslo: Norwegian Helsinki Committee, 2012.

Blaustein, Albert P., and Eric B. Blaustein, eds. *Constitutions of Dependencies and Special Sovereignties*. Dobbs Ferry: Oceana, 1994.

Boas, Gideon. *The Milošević Trial: Lessons for the Conduct of Complex International Criminal Proceedings*. Cambridge: Cambridge University Press, 2007.

Branch, Taylor. *The Clinton Tapes: Wrestling History with the President*. New York: Simon & Schuster, 2009.

Brent, Johnathan. *Inside the Stalin Archives: Discovering the New Russia*. New York: Atlas & Co., 2008.

Bulatović, Momir. *ICTY vs. Slobodan Milošević Neizgovorena odbrana*. Belgrade: Zograf, 2006.

Bulatović, Momir. *Pravila ćutanja*. Belgrade: Narodna knjiga, 2004.

Buruma, Ian. *Wages of Guilt: Memories of War in Germany and Japan*. New York: Plume, 1995.

Christenson, Ron. *Political Trials: Gordian Knots in the Law*. New Brunswick: Transaction, 1999.

Cigar, Norman, and Paul Williams. *Indictment in The Hague: The Milošević Regime and Crimes of the Balkan Wars*. New York: New York University Press, 2002.
Ćirić, Jovan. *Haški tribunal između prava i politike*. Institut za uporedno pravo. Beograd: Goragraf, 2013.
Cohen, Lenard J. *Broken Bonds: Yugoslavia's Disintegration and Balkan Politics in Transition*. Boulder: Westview Press, 1995.
Cohen, Lenard J. *Serpent in the Bosom: The Rise and Fall of Slobodan Milošević*. Boulder: Westview Press, 2002.
Cohen, Lenard J., and Jasna Dragović-Soso, eds. *State Collapse in South-Eastern Europe: New Perspectives on Yugoslavia's Disintegration*. Purdue: Purdue University Press, 2008.
Combs, Nancy Amoury. *Guilty Pleas in International Criminal Law: Constructing a Restorative Justice Approach*. Stanford: Stanford University Press, 2007.
Ćosić, Dobrica. *Piščevi zapisi: 1992–1993*. Belgrade: Filip Višnjić, 2004.
Dedijer, Vladimir. *Novi prilozi za biografiju Josipa Broza Tita*. Rijeka: Liburnija, 1981.
Dedijer, Vladimir, Ivan Božić, Sima Ćirković, and Milorad Ekmečić. *History of Yugoslavia*. New York: McGraw-Hill, 1974.
Denitch, Bogdan. *Legitimation of a Revolution: The Yugoslav Case*. New Haven: Yale University Press, 1975.
de Vlaming, Frederiek. *De Aanklager*. Leiden: Boom, 2013.
Doder, Duško, and Louise Branson. *Milošević: Portrait of a Tyrant*. New York: The Free Press, 1999.
Đorđević, Dimitrije, ed. *The Creation of Yugoslavia, 1914–1918*. Santa Barbara: Clio Books, 1980.
Douglas, Lawrence. *The Memory of Judgment: Making Law and History in the Trials of the Holocaust*. New Haven: Yale University Press, 2001.
Dragnich, Alex. *The First Yugoslavia: Search for a Viable Political System*. Stanford: Hoover Press, 1983.
Đukić, Slavoljub. *Milošević and Marković: A Lust for Power*. Montreal: McGill-Queen's University Press, 2001.
Eagleton, Terry. *Ideology: An Introduction*. London: Verso, 1991.
Elster, Jon. *Closing the Books: Transitional Justice in Historical Perspective*. Cambridge: Cambridge University Press, 2004.
Glenny, Misha. *The Fall of Yugoslavia: The Third Balkan War*. London: Penguin, 1992.
Goldhagen, Daniel. *Hitler's Willing Executioners: Ordinary Germans and the Holocaust*. New York: Alfred A. Knopf, 1996.
Gow, James. *The Serbian Project and its Adversaries: A Strategy of War Crimes*. London: Hurst, 2003.
Gow, James, and Ivan Zverzhanovski. *Security, Democracy and War Crimes: Security Sector Transformation in Serbia*. London: Palgrave Macmillan, 2013.
Gow, James, Rachel Kerr, and Zoran Pajić. *Prosecuting War Crimes: Lessons and Legacies of the International Criminal Tribunal for the Former Yugoslavia*. London: Routledge, 2014.
Gutman, Roy. *A Witness to Genocide*. New York: Macmillan, 1993.
Hagan, John. *Justice in the Balkans: Prosecuting War Crimes in the Hague Tribunal*. Chicago: University of Chicago Press, 2003.
Hazan, Pierre. *Justice in a Time of War: The True Story Behind the International Criminal Tribunal for the Former Yugoslavia*. Eugenia & Hugh M. Stewart '26 Series on Eastern Europe. Texas A&M University Press, 2004.

Hechter, Michael, and Christine Horne, eds. *Theories of Social Order: A Reader*. Stanford: Stanford University Press, 2003.

Helsinki Committee for Human Rights in Serbia. *Human Rights in Transition*. Annual Report. 2001.

Helsinki Committee for Human Rights in Serbia. *Self-Isolation: Reality and the Goal*. Annual Report. 2007.

Human Rights Watch. *Croatia: A Decade of Disappointment – Continuing Obstacles to the Reintegration of Serb Returnees*. September 2006.

Human Rights Watch. *Weighing the Evidence: Lessons from the Slobodan Milošević Trial*. December 2006.

Jović, Borisav. *Poslednji dani SFRJ*. Belgrade: Politika, 1995.

Jović, Borisav. *Knjiga o Miloševiću*. Belgrade: IKP Nikola Pašić, 2001.

Jović, Borisav. *Od Gazimestana do Haga: vreme Slobodana Miloševića*. Belgrade: Metaphysica, 2009.

Jović, Dejan. *Jugoslavija: država koja je odumrla*. Zagreb: Promotej, 2003.

Kadijević, Veljko. *Moje Vidjenje Raspada: Vojska Bez Države*. Belgrade: Politika, 1993.

Kennan, George F. *The Other Balkan Wars: A 1913 Carnegie Endowment Inquiry in Retrospect*. Washington, DC: Carnegie Endowment, 1993.

Kerr, Rachel, and Eirin Mobekk. *Peace & Justice: Seeking Accountability After War*. Cambridge: Polity Press, 2007.

Kershaw, Ian. *Hitler: Profiles in Power*. New York: Routledge, 2013.

Kirchheimer, Otto. *Political Justice: The Use of Legal Procedure for Political Ends*. Princeton: Princeton University Press, 1961.

Krieger, Heike, ed. *The Kosovo Conflict and International Law: An Analytical Documentation 1974–1999*. Cambridge: Cambridge University Press, 2001.

Kritz, Neil J., ed. *Transitional Justice: How Emerging Democracies Reckon With Former Regimes*. Vol. 2, *Country Studies*. Washington, DC: United States Institute of Peace Press, 1995.

Lampe, John R. *Yugoslavia as History: Twice There Was a Country*. 2nd edn. Cambridge: Cambridge University Press, 2000.

Laughland, John. *Travesty: The Trial of Slobodan Milošević and the Corruption of International Justice*. London: Pluto Press, 2007.

LeBor, Adam. *Milošević: A Biography*. London: Bloomsbury, 2002.

Magaš, Branka. *The Destruction of Yugoslavia: Tracking the Break-Up, 1980–92*. London: Verso, 1993.

Major, John. *The Autobiography*. London: Harper & Collins, 1999.

Manusama, Kenneth. *The United Nations Security Council in the Post-Cold War Era: Applying the Principle of Legality*. Leiden: Koninklijke Brill, 2006.

Masciulli, Joseph, Mikhail A. Molchanov, and W. Andy Knight, eds. *The Ashgate Research Companion to Political Leadership*. Surrey: Ashgate, 2009.

Meier, Victor. *Yugoslavia: A History of Demise*. London: Routledge, 1999.

Mesić, Stipe. *Kako smo srušili Jugoslaviju*. Zagreb: Globus, 1992.

Netherlands Institute for War Documentation. *Srebrenica: A 'Safe' Area – Reconstruction, Background, Consequences and Analyses of the Fall of a Safe Area*. Amsterdam: Boom Uitgeverij, 2002.

Nettelfield, Lara J. *Courting Democracy in Bosnia and Herzegovina: The Hague Tribunal's Impact in a Postwar State*. Cambridge: Cambridge University Press, 2010.

Orentlicher, Diana. *Shrinking the Space for Denial: The Impact of the ICTY in Serbia*. Open Society Justice Initiative, 2010.

Orentlicher, Diana F. *That Someone Guilty Be Punished: The Impact of the ICTY in Bosnia*. Open Society Institute, 2010.
Osiel, Mark. *Making Sense of Mass Atrocities*. Cambridge: Cambridge University Press, 2008.
Osiel, Mark. *Mass Atrocity, Collective Memory and the Law*. Piscataway: Transaction Publishers, 1997.
Owen, David. *Balkan Odyssey*. Oxford: Indigo, 1995.
Pavković, Aleksandar. *The Fragmentation of Yugoslavia: Nationalism and War in the Balkans*. London: Macmillan, 1997.
Pavlowitch, Stevan K. *The Improbable Survivor: Yugoslavia and its Problems, 1918–1988*. London: C. Hurst & Company, 1988.
Pavlowitch, Stevan K. *Tito: Yugoslavia's Great Dictator – A Reassessment*. Columbus: Ohio State University Press, 1992.
Petranović, Branko. *Istorija Jugoslavije, 1918–1988*. 3 vols. Belgrade: Nolit, 1988.
Popov, Čedomir. *Velika Srbija: Stvarnost i Mit*. Novi Sad: Sremski Karlovci, 2007.
Ramcharan, B.G., ed. *The International Conference on the Former Yugoslavia: Official Papers*. Vol. 1. The Hague: Kluwer Law, 1997.
Ramet, Sabrina Petra. *The Three Yugoslavias: State-Building and Legitimation, 1918–2005*. Bloomington: Indiana University Press, 2006.
Ridley, Jasper. *Tito*. London: Constable, 1994.
Roberts, Ivor. *Conversations with Milošević*. Oxford: Oxford University Press, 2013.
Ronen, Dov. *The Quest for Self-Determination*. New Haven: Yale University Press, 1979.
Sadat, Leila Nadya, and Michael P. Scharf, eds. *The Theory and Practice of International Criminal Law: Essays in Honor of M. Cherif Bassiouni*. Leiden: Martinus Nijhoff, 2008.
Samary, Catherine. *Yugoslavia Dismembered*. New York: Monthly Review Press, 1995.
Schabas, William A. *Unimaginable Atrocities: Justice, Politics, and Rights at the War Crimes Tribunals*. Oxford: Oxford University Press, 2012.
Scharf, Michael P. *Balkan Justice: The Story Behind the First International War Crimes Trial Since Nuremberg*. Durham, NC: University of North Carolina Academic Press, 1997.
Scharf, Michael, and William Schabas. *Slobodan Milošević on Trial: A Companion*. New York: Continuum International, 2002.
Sell, Louise. *Slobodan Milošević and the Destruction of Yugoslavia*. Durham, NC: Duke University Press, 2002.
Shklar, Judith. *Law, Morals and Political Trials*. Cambridge, MA: Harvard University Press, 1964.
Silber, Laura, and Allan Little. *Yugoslavia: Death of a Nation*. New York: Penguin Books, 1995.
Simmons, Beth A., and Richard H. Steinberg, eds. *International Law and International Relations*. Cambridge: Cambridge University Press, 2007.
Simpson, Gerry J. *Law, War & Crime: War Crimes, Trials and the Reinvention of International Law*. Cambridge: Polity Press, 2007.
Stambolić, Ivan. *Put u bespuće*. Belgrade: B92, 1995.
Stangneth, Bettina. *Eichmann Before Jerusalem: The Unexamined Life of a Mass Murderer*. New York: Alfred A. Knopf, 2014.
Stephen, Chris. *Judgement Day: The Trial of Slobodan Milošević*. New York: Atlantic Books, 2004.

Stevanović, Vidoslav. *Milošević: People's Tyrant*. London: I.B. Tauris, 2002.

Stover, Eric. *The Witnesses: War Crimes and the Promise of Justice in the Hague*. Philadelphia: University of Pennsylvania Press, 2005.

Subotić, Jelena. *Hijacked Justice*. Ithaca: Cornell University Press, 2009.

Suhrke, Astri, and Mats Berdal, eds. *The Peace In Between: Post-War Violence and Peacebuilding*. New York: Routledge, 2012.

Swart, Bert, Alexander Zahar, and Göran Sluiter, eds. *The Legacy of the International Criminal Tribunal for the Former Yugoslavia*. Oxford: Oxford University Press, 2011.

Teitel, Ruti. *Transitional Justice*. Oxford: Oxford University Press, 2000.

Thompson, John B. *Studies in the Theory of the Ideology*. Berkeley: California University Press, 1984.

Tomić, Oliver, ed. *Od Nirnberga do Haga: pouke istorije*. Beograd: Institute for Comparative Law, 2013.

Trifunovska, Snežana, ed. *Yugoslavia Through Documents: From its Creation to its Dissolution*. Dordrecht: Martinus Nijhoff, 1994.

Udovički, Jasminka, and James Ridgeway, eds. *Burn This House: The Making and Unmaking of Yugoslavia*. Durham, NC: Duke University Press, 1997.

Waters, Timothy, ed. *The Milošević Trial: An Autopsy*. New York: Oxford University Press, 2014.

Weber, Max. *The Theory of Social and Economic Organizations*. New York: The Free Press, 1947.

Weller, Marc, ed. *The Crisis in Kosovo 1989–1999*. Cambridge: Documents & Analysis Publishing, 1999.

West, Richard. *Tito and the Rise and Fall of Yugoslavia*. New York: Carroll & Graf, 1995.

Williams, Melissa S., Rosemary Nagy, and Jon Elster, eds. *Transitional Justice*. New York: New York University Press, 2012.

Williams, Paul, and Norman L. Cigar. *A Prima Facie Case for the Indictment of Slobodan Milošević*. Washington, DC: Alliance to Defend Bosnia-Herzegovina, 1996.

Winkler, Ingo. *Contemporary Leadership Theories: Enhancing the Understanding of the Complexity, Subjectivity and Dynamics of Leadership*. Berlin: Verlag, 2010.

Woodward, Susan L. *Balkan Tragedy: Chaos and Dissolution after the Cold War*. Washington, DC: Brookings Institution, 1995.

Zimmerman, Warren. *Origins of a Catastrophe: Yugoslavia and its Destroyers*. New York: Times Books, 1996.

Book and report chapters

Irvine, Jill A., and Patrice C. McMahon. "From International Courts to Grassroots Organizing: The Obstacles to Transitional Justice in the Balkans." In *Transitional Justice and Civil Society in the Balkans*, edited by Olivera Simić and Zala Volčič. New York: Springer, 2013.

Maier, Charles S. "Doing History, Doing Justice: The Narrative of the Historian and of the Truth Commission." In *Truth v. Justice: The Morality of Truth Commissions*, edited by R.I. Rotberg and D. Thompson. Princeton: Princeton University Press, 2000.

Marrus, Michael R. "History and the Holocaust in the Courtroom." In *The Holocaust and Justice*, edited by Ronald M. Smelser. Vol. 5, *Lessons and Legacies*. Evanston: Northwestern University Press, 2002.

Mason, Timothy. "Intention and Explanation: A Current Controversy about the Interpretation of National Socialism." In *The "Führer State": Myth and Reality – Studies on Structure and Politics of the Third Reich*, edited by G. Hirschfeld and L. Kettenacker. Stuttgart: Klett-Cotta, 1981.

Nice, Geoffrey, and Nena Tromp. "Bosnia and Herzegovina." In *The United Nations Security Council in the Age of Human Rights*, edited by Jared Genser and Bruno Stagno Ugarte. Cambridge: Cambridge University Press, 2014.

Tabeau, Ewa, and Jan Zwierzchowski. "A Review of Estimation Methods for Victims of the Bosnian War and the Khmer Rouge Regime." In *Counting Civilian Casualties: Introduction to Recording and Estimating Nonmilitary Deaths in Conflict*, edited by Taylor B. Seybolt, Jay D. Aronson, and Baruch Fischhoff. New York: Oxford University Press, 2013.

Tochilovsky, Vladimir. "Legal Systems and Cultures in the International Criminal Court: The Experience from the International Criminal Tribunal for the Former Yugoslavia." In *International and National Prosecution of Crimes under International Law: Current Developments*, edited by Horst Fischer, Claus Kress, and Sascha Rolf Lüder. Berlin: Arno Spitz GmbH, 2001.

Tromp, Nena. "War Crimes Tribunals and The International Criminal Tribunal for Former Yugoslavia." In *15 Years of Peace Building in the Western Balkans: Lessons Learnt and Current Challenges*, edited by Ernst M. Felberbauer and Predrag Jureković. Vienna: PfP Consortium of Defence Academics, December 2010.

Tromp, Nena. "A Troubled Relationship: The ICTY and Reconciliation." In *Regional Co-operation and Reconciliation in the Aftermath of the ICTY Verdicts: Continuation or Stalemate?*, edited by Ernst M. Felberbauer and Predrag Jureković. Vienna: PfP Consortium of Defence Academies, 2013.

Documents published by the United Nations

International Tribunal for the Prosecution of Persons Responsible for Serious Violations of International Humanitarian Law Committed in the Territory of the former Yugoslavia since 1991. Rules of Procedure and Evidence. No. IT/32/Rev.48. 19 November 2012. The Hague, the Netherlands.

United Nations. Charter of the United Nations and Statute of the International Court of Justice. October 1945.

United Nations. Updated Statute of the International Criminal Tribunal for the former Yugoslavia. September 2009.

United Nations General Assembly. Convention on the Prevention and Punishment of the Crime of Genocide. 9 December 1948.

United Nations Security Council. *Report of the Secretary-General Pursuant to Security Council Resolution 721*. No. S/23280. 11 December 1991.

United Nations Security Council. Resolution 237. No. S/RES/237. 22 May 1992.

United Nations Security Council. Resolution 743. No. S/RES/743. 21 February 1992.

United Nations Security Council. *Report of the Secretary-General on the International Conference on the Former Yugoslavia*. No. S/25015. 24 December 1992.

United Nations Security Council. *Report of the Secretary-General on the Activities of the International Conferece on the Former Yugoslavia*. No. S/25050. 6 January 1993.

United Nations Security Council. Resolution 808. No. S/RES/808. 22 February 1993.

United Nations Security Council. Resolution 819. No. S/RES/819. 16 April 1993.

United Nations Security Council. *Report of the Security Council Mission Established Pursuant to Resolution 819 (1993)*. No. S/25700. 30 April 1993.

United Nations Security Council. *Report of the Secretary-General on the Activities of the International Conference on the Former Yugoslavia: Peace Talks, Athens, 1–2 May 1993.* No. S/25709. 3 May 1993.

United Nations Security Council. Resolution 824. No. S/RES/824. 6 May 1993.

United Nations Security Council. Resolution 827. No. S/RES/827. 25 May 1993.

United Nations Security Council. *Letter from the Secretary-General addressed to the President of the Security Council.* No. S/26066. 8 July 1994.

United Nations Security Council. *Letter from the Secretary-General addressed to the President of the Security Council.* No. S/1994/1074. 19 September 1994.

United Nations Security Council. Resolution 1004. No. S/RES/1004. 12 July 1995.

United Nations Security Council. Letter from the Permanent Representative of the Russian Federation. No. S/1998/526. 17 June 1998.

United Nations Security Council. *Report of the Secretary-General prepared pursuant to Resolutions 1160 (1998), 1199 (1998) and 1203 (1998) of the Security Council.* No. S/1998/1068. 12 November 1998.

United Nations Security Council. *The Rule of Law and Transitional Justice in Conflict and Post-Conflict Societies.* No. S/2004/616. 23 August 2004.

Journal articles

"Army Commission for Cooperation with the ICTY Abolished." *Defence & Security*, no. 75 (April 2003).

Barria, Lilian A., and Steven D. Roper. "How Effective are International Criminal Tribunals? An Analysis of the ICTY and the ICTR." *The International Journal of Human Rights* 9, no. 3 (September 2005): 356.

Bass, Gary. "Victor's Justice, Selfish Justice." *Social Research* 69, no. 4 (winter 2002): 1035–1044.

Bataković, Dušan T. "Ilija Garasanin's Nacertanije: A Reassessment." *Balkanica* XXV, no. 1 (1994): 157–183.

Cassese, Antonio. "The Proper Limits of Individual Responsibility under Doctrine of Joint Criminal Enterprise." *Journal of International Criminal Justice* 5 (2007): 109–133.

Cheh, Mary M. "Should Lawyers Participate in Rigged Systems: The Case of the Military Commissions." *Journal of National Security Law and Policy* 1 (2005): 375–429.

Clark, Janine N. "The ICTY and Reconciliation in Croatia: A Case Study of Vukovar." *Oxford Journal of International Criminal Justice* 10, no. 2 (2012): 397–422.

Danner, Allison M., and Jenny S. Martinez. "Guilty Associations: Joint Criminal Enterprise, Command Responsibility and the Development of International Criminal Law." *California Law Review* 93, no. 1 (2005): 75–169.

de Graaff, Bob. "The Difference between Legal Proof and Historical Evidence: The Trial of Slobodan Milošević and the Case of Srebrenica." *European Review* 14, no. 4 (2006): 499–512.

Ford, Stuart. "Fairness and Politics at the ICTY: Evidence from the Indictments." *North Carolina Journal of International Law and Commercial Regulation* 39 (2013): 45–113.

Gaynor, Fergal. "Uneasy Partners: Evidence, Truth and History in International Trials." *Journal of International Criminal Justice* 10, no. 5 (2012): 1257–1275.

Glaurdić, Josip. "Inside the Serbian War Machine: The Telephone Intercepts, 1991–1992." *East European Politics and Societies* 23, no. 1 (February 2009): 84–104.

Hasani, Enver. "The 'Outer Wall' of Sanctions and the Kosovo Issue." *Perceptions* III, no. 3 (September–November 1998): 1–11.

Hendrickson, Ryan C. "Crossing the Rubicon." *NATO Review*, no. 3 (autumn 2005): 1–4.

Higgins, Gillian. "The Impact of the Size, Scope, and Scale of the Milošević Trial and the Development of Rule 73." *Northwestern Journal of International Human Rights* 7, no. 2 (Summer 2009): 239–260.

Humphrey, Michael. "International Intervention, Justice and National Reconciliation: The Role of the ICTY and ICTR in Bosnia and Rwanda." *Journal of Human Rights* 2, no.V4 (December 2003): 495–505.

Kostić, Roland. "Transitional Justice and Reconciliation in Bosnia-Herzegovina: Whose Memories, Whose Justice?" *Sociologia* LIV, no.V4 (2012).

Marković, Ratko. "Ustav naroda." *Pravni život* 38 (1988): 1179–1186.

Marković, Ratko. "Državnopravni Položaj Srbije i Njeno Opredelenje za Zajedničku Državu sa Crnom Gorom." *Pravni život* 42, no.V3–4 (1992): 373–380.

Menkel-Meadow, Carrie. "The Trouble with the Adversary System in a Postmodern, Multicultural World." *William & Mary Law Review* 38, no. 5 (1996): 5–44.

Nice, Geoffrey. "Trials of Imperfection." *Leiden Journal of International Law* 14, no.V2 (June 2001): 383–397.

Peterson, Jeremy D. "Unpacking Show Trials: Situating the Trial of Saddam Hussein." *Harvard International Law Journal* 48, no. 1 (2007): 257–292.

Popović, Srđa. "Proposal for Supplementing of Evidence Presentation Proceedings." *Helsinki Bulletin* 11 (March 2007): 1–24.

Power, Samantha. "Stopping Genocide and Securing 'Justice': Learning by Doing." *Social Research* 69, no. 4 (winter 2002): 1099–1113.

Quimpo, Nathan. "Trapo Parties and Corruption." *KASAMA* 21, no. 1 (January–February–March 2007).

Simpson, Gerry J. "Didactic and Dissident Histories in War Crimes Trials." *Albany Law Review* 60, no. 3 (1997): 801–839.

Swaak-Goldman, Olivia Q. "The ICTY and the Right to a Fair Trial: A Critique of the Critics." *Leiden Journal of International Law* 10, no. 2 (June 1997): 215–221.

Welsh, Helga. "Political Transition Processes in Central and Eastern Europe." *Comparative Politics* 26, no. 4 (July 1994): 379–394.

Wilson, Richard. "Judging History: The Historical Record of the International Criminal Tribunal of the Former Yugoslavia." *Human Rights Quarterly* 27, no. 3 (2005): 908–942.

Wilt, Harmen van der. "Joint Criminal Enterprise: Possibilities and Limitations." *Journal of International Criminal Justice* 5, no. 1 (2007): 91–108.

Yukl, Gary. "An Evaluation of Conceptual Weaknesses in Transformational and Charismatic Leadership Theories." *Leadership Quarterly* 10, no. 2 (Summer 1999): 285–305.

Zumach, Andreas. "US Intelligence Knew Serbs were Planning an Assault on Srebrenica." *Basic Reports*, no. 47 (16 October 1995).

Magazine and newspaper articles

"Dačić: Opstanak Republike Srpske mnogo važniji državni interes nego opstanak Kosova u okviru Srbije." *Blic.* 26 April 2013.
"Former 'Scorpion' Soldier Testifies about Links with Serbian Secret Police." *Sense Tribunal.* 14 December 2010.
"ICTY Lifts Seal from Supreme Defence Council Document in Momčilo Perišić Case." *Sense Tribunal.* 25 March 2011.
"Milošević Carries Off the Battle Honours." *Independent.* 29 June 1989.
"Radisavljević: Legija je otkrio ubice Ćuruvije; Vučić: Niko neće biti izuzet." *Blic.* 14 January 2014.
"Sarajevo Conference: Ode to Tribunal or Requiem for Justice?" *Sense Tribunal.* 27 December 2013.
"Shifting the Blame on a Family Clan in the 'Scorpions'." *Sense Tribunal.* 15 December 2010.
"Why Did Prosecution Fail to Prove What 'Everybody Knows'." *Sense Tribunal.* 7 April 2008.
Arslani, Merita, and Snježana Pavić. "Haaški istražitelji nisu htjeli tražiti dokaze protiv Miloševića." *Jutarnji list.* 10 September 2007.
Bilandžić, Dušan. "Najveća Razilaženja." *Nacional.* 25 October 1996.
Borger, Julian. "The Hunt for the Former Yugoslavia's War Criminal: Mission Accomplished." *Guardian.* 3 August 2011.
Danner, Mark. "Bosnia: The Great Betrayal." *New York Review of Books.* 26 March 1998.
Graff, James L. "Butcher of the Balkans." *Time.* 8 June 1992.
Gutman, Roy. "Ethnic Cleansing: Yugoslavs Try to Deport 1,800 Muslims to Hungary." *Newsday.* 3 July 1992.
Gwyn, Richard. "International Law Should Not Be Victors' Justice: Indicted or Convicted War Criminals Are All Citizens of Small, Poor Countries." *The Toronto Star.* 4 July 2001.
Harland, David. "Selective Justice for the Balkans." *New York Times.* 7 December 2012.
Ilić, Jovan. "Kako ćemo se razgraničavati." *Epoha.* 22 October 1991.
Izama, Angelo. "Kony is Not the Problem." *International Herald Tribune.* 21 March 2012.
Karić, Samir. "Od 200.000 Bošnjaka, u Foči ostale 3.000." *Oslobođenje.* 10 November 2013.
Katz, Lee Michael. "Peace Hope for Bosnia: Use of Force." *USA Today.* 19 September 1995.
Lane, Charles, and Thom Shanker. "In Bosnia: What the CIA Didn't Tell Us." *New York Review of Books.* 9 May 1996.
Miloradović, Ivana. "There Was Pressure on Our Work." *NIN.* 15 May 2008.
Milosevic, Sasa. "Fatal Privilege for Serbian War Criminal." *The World Post.* 29 January 2014.
Nice, Geoffrey. "Del Ponte's Deal." *London Review of Books.* 13 December 2010.
Nice, Geoffrey. "Neprofesionalna Del Ponte politizirala je tužiteljstvo." *Jutarnji list.* 16 September 2007.
O'Kane, Maggy. "Muslims' Nightmare under the Long Yugoslav Sun." *Guardian.* 29 July 1992.

Ronen, Dov. "End the Campaign to Spread Democracy." *New York Times*. 30 April 2013.
Roth, Kenneth. "A Tribunal's Legal Stumble." *New York Times*. 9 July 2013.
Sabalić, Ines, and Roland Kemp. "Marko Hoare: Bivši istražitelj Haškog suda." *Globus*, no. 854, 2007.
Schuessler, Jennifer. "Book Portrays Eichmann as Evil, Not Banal." *International New York Times*. 4 September 2014.
Simons, Marlise. "Serbia's Darkest Pages Hidden from Genocide Court." *New York Times*. 8 April 2007.
Simons, Marlise, and Alison Smale. "Slobodan Milosevic, 64, Former Yugoslav Leader, Accused of War Crimes, Dies." *New York Times*. 12 March 2006.
Traynor, Ian. "Slobodan Milosevic." *Guardian*. 12 March 2006
Zimonjic, Vesna Peric. "Serb 'Scorpions' Guilty of Srebrenica Massacre." *Independent*. 11 April 2007.

Index

Page numbers in *italics* denote tables, those in **bold** denote figures.

For Product Safety Concerns and Information please contact our EU
representative GPSR@taylorandfrancis.com
Taylor & Francis Verlag GmbH, Kaufingerstraße 24, 80331 München, Germany

www.ingramcontent.com/pod-product-compliance
Ingram Content Group UK Ltd.
Pitfield, Milton Keynes, MK11 3LW, UK
UKHW020017200926
475702UK00014B/1939
* 9 7 8 0 8 1 5 3 4 7 6 0 6 *